AT 12 MR BYNG
WAS SHOT...

Dudley Pope was the famous author of the best-selling Ramage Series and *Life in Nelson's Navy*. After service in the Merchant Navy during World War II, he went on to work for fifteen years in Fleet Street before settling down to become a full-time writer. In 1965 he set sail for the West Indies where he lived on his boat until his death in 1997.

Also by Dudley Pope

Flag 4: The Battle of Coastal Forces
in the Mediterranean

The Battle of the River Plate

73 North

England Expects: Decision at Trafalgar

The Black Ship

Fighting Sail

The Great Gamble: Nelson at Copenhagen

Harry Morgan's Way

The Devil Himself

Life in Nelson's Navy

AT 12 MR BYNG WAS SHOT...

Dudley Pope

'At 12 Mr Byng was shot dead by 6
Marines and put into his coffin ...'

Master's Log of HMS *Monarch*,
Monday, March 14, 1757

PHOENIX
PRESS

5 UPPER SAINT MARTIN'S LANE
LONDON
WC2H 9EA

A PHOENIX PRESS PAPERBACK

First published in Great Britain
by Weidenfeld & Nicolson in 1962
This paperback edition published in 2002
by Phoenix Press,
a division of The Orion Publishing Group Ltd,
Orion House, 5 Upper St Martin's Lane,
London WC2H 9EA

Phoenix Press
Sterling Publishing Co Inc
387 Park Avenue South
New York
NY 10016-8810
USA

A CIP catalogue record for this book is
available from the British Library.

Printed and bound in Great Britain by
Clays Ltd, St Ives plc

ISBN 1 84212 607 5

CONTENTS

CONTENTS

ILLUSTRATIONS

ACKNOWLEDGEMENTS

The author would like to thank the following for kind permission to reproduce illustrations in this book: The National Maritime Museum for numbers 1, 5, 7, 8, 9, 10 and 11; The Controller of HM Stationery Office (Crown Copyright) for number 2; The National Trust, Ickworth for number 3; Sir Danvers Osborn, Bt, for numbers 4 and 6; The Scottish National Portrait Gallery for number 13; *Musée de la Marine*, Paris for number 15; The National Portrait Gallery for numbers 16, 17 and 18; The British Museum for numbers 19 and 21.

AUTHOR'S NOTE

THE TRIAL AND EXECUTION of Admiral the Honourable John Byng was one of the most cold-blooded and cynical acts of judicial murder in the whole of British history. This is a bold statement to make; but few readers will disagree when they have read the remarkably incriminating letters written by those Ministers who actually contrived the disgrace and trial of the Admiral so that he should be the scapegoat for their tardiness, stupidity, and neglect.

In writing the story of Byng and his trial I have attempted to portray the situation as it appeared *at the time* to individual people in many walks of life. When I had the choice of describing an event in my own words or those of one of Byng's contemporaries, I have usually chosen 'the man on the spot'.

Fortunately my task was made easier because of the considerable number of contemporary documents which have survived to this day, some only recently coming to light. It has been a fascinating but in many instances a horrifying experience studying them, since they often showed the extent to which the Duke of Newcastle and his Government were prepared to sacrifice Admiral Byng. Nevertheless, I have tried to be objective. Byng, the only British Admiral ever to have been shot as a result of his shortcomings, had his faults, and they are described and analysed in detail.

Lord Anson, one of our greatest seamen, cuts a sorry figure in these pages, condemning himself for the most part with his own pen; but I wish to emphasize most emphatically that the affair of Admiral Byng and the related events in the Mediterranean were only a small (albeit discreditable) episode in a very distinguished career; and one must always bear in mind that as First Lord of the Admiralty he carried out, with ruthless determination, much-needed and long overdue reforms in the Navy.

Yet when letters arrived in England which might be useful to Byng, who was on trial for his very life, Anson's advice (given in writing) had been to 'sink them' as they 'would do harm at the court martial'—i.e. they might help Byng. Before the trial Anson drafted several harsh letters in the Board's name to the imprisoned

Byng, including one saying that the Admiralty wished to give him 'the earliest opportunity of acquitting yourself, if possible, from so heavy a charge'. His advice to his Government concerning the Mediterranean was lamentable.

In order to turn the anger of the Opposition and the mob on to Byng when the Admiral failed to relieve Minorca—a failure which was from the very beginning almost inevitable because of the Government's tardiness—the Ministers censored Byng's despatch heavily before publishing it in the *London Gazette*. Every word which might be construed in Byng's favour was cut out, along with everything that might, however remotely or obliquely, be read as a criticism of the Government. That Ministers resorted to this kind of forgery gives some idea of their fears for their own future.

These same Ministers had earlier recalled Byng in disgrace after the battle solely on the basis of an excerpt from the enemy's report, contained in a letter received by the Spanish envoy in London from his opposite number in Paris. The same Ministers hired hacks to write pamphlets in their defence; indeed one of them, David Mallet, had the Lord Chancellor to edit his work and was paid out of the Secret Service Fund.

The credit for being the first historian thoroughly to examine the case of Admiral Byng and to prove without any doubt that he was the victim of tragic and terrible circumstances, goes, of course, to Mr W. C. B. Tunstall, whose *Admiral Byng* was published in 1928. However, since his scholarly volume appeared certain new material has come to light giving us considerably more background. None of it, incidentally, throws any doubt on Mr Tunstall's basic conclusions, but it provides more than sufficient information to warrant a complementary volume aiming at giving a more personal story.

The new material includes the remarkable *Journal* of Augustus Hervey (who, apart from being a close friend of Byng, served under him in the battle, gave evidence at the trial, and fought hard to save his life); biographical matter concerning the Byng family, Admiral John Byng's private life in his Berkeley Square house and at Wrotham Park, and his mistress, Mrs Hickson; some of the letters he wrote and hundreds that he received; documents in the possession of the Duke of Devonshire; unpublished letters of the Admiral's sister Sarah; letters of Admiral Boscawen; private letters and diaries in the British Museum; and official Admiralty

and War Office letters, minutes, orders, intelligence reports, and
ships' logs and muster lists, in the Public Record Office. Since
most of the letters Byng wrote (though fortunately not the ones he
received) have failed to survive the years, he must remain a rather
shadowy figure. The new material has, however, enabled more of
his private life and personality to be sketched in, and I hope it will
help the reader to understand the almost terrifying inevitability of
some of his actions—and the courageous way in which he met his
death at the hands of a firing squad.

Byng was a staid and pompous bachelor, admiral and a Member
of Parliament, when he took a middle-aged widow, Mrs Hickson,
as his mistress, and her ill-timed death must have upset him considerably since it occurred only a short while before he sailed on
his last, tragic voyage. Since a man's official decisions—particularly
those taken in the heat of battle—must be conditioned by his
personality which in turn influences or is influenced by his private
life, I have, for instance, told all that can be discovered about Mrs
Hickson, and about the way in which Byng ordered his private life.

When quoting from contemporary documents I have in most
cases modernized the spelling and, in some instances, amended the
punctuation in order to make the meaning clearer. However, it
seemed a great pity to lose some of the quaint spelling in various
letters and ships' logs, and I have reproduced some of them in their
original form. Where I have interpolated a word or sentence to
make the meaning clearer in a quoted passage, it is contained within square brackets. For the numbers (referring to the Notes and
Bibliography Section, beginning on page 313) which are scattered
throughout the text I must apologize; but in a book which draws
on considerably more than a quarter of a million words of notes
taken from original documents, apart from dozens of published
works, it seemed highly desirable to give the chief sources.

Many people helped me in my research, but my greatest debt is to
my wife: faced with reading and copying scores of thousands of
words from contemporary documents, many in faded or execrable
writing, and translating old French documents, she kept her sense
of humour and patience and, above all, provided the encourage-
ment and incentive without which I should never have attempted
such a research project.

I am deeply indebted to Mr T. T. Barnard, MC, for much

material concerning the early days of the Byng family and the private life of Admiral Byng. The Hon David Erskine (and his publisher, William Kimber Limited) gave me permission to make use of the admirable *Augustus Hervey's Journal*, which he so ably edited, and he has helped in many other ways, particularly in making suggestions to improve my manuscript.

I must thank Lady Elizabeth Byng, who has allowed me to make full use of the Byng Papers in her possession and gave me such a hospitable welcome at Wrotham Park. Sir Danvers Osborn, Bt, has let me print many of the letters of his forebear, Mrs Sarah Osborn, who was John Byng's elder sister; and Lady Osborn gave me much help in going through the Osborn Papers.

I am indebted to the Duke of Bedford for permission to use papers and correspondence at Woburn relating to the fourth Duke; the Duke of Devonshire for allowing me to use some of the Devonshire MSS at Chatsworth; Lord Falmouth for permission to print some of the letters of Admiral Edward Boscawen; the Trustees of the British Museum for the papers of the Duke of Newcastle, the Earl of Hardwicke, Lord Anson and many others; and unpublished Crown Copyright material in the Public Record Office has been reproduced by permission of the Controller of HM Stationery Office.

The Admiralty Library contains many books and contemporary pamphlets and papers concerning Byng. The Head of Historical Section at the Admiralty, Cdr Peter K. Kemp, RN, gave me much advice and assistance; and his staff in the Library, particularly Mr Young, were as usual, unfailingly helpful and cheerful in the face of our demands on their time.

The staff of the Public Record Office, particularly Mr E. K. Timings, MA, and Mr R. Anslow, gave us much help. One can only wish that eventually both staff and students will have better surroundings in which to work, because the present conditions at the Public Record Office are a disgrace and made bearable only by the staff's unfailing patience and courtesy. The staff of the British Museum, particularly the Students' Room, and of the London Library have been most helpful.

I am greatly indebted to Mr W. C. B. Tunstall for his kindness in reading the proof of this volume and making many suggestions which have enabled me to improve it.

Professor Michael Lewis read the manuscript and made several valuable suggestions; Lt-Colonel Harold Wyllie, OBE, the Vice-President of the Society of Marine Artists and one of the foremost authorities on the days of square-rigged warships, has helped greatly with his friendship, information and advice, as did Cdr W. B. Rowbotham, RN (Retd). Mrs Anthea Barker readily came to my rescue when I found gaps in my research at a time when I was a thousand miles away from sources; and the Library staff of the Ministry of Marine in Rome have also been very helpful. My former colleague and old friend, H. Bailey, once again helped me by reading the proofs.

Porto Santo Stefano,   D.P.
(Grosseto), Italy.

For
MARIA AND MIREK

'To none will we sell, to none will we deny,
To none will we delay right or justice . . .'

—MAGNA CARTA

THE ADMIRAL AT HOME

THOMAS TRANTER, who was one of the Admiralty's three official messengers, stepped carefully across the odorous mosaic of putrefying rubbish and muddy puddles as he walked northwards along Berkeley Street. He was threading his way from the Admiralty in Whitehall, and he kept a cautious hand resting on the flap of his leather satchel, as a guard against the pickpockets whose light fingers were busy arranging what they considered to be a more equitable distribution of wealth among the jostling and noisy London crowd.

The crossing sweepers who posted themselves at strategic intervals along the street on this blustery day in March, 1756, were waiting for likely passers-by, for a few deft flicks with their brooms to clear a way across the cobblestones would produce a tip. However, they took one look at Tranter and stood back with their arms folded, for at a glance they could assess his salary (it was actually £30 a year) and guess that he had few spare coins in his purse.

Wayside hucksters busy selling everything from tea to corn salves, and hot eels to beetle wafers, shouted in enthusiastic discords the remarkable merits of their wares, which were displayed on stalls beneath the trees on Tranter's left; the costermongers hurled coarse greetings and invitations to the young milliners who hurried past, clutching bandboxes, their cheeks pink and ankles twinkling under looped and flounced skirts.

Taking care that his grey lisle stockings were not spattered with the water and mud thrown up by the wheels of passing carriages, Tranter turned left when he reached Berkeley Square and began to walk along the west side. The houses lining the square were modern; their size and the elaborateness of the lanterns and flambeaux-snuffers on their walls gave a further indication—if any was needed—that their owners were members of fashionable London society. They included Lady Pelham, for instance, widow of a former First Minister and the sister-in-law of the present one; and among her neighbours were the Earl of Darnley, and Major-General the Earl of Ancram, who had been wounded while serving with the King at the Battle of Fontenoy.

On each corner where Hill Street met Berkeley Square there was a matching house, three storeys high and with a three-sided bay jutting into Hill Street. Mr Robert Sayes Herbert lived in the one on the south side (now No. 42, but not numbered in those days) while an admiral, the Honourable John Byng, lived on the north side (now No. 41).[1] The house next to the Admiral was empty while beyond was the Duke of Ancaster who was Lord Great Chamberlain of England and also a major-general although—by a commission dated seven days later—junior to his near-neighbour, the Earl of Ancram. Beyond the Duke lived yet another Duke, this time of Manchester. One of his daughters—now unhappily a widow—had married a brother of Admiral Byng.

In Hill Street itself lived such diverse people as the Bishop of London and Mrs Chudleigh who, besides being the mother of the notorious Elizabeth, was still the housekeeper at Windsor Castle—the result, it was said, of a quickly-passing infatuation on the part of the old King. Other tenants included two more admirals, the Hon George Clinton, and Henry Osborn, whose elder brother had married Admiral Byng's sister.[2]

Mr Tranter made for the house on the north corner and pulled the wrought-iron bell handle. He was soon explaining that he had a letter from the Lords Commissioners of the Admiralty addressed to Admiral Byng, and he was conducted up the wide staircase to the library on the first floor.

The interior of the house was neat and well-furnished; the carpets underfoot were expensive; the furniture was of good quality. The only blemish to the casual observer was that a plaster statue of Venus standing shyly in a niche in the wall on the half-landing had been dropped recently, and her fingers had been broken off.

John Hutchens, the Admiral's valet, told Tranter to wait in the library until the Admiral was ready to receive him and sign the receipt for the letter. The messenger sat down and looked round curiously.[3] Thanks to the Admiral's will, we know what he saw. The leather-bound volumes gave a warm, nut-brown richness to the room which was emphasized by the bare, polished wood of the shelves on which they stood. Among the larger volumes was one which should have been in every intelligent admiral's library at that period—Father Paul Hoste's *L'art des armées navales; ou, Traité des évolutions navales*, which had been published in Lyons in 1697. (How a Jesuit priest came to write the treatise on naval strategy and tactics which was to remain a standard textbook for the next sixty years was explained in his own preface—for a dozen years he had served with three different admirals, and one of them de Tourville, 'has been kind enough to communicate to me his ideas, bidding me write on a matter which has, I think, never before been the subject of a treatise'). The book had the signature 'J. Byng' in sloping handwriting on the inside of the cover and every word of it had been absorbed by the Admiral, for it was among the best on the subject, even though it had not yet been translated into English.

There were many books on travel, history and geography; but the eye was caught by a row of seventeen tall and thick volumes. Although the numbers in gilt figures on the spines gave no clue to the contents, they contained hundreds of official letters written to the Admiral in the twenty-one years from 1727, when he was a twenty-three-year-old captain, until 1748, by which time he was a vice-admiral and had just hauled down his flag as the Commander-in-Chief in the Mediterranean. For the next seven years of peace the Admiral had lived on shore, devoting some of his leisure time to sorting out those letters, carefully dividing them into seventeen separate sections and compiling a careful index, using his favourite formula, 'Acquainting me that . . .'[4]

Among the letters were many from the leading personalities of the day, including the King's soldier son, the Duke of Cumberland and several people, French as well as British, who within a very few months of Mr Tranter's visit were to play a considerable part in determining the Admiral's fate.

Apart from a large desk and a few chairs, the rest of the furniture in the library consisted of two clothes presses which were, presumably, too big to go in the Admiral's dressing-room.[5] On one wall was a small painting of a naval officer. The uniform in which the artist[6] had painted him showed he was a captain, and on the bottom edge of the richly-gilded frame was the inscription 'The Hon Augustus Hervey'. The man portrayed, who occupies a prominent part in this narrative, was broad-shouldered, with widely-spaced sensuous eyes and a cleft chin. At this time he was serving in the Mediterranean in command of the frigate *Phoenix* while his brother, the Earl of Bristol, was at Turin as British Ambassador to the King of Sardinia.

Admiral Byng when he finally came into the library to see Tranter, appeared at first sight to be a man whose personality was laden with a pampered pomposity more suited to a middle-aged sultan. Of average height, he had a girth which betrayed good living and lack of exercise, a round face merging into a comfortable double chin, bulging, heavy-lidded eyes and the haughty expression which no doubt he considered became the son of a peer, a Member of Parliament and a senior flag officer in the Navy.

He was dressed with finicky and meticulous care. His coat, its flared skirt ending above the knee, had upward of a couple of dozen gilt buttons on its embroidered lapels; the sleeves widened into large and cumbersome cuffs, each turned back and decorated with more buttons and richly sewn. The white lawn neckcloth was neatly secured and tucked into the waistcoat—which was itself almost as long and quite as full as the coat, the bottom dozen buttons being left undone. Although his breeches, tightly-cut, had a becoming elegance, his stockings were embroidered with the clocks which were fast becoming unfashionable.

His wig, slightly larger than usual at this time, was tied in a single queue at the back. In an age when coats of shot-silk edged with bejewelled buttons and gaily-coloured satin waistcoats (often set off by breeches covered with silk net) caused no comment, the Admiral was dressed almost drably, at least as far as his choice of colour was concerned. Nevertheless, it was significant that although dressed soberly, he was dressed with remarkable precision.

Mr Tranter handed over to this impressive figure the letter which he had been carrying in his satchel. It was addressed to 'Vice Adml Byng' and marked 'Town', and the red wax which secured the letter against prying eyes bore the impression of the fouled anchor seal of the Board of Admiralty. Admiral Byng signed the proffered receipt book, and as soon as Tranter bowed and left the room the Admiral sat down at his desk and broke the seal.

Written from the Admiralty that same day, Thursday, March 11, the letter began with the usual polite flourishes and then said, as Byng had confidently expected:

'Having ordered Rear-Admiral West and the Captains of the ships named on the other side hereof to put themselves under your command, you are hereby required and directed to repair to Portsmouth, and take them under your command accordingly with all possible despatch. Given &c, 11th March 1756.—*Anson, Will, Rowley, R. Edgcumbe.*'[7]

He turned over the page and read through the list of ships' names with some annoyance because there were only ten of them. The Board had allowed him a small enough squadron, considering the task he was likely to be given.

A bachelor and just fifty-two years of age, John Byng was a lonely man: he was lonely at sea (for command, whether a small ship or a large fleet enforces isolation, apart from the fawning attention of flatterers and the necessary attendance of responsible officers) and now he was lonely on shore.

Being a member of a society which felt itself fully qualified to judge people at first sight, Byng was at an immediate disadvantage because, apart from the cultivated swagger, fashionable in a man in his position, his air of overbearing pride and superiority were, like a porcupine's spines, or a spinster's acidity, unconsciously designed to keep a potentially antagonistic and truculent world at a respectful and safe distance; but, unfortunately, a number of people, already intimidated by his manner, could become his enemies at the drop of a hint, for his was an age when service, political and social affairs were stirred up in the same cauldron as gossip, nepotism and intrigue.

Apart from the servants, who were kept in check by his valet Hutchens, the Admiral had lived by himself in the Berkeley Square house since the death of his middle-aged mistress. However, he had a widowed sister-in-law living a few hundred yards away in Brook Street, half-way to Tyburn Road, in whose three sons he took a great interest; and his sharp-tongued but affectionate sister Sarah Osborn, who was also a widow, lived about as far away in Stratton Street, with his aged mother, the Dowager Lady Torrington.

The death of his mistress, Mrs Susannah Hickson, was the last death but one in a series of bereavements that Byng had suffered in the past few years, as we shall soon see; and without her companionship and influence he quickly reverted to being self-centred and ridiculously precise over the small details that mattered not at all; he became something of a fussy old woman—a state of affairs not unusual in a middle-aged bachelor, especially one who had been endowed with a certain amount of authority for a number of years and was in a position to satisfy any whim.

Having an obsessional character, all the details of a particular problem tended to fascinate and almost hypnotize him. His difficulty was that when he had to make a decision he understood and had sympathy with every opposing point of view without being able to discriminate its importance: his judgment was bewitched by the trivial.

Byng's tragedy was that, metaphorically, his hesitation before going through a gate was not caused by fear of responsibility, making him timid, but because, once through it, he would have difficulty in deciding which way to turn: the merits of turning left, right or going straight on were equally great in his mind. And, like so many other sons of great men, he was fearful of losing even a particle of the greatness which he considered his rightful heritage.

Yet caution and indecision can in time of battle be interpreted by one's enemies as cowardice; and the apparently invisible armour which a man feeling insecure and insufficient wears in an attempt to hide his shortcomings—which are often only imagined —can be seen by the unfriendly as hauteur and conceit. Thus it seems that in John Byng were combined three distinct aspects of character—an ability to see all sides of a problem without being able to evaluate their relative importance (which made him slow to criticize or condemn, as this narrative will show); the desire to live up to the very high standard set by his father; and the basic fear that in this he might fail.

After that brief introduction to the Admiral at the moment when he received the first of a series of orders which were to lead to his trial and death a few months later in front of a firing squad—the first and only British admiral ever to be executed—we can now put the clock back a few years. First we must meet his forebears, to see what traits, good or bad, he inherited from them; and secondly we shall trace his career and investigate the three campaigns in which he served in the Mediterranean.

For the first of these he was a young and eager midshipman serving in a ship commanded by his uncle which formed part of a fleet commanded by his father. For the second he was an admiral who later became the Commander-in-Chief, picking up a small fortune in prize money. His third—and fatal—campaign in the Mediterranean was the result of the orders which Thomas Tranter had just delivered at Berkeley Square.

1

THE EARLY DAYS

THE BYNGS, of whom Vice-Admiral the Hon John was a proud yet lonely representative, were an interesting family: they had nearly all been decisive (though not always successfully), almost dashing in their actions; in times of crisis they acted swiftly and firmly—especially the women of the family. These traits, unfortunately, were missing in John Byng.

Since much of a man's personality consists of a quirkish and uneven mixture of parentage and environment, it is worth stepping back a couple of generations to look at the Admiral's immediate forebears, starting with the man after whom he was named, his grandfather John Byng.

When Grandfather John was in his teens he had been apprenticed, as a draper, to a director of the Levant Company, and after spending six years abroad he returned to London in 1654 to set up his own drapery business. After another six years, at the time of the Restoration, when Charles II entered London in triumph, John married Philadelphia Johnson, who was the daughter of a minor Court official of Charles I's day.

Unfortunately, by the time two sons had been born it was quite clear that his business was a failure (the Great Plague of 1665 cannot have helped much, depleting his few customers even further) and the erstwhile draper realized he soon would not have a shirt to his back unless something was done. He decided that if he was ever going to re-establish the family fortunes the time had come to look elsewhere.

John chose Ireland, and it was to Newtown, in Co. Cork that he took his family in 1666—fortunately missing the Great Fire which swept London that September—and started another business. But that too failed; within six years the creditors were pounding on the door of Byng the draper with rowdy ferocity and determination: so much so—since the penalty for debt was jail—that John had to leave his wife and children and flee secretly to England, where some cousins, the Hewets, gave him the hospitality of their home at Rickmansworth, in Hertfordshire.* While John fretted and worried at Rickmansworth, the creditors in Ireland were making it so unpleasant for Philadelphia at Newtown that she too had to flee, leaving the two younger sons behind and taking the eldest, George, with her to join her husband at Rickmansworth.

The immediate outlook for the refugee Byngs at Rickmansworth looked desperate; but thanks to a boyhood friendship made by John many years earlier, they were about to take a dramatic turn for the better. While his father had been in semi-hiding at Rickmansworth, afraid to move far from the Hewets' house in case someone with a writ for debt had him put in jail, the house across the river, Moor Park (now the celebrated golfcourse at Rickmansworth) had been owned by Robert Carey, Earl of Monmouth, and the Earl's son and a large number of Carey grandchildren lived there as well. One of them, Lady Martha, was two years younger than John, and at the age of eight or nine they were occasional playmates.

Lady Martha had married an old Scots general, the Earl of Middleton, but shortly before Philadelphia arrived at Rickmansworth from Ireland to join her husband, the old General had died. Philadelphia and John plucked up their courage and greatly daring—for by now the social gap was considerable—called on the former Lady Martha, who was now the Countess of Middleton and once again living at Moor Park, to offer their condolences. They had feared the newly-widowed woman might snub them; but the Martha of John's childhood was welcoming, and more than sympathetic when she heard of their financial plight.

Their greatest and immediate worry was, of course, the future of their elder son George, then ten years old, and they returned to the Hewets' house from their visit to Moor Park in a far happier frame of mind than when they left, for the Countess had decided to make herself responsible for George's education and upbringing.

Five years later, when George was fifteen, the time came to choose a career for him. He was intelligent, with more than a fair share of his mother's admirable qualities, and coupled with this was the determination of his father (who had long since given up

---

* They had done the same for his father some forty-seven years earlier when he too, with warrants out for his arrest for debt, had fled there for asylum.

any hope of ever restoring the family fortune) that the eldest son should enter a profession offering the best chance of social and financial advancement. The Countess and the Byngs chose the Navy; and, as events subsequently proved, they chose wisely.

George was a lucky boy—just as he was to prove a lucky man. The year was 1678: Charles II was still on the throne and Samuel Pepys was carrying out his widespread reforms as Secretary of the Admiralty. Pepys wanted young gentlemen of George's age for the Navy, to train as officers of the future. He would not take them under fifteen, and he did not like them older. But it was not enough for a fifteen-year-old boy to present himself at the Admiralty and demand a King's Letter to serve as a 'Volunteer-per-Order'* in one of His Majesty's ships. There was no shortage of applicants, so that to be successful a great many wheels of patronage had to be turned. Young George's case was no exception, and he provides a good example of 'influence' at work—'influence' being a word preferred, in the eighteenth and nineteenth centuries, to the harsher though more realistic 'nepotism'.

Lady Middleton was the first cousin of Lady Mordaunt of Avalon, who in turn was sister-in-law to the Earl of Peterborough. He was a close friend of the Duke of York, the former Lord High Admiral who as a Catholic had been forced out of office by the Test Act. The request for a favour for Lady Middleton's protégé thus reached the Duke who, to oblige his friend the Earl, mentioned the boy's name to Mr Pepys. Thanks to this chain of 'interest' the lad—who was later to become an Admiral, the First Lord of the Admiralty and a peer of the realm—was given a King's Letter and went to sea on May 30, 1678, a Volunteer-per-Order in the *Swallow*. It was none too soon: within a couple of years the Duke of York was in exile, the Earl of Peterborough had fallen from favour, and the size of the Navy was being reduced.

In these early years George's luck remained good, and he was intelligent enough to use every puff of it to get to windward in his naval career. But although charged with the task of filling the family coffers (and finding a rich wife was the surest method) he married when he was twenty-eight 'a lady of small fortune'. Yet

* Pepys had started the system two years earlier. A boy who made a successful application was given a letter from the Crown—a King's Letter—which he gave to the captain of one of His Majesty's ships, who then had to train him. The system found little favour among captains—the 'King's Letter Boys' crowded out their own favourites.

if Margaret Master, of East Langdon, near Dover, lacked a large dowry, she undoubtedly had a strong personality and George certainly married her for love. Very beautiful, very vivacious and not particularly intelligent, she was full of little 'whimsies' which delighted her husband but tried the patience of her children—who were, nevertheless, devoted to her. He soon took Margaret to Bedfordshire where, with some of the prize money which had accumulated from his captures, he bought some land at Southill and had a house built.

Although he had married impulsively for love and not fortune, the rest of George Byng's life was lived according to clear-headed thinking. He showed a particular skill in mixing naval and political life at a time when a knowledge of the correct ingredients was most necessary in order to gain advancement. In the years that followed there were various changes in the direction of the political storms; but Byng managed to weather them, and while he fought his battles—political ones at Court and naval ones at Barfleur, Malaga and Gibraltar—the Byng family at Southill increased and grew up under the care of their vivacious mother, Margaret.

The eldest was Sarah, born in October 1693, just after her father bought the Southill property. She was the only one of a very large family who inherited a full share of her father's many virtues, pleasantly blended with the spirit shown by her mother.

The next child and eldest son was Pattee (why did he have that absurd Christian name? One suspects it was one of his mother's 'whimsies'). His father had strong views about education: he had no use for public schools, or universities and he gave all his sons a Continental education, with tutors and periods of residence in French and Italian academies. Pattee was the one who benefited most: he started in Spain and then went to Italy, where he stayed in Siena. In 1713 he travelled with his tutor and his brother, Matthew, the Byngs' second son (who was actually the fifth child: a son and a daughter, born between Sarah and Pattee, both died at an early age), touring France, Germany and Italy. At Florence, however, Matthew was taken ill and died.

Margaret Byng's sixth child was George, destined for the Army, and a seventh child died within a few months of birth. Robert was born a year later, in 1703. Perhaps the most intelligent of the Byng brothers, he was to become the businessman of the family and to have a successful civilian career at the Admiralty under his father, becoming a Commissioner of the Navy and Comptroller of the Storekeepers' Accounts. He married Elizabeth Forward, younger daughter of Jonathan Forward, the 'great contractor of transports'. (Pattee, who had become a snob and later married a duke's daughter, wrote to Robert on his engagement deploring that he should be marrying into 'trade', but saying that of course other gentlemen did do that sort of thing, and if Robert thought it worthwhile, good luck to him).[1]

John, who was Margaret's ninth child and fifth surviving son, was born at Southill in 1704, and he was destined to become the main actor in the tragedy which this narrative attempts to describe. Jack, as the family called him, was two years old when Edward was born. Edward, usually known as Ned, was weak and sickly even as a child; his life was brief and was to end tragically in the cabin of his brother's ship.*

These, then, were the children born to the former bankrupt's son, as he approached the climax of his naval career.

The 'King's Letter Boy' of 1678 was, by 1718, Admiral Sir George Byng, one of the Royal Navy's more respected flag officers. A little earlier he had had to decide on a career for his fifth son, John. None of his four elder sons had shown the slightest interest in the sea or a naval life. However, John at the age of thirteen began to show a definite liking for the Navy, and once the boy had made up his mind the Admiral had only to find a suitable captain to take him to sea. The choice was easy—the obvious man was his wife's brother, Captain Streynsham Master, who was commanding the *Superb*. Young John joined his uncle on board just before his father was given the most important task of his career so far.

Because Spain and Austria were involved in a prolonged quarrel over their respective possessions in Italy, Britain fitted out a large fleet for the Mediterranean. Among the ships chosen were the *Superb* and command of the Fleet was given to Sir George, who thus had his brother-in-law and son serving under him. However, it was to become even more of a family affair, because he obtained the King's permission to take another son, Pattee, to the Mediterranean with him on his staff. Although this smacks of privilege—indeed it *was*—Pattee had all the qualifications for the job: he was

---

* Margaret had two more sons, Charles (born and died in 1707) and Osborne (born and died in 1710).

then nearly nineteen years old, intelligent, with all his parents' good looks and charm, and he spoke several languages (thanks to his father's attitude towards education), including Spanish and Italian, the two likely to be most in demand during the next few months.

Sir George's task was to try to persuade the Spaniards not to invade Sicily, but if this failed he would be free to attack them. The Fleet sailed for the Mediterranean, and Byng's victory at the Battle of Cape Passaro was the result. When he reported to the Admiralty that 'We have taken and destroyed all the Spanish ships which were upon the coast; the number as per margin', Pattee took the news to London, travelling from Naples to Hampton Court in only fifteen days.

Young John Byng and his uncle Streynsham Master had seen their fair share of the battle: indeed, the *Superb* managed to capture the flagship of the Spanish Commander-in-Chief. Thus John, at the age of fourteen, received his baptism of fire; and the effect it had on him cannot be overestimated since it was the only fleet action in which he participated until, nearly forty years later when he was himself Commander-in-Chief in the Mediterranean, he commanded at the disastrous Battle of Minorca.

Sir George was made Baron Southill and Viscount Torrington in 1721, and only one higher naval post was left to him. Full of nervous energy, active, decisive, patient when need be, he had had a successful life as a sailor; in love and in finance he had been lucky. An indication of his good fortune over prize money—and in his choice of wife—is given in a letter to his daughter Sarah in the autumn of 1725: 'Your mother now wishes she had not sent for me home from the Mediterranean when she did. Then she thought she had enough [money for a new house at Southill] but now thinks that £30,000 would have added beauty to the place . . . She grows younger and younger; rides out a-setting, is fond of the fields and calls all the partridges hers. Her new house pleases her too, so that in the main she seems to be as easy and happy as any wife I know and believe she thinks so too.'[2]

To have been able to write such a report on the woman who had married the penniless young captain in the sea service and borne him twelve children must have given the new Lord Torrington a great deal of satisfaction.

Meanwhile young John, armed with the necessary certificates of sobriety, diligence and capability, passed his lieutenant's examination in 1722, when he was eighteen; but he had to wait until he was twenty before being appointed a lieutenant. Obviously Lord Torrington was a wise father and determined not to rush his son's career, since almost any captain in the Navy would have been only too glad to welcome the son of the great Lord Torrington on board his ship; but the delay was also probably due to the long-dead Mr Secretary Pepys who, during his busy and fruitful life at the Admiralty, had attempted to cut down the more flagrant instances of boy officers getting command by making twenty—with at least three years' sea service—the minimum age for lieutenants.

John Byng was twenty-four when in 1727 he was given his first ship to command, the 28-gun *Gibraltar*. Meanwhile his elder brother Pattee had begun what appeared to be a promising career at home: he was a Member of Parliament* and in 1724 had been made Treasurer of the Navy, a £2000-a-year post. The salary was extremely useful, because this was the year that Pattee married, but unlike Robert who had married into 'trade', he chose the daughter (albeit the fourth) of the Duke of Manchester. Pattee's father, this same year, was appointed First Lord of the Admiralty, the highest naval post to which he could aspire.

John and Pattee's sister Sarah had by this time been a widow for eight years: she had not reached her seventeenth birthday when she married John, the eldest son of Sir John Osborn, Bt, who lived at Chicksands Priory, only three miles from the Byng home at Southill. Sarah's glimpse of happiness had been only brief because by the time she was twenty-five her husband had died of tuberculosis, leaving her with a young son, Danvers, who inherited the baronetcy. (But she was a resourceful woman: with advice from her brother Robert she ran the estate so well that when Sir Danvers was twenty-one she handed it over to him in a far stronger financial position than when her husband was alive.)

So the days passed: John exercised his lonely authority at sea; his father reigned supreme at the Admiralty; and Pattee, soon a Privy Councillor, quarrelled spasmodically with his soldier-brother George. Meanwhile the youngest of the brothers, the sickly Ned, lived with his wife in Grosvenor Street, London, on

* For Plymouth from 1721–7 and then for Bedfordshire.

what money the former Miss Bramston had been left after the death of her father. He was soon reduced, with almost monotonous regularity, to mortgaging the house.*

Captain John Byng was twenty-nine years old and in command of the 50-gun *Falmouth* when his father, Lord Torrington, died in 1733. Lady Torrington was to live for another twenty-three years, most of them spent with her daughter Sarah. Pattee succeeded to the title, and for the next ten years comparatively little of interest happened to the family. Sarah's son, Sir Danvers, married a daughter of the Earl of Halifax, and within three years his wife died giving birth to their second son.

Considering the enormous patronage and influence his father had wielded at Court and at the Admiralty up to the time of his death, Captain John's progress in the Navy was steady but not startling: however, there were few ships in commission at this period. For the next twelve years he remained a post captain, and during that time the war with Spain which was to be named after the ear of that rather dubious character Captain Jenkins merged into the War of the Austrian Succession. Byng was not involved in the opening rounds: he was sent out to Newfoundland in 1742 to inspect the fisheries, and there, as senior naval officer, he was also by custom the Governor of Newfoundland.

A year later he was brought back to the Channel—doubtless without any regrets at leaving the chilly Grand Banks—and given the command of the 50-gun *Winchester*; and then, in 1744, he obtained his largest command so far, the 90-gun *St. George*. In the August of that year, when the Young Pretender and his handful of companions sailed from Nantes to Scotland full of high hopes of rousing the Highlands to the Stuart standard and seizing the Crown—but in fact with little else for their aid and comfort— John Byng was made a Rear-Admiral of the Blue, lowest of the nine grades of admiral, but entitling him, at last, to hoist his own flag.

Byng was now forty-one years of age. He was already plump; he was confident and rather fussy. He had spent twenty-seven of those years in the Navy, almost continually afloat. He had considerable experience in ship-handling, ranging from the Mediterranean to the ice, fog and gales of the Grand Banks. He had made

* There are a dozen or more mortgages or changes of mortgages on the house between 1736–49 in the Middlesex Register of Deeds.

no mistakes, run no ships aground, become involved in no scandals. But as a flag officer Byng had one professional short-coming, albeit a common one at this particular time: he had never commanded a ship, squadron or fleet in action: his only practical knowledge of battle was still his experience as a fourteen-year-old at Cape Passaro.

Meanwhile, there had been another death in the family—that of his brother Robert, who had been made Governor of Barbados, but died a year after leaving England. His widow, with her three sons, one of them only a few months old, sailed back to London and settled in Brook Street, facing the problem of what to do with the two eldest boys. Her father, the old millionaire contractor of transports, stoutly refused to pay for bringing up the boys as 'gentlemen', so the rest of the family had to rally round. It was agreed that the eldest, George, would be educated 'as a gentleman' at Pattee's expense; Robert was to be brought up by grandfather Forward on the understanding that he should go into trade (he did—into the East India Company and, as will be told later, died in the Black Hole of Calcutta), while the youngest of the three sons, John, was 'adopted' by the new Admiral, after whom he had been named.

Rear-Admiral Byng hoisted his flag for the first time in the *Kinsale* and took a squadron to patrol the Scottish eastern coastline, with orders that he was to prevent any help reaching the Young Pretender and his gallant rebels by sea. In carrying out this task Byng co-operated with the King's son, the Duke of Cumberland who was commanding the troops, and their correspondence shows that the Royal soldier, no fool when it came to judging men, trusted him. One of several letters to him in the Duke's handwriting said, 'I am sorry you and the King's ships are exposed to so many hazards and hardships in those seas, at this very rough season of the year, and I hope you have good luck to escape one and struggle through the other. I am your affectionate friend, William.'[3]

With Byng's task fulfilled in those wild Scottish waters, two events occurred—the Battle of Toulon and its aftermath—which had a very considerable influence on his life and on the naval history of Britain. They both go a long way towards explaining the mystery of Byng's conduct ten years later.

2

TRIALS GALORE

ON APRIL 11, 1745, the outraged members of the House of
Commons resolved that a humble address be presented to the
King, 'that he will be graciously pleased to give directions that
courts martial may be held in the most speedy and solemn
manner', to inquire into the conduct of Admiral Mathews, Vice-
Admiral Lestock and six captains of His Majesty's ships 'in order
to bring to condign punishment through whose misconduct it shall
be found that such discredit has been brought upon His Majesty's
arms . . .'

This extraordinary resolution, to which the King agreed without
a moment's hesitation, was the result of the abortive Battle of
Toulon, fought ten months earlier. There were many reasons why
the battle had been abortive, but the main one was the then current
set of instructions governing the tactics used by British admirals.

In the previous fifty years the instructions had become as
stylized as those for the stately quadrille (which, with its four
couples and its five figures, was one of the favourite dances at this
time) and, the cynics might say, the resulting battles were about as
dangerous. But for an admiral the punishment for ignoring the
instructions—as the pending courts martial were to show—could
be severe.

The 'rules' which caused this situation—and many more like it—
were called the Fighting Instructions. They did not belie their
name but they were old and sterile, lacking in scope and allowing
no initiative. Nevertheless, they were the official instructions for
the way in which battles were to be fought, and both admirals and
the captains were supposed to abide by them. In effect the
instructions told both the admirals and his captains that 'When
you see the enemy do this, you do that; when you reach that position
you engage the enemy in this way.'

Up to a point they were reasonable and necessary; obviously

there had to be some sort of method in a battle, otherwise the admiral would have no control over his ships. The trouble was that the Fighting Instructions were usually out of date, and at the same time signalling was so crude that it was difficult, and often impossible, for an admiral to signal his exact intentions if it was not already listed in the Instructions with its particular flag signal. In addition the Instructions tied an admiral down to a few specific manoeuvres—yet a choice of several hundred would be none too many.

Originally an admiral drew up his own Instructions, which he issued to his captains when he took over command of a fleet. In 1691, when John Byng's father was only a captain, his patron, Admiral Russell, had issued a set of thirty Fighting Instructions,[1] and then in 1703 (a year before John was born) they were followed with a set issued by Admiral Sir George Rooke which were, however, almost identical with Russell's. In the following year Rooke fought and won his battle at Malaga, paying great attention to the line-of-battle.*

The admiral commanding the fleet would marshal his three squadrons or divisions—van, centre and rear—in the correct order and in a straight line and manoeuvre them so that they would attack their opposite numbers in the enemy's line—van ships versus van ships, centre against centre and rear against rear. The marshalling before battle reached such a state of refinement that it was usual, if the enemy had fewer ships, to 'fall out' one's own extra ships to preserve the delicate balance.

Even in the fury of battle it was considered vital to preserve the line: if a ship's gunfire drove her opponent to leeward out of battle, crippled and waiting helplessly to be finished off, the system prevented her from following: it was necessary to stay in the line. Thus the Instructions gave the enemy a sanctuary or funk-hole to leeward: if the battle became too brisk the enemy had only to drift out of the line to be sure of surviving.

Any chances the opponents of the 'line' style of fighting had of getting these indecisive tactics changed (in favour of less rigid rules) vanished in the smoke of Rooke's victory at Malaga: here indeed, it was claimed, was proof that the 'line' tactics were correct

---

* It is from this that the line-of-battleship—referred to from now on by its shorter and more modern title of battleship—takes its name, being a sufficiently powerful ship to take its place in the line of battle.

B

and therefore inviolate. Rooke's Fighting Instructions were based on the line; Malaga appeared to prove that his Instructions were sound. The Fighting Instructions were therefore given a more official status: from then on they were to be the only rules for battle: the Admiralty had literally, as well as figuratively, drawn a line of battle; and an admiral who deviated from the line did so at his risk and peril.

Thus the stage was set for two battles, the first of which was to end in a near-farce and the second in a complete tragedy.

The Commander-in-Chief of the British fleet at the Battle of Toulon was Admiral Thomas Mathews, a man who was plump, forthright, testy and conceited. At the time of the battle he was sixty-eight years old and had been sent to the Mediterranean after spending twenty years on shore in retirement. Politically, he was against the Government—this was important, as it happened—and the Ministers made up for this by their choice of his second-in-command, Vice-Admiral Richard Lestock: he was a supporter of the Government and he detested Mathews.

These two admirals, each convinced that the other was certainly a fool and possibly a knave as well, appear to have generated much more hatred for each other as they tacked and wore across the Gulf of Lions than for their common enemies, the French and Spanish. The third flag officer in this unhappy fleet, commanding the van squadron, was Rear-Admiral William Rowley, a brave and competent officer.

When they finally met the enemy, Lestock's rear squadron was not in position and had had a dispute the night before with the Commander-in-Chief. Mathews managed to get Rowleys' van squadron and his own centre squadron into a line-of-battle and waited for Lestock to complete it. Signals were hoisted, but Lestock made no move. Yet, under the Fighting Instructions, Mathews could not attack until the whole of his line—van, centre and rear—was complete and formed.

With the enemy likely to escape, Mathews made a bold decision: disregarding the Fighting Instructions and Lestock's absence, he left the line and his ship bore down for the enemy. Some of his captains followed, and some did not. Five of Lestock's captains left their admiral and went to Mathews's assistance, and Rowley too went into action.

The enemy escaped with little damage and thanks mainly—although not entirely—to Lestock's tardiness, only a few of the twenty-eight British ships got into action. Thus it was not surprising that Parliament suddenly took an interest in the affair.

Yet from the start the courts martial had a farcical ring about them. One of the dilatory captains, for instance, was Norris of the *Essex*, son of the Admiral of the Fleet Sir John Norris. After the battle he resigned his commission on the grounds of ill-health, but 'learning how much his character was aspersed by his officers' he applied to Rowley, who had taken over command of the Fleet from Mathews, for a court martial to inquire into his conduct. Rowley—apparently trying to shield Sir John Norris's son—decided that as Norris had resigned he could not be court martialled. Norris promptly applied to the Admiralty, who gave permission, but when the court assembled it too recorded its doubts whether it could try a man who had resigned and sent the minutes to the Admiralty.

Norris, in the meantime, started for home, and he had reached Gibraltar when he heard he was one of the captains named in Parliament's address to the King. His enthusiasm for courts martial immediately vanished: he took off his uniform, crossed the frontier into Spain, changed his name, and 'remained for ever in obscurity'.

So much for the background. The series of courts martial started in England with the trial of some lieutenants, who were acquitted of charges of giving their captain bad advice. The captain in question, when subsequently accused—among other things—of 'not engaging within a point blank', withdrawing from the fight, and not bearing down on the enemy despite two orders to do so, defended himself by saying (although the battle had been expected for four days) that he had no bags of powder filled for the guns. He was found guilty and dismissed from the Navy.

Another captain, facing similar charges, blamed defective eyesight, and was put on half pay; a third was said to be a good officer and his tardiness was put down to 'a mistake in judgment' which eventually cost him only a year's pay (he had been dismissed as well, but the King restored him to his original rank). A fourth, similarly charged and similarly sentenced, was restored by the King and put on half pay; the fifth, Captain Norris, was now fugitive in Spain; the sixth had died before the trials started.

However, five more captains were yet to be accused—not by Parliament but by Admiral Lestock, who appeared to be put out at the idea that any of his captains should have left the rear division and joined Mathews in the action. Two were acquitted and three were cashiered—but, as far as public opinion was concerned, this was 'deemed extremely hard and reprobated as severe', and the King restored them to his service. One of the three was Captain Temple West, who was to be Byng's second-in-command at the Battle of Minorca.

Finally it was the turn of the admirals to face their trials, and it is at this point that Rear-Admiral the Hon John Byng re-enters the narrative. The first to be tried was Lestock, and three admirals and fourteen captains received orders to form the court martial.* Strangely enough, two of the admirals had been members of the courts trying the captains; Byng was the only newcomer as far as the judicial aspect of the Battle of Toulon was concerned.

On May 6, 1746, the court sat for the first time on board the *Prince of Orange* in the Thames, and as the President was ill, Rear-Admiral Perry Mayne, who was senior to Byng, acted in his place. Lestock's main defence was that as the signal for the line-of-battle was kept flying along with the signal to engage, he could not obey the latter without breaking the former. For the whole of the rest of the month Byng and his colleagues sitting in the stuffy 'great cabbin' of the *Prince of Orange*, ears assailed by the constant drone of voices, nostrils assaulted with the constant stench of the Thames flowing softly but noisomely past the ship, heard the evidence—charges, counter-charges, excuses and explanations. At the end of it all Lestock was 'unanimously acquitted'.

Only one man then remained to be tried, and he was Admiral Mathews, who can have had little doubt about his fate since the court, by saying Lestock was not guilty, had, by inference, found Mathews guilty; and as if it was not enough to prejudice the case, thirteen of the fourteen captains who had acquitted Lestock, and both the admirals, Perry Mayne and Byng, were appointed to try Mathews.

The tardy Lestock was Mathews's chief accuser, making fifteen charges against him, when the trial began on June 16. It dragged on through a hot summer, until finally the last of the evidence was

---

* The number of officers forming a court martial was not limited to a maximum of thirteen until 1749.

heard. The court, of which Byng was the second-senior member, then decided *unanimously* on October 22 that 'Thomas Mathews, esquire, by divers breaches of duty, was a principal cause of the miscarriage of His Majesty's Fleet', and equally unanimously the court sentenced him 'to be cashiered, and rendered incapable of any further employ in His Majesty's service'.

So the man who *had* got to grips with the French but who had to break the line in order to do it, was blamed and sacked. Lestock, on the other hand, had disobeyed orders for three consecutive days in sight of the enemy, had betrayed his Commander-in-Chief and, what is perhaps worse, endangered the Fleet; but he had not broken the line. The quadrille was there to be danced, and he had been acquitted because he had kept in step.

Thus did the wicked prosper; thus did the doctrine of the line become even more deeply entrenched. And we must be absolutely clear about one thing: Byng played a considerable part in these two remarkable verdicts. He was an experienced officer, and since he was one of the two admirals forming the court, he could have exerted a great influence on the verdict. Despite the theory that justice was done at a court martial in the eighteenth century simply because, to avoid their being influenced by their seniors, the junior officers gave their verdicts first, it is asking a lot of human nature to think that the juniors would not, by the time a trial ended, have a shrewd idea of what their seniors thought, and often let their opinion be swayed accordingly. There was nothing to prevent the seniors being subjected to unspoken pressure from the Admiralty; after all, the admirals depended on the Government rather than on their ability for both employment and promotion.

From this it follows that the two verdicts, on Lestock and Mathews, represent fairly faithfully either the private opinions of both Perry Mayne and Byng, or Admiralty opinions they were prepared to endorse. But the tragic aspect of the verdicts was that neither Byng nor the rest of the court apparently gave a moment's thought of the effect their verdict would have on the future tactics of the Navy: in fact they had thrust an admiral further into a tactical strait-jacket and pulled the straps even tighter. For Byng, ironically, it meant that he had gone a long way towards subsequently condemning himself to death.

3

SARAH'S 'PERSENTIMENT'

WITH THE MATHEWS court martial over, Byng had gone back to his house in Berkeley Square in the early autumn of 1746 little realizing that within twenty-four hours he would receive orders which would send him abroad. After spending so many weeks on board the *Prince of Orange* moored in the Thames—for the members of a court were not allowed on shore while the trial lasted—he was glad to be back in his own house. During his absence the stables which he had ordered to be built next door in Hill Street had been completed, and he was informed that they raised the rateable value from £100 per annum to £116.

After buying the new house in 1741 'as it stands' from the speculative builders who were, with commendable artistry, constructing Berkeley Square, Byng had then commissioned Isaac Ware, the architect, to decorate the interior in the style expected of an admiral. Ware had been given a comparatively free hand by an enthusiastic Byng—'Have you seen Mr Ware?' he wrote to his brother Pattee from Portsmouth. 'How do you approve of what he is about? I mean as to the design, not ye expence, for that's out of the question, when if I live I am to enjoy it.'[1]

He had instructed Ware to install a wind vane on the roof which, by a series of spindles and gears running down the chimney, registered the direction on an elaborately-ornamented dial fitted over the fireplace in what Byng called the Red Octagon Room on the first floor. It was a copy of the one fitted in the Board Room at the Admiralty, although the plaster ornamentation surrounding it was more elaborate. Carved cherubs blew vigorously, their cheeks permanently distended with the effort; beneath the dial a pair of dolphins swam with lissome but static grace above Neptune with crossed oar and trident.[2] The rest of the room was furnished without ostentation: the floor was laid with an Indian carpet; a Dresden china clock decorated with flowers ticked away on a small table; an inlaid French commode sat among polished side-board, tables and chairs.

In the first few hours while Byng was relaxing in Berkeley Square, the First Lord of the Admiralty, who was the Duke of Bedford, was having to make a decision. He wanted an admiral to command a detached squadron in the Mediterranean, under the Commander-in-Chief, Admiral Medley, which would operate off the French and Italian Rivieras to prevent the French launching any attacks upon the possessions of Britain's allies in Italy. The need was urgent, and Rear-Admiral John Byng seemed the obvious choice: his illustrious father had made the Mediterranean almost a sea of his own; the son had seen much service there. In addition, his command of a detached squadron in Scottish waters, keeping a watch on the Young Pretender, had brought forth praise of the Duke of Cumberland. And he had been concerned in returning a 'correct' verdict on Admiral Mathews.

So the First Lord asked the King's opinion: did His Majesty consider that Mr Byng was a suitable man for the Mediterranean? His Majesty did, and so the Duke asked the approval of the Duke of Newcastle, who was Secretary of State for the Southern Province. Newcastle was in complete accord with the King and with Bedford. 'I entirely agree with you,' he wrote to the First Lord, 'that Admiral Byng is much the properest person that can be sent to the Mediterranean.'[3]

Thus instructions were despatched to Byng at his Berkeley Square house which sent him to the Mediterranean for the second of his campaigns—the one in which he was to pick up a small fortune. (The orders which were to send him out for the third and final campaign were not to arrive at Berkeley Square for another ten years). When he received the Duke of Bedford's instructions one might have expected him to be elated: his appointment was important and would be extremely interesting—and, thanks to prize money, lucrative as well. Yet Byng's letter of thanks to the Duke of Bedford betrayed neither elation nor enthusiasm but could, however, be read in one of two ways: either it revealed his own misgivings over his ability to do the job, or it showed him as a modest man—at least when dealing with dukes and First Lords. He hoped that he would 'behave in such a manner that your Grace will not repent the choice you have made', but 'I do not think myself equal to the task I am going to take. I can only assure your

Grace that nothing shall be wanting in me to forward His Majesty's service all that lays in my power.'

He could not restrain himself from grumbling that he was being sent off at such short notice and that he had to make his way to Genoa by land—'a road I have never been; and I am told I shall find it extremely cold before I get to my journey's end. My only fear is I shall be laid up upon the road, for I have now upon me the remains of the gout I brought with me from Scotland.'⁴

However, if one is going to consider Byng's letter to Bedford as 'defeatist', it should be read against another, hitherto unpublished, which he sent less than two years earlier to his brother George from Spithead when serving with the Channel Fleet. He wrote in great haste ('I am afraid I shall not save the post') and said that the Admiral 'goes on board this evening, and if ye wind will permitt our sailing we shall all go tomorrow. We all go with joyfull hearts to meet these people [the French]. To show you how intent we are, every ship at Spithead is as clear for action as any ships ever was, all ye cabbins of every ship is down [i.e. all bulkheads had been removed, leaving the decks clear for action], and sent on shore, all hands swing now in hammocks and not one chest on board—when ye seamen heard that the French were in ye Channel they took ye chests of their own accord out at ye ports and every-body seems to be cheerful.'⁵

As soon as he received his orders for the Mediterranean, Byng had tried to get his young friend and semi-protégé, Augustus Hervey, appointed to command the *Superb*, the ship in which he was to fly his flag. He wrote to the Admiralty, saying that in Hervey he 'never saw a more complete exact officer since I have had the honour of being in His Majesty's sea service,' and that 'as every admiral gone abroad have been indulged with the choice of his officers (especially his captain) I flatter myself in the opinion that Their Lordships will not make any difficulty in granting this request'.⁶ He flattered himself in vain.

Hervey and Byng had first met in 1742, when young Augustus joined Byng's ship as a junior officer just before Byng sailed for Newfoundland. By the time Byng left to command another ship a firm friendship seems to have sprung up between the two men, despite the difference in ages (Augustus was then only nineteen and Byng thirty-nine), in temperament, and in rank.

Augustus later, in August 1744, took an unfortunate step in

marrying Miss Elizabeth Chudleigh. She was beautiful and gay and her virtue was as easy as her laugh. Daughter of a former Lieutenant-Governor of Chelsea Hospital she was one of the Princess of Wales's six Maids of Honour: not that Miss Chudleigh was overburdened with honour, but what she had was available, at a welcome salary of £200 a year, to the Princess of Wales.*

The situation Byng found when he arrived in the Mediterranean was reasonably clear and straightforward and his squadron, operating off Toulon, was soon joined by Augustus Hervey. The rest of the Fleet, under the Commander-in-Chief, Admiral Medley, was away to the eastward off Savona, near Genoa. 'I heard strange accounts of Admiral Medley's conduct, who was totally devoted to a Piedmontese mistress he had, who was wife to an officer in the Army and,' wrote Hervey, 'it was thought left there purposely to command him and give accounts of everything he did. She was an artful, insinuating, interested woman,' he added darkly.[8]

However, despite the known beauty of the ladies from the Plain of Piedmont, and their deep understanding of the spiritual and physical needs of British admirals, Medley died suddenly on August 5. A ship was sent to look for Byng to tell him he was now, as his father had been a quarter of a century earlier, Commander-in-Chief in the Mediterranean. Byng's accession to this new command met with the approval of the great Admiral Anson, recently created a baron, for he wrote to the First Lord of the Admiralty, that 'I find a strong disposition in his Grace [the Duke] of Newcastle not to think so well of Byng as I am sure he deserves'.[9]

Hervey gives a picture of Byng, within a month of taking over as Commander-in-Chief, acting very decisively over Mr Arthur Villettes, who was the British Minister to the Court of the King of Sardinia, based on Turin. 'Mr Villettes,' wrote Hervey, 'began a correspondence with Admiral Byng in the same style he had

---

* Miss Chudleigh was ater to achieve a sensation by appearing at the Venetian Ambassador's Ball at Somerset House on May Day, 1749, as 'Iphigenia for the sacrifice, but so naked the high priest might easily inspect the entrails of the victim,' wrote Mrs Elizabeth Montagu. 'The Maids of Honour (not of maids the strictest) were so offended they would not speak to her.' Before marriage she had just ceased being the Earl of Bath's mistress. The marriage was in secret—'the ceremony took place at the dead of night by the light of a candle standing in the upturned hat of one of the witnesses.'[7] See *Augustus Hervey's Journal*, edited by David Erskine.

continued one with Admiral Medley, which was that of dictating and finding fault,' as if the Commander-in-Chief was supposed to act under his orders. Byng dealt swiftly with this erring envoy, because Hervey was sent to the King of Sardinia, to present the compliments of the new Commander-in-Chief, and at the same time tell Villettes that if he did not mend his ways, Byng would send one of his own officers to Turin to maintain contact with the Court of Charles-Emmanuel III, and would 'have no communication with Mr Villettes'.

War in the Mediterranean ended nine months after this little episode, with Byng getting orders on July 13, 1748, to suspend hostilities. Pleasantries and presents were now exchanged with former allies, and soon Villettes brought Byng a gift from the King of Sardinia—a painting of the King, set with diamonds and valued at £3000.*

With his task completed, Byng was ordered home. He was now forty-four, and had recently been promoted to Vice-Admiral of the Red, highest of the three grades of vice-admiral. He had achieved six of the nine steps in flag rank towards reaching the highest rank in the Navy. No one in authority had, as far as the author has been able to discover, made the slightest criticism of Byng's conduct at sea for the whole of the thirty years he had spent in the Navy (most of them afloat), and particularly during his last period as Commander-in-Chief in the Mediterranean. Byng himself was pleased enough; writing to the Duke of Bedford from Gibraltar he told the First Lord that he would be home by October, and would 'return you personally my sincere thanks for all the favours you have been pleased to show me; and the little fortune I have been able to pick up since having the command of His Majesty's fleet in these seas I shall ever gratefully attribute to your Grace'.[10]

Back in England with his 'little fortune', Byng hauled down his flag and went back to London to open once again his Berkeley Square house. Since he had been away there had been another death in the family: his brother Pattee, the second Viscount Torrington, had died a year earlier at the age of forty-eight. Although Pattee had been made a Commissioner of Greenwich Hospital (an unimportant sinecure) and Captain of the Yeomen of

* In his will Byng left it to his nephew, the fourth Lord Torrington.

the Guard, he had become a sad and embittered man. The hot-house atmosphere of his cosmopolitan youth, the responsibility as his father's aide in Sicily, his looks, cultured manner and un-doubted ability, had all combined to give him a very good start in life in London. But the posts he held were entirely those that one would have expected the son and heir of the illustrious Admiral Lord Torrington to hold: somewhere along the road Pattee took a wrong turning—the youth with all the promise became the man in early middle age who had not really fulfilled any of it.

The title had gone to brother George, the soldier, who was by now a major-general. The new Lord Torrington was a reserved man, and after receiving severe wounds some years earlier he had become withdrawn. He never got on well with the fashionable Pattee, but he exchanged affectionate letters with his brother Jack and no quarrels are recorded.

The Admiral settled down to the social round of London life, but found something missing—a country estate, a stately seat. While looking round for such a place he leased a country house in Finchley (and he was, in August 1750, knocked down and injured by one of the stags which went with it). He eventually found a suitable district for his proposed estate near Barnet and in 1750 started buying up various pieces of land, starting at Kit's End, a small hamlet. The first part, Pinchbank House and about 150 acres with various cottages and 'the sign of the Angel Inn', he bought for £6500; the rest of the land he wanted for his park must have cost him as much again.[11]

He sent for Mr Ware*, who had made such a satisfactory job of the interior decoration in the Berkeley Square house. Now the Admiral, a considerably richer man thanks to the 'little fortune' in prize money picked up in the Mediterranean, had a really big commission for him. Soon Mr Ware and the Admiral were walking over the Admiral's land, carefully choosing the exact site for the new house. They finally picked a piece of rising ground near the centre of the estate. The view across the gently rolling countryside was superb and somehow typically English: there were no spectacular hills and crags, just soft green ridge and furrow, rising and falling with easy grace, like the flight of the woodpecker.

---

* At this time Ware was busy restoring Chicksands, the Osborn home in Bedfordshire, for Sarah's son Sir Danvers.

The plan Isaac Ware finally produced for the Admiral's inspection allowed for a vast brick and stone house with a front two hundred feet wide. At each end was a minaret-like tower, while in the centre was a large portico held up by four great Ionic columns, each three feet in diameter. Two sets of steps, extending out imposingly from the portico like callipers, led to the main entrance. To Byng it seemed a house befitting a Vice-Admiral of the Red and former Commander-in-Chief in the Mediterranean (and a Member of Parliament, for since January 1751 he represented Rochester, an Admiralty borough, 'in the room of Sir Chaloner Ogle, deceased').*

When it came to naming his noble edifice, the Admiral recalled that the Byngs had their origins at Wrotham, in Kent, hard by the bulging chalk downs, and he decided to call it Wrotham Park. However, a nephew, John, refusing to be impressed by its vastness or Ionic columns, was to call it a 'stare-about pile'.†

Then once again the family was suddenly bereaved: three years after inheriting the Torrington title from Pattee, George Byng died. His successor, and the fourth person to hold the title in less than thirty years, was his eldest son, also called George. The new Lord Torrington was, of course Admiral Byng's nephew.

By the summer of 1751 the Admiral was well settled into the routine of life in London and Kit's End, staying at Knightlands, a house which he had leased, and a few months later bought, from the rector of Tilsey, in Surrey. Work on Wrotham Park was going ahead satisfactorily; he had more than £15,000 invested in bank annuities, a town house, Kit's End itself, various properties and mortgages on others, and his half-pay.

It was in this same year that the Admiral took Mrs Hickson as his mistress. We do not know exactly when and where they met, or much beyond the fact that she was poor, a widow, and socially

---

* It was usual for a high proportion of flag officers to be Members of Parliament: among Admiralty boroughs (i.e. those where Admiralty influence or pressure on its employees secured the election of its nominees) were Plymouth, Portsmouth, Rochester, Saltash, Queensborough, Sandwich and Hedon. The Admiralty controlled in all about a dozen seats at this time, but several other 'private' seats were under the control of naval families or families with naval connections (the Boscawens, for instance, controlled five seats, and the Edgcumbes five).[12]

† The whole house was stuccoed between 1815–20. Its present owner is Lady Elizabeth Byng.

well below the Admiral's station in life. But we do know, on the
excellent authority of his sister Sarah, that the Admiral was happy
with her. The house at Kit's End, where the Admiral and Mrs
Hickson often stayed—and walked over to Wrotham Park to see
how the builders were progressing with the big house—was also
a favourite spot for his three nephews, the sons of his dead
brother Robert. Another frequent visitor was the Admiral's
youngest brother Edward, who was a sick man and found the air
at Kit's End made a welcome change from the grime, soot and
mortgages of Grosvenor Street.

Sarah wrote in the autumn of 1751 to her son Sir Danvers, who
had just gone off to Nova Scotia for a six months' visit to the
Governor, that on Sunday 'brother Edward went to Kit's End for
some time, and I with him for a few hours' visit. I never see the
owner better, quite happy there, talks of keeping it warm the
whole winter, spends his time cheerfull [sic] and comfortable with
his Old Dame, as he calls her'. The next paragraph was perhaps
more revealing of herself than anyone else, showing she was broad-
minded and far from censorious of her brother Jack's conduct.
'What's matter what it is? If people can be happy at pushpin, 'tis
as entertaining to them as the most refind satisfaction to those of
a more exalted genius. Since happyness is not confind to any
situation, and it is a very vain pursuit, I conclude it praiseworthy
to let the mind fall till it sinks into nothing, and forget what God
created us for.

'Poor Edward I left there, I think worse than I ever saw him . . .
cannot eat, or has the strength or spirit left. Wether the Old Dame
can nurse him up or not I cannot say, but 'tis melancholy to see
him so'.[13]

Perhaps tired—apart from looking after the two Osborn boys,
she cared for her mother, and had been doing so for the past
seventeen years—she then wrote: 'Insted of growing hardend as
I grow older, I every day find myself less fit for this world. Such
a crowd of disagreeable reflections pressed upon me as I returned
from my visite, that I cannot even yet shake off the effect of it
from my mind.'

Five weeks earlier she had written to Danvers a letter[14] which
is remarkable for its prescience. 'My dear Danvers,' she said, 'I
have a persentiment [sic] of coming evil . . . to our family, why I
know not, but 'tis to be hoped I am mistaken. We have had

enough, God knows, but if it comes we must meet it with fortitude and resignation.'*

But while the Byng family moved on towards the evil days that were almost to engulf it, so England was in the grip of the same fate.

---

* Although it will be referred to later, it is worth noting here that within two years Sir Danvers was himself to be found shot dead in New York; two years later the Admiral's 'Old Dame' had died, followed seven months later by Sarah's mother; three months later her nephew was killed in Calcutta; four months later Sarah's brother Ned died and seven months after that her brother Jack was shot. The loss of her son, her mother, two brothers and a nephew in five years seems to bear out the presentiment of 'coming evil'.

4

RAISING THE ALARM

AFFAIRS IN EUROPE in the early days of 1756 had the same boisterous and noisy—yet curiously orderly—chaos of a London
Street, but while the quarrel between France and Britain had so
far been like that of two bickering neighbours, their voices were
becoming shrill, and many people could see they would soon come
to blows.

The root of the trouble was America, a country which was vast
and potentially rich, capable of paying a huge dividend to its
owner. But who was to own it? Were the dividends to be paid to
Britain or to France? In sovereigns or *louis-d'or*? There had already
been several small clashes between the two countries, but the
fighting was confined to the American continent: in Europe, the
British and French diplomats still met in the salons and danced
the friendly quadrille with each other's wives with all the guile of
their calling.

Britain's foreign policy in Europe was handicapped by the need
to safeguard Hanover, whose Elector had become George I and
which was also the beloved birthplace of his son, now wearing the
Crown as George II. In addition, the old Triple Alliance of Britain,
the Netherlands and Austria was slowly falling apart: the Dutch
had become weak while the Austrians were restless, eager to
exchange their old friendship with Britain for a new one with
France.

At the end of 1754, by which time the First Minister, Henry
Pelham, had died and had been succeeded at the head of the
Government by his brother, the Duke of Newcastle, the British
sent a reinforcement of a thousand soldiers to America. As soon
as they heard about it, the French decided they would send
three thousand.

At the beginning of 1755 the French suggested an armistice; but
the British Government, confident that they had the advantage,

demanded a treaty or nothing at all. At the same time Parliament
voted the King a million pounds to 'augment his forces by land
and sea' and secure his American possessions. The French replied
with a claim to the whole of the land in America which the two
countries were disputing—a claim which found so little favour in
London that the French Ambassador was soon reporting war
seemed almost certain. And the British King's much-detested
nephew, Frederick II of Prussia, watching the scene from Berlin,
told the French King's envoy sympathetically that if he was Louis
XV, as soon as his uncle declared war or committed any hostile
act against France, 'I would march a large body of troops into
Westphalia ready to carry it at once into the Electorate of Hanover.
It's the surest way,' he added, 'of getting a twist on that——.'[1]

While the diplomats argued, the French reinforcements were
still at Brest, waiting to sail in convoy across the Atlantic. The
British Government decided they must not be allowed to arrive
on the shores of America. Britain and France were—officially,
anyway—at peace; but Vice-Admiral Edward Boscawen was sent
to sea with a squadron of ships and a set of half-hearted orders
which the Government had deliberately made vague, although it
was intended that Boscawen should capture the whole convoy.
The French convoy eventually sailed and, a week or two later,
Boscawen found three ships which had become detached from
the rest and he captured two of them. When the British Government heard that, instead of seizing the whole convoy, Boscawen
had taken only two ships, it was realized that they were now
morally in the wrong—without having the strategic compensation
of having seized all the French troops and the ships that were
carrying them. 'We have done too much or too little,' commented
the Lord Chancellor, Lord Hardwicke. And Boscawen himself, a
far from imaginative admiral, wrote to his wife Fanny that 'To
begin a war between two great and powerful nations without an
absolute order or declaration for it, now and then gives me some
serious thoughts.'[2] And well it might. The French Government
recalled its Ambassador from London; and the British promptly
sent out another squadron under the command of Vice-Admiral
Hawke.

Very soon Admiralty orders arrived at Berkeley Square for
Byng—he was to take another squadron to sea and operate in the
Western Approaches, with Rear-Admiral Temple West as his

second-in-command. If the British Government's original instructions to Boscawen had been half-hearted, there was no ambiguity
about Byng's orders—or in the fresh orders sent to Hawke: they
were to capture as many French ships they could.

Byng said goodbye to Mrs Hickson and put to sea for the first
time since he returned from the Mediterranean seven years earlier.
He was, of course, highly successful: unsuspecting French merchantmen, returning from the four corners of the earth, found
that a strange sort of peace had broken out; and instead of ending
their voyages in bustling French harbours they found a British
prize crew put on board and a course set for British ports.

For the moment, the French did nothing, and it did not take the
British Government long to find out why, even though their
Ambassador to France had returned. Fortunately, thanks to a
British agent, they still had ears and eyes in the highest diplomatic
circles in the French Court, where one of the most favoured of the
foreign diplomats, the Swedish Minister, Bunge, was basking in
the warmth of France's special friendship with his homeland.
Naturally the secret dispatches which Bunge wrote to his Foreign
Minister in Stockholm were of more than passing interest; and the
British agent was very cleverly intercepting them on their way to
that northern capital and copying them out.

Thus it was from Bunge that the British Government learned
that the French were for the time being waiting to see what Britain
was going to do with the captured ships. This news was followed
shortly afterwards by a memorial from the French Foreign Minister
to the British Government saying that although the French wanted
peace, Boscawen's capture of the two French ships was 'a public
insult', and the recent events in the Channel were 'pirateries' and
'brigandages'. The captured ships (for by now Hawke and Byng
had taken more than 300) must be returned to France, and if this
was done France would negotiate over America. A refusal, however,
would be a declaration of war '*la plus authentique*'.[3]

Henry Fox, the Secretary of State for the Southern Province,
writing to the Duke of Devonshire,[4] commented: 'All agree that
a war is unavoidable but the Ld Chancellor and the D. of Newcastle are for a little paper war first.'

However, the British Government's confidence soon had a rude
and sudden shock: the French, finally exasperated by the events
of the past year, were apparently planning to invade the British

Isles. 'We first engaged in a war, and then began to prepare ourselves,' commented Lord Waldegrave.

While the Duke of Newcastle fretted at Britain's unpreparedness
for a situation he had done as much as anyone to bring about,
John Byng was facing a personal crisis. Finishing his cruise in the
Western Approaches, he returned to England on November 21 to
find that his beloved Susannah, whom he had left happily estab-
lished in the Berkeley Square house, had been taken ill, and the
doctors seemed to hold out little hope for her recovery; indeed,
they had almost despaired of her life two months earlier, and she
had even sent for a lawyer to draw up her will. It was a pathetic
document in which she described herself as a widow of the parish
of St George's, Hanover Square, and asked that she should be
buried in the grave of her deceased husband at Woolwich. She left
£10 each to her two aunts living in Greenwich, and £50 to 'the
Right Honourable Admiral Byng' for him to buy a ring. The resi-
due went to a relative serving as a carpenter in the Navy.

Byng had not been back at Berkeley Square more than a few
days before Susannah died, and on December 12 he had the
melancholy task of attending her funeral at Woolwich. Her death
was a great blow—he had found personal happiness late in life,
and in less than five years he had lost it again. He continued calling
her bedroom at the Berkeley Square house by the name of 'Mrs
Hickson's Room', and because there was eleven months' delay in
proving the will[5] (her relative had since died on board his ship
in the East Indies) the Admiral had the mourning ring made even
before he received the legacy, and he wore it in her memory.

Meanwhile Britain's unfortunate legacy, the Duke of Newcastle,
continued to fret, for the news he was receiving almost daily from
his ambassadors, consuls and spies the length and breadth of
Europe would have alarmed even the calmest of men; and even
the most fawning parson depending on His Grace for a rich living
would never have called him calm.

Dozens of intelligence reports were flowing in about the French
plans and activities—far too many for us to consider all of them
individually. However, it is vital to this narrative to see what the
British Government knew—or thought it knew—of French plans
as the year 1755 bowed itself out in favour of 1756. They referred
to two distinct areas—the English Channel and the Mediterranean;

and we will deal first with those reports coming in during the last five months of the old year which concerned the Channel.

In August the British Minister at The Hague—who was Colonel Joseph Yorke, son of Lord Chancellor Hardwicke—sent a dispatch which faithfully reflected the air of confusion existing in the French Court at Versailles: the Ministers of France, he said, were never more perplexed, and although they were angry they could not agree on a policy. 'Councils are held upon councils, but nothing resolved.'

A month later came intelligence that there was talk in France of an invasion attempt, with Scotland as the target. 'The Pretender is said to be in Paris,' the agent added. In London the memories of the '45 Rebellion were, of course, just ten years old; the capital remembered the shock it had received when the Young Pretender roused the clans and gave the redcoats a long run for their money before being forced to flee.

By October the Duke of Newcastle was reading more dispatches from Europe which provided a slight variation on the main theme: a French invasion of Ireland was now being proposed, and this would take place at the same time as the attempt on Scotland, but 'on examination many difficulties arose.'

November brought talk of an attempt to invade England and for this task French troops were reported to be arriving at Dunkirk, while sixty ships—all merchantmen—were waiting at Boulogne and another thirty at Calais. For the invasion of England it was proposed to collect the troops and ships to transport them at one or two ports, and then the Brest Fleet would sail up Channel to protect them while they 'jumped the ditch'. However, the agent reporting this added that 'Probably no resolution has been taken yet except that of alarming and putting our Court to a great expense'.

The prospect of an invasion created a great deal of alarm in Britain and the First Minister (a position later referred to as Prime Minister) was writing that he always thought it would be difficult to make France confine the war to the sea and to America, and probably dangerous as well, since the French would strengthen their Navy, 'which they now actually do; and are, or I am afraid will very soon be, superior to us at sea. In what condition will this country be then?'[6]

In December, the month in which Byng attended Mrs Hickson's

funeral, it was reported to the Duke that seventy or eighty thousand troops were expected at Dunkirk—but the account was vague and more credence could be placed on a dispatch from The Hague which said that 'All the search that is possible hath been made, and it cannot be found that any plan has been found by the Council of France for invading England or Ireland ... Hitherto nothing has been done in France but to alarm and distress the Court of England.'

Thus the keynote of the Channel intelligence for the last five months of 1755 was that much was expected but nothing concrete had actually occurred. However, the news which had been coming in from the Mediterranean during the same period was more definite and more disturbing. The reports came from widely-spaced ambassadors, consuls and agents,* and the first of any importance came with a rush at the middle of September, two arriving in the same post on the 16th. One was from Consul Cabanis at Nice, saying that the French Government had just given orders to fit out sixteen men-of-war at Toulon; the other, from Mr Birtles at Genoa, confirmed this by saying a courier had arrived at Toulon with orders to fit out seventeen warships 'with the utmost diligence'.†

Two days later a report from a British agent in Marseilles reduced the total number of ships to a dozen, but added that they were to be ready within eight weeks. Then, at the end of September, some ominous news came from Consul James Banks from Carthagena: a hundred French battalions were marching into the Roussillon—the area on the eastern frontier with Spain—and 'are designed against Minorca'. They were to embark at Toulon and the squadron of warships then would escort them to the island, a distance of less than 225 miles. This piece of intelligence was important and, as it transpired later, one hundred per cent accurate.

In the next month, October, further reports from Cabanis at

---

* The main sources in the Mediterranean were Consul John Birtles (Genoa); Arthur Villettes, British Minister at Bern (the same Villettes whom Byng had chided at Turin); Consuls James Banks (Carthagena); John Dick (Leghorn); Lewis Cabanis (Nice); James Miller (Barcelona); Augustus Hervey's brother the Earl of Bristol, the British Minister at Turin; and Sir Benjamin Keene, the Ambassador in Madrid.

† This intelligence was accurate: the French Navy minister had issued the orders in the middle of August for twelve battleships and five frigates.

Nice and the Earl of Bristol in Turin gave the actual names of the warships; while for good measure Cabanis also added that the Toulon squadron, when it was ready, would be commanded by the Marquis de la Galissonnière.

At the beginning of November the man commanding the Royal Navy's small squadron in the Mediterranean, Captain George Edgcumbe, reported to the Admiralty that he too had just received intelligence that the French were fitting out a dozen battleships in Toulon. The agent at Marseilles wrote that seven of them now had their masts in, and this was followed up by a later letter from Edgcumbe saying that the dozen battleships, as well as five frigates, would be ready to sail by February or March. The last report of any importance received in 1755 came from Mr Villettes at Bern and said: 'Money is wanting [at Toulon], the workmen withdraw for want of pay, and the work goes but slowly.'

From the above brief summary, we can sum up what the British Government knew—or ought to have deduced—by the end of the year. As far as the Mediterranean was concerned, there should have been no doubt in anyone's mind that the pot was coming to the boil at Toulon: the reports received came from such places as Marseilles, less than thirty miles away, and Nice, a bare seventy-five; yet other cities—ranging over a distance of a thousand miles, from Carthagena in southern Spain, to Turin in northern Italy and Bern in Switzerland—had heard the same news: men had gone to the British envoys and consuls because of patriotism or in return for hard cash to tell what they knew or had heard.

In deciding whether or not the information was true, or just misleading tales put out by the French, the very fact that at first the early reports contradicted each other over the exact number of battleships being prepared at Toulon made it more likely that it was true: an alarmist story put out by the French for the benefit of British agents would at least have been consistent.

So, by New Year's Day, 1756, the information sent to the British Government concerning the Mediterranean told them this much: the French were preparing twelve battleships and five frigates (all of which were named in the reports); they would be ready by February or March; they would be commanded by the Marquis de la Galissonnière; a hundred battalions of troops were marching into the Roussillon to be embarked on board transport ships; and that these transports were to be escorted by the dozen battleships to capture the British-owned island of Minorca.*

This information (every item of which was, in fact, quite correct) should in any case have frightened the British Government: to defend Britain's interests in the Mediterranean there was at this time only the small British squadron consisting of one 60-gun ship, one 50-gun ship and four frigates.† The squadron was usually based at Port Mahon, in Minorca.

Minorca, the easternmost of the Balearic Islands, was strategically an extremely well-placed naval base: less than 225 miles north-north-east was the French main base of Toulon; a little more than 100 miles to the north-west was the Spanish port of Barcelona. And 150 miles to the south lay the great sea highway leading from the Strait of Gibraltar to the rich harbours of the Mediterranean— Genoa, Leghorn, Venice and Alexandria, as well as the Levant, whose harbours were then the trading sally ports for the riches of the East.

Minorca, placed by a lucky quirk of Nature almost midway between this highway and the French base of Toulon, was thus well-placed to protect it; in addition it was an ideal base for a British squadron wanting to blockade Toulon.

In other words, for a maritime nation already in possession of Gibraltar and wanting to protect its trade in the Mediterranean as well as hold down the French Fleet in Toulon, Minorca was the best possible base. But Minorca's value was only as a naval base: if there was not a powerful squadron in the Mediterranean to make use of it, then Minorca was an expensive luxury: a cannon without powder or shot. It was off the main trade routes, only just self-supporting and incapable of exporting anything.

Minorca, shaped like a miniature Australia, measures some thirty-three miles from west to east, and its average width, north to south, is ten miles. It has a mountainous backbone and then had only a few roads. Its former capital, Ciudadela, is at the western end, and its present capital, Mahon, is at the eastern end and has a magnificent natural harbour shaped roughly like a bottle: although

* For a divergent view on the significance of this information, see note 6 on page 315.

† The strength of a fighting ship was usually calculated by the number of guns she carried. At this time the smallest line-of-battleship was reckoned to be a 64-gun ship.

the entrance is only 250 yards across it soon widens out to more than 800 yards, and is more than three miles long.

To protect the harbour entrance there was a huge fortress, St Philip's, on the south side. The town of Mahon, at the far end of the harbour and more than three miles inland, could not be covered by Fort St Philip, and in the event of an attack it was planned that everyone should retire into the fortress, which had originally been well designed and strongly constructed.

It might be thought that this magnificent natural scabbard for Britain's offensive sword in the Mediterranean would have been well kept; but those better acquainted with Britain's inveterate unpreparedness in times of danger will not be surprised to learn that Minorca in 1756 was no exception to the rule of too little and too late. Its condition on New Year's Day, 1756, in the face of an open threat of invasion was so bad that had it been the twentieth century the leading politician responsible would have been granted an immediate earldom, while his bureaucratic advisers would have been showered with various minor orders of knighthood.

The defences of Fort St Philip had been allowed to decay; even the wooden platforms for the guns were rotting. Yet if the Fort was in a poor state, so was the island's garrison. It had an 'on paper' strength of four regiments, totalling 2860 officers and men, but on this New Year's Day no less than forty-one officers were absent in England, instead of being at their posts on the island. They included the Governor, Lord Tyrawley; the Governor of Fort St Philip; all the colonels commanding the four regiments; nine other officers, and nineteen subalterns who had been appointed to the regiments but had not yet joined. Left in command of the island was the eighty-two-year-old Lieutenant-Governor, who was Lieut-General Blakeney. The next senior officer to him was a lieutenant-colonel.

That, then, was Britain's strength in the Mediterranean: a blunted and rusty sword consisting of six small warships; the bent scabbard of a virtually defenceless island. Nor was the garrison at Gibraltar in a better condition. Although a parsimonious Government allowed them no money for the postage, it is to the credit of several of the consuls ranged round the Mediterranean coastline that they occasionally sent duplicates of their dispatches to General Blakeney, and the news they contained did little to comfort him; but unfortunately, they did little to animate him either.

Having surveyed the intelligence reports received in London up to the end of December 1755, and the state of the island of Minorca which the reports said was threatened, there remain only two other aspects to complete the picture of the situation: what the French were actually planning to do, and what the British were proposing to do in reply. Both can be explained briefly and simply.

To meet the alleged invasion threat in the Channel, the Royal Navy in December had eighty-three battleships in commission. Of these, sixty-five were in home ports or cruising in home waters; eleven others were in American and West Indian waters. Since the Admiralty maintained that forty battleships were necessary to defend Britain and the British merchant ships in home waters, there was an 'excess' of twenty-five battleships which could be used elsewhere.

In addition to the fact that this excess existed, there was absolutely nothing in the intelligence reports received up to the end of December, as we have already seen, to indicate the French had done anything more than talk about an invasion of Britain. The ninety ships reported to be in Boulogne and Calais soon proved to be weatherbound merchantmen; and there was no sign of other ships suitable for an invasion being assembled in any of the Channel ports. Nor had the reports of troops due along the French coast proved to be anything more than expectations: none had actually arrived.

So, with its excess of twenty-five battleships, and the fact that there were forty battleships available to defend the British Isles from a threat it was clear did not exist, it should have been easy to send out a powerful squadron to the Mediterranean by New Year's Day, 1756, to watch and blockade the Toulon squadron, and to guard Britain's position in the Mediterranean. The King's son, the Duke of Cumberland, already realized the danger to Minorca and eight months earlier had wanted to send recruits to Minorca and Gibraltar.[7]

Why, then, was nothing done? The answer is not hard to find: Lord Anson, who was the First Lord of the Admiralty, and his father-in-law, Lord Hardwicke, who was the Lord Chancellor, were against sending any ships because of their fears for the safety of Britain. As late as the beginning of December Lord Anson repeated his views in writing, and the letter still survives. He had received permission to go to Bath for a few days' course of the mineral waters for which that city was famous. Writing from there on December 6 to Lord Hardwicke he first assured him that 'I think the waters have agreed very well'—and then referred to a letter he had received from the Secretary to the Board of Admiralty. 'Mr Clevland has transmitted me a paragraph of intelligence from Toulon.* I think it would be a dangerous measure to part with your naval strength from this country which cannot be recalled if wanted, when I am strongly of opinion that whenever the French intend anything in earnest their attack will be against this country. This I should be glad the Duke of Newcastle should know; if his Grace is of another opinion I shall be ready to obey his command.'[8]

Lord Anson's advice was accepted by the Duke of Newcastle though, if the Duke's subsequent protestations are to be believed, against his better judgment and that of Henry Fox, the Secretary of State for the Southern Province.

By the end of December the French Government's plans were still in a muddle. The British agents had been quite correct in reporting that the Ministers were having meeting after meeting without deciding which plan to adopt. The only facts they omitted were the reasons for the repeated meetings. One was the King's mistress; the other was the scheming of the Ministers. The policy for any action against the British had to be agreed between Louis and Madame Pompadour on one hand and the Ministers on the other. The situation was confused even further because the Ministers were busy plotting among themselves and against each other. However, most of the responsible people in France were at least agreed on one thing—that France had been left well behind; the British held the initiative.

While the arguments were going on at Versailles, the Minister of the Navy, Count Machault d'Arnouville, was doing his best to

---

* From Captain Edgcumbe: he said five frigates would be ready to sail within a week, but work on the twelve battleships 'is going on but slowly' though they would soon be ready if fresh orders arrived to speed up the work. In any case, it was generally believed they would not be ready before the spring.

fit out three squadrons of warships—two at Brest and one at Toulon. The orders for the Toulon squadron to be prepared, as we have already seen, were given by him during August. Machault was one of the Pompadour's favourites, and her influence on the King was considerable at this time: each evening, before he saw his Ministers, Louis usually went to Pompadour's red-lacquered sitting-room for a talk about state affairs. The Navy was therefore in a happier situation than the Army, because the Minister for War, the Count d'Argenson, although an old friend of the King, was an old enemy of Pompadour. With his mistress, Countess d'Estrades, the Minister continually schemed and plotted to get rid of Pompadour—although in the end she won. (D'Argenson was in his bath when eventually he received the King's order of dismissal, banishing him to his estates.)

Work on the Toulon squadron was well advanced and the hundred battalions were in their camps in the south by the time the King decided to call the elderly Marshal de Belle-Isle to Versailles and give him command of the whole of the Channel coast, from Bayonne in the south to Dunkirk in the North. On New Year's Eve the Marshal Duke de Richelieu, the veteran of many victories in both boudoir and battlefield, was given command of the French Mediterranean coast from Port Vendres on the Spanish border, where the Pyrenees met the sea, round to Antibes.

A plan which had been under consideration for some time, was now to be carried out. It was quite simple: all the intelligence reports reaching Versailles from the British capital showed that the British feared a French invasion of their sceptr'd isle, so some judicious sabre-rattling along the Channel coast, and some cleverly-propagated rumours, should increase that alarm considerably. In the meantime, the French would capture Minorca, using the Toulon squadron to carry across the troops which were already waiting in the Roussillon.

The capture of the island would rid France of a British base uncomfortably near Toulon but, more important, it would cover her flank to seaward—while she carried out the second phase of the plan, which was to annexe Corsica. Once captured, Minorca would be a good bait to hold out to Spain, because in return for Minorca the Spanish might be enticed into joining the war against Britain.[9]

Count Machault, finding his orders of the previous August were not being carried out with sufficient expedition, now sent orders to the commander of the port of Toulon to speed up the work on the twelve battleships. But it was, as the intelligence reports reaching London already indicated, a difficult task. At Toulon they were desperately short of skilled men—the shipwrights, caulkers, riggers and sailmakers needed to get the ships into commission. When eventually they found the skilled men they were short of money to pay them and buy the necessary materials; when they obtained the materials—including such items as timber for the spars—it was frequently too dangerous to ship them round to Toulon by sea because of the English privateers harrying the French coastal shipping from their base at Villefranche which, like Nice, was of course not then French territory.

5

HIS GRACE'S AGENDA

NEW YEAR'S DAY OF 1756 was a mournful Thursday for those thoughtful people in Britain who feared the coming war, but nevertheless in London the Poet Laureate, Colly Cibber, arrived at St James's Palace in company with several score diplomats, ministers and courtiers, all of whom were intent on paying their respects to His Majesty. Promptly at noon, before an expectant audience which included the noblest in the land, Mr Savage (to the accompaniment of Dr Boyce's music) read Mr Cibber's 'Ode to the New Year', the Poet's atrocious attempt to justify his salary of £100 a year.

'Hail, hail, auspicious day' declared Mr Savage; but rather nearer reality than Mr Cibber's poetry was a warning being given that very day to the people living in a street near Chatham Dock: because of the danger of a French invasion they had thirty days in which to leave their homes, which were to be demolished and 'intrenchments thrown up in their room'.

Yet the majority of London folk still bustled about their business without bothering overmuch about the bickering of Governments. The booksellers busied themselves trying to sell Dr Johnson's Dictionary for ten shillings a copy—and one had to admit it was a bargain compared with Mr William Payne's *An Introduction to the Game of Draughts* which cost three shillings and sixpence. The City of London was busy petitioning for a new bridge over the Thames 'at or near the Fleet Ditch' (they eventually got it, much to the annoyance of the boatmen working the ferries and it was called Blackfriars Bridge) while 'diverse merchants, tradesmen, citizens and inhabitants of London and Southwark' wanted London Bridge to be widened by removing some of the houses built on it.

The Government, however, were not interested at the moment in building a new bridge over the Thames: they were more con-

44

cerned that France might use her ships to bridge the Channel and march a few hundred regiments up the road to London. The Ministers' peace of mind was disturbed by the intelligence reports which continued to arrive in London from all over Europe, and there was a good deal of gossiping and speculating in the coffee houses, for the newspapers were almost as well informed as the Government; indeed, as we shall soon see, their information was often earlier and more accurate.

Admiral John Byng, still grieving for Mrs Hickson, stayed at Berkeley Square: it was less lonely for him than the big house at Wrotham Park, and in any case he wanted to be in London so that he could call at the Admiralty from time to time to find out the latest news.

The information which reached London from the network of agents and envoys during January and February was great in quantity and much of it confused in content; but a competent Minister watching the trends and refining the crude ore would soon have found himself in possession of much valuable material. It did not take long for news of the appointment of Marshal de Belle-Isle to the Channel command and the Duke de Richelieu to the Mediterranean to reach London—the letters reporting it arrived on January 12 and several more confirmed it within a few days.

In making a brief survey of the intelligence reports received in January and February, we can once again divide them into those referring to the Channel and to the Mediterranean. The first concerning the Channel reported Belle-Isle's appointment and said that 'The moderation of the French King is at an end'. All Paris was talking about an invasion, although "They agree it must be attended with insuperable difficulties,' so much so that the citizens of Paris had concluded, said the agent, 'the great preparations that will be made for the invasion are intended to alarm the nation, distress our credit, and prevent our transports being sent abroad.'

By February an agent was reporting that Marshal de Belle-Isle had advised the King not to attack any Continental Powers yet, but to assemble large armies to keep the powers 'in check and suspense'. After that, an invasion of England or Ireland 'must be seriously attempted'. Another agent said that the troops intended for an invasion of England would embark at Brest and Le Havre and added that at the latter port the French had assembled 'a vast number of flat-bottomed boats'. However, when a British warship was dispatched to count them her captain reported there was none in the harbour.

On February 14 Colonel Yorke wrote from The Hague that the French Court had approved a plan by Marshal de Belle-Isle to assemble 100,000 men on the Channel coast for three attacks on the British Isles, but two of them would be feints. The Marshal, said Yorke, was demanding 600 transports and intended using British smugglers from Kent, Sussex and Hampshire to pilot his ships, which would sail in a fresh southerly wind, on a dark night, or in a fog, 'because in each of these cases the fleets of England could not come to intercept their passage' (a very fallacious deduction on the part of the Marshal).

'It is further reported,' said Yorke, 'that this project is to be seconded with an embarkation upon the coast of Provence, where 30,000 men are ordered to assemble and to make an attempt upon the island of Minorca.' This piece of information, coming as it did in the middle of February, formed a direct link with earlier material from the Mediterranean—particularly the report from Consul Banks at the end of September that 100 battalions 'designed against Minorca' had arrived in the Roussillon. Since then Consul Birtles had written from Genoa in January that a 'positive order' had been given to get the Toulon squadron ready at once 'and it is whispered they intend to make a descent ... to surprise the island of Minorca'. Consul Banks had written again to say that most of the Provençal ports were crowded with local craft hired by the French Government; and several other agents constantly referred to a threat to Minorca.

However, as far as the Duke of Newcastle was concerned, the most usful piece of information arrived on his desk on February 25: it was a copy of a despatch from the faithful Swede Bunge, intercepted on its way to his master in Stockholm. It gave more news of Marshal de Belle-Isle's plan: 'This plan,' said Bunge, 'consists properly in two articles. (1) A landing in England; and (2) another in Minorca, in order to take Port Mahon.' It was known, he added, that Mahon was not particularly well fortified on the land side.[1] This confirmed the information received eleven days earlier in Colonel Yorke's dispatch. However, the Duke of Newcastle did nothing until a third letter arrived a few days later, this time from Mr Cressener. As soon as he read it the Duke became very agitated. He finally called for a meeting of the Inner Committee next day, March 9, and in the meantime (apparently, as a result of discussions with Fox, Hardwicke and Anson) told the First Lord that, pending the Inner Committee meeting, the Admiralty should prepare a squadron for the Mediterranean.

The Board of Admiralty consisted of seven 'Lords Commissioners for Executing the Office of Lord High Admiral of Great Britain and Ireland', and whereas the majority of its members today are serving naval officers, in the eighteenth century it was more usual for them to be outnumbered on the Board by civilians.* These civilians were not men with any special knowledge—or, indeed, any knowledge at all—of the sea or of administration; for the most part once a man was appointed a member of the Board he could treat it as a £1000-a-year sinecure if he so wished, or could be quite active.

Usually Lord Anson was at the Admiralty each day, and at least two other members of the Board called in during the morning for a Board meeting (which was usually quite perfunctory because of Anson's ability and the strength of his personality), returning in the afternoon to sign orders which required the signatures of three members of the Board.

After hearing from the Duke of Newcastle about Cressener's letter, Lord Anson called a Board meeting late in the day, which two other members attended. They were Lord Bateman and Mr Thomas Villiers. Bateman, thirty-five years of age, was formerly Member of Parliament for Oxford and was then one of the two representatives for Woodstock. Villiers, then forty-five years old, was the Member for Tamworth and formerly a British envoy at Dresden. Neither men had any knowledge of maritime affairs, which of course meant that Anson held complete sway at the meetings.

It was John Clevland's job, as Secretary, to draw up an agenda for each Board meeting, and to take notes and keep the minutes. A Scotsman and the son of a former naval officer, he had been in the Admiralty's service for thirty-four years, with the result that, as he was later to petition the King, his 'health and eyesight is greatly impaired by the incessant application to the faithful

---

* In the present electronic age the composition of the Board is equally ridiculous, having no engineer specialist among the members. On the other hand, the Secretary and clerks of the eighteenth century had, mercifully, considerably less power than they have gained for themselves in the twentieth century.

discharge of his trust'. He also had 'a wife and great number of children' to worry him. One son was an Admiralty clerk.*[2]

Seated round the long, well-polished table, with its inset legs, the three Board members, Anson, Bateman and Villiers—with Clevland sitting among them, quill poised ready to take notes—discussed the Mediterranean situation. The Duke had said a squadron was to be prepared and the Board had only to choose the ships. However, since the names would have meant as much to Bateman and Villiers as the runners in a local horse-race, we can safely assume that they were picked by Anson. The *Ramillies*, in which Byng had flown his flag last winter, would make a good flagship. The *Buckingham* (which had been Temple West's ship) would do well for the second-in-command. From the other ships available, eight more were chosen. When they joined the ships already in the Mediterranean they would form a squadron of thirteen battleships, though several would be only 64-gun ships.

To each of the captains instructions[4] were sent saying that 'Having ordered His Majesty's ship under your command to be fitted out for a voyage to the Mediterranean,' he was to 'get her ready for the sea accordingly, as soon as possible, and hold yourself in constant readiness for sailing . . .'

The Army's interest in Minorca had already started, because the King (no doubt under the influence of the Duke of Cumberland) had ordered all the absentee officers to get to their posts on the island as soon as possible. The Admiralty were warned to provide a ship to transport them[5] and soon a messenger brought a letter from the Secretary at War, Lord Barrington, at the War Office next door, giving the total number of officers, servants and troops to go to Minorca.[6]

Next morning, March 9, the Board met again to decide who should command the squadron. There was not a wide choice; indeed, the obvious man was John Byng, since he had already

---

*The name Clevland has often been written with a second 'e' but both men always signed their names without one. The Clevlands afford a good example of 'interest' at work: the Secretary's eldest son, already a clerk in the Admiralty at £70 a year, was within five years a clerk at £100, Deputy Judge Advocate at £146, a Commissioner for the sale of Prizes (from which he took a percentage), and an Agent for Marines. By 1766 he was also MP for Barnstaple, a seat which he eventually held for thirty-six years. His father in 1756 was MP for Sandwich —which was another Admiralty borough, inasmuch as the Admiralty nominated one of its two members.[3]

acted as Commander-in-Chief in the Mediterranean in the last war. His period in command had not been marred by any unpleasant incidents; his recent cruise in the Atlantic, with Rear-Admiral Temple West as his second-in-command, had gone off smoothly. So once again Clevland noted down the decision of the same three members of the Board: 'Vice-Adml Byng is to be directed to take the ships lately ordered to fit for the Mediterranean under his command.'[7]

After receiving Cressener's letter and calling a meeting of the Inner Committee, the Duke of Newcastle scribbled down in his almost indecipherable, jerky handwriting, a few notes in two columns on a blank sheet of notepaper. These were to form the agenda, and later his secretary, Hugh Valence Jones (who was the nephew of Lord Hardwicke, the Lord Chancellor) copied them out for His Grace to take to the meeting. Headed

Business for the Meeting this evening March 9th, 1756.

the agenda finally ended:

Advices from Spain—Port Mahon—Squadron for the Mediterranean

Cressener's Intelligence—Port Mahon—Canada—8000 men—Invasion . . .

Armed with this, His Grace set out in his carriage bound for the Cockpit, the name given to the building on the park side of what is now the street of Whitehall, and which contained the offices of the Secretaries of State and also the Council Chamber. There were seven men at the meeting of the Inner Committee that evening (for the whole Cabinet was large and seldom met) and they were making or confirming for the first time as a group, as far as we can tell from the minutes preserved among the Newcastle Papers, the Government's decisions over the French preparations in the Mediterranean. These men are important to this narrative because they were responsible for sending Byng to the Mediterranean; they were responsible, in part at least, for what subsequently happened then; and they were completely responsible for the tragic aftermath.

The first of the seven men was Philip Yorke, the Earl of Hardwicke and Lord Chancellor, a self-made man who had become an eminent judge, and who was the cold, incisive and worldly brain behind the fretful Duke of Newcastle. The second was the Lord

c

President, Lord Granville, a cultured man of the world, a skilled diplomat, and a remarkably good classical scholar, who in the words of Lord Shelburne, 'had a rooted objection to Lord Hardwicke and to all his family. I don't know precisely for what reason, but he got the secret of cowing Lord Hardwicke, whose pretensions to classical learning gave Lord Granville, who was a very fine classical scholar, a great opportunity.'[9]

The third man at the table was his Grace the Duke of Newcastle. Although First Minister, he was very much the hesitant velvet hand in the iron glove of the Whig Government. Superficially, His Grace was a comical figure: Lord Wilmington in a judgment that was to become famous, said the Duke 'always loses half an hour in the morning which he is running after the rest of the day without being able to overtake it.' He lived—as his voluminous correspondence shows—in a state of perpetual alarm: his mind was a playground for a host of homeless political hobgoblins who rang the alarm bells in his brain at the same pitch whatever the cause—to the annoyance of his friends and the delight of his enemies.

Horace Walpole, certainly no friend of the Duke, later described his conduct at the funeral of George II at Westminster Abbey in these terms: 'He fell into a fit of crying at the moment he came into the chapel, and flung himself back in a stall, the Archbishop hovering over him with a smelling-bottle; but in two minutes his curiosity got the better of his hypocrisy, and he ran about the chapel with his glass to spy who was or who was not there, spying with one hand and mopping his eyes with the other. Then returned the fear of catching cold; and the Duke of Cumberland, who was sinking with heat, felt himself weighed down, and turning round, found it was the Duke of Newcastle standing upon his train, to avoid the chill of the marble.'

His Grace, before venturing from home, always sent instructions to his prospective host that the beds intended for himself and the Duchess were to be slept in the night before they arrived, to make sure they were well-aired. Melodramatic, jealous of any possible political rival or of anyone with ability which outranked his, querulous, frequently childish and certainly unbalanced, he nevertheless proved to be necessary to nearly every Government for more than forty years. The reason is not hard to find: he was an extremely energetic man, prepared to devote all his time and nearly all his not inconsiderable fortune to control the party machine. In this he had experience of home politics, politicians and their prices, which was probably unrivalled. How he wielded some of this power will soon be seen.

The fourth man in this Whiggish septet was Lord Hardwicke's son-in-law, and if the Lord Chancellor was the grey eminence of the Whig Government then the man who married his daughter Elizabeth was its Neptune. George, Lord Anson, the First Lord of the Admiralty was strong and silent, fitting the popular idea of a sailor, with all the professional seaman's suspicion of politics and politicians. He had commanded the *Centurion* during her cele- brated voyage round the world and appeared to a Royal prince as a good man who, though not brilliant, 'improved the building of our ships, made more good officers, and brought others forward in the Seven Years' War, than any of his predecessors had done.'[10]

One of his brothers-in-law, writing that he was at first shy and reserved, admitted he 'loved reading little, and writing or dic- tating his own letters less, and that seeming negligence in an office, which must be attended with applications to the First Lord in person, to which answers are always expected and are often proper, drew upon him the ill-will of many'. But nevertheless, he had 'a remarkable quickness in making dispositions of ships and appoint- ing them to the services for which they were fittest', and con- ducted the business of a very complicated department 'with uncommon vigour and despatch'.[11] Horace Walpole, commenting that he was reserved and proud, said he was 'so ignorant of the world that Sir Charles Williams said he had been round it but never in it'.

Born the second son of a Staffordshire barrister in the parish of Colwich, Anson was now seven weeks short of his fifty-ninth birthday and at the height of his power.* That he was a great seaman is shown by his famous voyage; contemporary verdicts indicate his ability as an administrator. Unfortunately, as a strategist in the period 1755–56, he left a lot to be desired. It is worth noting that as First Lord of the Admiralty he had a very difficult task, because he was at the head of a service in which no

---

* Anson and his wife Elizabeth had lived since 1751 at Moor Park, in Hert- fordshire, the former home of the Careys, where more than a century earlier another John Byng had begun a childhood friendship with Lady Martha which was to start his son, later Lord Torrington, on his naval career.

one had a great deal of confidence: the Navy's great reputation was yet to be made. For the time being Anson was more concerned in producing a Navy which could fight battles which did not end up with chaos and courts martial, and he began by having little or nothing to do with the Duke of Newcastle's tangled web of political patronage. A typical example was the occasion when the Duke wrote to him claiming that the Corporation of Okehampton was interested in a certain lieutenant, and unless he was promoted, 'the corporation is lost and with it one, or perhaps two Members [of Parliament]'. Anson replied that he 'always do attend seriously to whatever your Grace recommends,' but, he added rather sourly, 'I must now beg your Grace will seriously consider what must be the condition of your Fleet if these borrough recommendations, which must be frequent, are complyed with . . .'[12]

The fifth man attending the meeting of the Inner Committee was not bothered with attacks of scruples: Henry Fox, the Member of Parliament for Windsor, was Secretary of State for the Southern Province, and whereas his great rival Pitt was haughty and arrogant with friend and enemy alike, often making enemies without purpose, Fox was just the opposite. Whereas Pitt's great knowledge and understanding of foreign affairs and the strategy of war let him see how policy should be formed on the grand scale, Henry Fox relied on his knowledge of men: men with all their ambitions, fears and weaknesses, their abilities and shortcomings. This knowledge of human nature (and few if any of his political contemporaries had greater—except perhaps for the Duke of Newcastle, although usually his Grace knew more about a man's price than his personality) made Fox, with his considerable experience and ability as a speaker, the Duke's strongest weapon in the House of Commons.* As a Secretary of State 'he shone in administrative detail rather than in original conception'.[13] His morals, as a politician, were no better and no worse than those of his contemporaries.

The other Secretary of State, for the Northern Province, was Robert d'Arcy, fourth Earl of Holdernesse. At the age of thirty-

---

* The majority of the important Ministers were in the House of Lords. In addition to the Duke of Newcastle, there were Lords Hardwicke, Granville, Anson and Holdernesse. In the Commons, in addition to Fox, was Lord Barrington, the Secretary at War, (a comparatively minor post), who was not a peer.

eight, Lord Holdernesse was a colourless man, pliable and sufficiently lacking in individuality and opinion to be a favourite of the
Duke, whose first reaction some years earlier to working with him
had been that 'though a d'Arcy, he is not proud, you can tell him
his faults and he will mend them'.[14] However, when removed
from office Holdernesse faded from the political scene into the
obscurity from which, one might be forgiven for thinking, he
ought never to have emerged.

The last man at the meeting was Sir Thomas Robinson, MP for
Chislehurst, a pompous and long-winded former diplomat (he
had been the British ambassador at Vienna for eighteen years),
and now Master of the Great Wardrobe.

These then, were the seven men who sat down at the Cockpit
on Tuesday evening, March 9, to decide the next moves in this
particular round of the game of diplomacy which was, within a
few weeks, to lead to the Seven Years' War.

They had a considerable amount of information on which to base
their opinions. Apart from the intelligence reports already described (including Consul Bank's warning of September 27 and
Birtles's of February 4, both saying the French planned to capture
Minorca; Yorke's of February 14 reporting Bell-Isle's plans to
invade England; and Bunge's of February 25 giving the plans to
invade England and Minorca) there were later ones covering the
first nine days of March—up to the time the Inner Committee
met. The more important of these were from Captain Edgcumbe,
saying that the Toulon squadron was ready, 'a considerable number' of French troops were marching to the coast, and 'It is generally thought the French mean to surprise Minorca'; Sir Benjamin
Keene in Madrid, who declared that he was apprehensive about
Minorca because of all the reports of French troop and ship
concentrations; and General Blakeney in Minorca, who wrote that
there was 'reason to believe the French intend very shortly to make
an attack on this island'.

There was, however, one other piece of information for the
Ministers to consider, and it was the item noted down on the
Duke's agenda as 'Cressener's intelligence', and which was, of
course, the reason why the Ministers had been called to the
meeting. Cressener, although a British agent, was a Frenchman
living at Versailles. He apparently had access to the French Court
and diplomatic circles, and his information was highly valued by

the Duke. His letter, which had so agitated his Grace the previous day, said that France badly wanted Spain's help in the coming war, and was bidding high for it. Louis's offer to King Ferdinand, he reported, was going to be quite simple: if Spain came into a war on France's side, Louis would in return give Ferdinand the island of Minorca (after capturing it from its present owners); and if Spain further co-operated by providing fifteen battleships, she could have Gibraltar as well.[15]

Spain's present friendship for Britain was largely the result of the work of three men—her pro-British premier, who was the Irish-born General Wall; the British Ambassador, Keene; and also the present Spanish Ambassador in London, Count d'Abreu, who was well-liked and well-trusted in the British capital. But the question the British Ministers could not answer was whether Spain's friendship would be strong enough to withstand the temptation of acquiring Minorca and Gibraltar for virtually no cost, and at no risk. Cressener's warning letter had been written from Versailles on February 22, and it was now March 9. The Toulon squadron could have sailed for Minorca a fortnight earlier; the French army might have been in the island for a week . . .

The Inner Committee considered the various reports and their implications, and then made up its collective mind. The minutes recording its decisions said that 'Their Lordships are humbly of opinion that as strong a squadron as can be spared from hence be got ready to send into the Mediterranean'.[16]

No mention was made of the size of the squadron*; nor was a date fixed by which it should sail. Both points were important, it later transpired. Anson had, of course, already been told to prepare a squadron. Since the Inner Committee uses the phrase 'as strong a squadron as can be spared', without specifying the number of ships, it seems probable that it had been left to Anson to decide on the strength; otherwise, as the squadron had in fact already been chosen, the Committee might have been more specific. Letters written subsequently by Newcastle and Fox imply that Anson made the choice.

However, having at long last admitted that a threat to Britain's

---

* The Admiralty and Byng referred to the ships as a 'squadron' and also a 'fleet', often in the same sentence. Since they were 'a detachment of ships employed on a particular expedition', squadron is used where possible in this narrative.

position in the Mediterranean actually existed, and made their desision accordingly, the seven men said their farewells and left the Cockpit.

Two days after the meeting Lord Anson had the task of drawing up two sets of orders. The first, delivered by Thomas Tranter, was the one addressed to Vice-Admiral Byng which, as we saw in the Prologue, ordered him to embark for what was to be his third and fatal Mediterranean campaign and 'required and directed' him to go to Portsmouth and take the squadron under his command. The second was commendably brief and addressed to Rear-Admiral Temple West, who was to be second-in-command, and to the captains of each of the ten ships, and followed the traditional wording: 'You are hereby required and directed to put yourself under the command of Vice-Admiral Byng and follow his orders for your further proceedings.'[17]

Byng was soon busy settling his own affairs before going to Portsmouth. Wrotham Park had to be closed up—for it was obvious he would not be back for many months—and, when he had left, the Berkeley Square house as well. The man who looked after his affairs was his first cousin, Edmund Bramston (whose mother had been Isabella Master, sister of Byng's mother: he was trustee, executor and friend to several of the Byngs).

The Admiral was still busy the following Wednesday, March 17, when the Board met and discussed the question of promoting him. He was by then senior of the vice-admirals, and the Board finally agreed 'That the Honble John Byng be appointed Admiral of the Blue Squadron of His Majesty's Fleet.'[18] In prestige, Byng took another step forward. Materially he was a good deal better off—his daily pay as Vice-Admiral had been £2 10s. but now, as a full admiral, it would be £3 10s. That afternoon—for the Board meeting was held in the morning, and a message was sent summoning him to the Admiralty—Byng was sworn in, taking the oaths of allegiance and supremacy required under the Test Act, and receiving his commission appointing him Admiral of the Blue.[19]

Next day he said his farewells: first to his mother, old Lady Torrington, and to Sarah, living in Stratton Street; and then to his sister-in-law Elizabeth, widow of his brother Robert. He also collected his nephew John, whom he had taken to sea for the first time as a midshipman in the *Ramillies* during the cruise the previous winter, and whose name had been on her muster list ever since.*

Finally, on the 19th, the horses in the stable were harnessed and the Admiral and the Midshipman climbed into the carriage: at last they were bound for Portsmouth, but there was a sea of trouble awaiting the Admiral on the other side of the Portsdown Hills.

* His name is entered on September 27, 1755, on the line beneath that of the Admiral. [20].

THE ISLAND OF DESPAIR

THE BRITISH IN MINORCA at the beginning of the year had been anxious men, because the news reaching them from France and Spain was grave, and the island was short of every commodity except despair. The garrison was well under strength and there was no indication from London that more troops or ships were to be sent out to help them.

Augustus Hervey had been in the Mediterranean since 1752, commanding the *Phoenix*, which formed part of the small British squadron. He arrived at Port Mahon on New Year's Day and was fortunate to find at least one bright spot: he was, he wrote, 'lucky enough to get in with a very pretty girl, daughter of Smallridge that kept the tavern. She and I agreed very well, and I kept her all the while, and a sweet pretty girl she was.' However, life also had its serious side: 'I hove down the ship here and prepared for sea as soon as I could, expecting a war every minute.'[1]

General Blakeney, who had assumed command of the island in the absence of the Governor, Lord Tyrawley, finally became alarmed at the French threat and called a council of war. It met for the first time on February 5 and sat nearly every day for the next three weeks, talking much and achieving little. Hervey was second in seniority among the nine other members,[2] but even his restless, questing brain and forceful personality could make little progress against the age-induced lethargy of an eighty-two-year-old General.

Hervey wrote that the council was making resolutions upon resolutions, but none was ever put in execution 'from the great indolence of the General and his ill-judged tenderness to the inhabitants, who were all this time betraying us to the French, inviting them over, and making ready to assist them when they came. We had good accounts of the French forces and their designs, and yet nothing was done here. The island was in a very bad condition for want of stores, of officers, of men, of provisions, and in short had been much neglected.'

On February 25 Hervey sailed in the *Phoenix* for Villefranche and Nice to see what news he could pick up, and he returned to Mahon on March 10 with a very disturbing report about the advanced French preparations, which he delivered to a specially-summoned council of war.* It thanked him for his diligence, but did nothing, so Hervey finally delivered himself of a tactful but tough speech pointing out that 'I look upon every man here responsible for his conduct and liable to be called to an account if any accident happens to this island, which has cost so much obtaining and such infinite sums to maintain to the Crown . . .'

The General, he said tactfully, was too kind to the local inhabitants. 'Have the magistrates shewn their activity in putting your orders in execution? Have the clergy been known to preach up and propagate to the people a spirit of heartily joining His Majesty's troops, and giving all assistance cheerfully? Have they not done the reverse?'

Hervey's exasperation was understandable: he had so far suggested—without anything being done about it—that all the local people who had worked in the caves forming the main defences of Fort St Philip should be encouraged or forced to serve in the Fort, since with their knowledge they would be sources of danger in the hands of the French; that the town of St Philip's be destroyed because it was a threat to the castle, giving cover to the enemy almost up to the walls; that all the cattle should be driven in; and that the island be put under martial law. They were all necessary measures if the Fort was to stand a siege, but by now Hervey was being regarded as a nuisance by the old General, and he noted: 'This evening I was ordered [to cruise] off the island for seven days to give notice of the enemy's approach, tho' it had been proved useless at the Council . . . The fact was,' Hervey added wryly, 'the General wanted to get rid of me out of the council now.'[3] He had no sooner returned from the cruise than he was sent off once again, this time to Villefranche or Leghorn for intelligence.

As soon as he arrived in Portsmouth, Admiral Byng was taken out in his barge to Spithead, where he boarded the *Ramillies* amid the

---

* Next day Thomas Tranter called on Admiral Byng in Berkeley Square to deliver the Admiralty's orders to fit out the squadron.

usual salutes. It did not take long for him to discover that most of the nine ships of his squadron which were already at Portsmouth and Spithead (the tenth, the *Intrepid*, was coming round from the Medway) were desperately short of men. Normally this would not have presented any problem because the Admiralty could have ordered him to take men from some of the other warships at anchor nearby which were not under sailing orders.

But two letters from the Admiralty, which Byng found waiting for him at Portsmouth, prevented him from doing this. The first letter said he was 'not to meddle' with any of the crews of six named ships, which were wanted 'on the most pressing service'; the second told him to hurry with the fitting out of another ship, the *Stirling Castle*, which was not part of his squadron but which was also wanted 'on the most pressing service'.[4]

It might be thought that the 'most pressing service' which took priority over the dispatch of a squadron to the Mediterranean to counter the French threat to Minorca was at least concerned with the safety of Britain; but this was far from being the case. Instead, five of the six battleships were wanted to intercept a French coastal convoy—when it was found.

Admiral Byng sat down in the great cabin* of the *Ramillies* to work out exactly the situation concerning crews. He was appalled to find that his squadron (excluding the *Intrepid*) was short of 722 men. This total was made up of 290 men lent to other ships not in the squadron, 192 sick in hospital, and 240 short of complement.[6] The *Ramillies* was herself short of 222 men, the majority of them lent to the *Ludlow Castle*, which was at sea. That was bad enough, but five of the ships which he was forbidden 'to meddle' with were fully manned and the sixth had more than her complement on board.

As soon as he had found out how many men the rest of the ships in the anchorage had on board, Byng wrote to the Admiralty. He pointed out that while his ships were short of men there were twelve other ships at Spithead, all of which were fully manned;

---

* Now more comfortable than when he had flown his flag in her the previous autumn: anticipating that he might be going to sea in her again, he had complained to the Admiralty a few weeks earlier that his secretary's office was so dark 'the clerks cannot see to do their work', and his 'own bed-place was so dark' with the port shut that he was 'obliged to burn candles in it, even in the middle of the day.' The Admiralty had since told the Navy Board to have scuttles cut to let in some light.[5]

indeed, three of them had more than their complement. Nine of
the thirteen battleships in Portsmouth were fully manned and one
had a surplus. [A complete list is given in Appendix I, page 303].

This letter had hardly reached the shore on its way to London
before a boat fought its way out to Spithead in a strong south-
westerly gale which had just sprung up. It brought Byng another
letter from the Admiralty which said that by the enclosed intelligence, he would 'perceive the necessity' of his squadron sailing
for the Mediterranean with 'the utmost despatch'. He would
receive his sailing orders by March 24 (it was then the 21st) and
he was to use the 'utmost diligence in getting everything in the
greatest forwardness for sailing that is possible'.[7]

The intelligence report was a letter from Augustus Hervey's
brother, the Earl of Bristol, who was the British Minister in Turin.
It said that he had just heard eleven French ships were on the
point of sailing from Toulon and 'the report of an invasion of the
island of Minorca is very strong'.[8]

Byng was now in an absurd position because, although he was
enjoined to prepare to sail with 'the utmost diligence', the six
ships wanted to intercept the French convoy still had priority.
Since the Government was later to claim that Byng's squadron
could not have sailed earlier than it did, it is worth noting that the
Admiralty sent thirteen other battleships to sea between March 8
and April 14 on considerably less important tasks, and that the ships
allocated to Byng were almost the only ones in Spithead and
Portsmouth which were short of men. Six of the battleships
already cruising off the French coast while Byng tried to man his
ships were not there to watch for an invasion attempt: they were
hunting for a French coastal convoy—the same convoy the other
six battleships at Spithead were also intended to intercept.

Thus while Byng struggled to man nine of his ten ships which
were supposed to be sailing to secure Britain's position in the
Mediterranean, eleven other fully-manned battleships—any of
which could have been attached to Byng's squadron or ordered to
supply him with men—were at sea or waiting in harbour to deal
with an unimportant French convoy. It is quite clear that Byng
could have sailed earlier—and with more ships—without the
slightest risk to the safety of the British Isles.

Byng wrote to the Admiralty saying that he expected his
squadron to be ready for sea in seven or eight days 'in every respect

excepting men'. He also enclosed his list of all the ships at Portsmouth and Spithead showing how many men they had on board. In the meantime, he had press-gangs combing the streets of Portsmouth and roaming round the surrounding villages looking for likely men, while on board his ships the crews were busy stowing stores, fresh water, powder and shot.

The squadron would, of course, carry out the Army officers who had been ordered to return to their posts in Minorca, and some recruits, as well as some soldiers due to go to Gibraltar. On March 23, Admiral Byng received orders to take the Earl of Effingham and his family and servants on board the *Revenge* while General Stuart with his attendants were to go on board the *Culloden*, and various other officers and recruits were to be distributed in the ships 'as you shall think proper'.[9]

No doubt Byng smiled wryly at the phrase 'and family' after the Earl of Effingham's name. Thomas Howard, second Earl of Effingham and eighth Baron Howard, was now forty-two years old, and had married Elizabeth Beckford, sister of the Sheriff of the City of London. Although the Earl's eldest son was only nine years old, and there were other children, the Countess and her servants—five of them—were going to Minorca as well.[10] Captain Cornwall, commanding the *Revenge*, would look askance when he received Byng's order to receive them on board: he would have to give them his cabin. Perhaps he would be recompensed by the knowledge that his guest was descended from Charles, Lord Howard of Effingham, who had commanded the British fleet which had defeated the Spanish Armada. This particular descendant had not, however, the same facility for being in the right place at the right time.

Earlier in the month the Duke of Newcastle had made some inquiries about Lord Tyrawley who, far from being in the Governor's house in that Mediterranean paradise, was at his house on Blackheath. One Sunday morning the Governor sat down and replied to the Duke, saying 'I thank God, I am quite recovered, and hope very soon to have the honour of waiting on you . . .'[11]

Byng noted in his journal that he was to carry twenty-eight officers (including another Colonel, Cornwallis), thirty-two recruits and eight deserters to Minorca, and sixteen officers and thirty-six other ranks to Gibraltar. Next day, Wednesday, March 24, brought another gale sweeping across Spithead and yet another 'express' arrived from the Admiralty. It did not contain the sailing orders previously promised for that day: instead Byng was instructed to send three battleships and two frigates to sea under the command of Captain the Hon Augustus Keppel 'with all possible dispatch'. Keppel was to take what men he needed to complete his ships from one of the ships which Byng had been forbidden to touch. The reason for the haste was that the French coastal convoy had at last been reported off Cherbourg.*[12]

On Thursday, the gale brought snow and sleet, and four more letters arrived from the Admiralty. One of them told Byng to send the *Stirling Castle* to sea—completing her crew by using men left over from Keppel's Squadron, those 'discharged from hospital', and the first of the men brought in by the press gangs.[13]

The second letter told him that for his own squadron he could take 101 men from the *Augusta*, and that the *Ludlow Castle* had been ordered to return to Portsmouth with the 199 men she had borrowed from Byng's flagship. Their Lordships hoped they would be 'sufficient to complete the complement . . . of your squadron'.[14] It was a pious hope, and the Board knew it; they were giving Byng exactly 300 men, yet they already knew he was short of 722. The third letter told him, notwithstanding the previous order, to take back from the *Stirling Castle* the men he had just been told to put on board, 'and apply them towards completing the complements of the ships of your squadron'.

The fourth letter[15] showed Byng there had been a complete change in Government policy: he was to send all the Marines in his squadron to other ships and take soldiers on board in their place—Lord Robert Bertie's regiment of Fusiliers, 'consisting of about 900 people, including six women and six servants per company allowed to proceed with them,'—and he was to do this 'without a moment's loss of time'.

The orders the War Office had given concerning Lord Robert Bertie's Fusiliers were a muddle from the beginning and became one of the contributory factors in the loss of Minorca. One of the reasons for the muddle was undoubtedly the personality and inexperience of the Secretary at War, Lord Barrington. Walpole's verdict on this wretched man is interesting: he was 'always

---

* Keppel's squadron returned to Spithead on April 9, three days after Byng had sailed.

assiduous to make his fortune', and aimed at making not friends
but patrons. He had 'a lisp and a tedious precision that prejudiced
one against him; yet he did not want a sort of vivacity that would
have shone oftener if the rind it was to penetrate had been thin-
ner'.[16]

One can only regret that Barrington, who was MP for Plymouth,
did not apply some of that 'tedious precision' to his orders: had he
done so the effect on Minorca would have been far-reaching. He
was instructed by Henry Fox to arrange for Admiral Byng's
Marines to be replaced by troops. That appears simple enough,
but Barrington misunderstood it. He ordered Bertie's Fusiliers to
join Byng's ships, but then wrote a curious letter to the Governor
of Gibraltar, Lt-General Fowke, telling him, of all things, that
the regiment of Fusiliers was to be landed in Gibraltar, and that
Fowke was then to take a battalion from the Gibraltar garrison
which was to be embarked on board Byng's ships for Minorca.

It is impossible to understand the reason for Barrington's
proposed musical chairs or why he mentioned Minorca, but the
letter was given to General Stuart—who was just leaving for
Portsmouth to join his ship—to deliver to Fowke when he reached
Gibraltar. However, Anson protested as soon as the Admiralty
heard about Barrington's reference to carrying the Gibraltar
troops to Minorca, pointing out that it was impossible to send
the squadron to sea unless the Fusiliers remained on board as part
of the ships' crews, since they were replacing the Marines.[17]

After deciding that Minorca would need reinforcements only
if the French were actually invading, Fox told Barrington to order
that the Fusiliers were to stay on board, and to instruct Fowke to
send an additional battalion on board from the Gibraltar garrison
only if Minorca 'should be in any likelihood of being attacked'.
Barrington therefore wrote a second letter to Fowke to this effect
—without mentioning the first one—and sent it down to General
Stuart at Portsmouth for him to deliver. But since Barrington did
not cancel the previous order, Fowke was thus told in the first
letter that the Fusiliers were to land at Gibraltar and he was to
put a battalion on board Byng's ships for Minorca, and in the
second he was ordered to put a battalion on board only if Minorca
was threatened. To add to the confusion the maladroit Minister
sent yet another letter to Fowke, making no reference to the other
two, and telling him to 'receive into the garrison . . . such women

and children belonging to the Royal Regiment of Fusiliers as
Admiral Byng . . . shall think fit to land there'. (The Orders are
given fully in Appendix II.)

Down at Portsmouth Byng distributed his Marines to other ships
on March 29, hampered by gales and snow squalls, and next day
the ships' boats ferried out the Fusiliers, who were seasick, wet
and frozen long before they arrived on board. The task was completed by nightfall, except for one company left on shore for the
Intrepid, which had not yet arrived from the Medway.

The Fusiliers' commanding officer, Lord Robert Bertie, was
given a cabin in the *Ramillies*. He was probably already acquainted
with Admiral Byng because apart from anything else his father,
the Duke of Ancaster, was a neighbour of the Admiral's in
Berkeley Square. The Duke was Lord Great Chamberlain of
England—a post which gave him the King's ear, and thus helped
his son's military career.

April Fool's Day brought a change in the weather, for which
Thomas Tranter, the Admiralty messenger, was thankful since he
had to take a boat out to Spithead with a packet of their Lordships'
orders for Admiral Byng. The first of several letters in the packet,
signed by Clevland and marked 'per Express at twelve midnight',[18]
enclosed 'the whole of your Orders and Instructions', and told
Byng that as it may be 'of the utmost consequence to the welfare
of this nation that the Squadron under your command should
immediately put to sea', the Board signified their direction 'in
the strongest manner, to put to sea the moment the wind comes
fair, and not to suffer the least time to be lost'.

The instructions,[19] (which, as an indication of the urgency,
had arrived nine days late) had been drawn up by Anson and
covered four large pages. (See Appendix III.) The curious thing
about them was that despite all the intelligence reports saying
the Toulon squadron was to operate against Minorca, Anson considered it was more likely to be intended for America: he clearly
considered the threat to Minorca was slight.

Byng was told to put to sea with the ships that were ready,
leaving the rest to follow as soon as possible. On arriving at Gibraltar he was to find out whether the French ships had passed through
the Strait, as 'it is probable they may be designed for North America'. If they had, Byng was to reinforce a British squadron cruising

off the American coast by sending enough of his own ships to make it superior to the French. He was then to take his remaining ships to Minorca, 'and if you find any attack made on that island by the French, you are to use all possible means in your power for its relief'.

However, if Byng found that the French had *not* gone through the Strait of Gibraltar, he was to go 'without a moment's loss of time to Minorca', and if that island had not been attacked he was to go on to Toulon and prevent any French ships getting out. He was also 'to exert your utmost vigilance therein, and in protecting Minorca and Gibraltar from any hostile attempt'.

Despite the emphasis on America, the strangest thing about the orders was that they did not give any clear-cut instructions covering the most *likely* situation—that Byng would arrive and find that the Toulon squadron had already escorted an invasion force to Minorca and was cruising off the island to protect it. The Admiralty had no excuse for this glaring omission: the Board knew that the island might well have been invaded, and Anson had twenty-two days in which to draft the orders. The Government's reason for sending out the squadron was that Minorca was threatened, not America. This was made clear in the preamble to Byng's orders, which said the Government had ordered his squadron to sail in view of reports relating to the supposed intention of the French to attack the island of Minorca.

Another letter in the packet delivered by Tranter told Byng that the Fusiliers were to serve on board the squadron, but that they should be landed in Minorca 'in case the Governor shall think it necessary for its defence'. They added (and it was to be important, as it happened) that the Governor of Gibraltar had orders, in case Minorca needed further reinforcements, to send a battalion from his garrison. In addition, Byng was told to 'assist with as many gunners and men from your squadron as may be serviceable, and the ships can possibly spare'. Despite Anson's protest over Barrington's orders, the Admiralty had ignored the fact that if the Fusiliers were landed, the ships would be so short of men (more than 800) that they would not be able to risk a battle with the French.

As soon as he read the letters and instructions, Byng ordered his captains to collect from the hospital every one of their men who was fit to serve, and to tell him as soon as possible the number of men they were deficient. It was late at night before the last of the returns had been sent in, and Byng then sat down and wrote to the Admiralty. 'With regard to the instructions I have received,' he said, 'I shall use every endeavour and means in my power to frustrate the designs of the enemy, if they should make an attempt in the island of Minorca,' but, he added gloomily, 'shall think myself the most fortunate if I am so happy to succeed in this undertaking.' His squadron was ready for sea except that it was still short of 336 men, and he 'desired their Lordships final orders with regard to them.' He also requested that as he was to command all the ships in the Mediterranean he should be made the Commander-in-Chief.

At sunrise next day, April 2, as Byng noted in his journal, 'loosed the foretopsail and hauled home the sheets' [the signal for sailing]. A few hours later the *Intrepid*—the last ship of Byng's squadron—was reported to have arrived from the Medway.

The *Intrepid's* short voyage had been unpleasant and tedious.[20] At the beginning of the year she had been refitted at Chatham at a cost of £5,600[21] and, soon after Captain James Young received orders to 'put yourself under the command of Vice-Admiral Byng', she sailed for Spithead. But she had been at sea less than twelve hours, heeling in a gale, when she began to make 'a deal of water at the lee ports'. In fact so much squirted in round the edges of the port lids, even though the crew had caulked them, that it was beginning to affect the ship's stability, and Captain Young gave the order for the decks to be scuttled. The carpenter, William Foster, and his crew then cut holes in the deck planking so that the water drained down into the bilges from where the pumps could suck it out and pump it over the side.

The voyage to Spithead eventually took more than a fortnight, and as soon as the *Intrepid* was safely at anchor Captain Young went over to the *Ramillies* to receive his orders from Admiral Byng. He was startled to find that the squadron was bound for the Mediterranean and, Byng noted in his journal, 'represented that the *Intrepid* was not fit for a foreign voyage . . . and had neither water, provisions nor stores for that purpose'.*

---

* The explanation for this was that Young's copy of the Admiralty order to fit out for the Mediterranean had not been sent to him at Chatham: it was waiting for him at Portsmouth. No one thought it worthy of comment that a ship was 'unfit for foreign service' within a few weeks of a dockyard refit.

Since Byng was waiting for the Admiralty's reply about men, he ordered the boats of the other nine ships in the squadron to help the *Intrepid* get more stores and water on board. Finally Byng took thirty men from the *Stirling Castle* and seventy men from the *Cambridge*. He was still short of men but, as he noted in his journal on April 6, 'The squadron weighed . . . and stood out to sea'.

Bunge's intercepted letter had been received in London on February 25, and Cressener's intelligence on March 8. The ten ships of Byng's squadron had been ordered to prepare on March 8, and since joining the squadron on March 21 the Admiral had—despite the Admiralty's prohibitions—made good much of the deficit of 722 men, manned and sent off Keppel's squadron, and dealt swiftly with the *Intrepid*'s difficulties. And in view of the fact he was subsequently accused of dallying, it is worth remembering he did not receive his orders until April 1.

7

THE FRENCH INVADE

AT TOULON THE MARQUIS de la Galissonnière had, like Byng, experienced great difficulty in preparing his squadron for sea: the French Court had been lavish with the orders for the dozen battleships but not with the money.

Galissonnière had arrived at Toulon to take over the squadron on March 2, and Richelieu joined him on the 25th to command the troops. No two men could be less alike. Richelieu was a handsome rake, worldly and suave and perfectly at home in the heady atmosphere of the French Court. Roland-Michel Barin, Marquis de la Galissonnière, was hunchbacked and small, physically insignificant and quiet in manner, but he had considerable ability.

He came from a naval family and was born in 1693 at Rochefort, within the sound of the Atlantic rollers which rounded the Ile d'Oleron to thunder against the cliffs and swirl over Belesbat, the legendary submerged city nearby. His childhood was spent in this region, where a quirk of the atmosphere gives the light a curious, at times seemingly-solid whiteness. His father had commanded at Rochefort; his grandfather had been a famous naval administrator under Louis XIV; an uncle and cousin had been killed in battle while serving in the King's ships. Ninety-eight years earlier, one of his ancestors had been created marquis and took his title from La Galissonnière, the name of an estate near Nantes.

Roland-Michel had gone to sea as a cadet nine days before his seventeenth birthday; yet he was not made a captain until he was forty-five—perhaps due to the fact that he spent more time at sea than at Court. After that, promotion came more quickly: in February 1745 (while Captain John Byng was still commanding the *St George* in the Channel and two months before Parliament petitioned the King to court martial Mathews and Lestock), he was made Commissioner-General of Ordnance at his home town of Rochefort. Then, two years later, he was made the Governor of Canada.

Back in France he made a name for himself as a tactician as a result of two training cruises in the Mediterranean. He was, therefore, an obvious choice for the command of the French ships intended for the capture of Minorca, and when he hoisted his flag at Toulon he was sixty-three years of age. He had served in the Navy for forty-five years.

Richelieu had brought Galissonnière's orders from Versailles, and also a letter for him from the King. The orders had one main theme, which was emphasized repeatedly: Galissonnière must take no risks with his ships. Machault, the Minister of Marine, told him that the King had 'positively forbidden' him to endanger the squadron, or the troops it was to carry by any action against a stronger British force. Galissonnière was to choose the date for invading Minorca with this in mind, and if the expedition was threatened by a superior British force before it could land its troops, then he must take 'prompt measures' for its safety by retiring into a French or Spanish port.

The King's letter to the French Admiral expressed the same caution: by the orders* he was sending him, Louis said, 'You will see that my intention is that you should principally attend to the safekeeping of my squadron and the troops I have ordered for this expedition'.[1]

Galissonnière had found there was much work to be done before the squadron could sail, but the soldiers were becoming impatient. The Marquis de Maillebois, for instance, who was one of Richelieu's two deputies, had been in Toulon only a day or two before he called on Galissonnière, asking when the squadron would be ready, and when it would sail. Galissonnière would make no guesses, and in a letter to Machault describing the Marquis's visit he commented, 'Our profession is filled with uncertainties, and those who are not accustomed to it are always astonished'.[2]

On April 10, four days after Admiral Byng's squadron left Spithead, a crisp, chilly wind came off Mont Faron and the grey-capped heights of Le Coudon and blew seawards across the bay of Toulon, ruffling white spray against the guardians of its great

---

* Richelieu's orders were pitched on a grander note: 'The moderation which the King has exercised for a long time has not stopped the piracies of the British Navy ... His Majesty, after a fruitless attempt to lead the London Court to give him satisfaction for this highway robbery, plans to take august vengeance against them by taking possession of the island of Minorca.'

entrance, Cap Cépet and Pont de l'Hermitage: at last Galissonnière had the north wind for which he had been waiting.

The troops, 15,000 of them, were already embarked in 173 transport ships; on board Galissonnière's flagship, the *Foudroyant*, the Duke de Richelieu was impatient to be under way—a view shared by his two companions the Duke de Fronsac, who was his son, and Count d'Egmont-Pignatelli, his son-in-law. The wind was as fair for Minorca as it would ever be, and Galissonnière gave the order for the squadron and its convoy to weigh anchor.

But the last of the mass of ships, ranging from the huge *Foudroyant* to tiny lateen-rigged tartans, had hardly cleared Cap Cépet than the wind backed south-west—foul for Minorca. Galissonnière gave the order to bear away for Hyères, where they could anchor under the lee of the islands and shelter until the wind changed.

Richelieu's two seconds-in-command were rowed across to the *Foudroyant* to discuss the delay—Count de Maillebois from the *Couronne* and the Marquis de Mesnil from the *Redoutable*. The Duke soon had them settled down round a table playing a friendly game of whist. Nevertheless, he was anxious.

'How long do you think this foul wind will last?' he asked Galissonnière, adding that it was just the wind to bring the British squadron into the Mediterranean.

Galissonnière's reply gave him no comfort: 'It has taken me three days to return from the Strait of Gibraltar after taking three months to get there: that is all the reckoning it is possible to make at sea . . .'[3]

Two days later the convoy was under way again, but the wind was soon blowing so strongly that several ships were damaged and others became scattered across the Gulf of Lions. More headwinds delayed them, and it was not until the 17th, Easter Saturday, that they sighted the hills and mountains of Minorca, purple and almost menacing in the evening sun.

Since it was essential to capture the harbour of Mahon and its guardian, Fort St Philip, as soon as possible, Richelieu and Galissonnière wanted to put the Army on shore at the nearest suitable place. They had two possible areas in mind—the tiny island of Aire*, just off the south eastern tip of Minorca and three miles south of Fort St Philip; and Fornells, a small port on the north side of the

---

* Isla del Air, whose name was variously spelled and which was often called the Lair of Mahon.

MINORCA

CHARLES GREEN

island which is more than twenty-five miles by road from Fort St
Philip. Neither was ideal, but Minorca was rocky and mountainous,
giving no geographical assistance to an attacker. Nor were the
French helped by their maps of the island, which were inaccurate
and out of date.

Both Richelieu and Galissonnière had one great fear: that a
British squadron would appear on the scene while the French
troops were being put on shore. This meant that neither man
wanted there to be any delay once they reached Minorca. However,
the headwinds and bad weather had played havoc with navigation,
and when the invasion fleet sighted Minorca, they found they were
approaching its western coast—the opposite side to Mahon and
Fort St Philip—and they sailed in close to the shore just as the
wind dropped. Richelieu wrote later that 'the calm brought us
face to face with Ciudadela . . . we found the town clear of the
English, who had fled at the sight of our Fleet.'⁴ He had a hurried
conference with Galissonnière and they decided to change their
plans and land troops at Ciudadela, even though it was thirty-two
miles from Fort St Philip, and the French troops would have to
march the length of the mountainous island before reaching their
objective.

One of the French officers wrote later, 'It was one of the most
beautiful spectacles I had ever seen in my life. Our squadron
anchored in a crescent shape, having behind it all our transport
ships . . . I saw with my telescope many women, which did not
give me much of an opinion of the resistance which would oppose
the invasion force.'⁵

The first of the 15,000 soldiers to land met with no resistance,
and by the evening Richelieu and all his senior officers were
attending the church which was soon echoing to the sound of the
Te Deum. After the service the Duke received the oath of allegiance
from the senior officers, and also from all the clergy in Ciudadela.
'I was busy the rest of the day,' wrote Richelieu, 'arranging the
disembarkation of the rest of the troops and some of the artillery
and ammunition.'⁶

Despite the resolutions of his council of war, Blakeney, as we have
seen, had done little to get the garrison prepared for the long-
anticipated invasion. Late on Easter Saturday he received a report
that the French squadron had been sighted; late on Sunday a

party of Rich's Regiment 'brought the news that the French had
landed at Ciudadela'.[7] This was followed by a letter from Captain
Thomas Noel, commanding the *Princess Louisa*. Noel had gone
on shore and climbed up to a vantage point at the western end
of the island, from where he had seen the French invasion fleet
arrive. 'There are now at anchor off Ciudadela one hundred and
twenty vessels of diverse sorts and sizes . . . about thirteen only
be men-of-war, but not above seven appear to be of the line,' he
wrote.[8]

Rich's Regiment had been stationed at Ciudadela and had, at
the sight of the French invasion force, prudently withdrawn—
accidentally losing a corporal, who was taken prisoner by the
French—eastwards across the island to Port Mahon, ripping up
the road as they went. With a garrison of less than 2500 and facing
an enemy who had landed 15,000 men, Blakeney could only withdraw into Fort St Philip and prepare for a siege. Writing to London
on Easter Monday, Blakeney said 'I am informed they propose
being at Alayor this evening, about eleven miles distant from hence,
so that I have much reason to believe that they intend to attack us
herewith . . . as their main body is now on their march'.[9]

Captain Edgcumbe was still in Port Mahon with his squadron,
consisting of the *Deptford*, *Princess Louisa*, *Portland*, *Chesterfield*
and the tiny *Proserpine* and *Dolphin*. Fearing that the French
would make an assault on Mahon itself, he had ordered the four
big ships to be moored bow to stern across the narrow harbour
entrance, making a defensive boom, and some of their guns were
landed, sited on the cliffs and manned by Marines.

Edgcumbe called all his captains to a council of war at sunrise on
Easter Monday, since any minute the French squadron might
appear off Mahon and trap them in the harbour. He asked them
to consider how the ships 'could be disposed of most advan-
tageously'. The captains resolved unanimously that they could not
help the garrison by remaining in Mahon; indeed, if they waited
they risked losing all the ships—a loss which might be 'of infinite
prejudice to His Majesty's service as any admiral coming out of
England must count these as part of his squadron and consequently depend upon that additional strength'. They should
land as many seamen and Marines as they could spare to help the
garrison and, leaving the fireships *Dolphin* and *Proserpine* in the
harbour, sail for Gibraltar 'without loss of time'.

Edgcumbe took the resolutions to General Blakeney, whose own council of war opposed them. Edgcumbe called his captains together again and told them that the General's council thought that by using all the crews as soldiers the garrison could hold out longer—perhaps until they were reinforced by a squadron they had been told was coming out from England.

But the sea captains were adamant—the French troops were now less than ten miles away, and they repeated that any British admiral arriving in the Mediterranean would need the ships. The captains were perfectly correct: for the only time in the whole of the Minorca campaign, a council of war had made a faultless decision, because of course the Admiralty had given Byng only ten ships, anticipating that on arriving in the Mediterranean he would be reinforced by Edgcumbe's squadron. Sailing for Gibraltar next day, April 20, Edgcumbe's squadron left 286 Marines and soldiers behind on the island, with ten guns, and all the powder, shot and food they could spare, under the command of Captain Scrope of the *Dolphin*.

Augustus Hervey, in the meantime, had called in at the Tuscan port of Leghorn on April 10 in his hunt for news of the French, and learned incidentally that Admiral Byng was coming to the Mediterranean with ten ships, although 'I feared he would be too late to hinder the descent, and too weak to conquer their fleet'.

The next day he received a report that he expected but dreaded: 'We had news that the French had sailed the 10th from Toulon.' That afternoon he captured a French ship off the island of Hyères which carried some letters 'which I opened and found the French sailed the 13th, with a whole detail of their fleet for Mahon'. He added that 'It was amazing to all Italy that as long as this armament had been fitting and declared for Minorca that England was so long without sending ships out ... Had the fleet sailed from England a month sooner, the French would never, I may venture to say, have landed at Minorca. This is a fatal and dishonourable stroke to England, for which the leading Ministers deserve to lose their heads.'[10]

Next day he took the *Phoenix* into Nice and wrote three warning letters—to the Admiralty, to Henry Fox, whom he knew well, and to 'my Brother Bristol' in Turin.

THE DUKE'S GO-CART

FROM THE TIME THAT Admiral Byng had sailed from Portsmouth the hurly-burly in the capital had an undercurrent of increasing apprehension. A proclamation which was made throughout the Kingdom did little to calm the people's fears, since it said that at the first sign of a French invasion all horses, oxen and cattle 'which may be fit for burthen, and not actually employed in the King's service' were to be driven 'twenty miles at least from the place where such hostile attempt shall be made'.[1]

However, Horace Walpole continued to play his usual role of detached and flippant observer. Writing to his cousin General Conway he said that the Duchess of Norfolk was to give a great ball in a week's time to the Duke of Cumberland, 'so you see that she does not expect the Pretender, at least this fortnight', while at Lady Hervey's the previous night Mrs Dives had expressed great panic about the French. Lady Rochford, looking down her fan, said with great softness, 'I don't know: I don't think the French are the sort of people that women need be afraid of'.

The Duke of Newcastle, however, did not share Lady Rochford's view, and on April 10, the very day that the French squadron weighed anchor in Toulon, and while Byng was fighting a gale thirty miles off Plymouth, he wrote to the Duke of Devonshire that the French 'certainly have designs to attack Minorca. If Admiral Byng gets there in time enough, that will be safe also.' The Duke had continued to hope in the days that followed; but on April 25 a copy of another of Bunge's dispatches, intercepted on its way to Stockholm, arrived on his desk to tell him that an expedition against Minorca was thought by the French to be the only way of making Britain mend her ways, and 'the inattention of the English to cover that island in time' was the main reason why the French were attacking it immediately 'without waiting for the great expedition against England'.[2]

A few days later, the newspapers began printing reports that the French had actually sailed, and 'all faces lengthen here upon it, and the greatest face of all [the Duke of Newcastle's] could not forbear to take the same dimension', according to George Grenville's wife when she sent her husband the capital's latest news.[3] Horace Walpole wrote ironically to a friend that 'The French are said to be sailed for Minorca, which I hold to be a good omen of their not coming hither; for if they took for England, Port Mahon, I should think would scarcely hold out'.[4]

Henry Fox was frankly disturbed by the news. Some people, he wrote to the Duke of Devonshire, thought Minorca would be able to hold out until Byng arrived, and that he would save it, but nevertheless he wished Byng had been sent sooner.[5] Lord Lyttelton, telling his brother in America that Byng had left with ten battleships, said 'You will ask why he was not sent out with more strength. I can make you no answer but that Lord Anson thought he had no more to spare, and it was hoped that he would arrive at Minorca before the French could get thither.'[6]

Letters took from two to six weeks to arrive in London from the Mediterranean, and the news that the French had landed on Minorca on April 17 eventually reached London on May 6 through the Spanish Ambassador, Count d'Abreu, who sent a hurried letter round to the Duke of Newcastle on that day saying he had just heard about it from his colleague in Paris.

His Grace was much depressed—a fact which George Bubb Dodington, a former Treasurer of the Navy and one of the most barefaced political opportunists of the day, recorded in his diary.[7] Dodington chanced to meet the Duke who told him, 'with much warmth and anxiety' of the news just received, and added that after covering the landing the French squadron had stood out to sea again to intercept Byng, so that there must already have been a naval action.

Dodington was in no mood to comfort his Grace. 'It is astonishing that Byng was not there a month ago,' he commented. The Duke replied that Byng had not been ready, and he was obliged to stay two or three days for his last two hundred men.

'Why were you not ready?' asked Dodington. 'Why have you not more ships and more men?'

They were questions which deserved more intelligent answers than they received. The Duke said he did not direct the Navy and, according to Dodington, 'His Grace laid a great deal of blame there, and without naming Lord Anson he showed himself extremely dissatisfied with him'.*

That evening, in answer to an urgent request by the Duke for a meeting of the Inner Committee, the same seven men met at the Cockpit who had a few weeks earlier decided at long last to send Byng's squadron to the Mediterranean. The meeting was brief and this time they resolved, in view of the reports of the French landing in Minorca, that 'four large ships of the line should be sent forthwith to reinforce the squadron under the command of Admiral Byng; and that three or four battalions should also be sent to relieve the garrison of Port Mahon'.[8]

These were belated decisions, considering the danger; and no one was more acutely aware of this than Henry Fox. Indeed, it was the very next day that the ship of state sprung its first leak, and Fox was the man responsible. It began with William Pitt making a powerful attack in the House of Commons on the Government's policy; then later in the day the letters written from Nice by Augustus Hervey, when he found the French Toulon squadron had sailed, arrived in London. Fox sent a copy round to the Duke of Newcastle, and in a covering letter took the opportunity of dropping a hint to the Duke that as far as he was concerned the wind was changing. 'Mr Pitt has taken the liberty to blame your Grace as well as others today,' Fox wrote. 'I answered as well as I could, but the loss of Minorca is a weight that it is not easy to debate under.'[9] His assumption at this early stage that Minorca was already lost is worth noting; the reference to the weight under which he had to debate brought home to the Duke once again that Fox was—apart from the Attorney-General, William Murray—virtually his only spokesman in the Commons, and that the Secretary of State therefore held most of the court cards in a no-trumps hand.

While his letter was being delivered to Newcastle House, Fox had a visitor—the irrepressible Dodington, who recorded the meeting in his diary, saying that Fox was full of concern. 'He would have sent the squadron, and a strong one, the first week in

---

* It is worth noting that no blame was attached to Byng at this stage: indeed, the Duke seems to have understood Byng's difficulty. Had he blamed Byng undoubtedly he would have told Dodington at this point. Instead, he blamed only Anson, the First Lord of the Admiralty.

March, but could not prevail. Lord Anson assured him and put it
upon himself that Byng's squadron would beat anything the
French had, or could have in the Mediterranean.'[10]

By now the Duke was deeply suspicious of Fox's letter and
deeply hurt by Pitt's attack. Succumbing to an excess of tremu-
lous anxiety, his Grace wrote an urgent letter to Lord Hardwicke,
his old friend and stand-by on such occasions who, he said, would
have heard of 'the extraordinary debate in the House of Commons
yesterday where I think Mr Pitt laid everything that was blamed
upon me, though he varied his discourse at times. He made great
compliment to my Lord Anson, all at my expense,' he complained,
as if Hardwicke was responsible for the apparent merits of his
sailor son-in-law. 'I am not able to bear this weight, especially for
measures where *others* have the principal, if not the *sole* direction.
Mr Pitt went so far as to charge the loss of Minorca as a design to
justify a bad peace.'[11] He enclosed a copy of the letter he had
just received from Fox, with the comment that 'I see plainly where
Mr Fox would lay all blame'.

Having sent out his message of distress, the Duke replied to
Fox. He said that Lord Anson had thought Byng's squadron was
undoubtedly strong enough; and that 'in all probability the French
would not stay to meet him'. As far as the safety of Gibraltar was
concerned, 'I cannot apprehend any danger: Spain will not attack
it, and France, I suppose, has employment enough at Minorca.'

Having first struck a confident note, his Grace then waxed
indignant. 'I don't remember that I ever differed in opinion from
the rest of the King's servants in relation to Minorca,' he wrote.
'I don't think the defence of what was done, difficult; though,' he
hastened to add, 'I am not more concerned to defend it than others.
You must remember what was constantly said whenever this question was before us. That the *heart* must be secured in the first
place.' France's naval strength could not be as strong as they
represented, nor could it be ready so soon. A naval battle in the
Channel in which Britain had an inferior fleet 'would have been a
more fatal thing than in the Mediterranean, and then the Ministers
would have been represented as fools, knaves, that did not see the
preparations in Toulon were only a feint'.

At this point in the letter the Duke's confidence vanished,
taking his indignation with it, and he confessed that 'the occasion
of all our misfortunes, and that will increase every day, is that we

are not equal to the work we have undertaken; we are not, singly, a match for France; we cannot provide for all services and all places where they might attack us; and rather than own this truth when any misfortunes happen, which may, in itself have been unavoidable, the Ministry are to be blamed . . .'[12]

And the blame was not long in coming. Within a few hours in the House of Commons, Pitt dealt with the main point of the Duke's confession. The Government, under the Duke's leadership, had 'provoked before we could defend, and neglected after provocation' he declared. Britain was 'left inferior to France in every quarter'. Could he arraign the Government every day and yet continue to trust it? If he 'saw a child [the Duke of Newcastle] driving a go-cart on a precipice with that precious freight of an old King and family,' surely he was bound to take the reins out of such hands? He prayed to God that His Majesty might not have Minorca, like Calais, written on his heart.[13]

A little later Henry Fox met Dodington again in the House of Commons, and admitted that he 'was very uneasy at the posture of public affairs and, particularly, with his own situation'. He described a conversation he had had the previous day with the Duke of Newcastle when his Grace had come to dinner with him—and had been 'unusually light and trifling' into the bargain.

The Duke had claimed that no one blamed him over Minorca; that the City 'imputed nothing to him, as the sea was not his province'. This had been too much for Fox, who asked him from where he had received that news. The Duke said it came from Garraway's Coffee House, whereupon Fox told him bluntly that he had heard the City were extremely displeased that Minorca had been left exposed; and that when Pitt had blamed the Duke in the House of Commons for the loss of Minorca and Fox had defended him, all their friends had hung their heads, 'and not a man of them was, or seemed to be, persuaded that a squadron could not sooner be sent, or that all had been done which could be done'.

Having related all this to Dodington with suitable indignation, Fox then asked him if it was not true that the head of an administration 'would always be the most obnoxious?' Dodington agreed that he would—unless they had someone else to make a scapegoat. Fox saw at once the explosive possibilities of this political canon, and they alarmed him. Did Dodington think him

likely to be made the Duke of Newcastle's scapegoat? he asked
'and dwelt upon the expression'. He told Dodington that he had
always hinted at sending a squadron to Minorca earlier, and the
Duke of Cumberland had pressed it strongly so long ago as last
Christmas.

While Fox and the Duke alternately confided in Dodington, the
letter-writers were busy. To Sir Horace Mann in Florence, Walpole commented on May 16, 'We are to declare war this week; I
suppose in order to make peace, as we cannot make peace till we
have made war,'[14] and Admiral Boscawen, out in the Atlantic
with his squadron waiting for the French Fleet to make a move
towards America, wrote to his wife that the only news he had
received came from Dutch ships which had recently left France.
'If we believe them, Mahon is taken and Mr Byng not yet got into
the Mediterranean . . . I believe he has been tardy, and don't think
he could have thought of so much business when he asked for that
station.'* A few days later he added that from what he heard
from France they had little chance of taking Minorca. 'If Byng
relieves it, he will strut not a little, and I know he will get more
money (his talent is that) and, you'll say, of spending it. By what
we saw at Wrotham Park, I would not have such a house if he would
build it [for] you.' (His criticism of any financial advantage that
Byng might have acquired was rather hypocritical since at the
beginning of the letter he said 'If these French gentry do not
escape me this time, they will pay for the house and furniture too,
besides something to save hereafter for all our dear children.')[15]

As the Admiralty busied itself preparing the little squadron to
send out to Byng, the Government finally declared war against
France, as Walpole had forecast. The King signed the declaration
on May 17 when the Privy Council met at Kensington Palace and
next day in sunny weather, with a north-easterly breeze ruffling
the heralds' hats, the declaration was proclaimed with due solem-
nity at several places in London. At St James's Palace the Garter
Principal King of Arms, Mr Stephen Leake, appeared resplendent
in his ancient garb of office on the balcony over the gateway and

---

* This is the only important reference the author has been able to trace
saying that Byng actually asked for the command. Boscawen was in a position
to know; but in any case Byng was the obvious choice. Boscawen, as will
become apparent later, disliked Byng.

while he read the proclamation the old King, to the delighted cheers of the waiting crowd, 'appeared with his sword drawn at the window of the room overlooking the gateway', and watched the proceedings.

Two days later, on May 20, Rear-Admiral Thomas Broderick, newly-promoted for the occasion after being chosen by Anson, sailed with the reinforcement for Byng. It consisted of five ships— the Admiralty added an extra one at the last moment.* That the Government's subsequent protestations that Byng could not originally have been given a large squadron were lies is shown by the fact that two of Broderick's ships (the 80-gun *Prince George* and *Nassau*) were at anchor in Portsmouth when Byng sailed, and were included in the list he sent to the Admiralty among the fully-manned ships of 64 guns and over.

Byng had sailed from Portsmouth, as we have seen, four days before the French expedition left Toulon bound for Minorca, and Broderick sailed on the same day that Byng fought his last battle. Once again, and for by no means the last time in history, the British Government had been too late in letting slip the dogs of war which, in this case, were too undernourished to do much more than bark while their owners cried 'havoc' in voices which sounded more hopeful than assured.

Byng's voyage to the Mediterranean had been long and wearisome. The squadron had hardly cleared the Isle of Wight when a violent north-westerly gale swept the Channel, and a second one, which hit the squadron between Ushant and Finisterre, brought the *Intrepid*'s maintopmast crashing down with its yard, on which six men were working. The *Trident* had gone to stand by her, and the wind soon eased up to leave, in the words of young Usher Ellis, one of the *Intrepid*'s midshipmen, 'a very great sea and light airs' so that the ship, robbed of the steadying pressure of the wind, rolled and pitched violently—the worst possible conditions for the men struggling to get 'the riggin fitt'.[16]

For most of the landsmen recently pressed into the Navy these days when Byng's squadron laboriously worked its way southward were a blurred, shivering and retching miasma of misery. For

---

* The five ships were the *Prince George* (80), *Hampton Court* (64), which was intended for Augustus Hervey to command, *Ipswich* (64), *Nassau* (64) and *Isis* (50).

D

trained seaman—a species of which every ship was in short supply
—they were days of back-breaking labour with little or no sleep:
what rest they could get was taken in hammocks soaking wet from
leaks through the decks, and there was no hot food to give them a
little stamina to bear up under the cursing petty officers and their
bruising canes. Three more gales and a spell of fog had to be
weathered before, at noon on May Day, Cape Trafalgar bore due
east, eighty-one miles away. However, although there was another
gale next day the crews were more cheerful: as Midshipman Ellis
noted in his journal, 'At noon, all the fleet running in for Gibraltar
Bay.'

Byng, of course, had been at sea for a month, and knew nothing
of the recent French activities. However, the sight of ships from
Captain Edgcumbe's little squadron waiting at anchor must have
warned him of bad news to come since otherwise they would have
been at Port Mahon. The thunder of the *Ramillies*'s reply to their
17-gun salute had hardly died away before Edgcumbe's boat was
alongside the flagship and Byng was hearing at first hand how the
French had invaded Minorca. Edgcumbe told Byng that according
to the observations of Captain Noel of the *Princess Louisa* the
enemy's squadron consisted of about thirteen men-of-war, 'but
not above seven appear to be of the line'.[17]

While Edgcumbe was making his report to the Admiral, General
Stuart went on shore to see the Governor of Gibraltar, Lieut-
General Fowke, and to deliver the letters from the Secretary at War.
At the same time Byng ordered his ships to complete their provisions and water 'with the utmost expedition'—an order anticipated by Captain Young, for the *Intrepid*'s longboat, loaded with
empty casks, was already pulling for the shore.

Apart from provisioning his ships, Byng had several other tasks,
each one of which was to give him an unpleasant shock. Since
Gibraltar would have to be his main base now that Minorca was
besieged, he set about making sure it was in a good condition.
Here, he had assumed, he would be able to get all the naval stores
he wanted: all the large quantities of rope, canvas, food, water,
powder and shot needed to keep a squadron of the King's ships in
fighting trim. Here, he assumed, he would be able to repair his
ships and careen them when their bottoms became encrusted
with weed and barnacle. However, all his assumptions, although
reasonable enough, were wrong.

It did not take the Admiral long to discover that the dockyard was a decayed wreck, bereft of naval stores; nor was he impressed with the capabilities of Henry Blankley who was the storekeeper, clerk of the checque and clerk of the survey—three posts offering almost unlimited opportunities for curruptly supplementing an official salary of £200 a year. Fortunately, Edgcumbe had brought with him Milburn Marsh, a naval officer who had been stationed at Port Mahon, and who was a qualified shipwright. Byng at once gave orders that he was to act as master shipwright at Gibraltar and, with Blankley's help, give him an immediate report on the situation in the dockyard.

When it was delivered to Byng the report made depressing reading for an admiral who had to maintain a squadron of battleships and frigates, particularly as it was almost certain that they would soon have battle damage to repair, in addition to normal wear and tear. And Byng probably reflected that 'normal' would soon become 'abnormal' if the squadron had the misfortune to run into a brisk Gulf of Lions gale, for they had a well-deserved reputation for tearing sails and treating masts and yards with the scant courtesy which an elephant affords bamboo shoots beneath its clumsy feet.

Marsh and Blankley reported that the mast-house, boat-house, pitch-house, smith's shop and cable-shed, whose very names indicated their importance to a dockyard, were 'all decayed and tumbling down'. The sheds used for repairing sails and for the artificers to work in were both falling down; capstans were rotting away; and 'In case there may be a necessity to careen or caulk any of His Majesty's ships there is neither floating stages for that service, nor any boat for the officers to attend to their respective duties.' The list of stores 'of which there is few or none of in His Majesty's magazines' was a list of just about everything that was necessary—from pitch to lanterns, and caulking cotton to canvas.[18] The dockyard was, in other words, a monument to the destructiveness of Government complacency and neglect, service corruption, bureaucratic lethargy and dry rot.

Having found out how little reliance could be placed on Gibraltar's dockyard, Byng's next discovery was how much reliance could be placed on its Governor, General Fowke, who had in the meantime read the three letters addressed to him by the Secretary at War. As we have seen, the first told him to take Lord Robert

Bertie's Fusiliers into the Gibraltar garrison and give Byng a battalion in its place to take to Minorca; the second, written after the Admiralty protests at this musical chairs, said that if there was any chance of Minorca being attacked he was to give Byng a battalion to take to its relief; the third said he was to take the Fusiliers' women and children from the ships and receive them in the garrison. But Fowke then discovered that Admiral Byng regarded the Fusiliers as part of the crews of his ships, and had Admiralty orders to that effect.

Thanks to Barrington's stupidity, however, the orders to Fowke did not cover the most likely situation—and the one that actually occurred: that by the time Byng's squadron arrived at Gibraltar the French would have actually landed in strength on Minorca and would be covering their supply lines with a powerful squadron.

General Fowke, reflecting on these elaborately-worded contradictions, finally decided that the safety of Gibraltar was his supreme responsibility and something which had priority over all other considerations. He already had what he considered to be the bare minimum of troops for its defence—four battalions, under 3,000 men. Since the French had invaded Minorca with 15,000 men, he appears to have thought that supplying Byng with a battalion, 700 men, to take to Fort St Philip would not make much difference to the besieged Blakeney, whose days were obviously numbered, and would only swell the number of prisoners the French would take; whereas 700 men in Gibraltar represented nearly a quarter of the garrison.

If he had not received any orders at all from London, one can understand why Fowke took this view though not necessarily agree with him; but, contradictory though they were, Fowke did have orders, and he found them extremely disturbing; so much so that he set about rigging an elaborate charade which, he hoped, would provide him with a legal excuse for disobeying them. To begin with he sent for three Army officers whom he knew were well acquainted with Minorca, and especially with Fort St Philip. They were Major James Mace, of the Artillery, who had come out in the *Intrepid* and was under orders to go to Minorca to join the garrison; Archibald Patoun, the Chief Engineer at Gibraltar; and Captain Alexander Leith, also one of the Gibraltar garrison. When these three worthies arrived in Fowke's office he gave them a written question and told them, in the light of their knowledge, to consider it and then bring him their written answer. The question was: 'Whether or not it is practicable to throw succours into St Philip's Castle, supposing the enemy to have erected batteries on the two shores near the entrance of the harbour, an advantage scarce to be supposed they have neglected.'

The three men deliberated and returned to Fowke's office, where one imagines he greeted them as if they were so many Jasons bringing him the Golden Fleece. Their answer—which was to bring Fowke as much ill-fortune as if it had been spoken by Medea —was that 'Unless the batteries can be silenced, it will be extremely dangerous, if not impracticable; as the sally ports, by which succours must enter, according to the best of our recollection, are so entirely exposed that their guns may destroy any boats employed on that attempt.'[19]

To complete the hand of cards he wanted to play, Fowke sent a boat off to the *Ramillies* to ask for copies of all of the Admiralty's orders and instructions to Byng, which the unsuspecting Admiral naturally handed over without question. Fowke then called a council of war consisting of ten Army officers, including General Stuart and the three colonels sailing with Byng. General Fowke acted as president and opened the proceedings by reading out the three contradictory letters from Lord Barrington. After this recital, which drew attention to their only merit, which was brevity, he read the Admiralty's instructions to Byng, followed by the report on the chances of succouring Fort St Philip, and the latest intelligence reports received.

If Barrington's orders had been considered in the light of the Admiralty's orders to Byng, relating to the Fusiliers, the Secretary at War's intentions could be understood without any difficulty, and it is ridiculous to suppose that Fowke had not already compared them and realized he ought to give Byng an extra battalion. In any case, he must have known that Byng was conversant with the Government's intentions. However, Fowke clearly did not want any enlightenment, and his council of war soon recorded that since the French had landed 13,000 to 15,000 men on Minorca and that the British had retired into Fort St Philip, they 'are humbly of opinion that the sending a detachment equal to a battalion would evidently weaken the garrison of Gibraltar, and be no way effectual to the relief of Minorca'. In addition, since the Toulon squadron appeared to be equal in strength, if not superior, to Byng's force, the garrison of Gibraltar would be exposed to imminent danger if the British squadron was 'weakened by an engagement, or any other accident'.

Although the General was later to claim that he could not understand the Secretary at War's orders, the ten soldiers had nevertheless collectively and openly disobeyed them; and they had discreetly invited Byng not to get involved in any fighting (and, one can only assume from the reference to 'any other accident', not to risk running into a gale) lest Gibraltar should be put in hazard. But they had also put their own careers in hazard, too, because although a council of war was a method by which officers discussed and concerted action against the enemy, usually in the absence of direct orders, it was certainly not a vehicle for collective disobedience to direct orders, as Fowke was soon to find out to his cost.

However, the most startling thing about the council's deliberations is not Fowke's chicanery but his stupidity. Neither he nor his nine fellow members of the council realized that the only way the French could possibly attack Gibraltar was by using its Toulon squadron to escort a convoy carrying troops. If Byng could destroy or cripple the French squadron, then Gibraltar was absolutely safe.

Thus in his handling of the situation Fowke was both a fool and a knave; but some of the blame must be laid at the door of Byng's cabin, for the Admiral might still have saved the day. Had he brought any pressure to bear; had he pointed out with all the tactful vigour that he could muster the effect of abandoning Minorca to its fate, then Fowke might have been persuaded—or shamed—into doing his duty and carrying out the spirit, as well as the letter, of his orders from Barrington.

But Byng was not that kind of man: he could see Fowke's point of view—although not agreeing with it—and he was only too ready to have his own pessimism reinforced by Fowke's. He had already been humbugged by the Admiralty—forbidden to take seamen by one express, urged to sea by the next, and his main base at Gibraltar was a complete ruin; and he had been humbugged by the weather all the way from Portsmouth to the Pillars of Hercules—four strong gales in a month, interspersed with fogs and calms, were too much considering the condition of the ships that the Admiralty had given him. Now, at the end of all that, he was being humbugged by the Army—ranging from the Secretary at War who was, from the maladroit way he dictated orders, a lisping idiot, to the General receiving them, who was a frightened one.

If John Byng, in his haughty and precise fashion, had mentally consigned them all to the devil—Admiralty, War Office, Fowke, the trio of lugubrious experts on Fort St Philip, and now the council of war which had (apparently) given Fowke a cast-iron excuse for doing nothing, it would be hard to blame him. Yet a cleverer admiral would have had Fowke eating out of his hand.

Byng did in fact have a chance of asserting himself, if Fowke is to be believed, but he wrapped himself up in his pride. The circumstances were described at Fowke's subsequent court martial by the General himself and by Byng's second-in-command, Rear-Admiral Temple West. Fowke claimed that he had told Byng, in front of West, that 'notwithstanding the order of the council which Admiral Byng had read, he would furnish a battalion if desired'. When asked to confirm this, West said he did not remember that Byng had read the report, but he recalled Fowke's offer, and Byng had answered either that he did not desire it, or he did not think it necessary, but at the time 'very little was said upon it', and it seemed to West 'as if Admiral Byng considered himself no further concerned in the question than to carry such detachments to Minorca as should be put on board him'. West considers that 'The Admiral did not think himself called upon to take any part in the determination.'[20]

West's evidence rings true: one can picture the pedantic and now thoroughly angry Byng declaring to himself that what the Army did was an Army affair and nothing to do with him: he had his orders—such as they were—and he was going to obey them, and if General Fowke chose to behave differently that was his concern. A greater man would have taken a broader view; but the Hon John Byng was, unfortunately, only the son of a great man.

Byng went back to the *Ramillies* and composed a dispatch to the Admiralty to tell their Lordships what was happening. He had, over the years, evolved a curious formula for his letters which could be interpreted as either modest or defeatist.* This time he

---

* 'I do not think myself equal to the task I am going to take,' he had written to the Duke of Bedford when appointed to the Mediterranean ten years earlier; 'I shall use every endeavour . . . to frustrate the designs of the enemy . . . but shall think myself the most fortunate if I am so happy to succeed in this undertaking' he wrote to the Admiralty before sailing from Portsmouth for Minorca.

wrote, 'If I had been so happy to have arrived at Mahon before the French had landed, I flatter myself I should have been able to have prevented their getting a footing on the island', but now, because of the number of troops the French had put on shore, he was firmly of the opinion that landing British troops to reinforce Fort St Philip would only enable it to hold out a little longer and result in more prisoners for the French, 'for the garrison in time will be obliged to surrender, unless a sufficient number of men could be landed to dislodge the French or raise the siege'.

Judging Byng's reasoning in the light of a twentieth-century knowledge of strategy, one is appalled that a man sent out to be Commander-in-Chief in the Mediterranean should, like Fowke, be incapable of realizing that the best way of defeating the French was to defeat Galissonnière's squadron, and then blockade the island to starve out Richelieu's army. But if we judge Byng only by the standards of his day, the fact is that although the dispatch he was writing was subsequently criticized by the Government, no one found fault with this particular passage and the ideas it contained when everything possible was being used to blacken and condemn him.

Byng brightened up in the next paragraph of his dispatch: he was determined, he said, to take the squadron up to Minorca, where he would be better able to judge the position and 'will give General Blakeney all the assistance he shall require' though, he pointed out rather illogically, 'I am afraid all communication will be cut off between us'. (The authority he gave for this statement was the report of Fowke's trio of 'experts'.)

He added that, if he could not relieve Minorca, he would regard the security of Gibraltar as his next task 'and shall repair down here with the squadron; and hope their Lordships will approve of that measure'. He concluded by describing the appalling condition of the Gibraltar dockyard; reporting on Fowke's council of war and its decisions; and assuring their Lordships that 'We are employed in taking in wine and completing our water with the utmost dispatch, and shall let no opportunity slip of sailing from hence'.[21]

Since we have been critical of Byng's ideas, it is necessary to make a brief survey of his situation and first of all, consider his orders. We have already seen that they had been framed by Anson in the mistaken belief that the French Toulon squadron was much more likely to make its way to America; or alternatively, that at the worst Byng would arrive in the Mediterranean after only a small French force had attacked Minorca. Out of more than 700 words of orders, only twenty-five referred to this eventuality— 'If you find any attack made upon that island by the French, you are to use all possible means in your power for its relief'.

From Byng's point of view these twenty-five words were all he had to guide him in the task of relieving an island which had been invaded by 15,000 French troops. In estimating his chances of relieving Minorca, Byng appears to have put all the French and all the British forces on the scales: a battalion of Fusiliers and thirteen battleships (one of them, the *Deptford*, was in fact of only 48 guns) against 15,000 French troops and twelve battleships.

Yet the very impossibility of taking any military action on shore against the French should make any admiral realize that Galissonnière's squadron—the shield protecting Richelieu's army— was his first target; that once the French squadron was destroyed, crippled or simply driven off, the British could blockade the island and starve Richelieu's army into an ignominious submission.

By a remarkable coincidence, Byng's father had as Commander-in-Chief in the Mediterranean faced a similar situation when dealing with the Spanish threat to Sicily; and—ironically enough— had written from Port Mahon a dispatch which described, in a single sentence, what he was going to do at Sicily in 1718 and what his son ought to have done at Minorca in 1756: 'Since we cannot come time enough to prevent their [the Spanish] landing and they will not withdraw their troops, I intend to attack their fleet and render them useless from either covering their army or bringing more succours to them . . .' He carried out this plan brilliantly, for it resulted in the victory of Cape Passaro.

Did Byng later recall his father's victory? Did plain commonsense tell him that the opinions he had given in his letter to the Admiralty were rubbish? As the narrative will soon show, he eventually met the French squadron and engaged it; but in view of the opinions expressed in his letter to the Admiralty, we can conclude that although he did the right thing it was for the wrong reason: he engaged the French ships because they were in sight, not because he realized that they were Richelieu's lifeline.

While Byng was finishing his letter to the Admiralty, General Fowke was writing a cunningly-contrived letter to the Secretary at

War. The General no doubt thought that if there was going to be any trouble, then Byng should share in the blame. Making no mention whatsoever of the Minister's orders (though he made great play of them at his court martial and drew some damaging admissions from Barrington), he implied that Byng had refused to take a battalion of troops with him by quoting him as saying 'he did not think so large a detachment was necessary, and that he only required a sufficient number to put the ships late under Mr Edgcumbe's command in a condition to act against an enemy'.[22]

9

WARM BEER FOR THE DUKE

THE FORTY-TWO WOMEN and children belonging to Lord Robert Bertie's Fusiliers were taken on shore by the ships' boats after tearful farewells. Since the soldiers were part of the crews of Byng's ships or, in an emergency, to be landed on Minorca, it is hard to understand why the War Office allowed them to be embarked in the first place; but the wives knew only too well that once abroad, a regiment was often forgotten—like the 38th Foot, left in the Leeward Islands for sixty years without being relieved, while the 13th Foot went to Gibraltar in 1710 and stayed for twenty-eight years. To allow a soldier husband out of her sight often meant, in those days, he went out of her life for ever.

On May 3, the day after arriving in Gibraltar, Byng ordered all his captains to send in reports of the condition of their ships, so that he could see the state of his squadron. His flagship, the 90-gun *Ramillies*, was the largest. She was originally built in 1664 at Woolwich and named the *Royal Katherine*, an 82-gun ship of 1,086 tons. She was rebuilt* in 1702 and later renamed the *Ramillies*, and rebuilt yet again forty years later. On this day the *Ramillies* mustered 768 men and there were forty-three sick on board, plus seventy-two soldiers and five officers. As far as food was concerned, stowed away in bags, barrels and casks were twelve weeks' supply of bread and only one day's beer, twelve weeks' of beef, twenty of pork, eight of flour, and at least ten weeks' supply of everything else. Her hull had been cleaned in January, and against the question 'Condition of ship' her captain, Arthur Gardiner, had entered 'Fit for sea.'

Byng had a complete trust in Gardiner; indeed, he had known him since he was a boy and helped train him, because three of the six years Gardiner served at sea before getting his lieutenant's

---

* 'Rebuilding' could mean anything from stripping a ship down to its keel to a large-scale refit.

certificate were spent in the *Falmouth* under Captain John Byng.

At anchor nearby was the *Buckingham*, flying the flag of Rear-Admiral Temple West. She was a 68-gun ship which had been launched at Deptford in 1748. Commanding her was Captain Michael Everitt, and she was short of seventy-three men. Stowed below she had bread for twelve weeks, beef for sixteen and pork for twenty, but only eight days' supply of beer.

When the squadron went into battle it would be divided into two divisions—the van under Temple West and the rear under Byng. The ship that would lead the line of battle—in other words the leading ship in West's van division—was the 60-gun *Defiance*, commanded by Captain Thomas Andrews. She was another of the ships built on the banks of the Thames, and had been refitted at Plymouth the previous December.

The second ship in the line was the *Portland*, commanded by Captain Patrick Baird who, as a lieutenant, had served in the *Gloucester*, one of the six ships which had set out with Anson in 1740 for his great voyage round the world. Baird was a brave man; he had been severely wounded when with his first command, the sloop *Fly*, he had put up a very gallant fight against a much larger French privateer. The *Portland*, too, was a Thames ship: Thomas Snelgrove had built her at Limehouse, and launched her in October 1744. She had not been refitted nor had her bottom scrubbed for a year—since she left Plymouth in May 1755 to join Edgcumbe's squadron in the Mediterranean.

The *Lancaster* was the third ship, and she had been brought out for Edgcumbe to take over. Edgcumbe had gone to sea at a very early age and obtained his first command when he was twenty-three—due no doubt to the Parliamentary 'interest' of his father. At the age of twenty-four he was given the command of the 50-gun *Salisbury*, and within a couple of years he was bringing the French East Indiaman *Jason* into Plymouth—Edgcumbe's home—as a prize with eight cases of silver in her holds. He was at present one of the two Members of Parliament for Fowey, and his brother Richard sat for nearby Penryn, as well as being a member of the Board of Admiralty. Edgcumbe's present command, the *Lancaster*, was originally built as an 80-gun ship at Bursledon, in Hampshire, by Wyatt and Company* in 1693, but when she was rebuilt

* Wyatt's built at Buckler's Hard three of the ships which were at Trafalgar—see the author's *England Expects*, pp. 64–6, Weidenfeld & Nicolson, 1959.

for the second time in 1749 she was reduced to 66 guns. Her last refit had been at Portsmouth in October 1755.

The *Lancaster* would be followed in the line by the *Buckingham*; astern of her would be the 64-gun *Captain*, commanded by Captain Charles Catford. He had been one of the officers who, with Byng, had tried Admirals Mathews and Lestock after Toulon. The *Captain* had been launched at Portsmouth in 1746 as a 70-gun ship, but she had later been cut down to a 64. According to Rear-Admiral West she was now 'a very complaining ship, was always leaky, and always sickly; and was, in my opinion, a very unfit ship to have been sent abroad on service'.[1]

The *Intrepid* was the last ship in West's division. She had been captured from the French, and the only noticeable alteration made before putting her into service with the Royal Navy appears to have been the dropping of the final 'e' from the French rendering of her name. Her captain, James Young, had spent several years commanding ships in the Mediterranean, some of the time while Byng was Commander-in-Chief after Medley's death.

Byng had chosen the *Revenge* to be the leading ship of his division, and she was commanded by Captain Frederick Cornwall. An interesting glimpse of Admiral Byng and Cornwall is given by one of Lord Robert Bertie's young officers, Captain John Hylyn. He wrote that the Army officers had been appointed to their individual ships. 'I was to sail in the *Revenge*, but I had a great desire to go in the *Culloden*, as in that ship I should have enjoyed the company of two or three intimate friends. To make this point I waited upon Admiral Byng, but the arrangement having been made I was told I must abide by it. I must here observe that if "outward and visible signs" were always genuine and decisive marks of the inward man, you might have concluded from the appearance of the Admiral that he was a hero. His face, his person, and his manner, were manly and noble ...

'I must confess I met with nothing agreeable to my particular taste when I went on board the *Revenge* ... Captain Frederick Cornwall, her commander, seemed about sixty years of age: he had the manner of a gentleman; he had a good person and a good face, but there was a natural haughtiness in him which had not been softened by the naval school of those days. He had lost an arm when a lieutenant on board the *Marlborough* in the engagement of Mathews and Lestock ...' (It is a pity the young officer did not find the company 'very agreeable' in the *Revenge*: his fellow passengers were the Earl of Effingham and his good lady.)

The second ship in Byng's division was Captain Thomas Noel's *Princess Louisa*, which had been built at Robert Carter's yard at Limehouse in 1744, and although fitted out in August 1755 before going to the Mediterranean she had not been refitted since. Her masts were in such a bad condition that they had been condemned, but no replacements were available. She was short of sixty-four men and, since she had not been scrubbed for nine months, her bottom was foul.

The 64-gun *Trident*, astern of the *Princess Louisa* in the line, had been captured from the French in 1747 and was now commanded by Captain Philip Durell, one of Byng's most senior captains. He was far from pleased with life at that moment: his first lieutenant was on shore sick, the second was in another ship, the gunner had died and the chaplain was also on shore sick. Thus his mainstays for sailing, repairing guns and repairing souls were missing at a time when their services were most wanted. His ship was also sixty-seven men short of her complement.

The *Ramillies* followed the *Trident* and was in turn followed by the 74-gun *Culloden*, another Thames-built ship, commanded by the senior of Byng's captains, Henry Ward. In 1741 he realized the young captain's dream by capturing a rich prize, the *Nuestra Señora del Rosario*, and carrying her into Jamaica.

A ship named the *Deptford* came next, and appropriately enough she was built at Deptford in 1729 costing £12,985, and rebuilt in 1750. She was the weakest ship in the line, carrying only 48 guns —indeed, she ought never to have been in the line at all. Commanding her was Captain John Amherst, son of a bencher of Lincoln's Inn. Now aged thirty-nine, he had been a protégé of Vice-Admiral Thomas Smith (who enters this narrative later as the president of the court which tried Byng). His marriage had been a complete failure and when he had left his wife he had written to Smith saying that 'Indeed I have not one thing to blame my self for; except it was a fault loveing hir to much. I thought myself retired with content, and tho' poor was happy, till it pleased God to bring this misfortune upon me . . . We are parted by articles, and I never will see hir more'.[2] This parting had a great effect on Amherst, and a year later he wrote to the Admiral that 'I care little for the world and less for the people that are in it, and would, if I could help it, not love you. My ship I shall soon have ready for the sea, and suppose as soon as some damned voyage can be found for me, you will hear of my being at sea. I hope you will take care of your health, for if I should loose [sic] you, I shall loose my faith of their being one honest man in the world'.[3]

The last ship in the line was the *Kingston*, commanded by Captain William Parry, who was described as a 'descendant of a very noble and ancient Welsh family'.[4] Most of the squadron were still short of men, according to the musters on May 2 and 3, (they had also landed a number of sick). The *Intrepid* was short of eighty-three seamen, the *Captain* eighty, and the *Lancaster* sixty-seven. The other nine ships were short of more than 500 men.[5]

Just before Byng sailed he received more news about the situation at Minorca: the *Dolphin* under young Lieut O'Hara's command, arrived from Mahon on May 5. She had, of course, been left behind by Edgcumbe, but O'Hara persuaded General Blakeney to let him have thirty men[6] in order to take the *Dolphin* to Gibraltar and thus save her from certain destruction. Admiral Byng ordered several ships to provide some seamen to bring her crew back to full strength, and he then put O'Hara—the son (Augustus Hervey called him 'the worthless son') of Lord Tyrawley, the absentee Governor of Minorca—in command of the little *Lovel* and ordered him to go to England with duplicates of his letter to the Admiralty.

Up to now all the ships in Byng's squadron had been busy each day trying to get more water on board, but on the 8th the squadron finally sailed for Minorca 'Without', as Byng noted in his journal 'waiting to complete the watering of the Fleet, because tedious, on account of the small quantity of water furnished by the springs at Gibraltar and the great number of ships to be supplied'.

All the Duke de Richelieu's hopes of a swift victory in Minorca soon shrivelled up with the grass in the heat and dust of early summer: having let impatience overcome his carefully-laid plans and landed his invasion force at the opposite end of the island to his objective, he now had to pay the price for what now proved to be ill-judged urgency. His intended swift blow had fallen on thin air. His maps of the emplacements at Fort St Philip were long out of date and he had already been forced to appeal to France for more men and more guns to begin a siege.

The road to Fort St Philip runs beside the island's mountain spine and although its surface at the best of times was atrocious, the retreating British had done their best to make it worse. As the French trudged eastwards, thirsty and perspiring, British scouts kept a watch on them, and reported back to Blakeney. When they had reached Alayor, only a few miles from the Fort, the General sat down and wrote an indignant letter to the Duke de Richelieu— for of course Britain and France were still, officially, at peace— demanding to know 'the reason of the French King's troops landing in a hostile manner in His Majesty's island of Minorca'. It was late in the day to bother about such legal niceties, but the letter was sealed and given to the Drum-Major of Cornwallis's Regiment who marched off out of the Fort and down the road to Alayor 'in full military form' to deliver it to the Duke.

A few days later Richelieu sent his reply—a polite prevarication —by a French drummer who struck his way up to the gates of the Fort. The drummer also brought a present from the Duke for General Blakeney—some dried fruit. Not to be outdone, Blakeney sent the Duke six bottles of warm beer with his acknowledgement. Three days later, on April 30 the British guns at the Fort opened fire on the enemy for the first time as they came in range: the siege had now begun.*

The efficiency of the British gunfire was partly due to the energy of a Scotsman, Captain William Cunningham who had spent nearly all his own money to strengthen the timber platforms of the batteries. Cunningham was originally the second engineer at the Fort and when the chief engineer left, took over the post temporarily while General Blakeney applied to the War Office for him to have it permanently. Instead, a new chief engineer was sent out from London—a man described as 'an old decrepit German'.

Cunningham resigned in disgust, intending to return to his regiment in England. The young captain left the island with his wife—who was pregnant—and two children and they waited at Nice while Mrs Cunningham's baby was born. Cunningham then heard of the French plans against Minorca. 'Recollecting that the platforms of the batteries at Fort St Philip were in such a rotten and ruinous condition that they would not stand any hot service', he promptly spent all the money he had, about £1,600, on buying

---

* Before it ended, the garrison had fired 32,706 round shot, 28,250 shells and hand grenades, 959 grapeshot and 332 double-headed shot.

timber to repair them. He then hired a ship, had the timber loaded, and sailed with it for Minorca, leaving his family behind at Nice. It was reported that 'his arrival with such a supply at such a critical juncture gave General Blakeney infinite pleasure'. To show his gratitude, Blakeney consigned the War Office to perdition, sacked the new chief engineer, and gave Cunningham the job.[7]

While the French were advancing across Minorca and Byng wrestled with his problems in Gibraltar, Augustus Hervey, after calling in at Nice to send warnings to the Admiralty, Henry Fox and 'my brother Bristol', tried to get back to Port Mahon with another vessel in company. This was a settee, a small and fast lateen-rigged craft, commanded by Captain Ourry, who had also been sent out from Mahon to get news of the French. However, nature joined Hervey's enemies, and as he recorded in his *Journal*, he fell sick almost at once.

'I was ill with rheumatism and took James's powders, and sailed on for Mahon,' he wrote. 'The 19th [of April] I was in such pain in the night that I was blooded.' He stayed in bed for the next four days while the *Phoenix* made her way towards Minorca, with Captain Ourry's settee in tow. But at dawn on the fifth day he received a rude awakening which soon fetched him from his bed: the lightening of the sky showed some faint patches in the grey monochrome—the sails of ships. The *Phoenix* had strayed into the middle of Galissonnière's squadron. They did not spot her at once but as soon as daylight came—just as Hervey made out Galissonnière's flagship busy making signals—three of them gave chase. The settee was hurriedly cast off and Captain Ourry was told to try to make his escape by steering in a different direction.

Hervey decided to make for Majorca, the largest of the Balearic islands and lying south-west of Minorca. Fortunately for him, after chasing the *Phoenix* for several hours without gaining on her, the French ships finally gave up and turned back, but his troubles were not at an end: 'The next day I felt a violent pain in my left great toe, which I found was the gout got down there.'

After capturing a French ship which was carrying twenty live bullocks intended for Galissonnière's squadron—they made a welcome change of diet for the British seamen—the *Phoenix* arrived in Palma, in Majorca, on April 29, twelve days after the French landed on Minorca and three days before Byng arrived at

Gibraltar. Majorca was owned by the Spanish and therefore neutral in the present conflict, and Hervey sent an officer on shore to pay his compliments to the Viceroy, the Marquis del Cayro, and to the British Consul, Mr Samuel Scot. The officer returned to report that Scot 'was a poor old man not able to move from age, and the Vice-Consul a fellow of the island in the French interest'.[8]

Hervey later went on shore to meet the Viceroy, who told him that he was determined to maintain a very strict neutrality between the two nations. However, the young captain was too well informed to be taken in by fine words, and answered that although he was well satisfied with the neutrality of the Court of Spain, he could not help commenting on the fact that he had seen 'great proofs of the reverse here, for every possible partiality is shown to the French'. Everything they wanted in Minorca was sent over to them, including horses.

A warning was sent to Hervey next day that several French warships were cruising off the island, and that they had stopped and boarded fishing boats in an attempt to get information about the *Phoenix*. Within a few hours two French warships, the 64-gun *Hippopotame* and the frigate *Gracieuse*, arrived in Palma Bay and anchored.

The reason for the arrival of these unwelcome visitors is not hard to find: as soon as Galissonnière had heard that a ship bringing him twenty bullocks had been captured—'by a pirate', according to one report he received[9]—he ordered the *Gracieuse* to investigate. She was commanded by Captain de Marquisan, a Provençal and son of a former lieutenant in the Navy. He sent a rather curious report to Galissonnière, claiming that he had found and chased the *Phoenix* 'and obliged her to anchor in the roads at Palma'. Since he arrived in Palma six days after the *Phoenix* it is unlikely that there was any more truth in the other claim he made, which was that he had challenged Hervey to come out with him but that the British captain had refused.

Hervey was in a very unpleasant situation: although the *Hippopotame* had sailed, the *Gracieuse* was still anchored nearby and other French warships were cruising round the island, so that he was trapped; in addition he had no idea what had happened to Edgcumbe and the rest of the little squadron. Had they all been destroyed by the French? Or were they blockaded in Mahon just as he was trapped in Palma? Or had they escaped? And why had no reinforcements arrived from England?

Hervey had been in Palma twelve days before he heard a report that Admiral Byng was certainly on his way to the Mediterranean —thus confirming the information he had obtained at Leghorn— and this made him decide to sail for Gibraltar with the first strong easterly wind, risking being captured by Galissonnière's ships. Byng had in fact already arrived at Gibraltar and sailed again three days earlier, heading for Palma, although of course Hervey knew nothing of this until Captain Ourry arrived from Barcelona with the news that a British squadron had anchored in Gibraltar.

Hervey went on shore to call on the Viceroy and tell him that the *Phoenix* had observed a strict neutrality since she had arrived in Palma; that he now intended to sail next morning, and 'if the *Gracieuse* came near me I was determined to engage her, which I hoped to do in sight of his town tomorrow'. The Viceroy tactfully pointed out that the *Gracieuse* would be too strong for the *Phoenix*, since she had 36 guns and a crew of 300. Hervey replied that 'We will try'. (The *Phoenix* had only 24 guns and a crew of 107—she was short of fifty-three men.)

Having delivered his warning, Hervey returned to the *Phoenix* for a meal, taking a friend with him. However, before they started eating one of the officers came in to Hervey's cabin to tell him that the *Gracieuse*, which had earlier weighed anchor, was now sailing 'with all she could crowd and making many signals'. Hervey wrote that 'Soon after this from our masthead we saw two sail standing in, and at five we saw seventeen sail . . .'[10]

10

'ENEMY IN SIGHT'

ALTHOUGH THE MEDITERRANEAN can justly claim to have been for centuries the gentle cradle, the happy playground and the all-engulfing battlefield of many vigorous and colourful civilizations, it can be a wilful sea. Not for nothing have many of its winds been given special names—the bora, for instance, which suddenly hurtles down the Adriatic like a giant's sneeze; the Levanter, blowing raw and easterly out through the Strait; the tramontana coming cold across the mountains, its chill soaking into flesh and spirit like the words of a death sentence; and the hot and humid sirocco which carries the heat of Africa's sands to the southern fringes of Europe, picking up an enervating dampness as it crosses the sea.

The Mediterranean was certainly in no mood to give Admiral Byng a joyous welcome when he returned through the Pillars of Hercules after an absence of nearly eight years: instead of a boisterous westerly wind which would speed the squadron on its way up to Minorca there were only baffling calms; and Byng reflected bitterly that for the first few days the only easting made by the squadron had been due to the current caused by the water continually overflowing into the great inland sea from the Atlantic.

The Admiral's nephew John, entering the Mediterranean for the first time and watching the coastline of Granada to larboard rising into the blue-grey of the Sierra Nevada, was experiencing the same excitement that had gripped Byng when, so many years earlier, he had sailed to the Middle Sea as a youngster on board the *Superb* under the command of his uncle, Streynsham Master. Then, his father had been the Commander-in-Chief, on his way to fight and win the Battle of Cape Passaro; then—it was thirty-eight years ago—he had borne no responsibility; like his young nephew he had been carefree, eager-eyed and expectant, happy in the midshipmen's berth and secure in the knowledge that his father commanded all the ships in sight from the *Superb*'s quarter-deck.

Now every ship in sight from the quarter-deck of the *Ramillies* was his responsibility and his alone. In addition the safety—rescue, rather—of Minorca and, indeed, the safety of Britain's whole position in the Mediterranean, rested on his shoulders. A false move on his part, an omission, a forgotten factor, a slight change of wind should he meet the enemy's squadron, a vicious gale—any one of these things, and many more too, could bring utter and complete failure. It was a heavy responsibility and one that had sat more easily on the shoulders of Sir George Byng than his son.

John Byng may well have reflected on the confusion that existed: for instance, eight months ago he had been out in the Atlantic capturing French ships without a declaration of war; why, even now, war had not been declared—as far as he knew, anyway—and here were the French besieging Fort St Philip. It was highly irregular. The Admiralty had taken away his Marines and given him soldiers instead—what good did that do? Anson had given him old ships, for the most part, and kept him short of men. And his orders were vague. Was this the way to save Minorca?

He was very disgruntled, but had no one in whom he could confide his indignation, and as the ships of the squadron hurriedly trimmed their sails for every puff of wind, he considered his next move. The most important thing, he thought, was somehow to get in touch with General Blakeney at Fort St Philip to find out the situation on the island, and see what the General wanted him to do with the handful of Army officers and recruits who were supposed to be joining their units on the island. Secondly he had to discover the whereabouts of the French squadron under Galissonnière. He had none too many frigates to send out searching ahead, but neutral merchantmen were passing the squadron daily, and they were usually talkative. Apart from them, there might be some British merchantmen at sea whose information would be more reliable. A few might be sheltering at Majorca, and since his own squadron would have to pass close to that island, Byng decided he would send a ship into Palma. For Augustus Hervey this was a fortunate decision because as the British squadron was sighted at Palma, his unwelcome watchdog, the French frigate *Gracieuse*, made off to warn Galissonnière.

The fleeing *Gracieuse* was seen from Byng's flagship, but the Admiral knew that the French were bound to have frigates on the lookout, and she was too far off to be pursued. He ordered the *Experiment* to go ahead and call in at Palma to see what she could discover. This was, of course, the morning that Augustus Hervey, after warning the Viceroy that the *Phoenix* would sail shortly, had taken a friend back on board for a meal—one which, as we have already seen, was never started because the *Experiment* and Byng's squadron were sighted from the *Phoenix*'s masthead immediately after the departure of the *Gracieuse*.

'I rowed out and met the *Experiment*,' wrote Hervey, 'who gave me the account of Mr Byng being those ships in sight and that he came here for intelligence.' From the quarter-deck of the *Ramillies*, Byng watched the *Experiment* returning from Palma and saw that with her was another ship, a frigate, which soon hoisted the signal to speak with the Admiral. 'At six she joyned,' noted the *Ramillies*'s log, 'and proved to be His Majesty's ship *Phoenix*. She saluted with thirteen guns. Returned thirteen guns.'

The Admiral was delighted to see Hervey: apart from a natural pleasure at seeing his young friend and protégé again, he at last had someone in whom he could confide his troubles—and with whom he could release some of his indignation. Hervey soon related all he knew about the French naval and military activities, and the conversation turned to Byng's ships. Having hoped that Byng would have had a larger squadron, Hervey commented that 'I was extremely sorry to see him so thinly attended, that I thought two or three more ships would have done the thing completely, and it was an object that deserved preference'.

Byng was in no mood to minimize his difficulties or gloss over the way he had been treated, telling Hervey that ' 'twas worse than I saw, for his ships being almost all the worst of the fleet, that even they were not manned, that the troops of Lord Robert Bertie's Regiment, which were to be landed at Mahon, made up the compliment [sic] now of the fleet; such was the situation of this fleet, and that his instructions were to secure Gibraltar as well as relieve Minorca.

'In short,' wrote Hervey, 'Lord Anson, the First Lord of the Admiralty only sent the very worst of the fleet whilst he kept the rest cruising at home, no hospital ship, no fireship, no storeship, nor any tender, and if the Mediterranean squadron [i.e. Edgcumbe's ships] had been cut off and kept into Mahon, as it might have been, where then could he have shown himself? What a reflection on

Government!'[1] When he visited the *Ramillies* again next day, Hervey recorded, he lamented once again that the Admiral did not have more ships, and Byng told him that 'Ld Anson sent all the best ships cruising with his favourites*, and all he could do, he could not obtain two or three more, though he might with ease have brought them'.

While the squadron worked its way south-eastwards to round Cape Salinas before heading up north-eastwards for Port Mahon, there was one fear in the back of Byng's mind: that Fort St Philip had been obliged to surrender to Richelieu's army.

After a day of calms on May 18, the breeze came up at sunset and by midnight the topmen in each of the ships in Byng's squadron were scrambling out on the yards to reef and furl in the first warning gusts of a north-easterly gale. Apart from the weather, there was no rest for Byng: even though he now had a headwind for Minorca he could expect to reach the island in the morning. What awaited him he knew not: certainly the French squadron warned by the *Gracieuse*, would not be far away. But would he find British colours flying over Fort St Philip or the French standard?

He paced up and down his cabin dictating various orders to his secretary, George Lawrence, and making sure that the clerks made correct copies. He decided to send three frigates ahead under the command of Augustus Hervey, who was reliable, had plenty of initiative, and of all the frigate captains knew best the Admiral's way of doing things. The frigates were to make for the entrance to Port Mahon and Hervey was to use his 'best endeavours' to land a letter for General Blakeney, bringing or sending back the General's answer. He was also to range along the coast, 'observing any enemy batteries or posts that could interfere with communications between St Philip's and the Fleet'.[3]

The Admiral's letter to Blakeney was written in his usual despondent style. He was extremely concerned, he said, to find

---

* This certainly appears to be true as far as Keppel's squadron was concerned. It will be recalled that before leaving Portsmouth and while still very short of men, Byng had to man Keppel's ships so that they could seek an unimportant French coastal convoy. Keppel's biographer, the Hon Thomas Keppel, said that if Byng had been able to use those men to complete his own ships, or if he had been given Keppel's ships as well, he might have arrived in sufficient time and force to hold Minorca. Keppel was in fact one of Anson's favourites.[2]

that the French had landed and that Fort St Philip was besieged, 'as I flattered myself, had I fortunately been more timely in the Mediterranean, that I should have been able to prevent the enemy getting a foothold on the island'. He asked for Blakeney's instructions concerning the thirty or so officers and some recruits on board the ships of the squadron who were due to rejoin their regiments on the island. Byng then mentioned that he had Fusiliers on board, but that they had replaced his Marines and were intended to serve in the ships unless it was thought necessary—in consultation with Blakeney—to land them to help defend St Philip's. However, warned Byng, if this was done it would 'disable the squadron from acting against the enemy, which I am informed is cruising off the island'.[4]

The letter and the orders to Hervey were sent off to the *Phoenix*, and then at 4 a.m., while it was still dark, Byng made the pre-arranged signal by lamp for Hervey to go ahead with the frigates, taking the *Experiment* with him as well, as she was to stay between the *Phoenix* and the *Ramillies* to repeat signals. The four ships hardened in sheets and braces and in a welter of spray began the long flog to windward round the Lair of Mahon, the island off the south-eastern tip of Minorca which Richelieu had originally considered as a possible landing place for his invasion force.

It took four hours for the ships to work their way up to 'within pistol shot' of the Lair, but as they rounded it the wind, which up to then had been blowing a gale, suddenly dropped away and the *Phoenix*, which was the closest inshore, began to drift towards the cliffs with her sails flapping. Hervey had to order the boats to be lowered and within a few minutes, like ants pulling at a dead beetle, their crews were straining at the oars to tow the frigate clear.

Fortunately for them a breeze soon sprang up and the frigates got under way once more. As the frigates moved along the coast, with the squadron just in sight astern, Hervey watched through his telescope for signs of French batteries, but he saw none. Finally Fort St Philip came in sight and much to his relief Hervey could see quite clearly that 'The English colours were still flying on the castle of St Philip's, which the enemy were firing on from all parts, and the French colours on Cape Mola [on the other side of the harbour entrance from the Fort] and many other parts of the island'.[5]

Hervey ordered a signal to the Fort to be hoisted. The flags were run up and he waited for a reply from the besieged soldiers, but there was none; nor could he see any boat putting off from the shore. He therefore ordered a white flag to be hoisted and the foretopgallant sail to be hoisted and clewed up. This was the signal Byng had ordered him to make 'If I perceive any fire at St Philip's, or thereabouts, to suspect its being attacked'. A gun was then fired to draw the *Experiment*'s attention, and she was soon repeating it back to the *Ramillies*.

Byng's squadron had lost the wind at the same time as the frigates, and for some time the boats had to be used to tow the ships. By 10 a.m. however, they were within six miles of the Fort. 'Saw ye Union flagg flying on the Castle at St Philip's,' it was noted in the *Ramillies*'s log. 'At the same time saw a French flagg flying supposed to be on Marlborough Fort cannonading each other.'[6]

In Fort St Philip it had been a noisy morning. One 13-inch French shell spluttered down in Castle Square and exploded on a house where some of the sailors left behind by Edgcumbe were billeted; another blew up two barrels of gunpowder. Then, according to one diarist,[7] 'All our garrison was in great spirits by ye seeing our English fleet come from the west . . . but very little service they did us. It's true they fired three guns to the leeward as friends, but they never after gave us any proof of their friendship, which made us believe it was some of the French policy to alarm us, knowing that our strength in the garrison was small.'

However, only one man in the whole garrison showed any signs of activity at the approach of Byng's squadron, and he was Robert Boyd, the storekeeper*, who was acting as ADC to Lieut-Colonel Jefferies. As soon as he saw the British ships he went to Jefferies and volunteered to be rowed out with a message. It was then before 10 a.m., and Jefferies, displaying an extraordinary lethargy, replied that he would raise the matter at the afternoon's council of war. Boyd was finally called before the council and told to get ready to take a letter out to Admiral Byng which would 'make him a compliment upon his arrival before Minorca', and to tell him that Boyd could describe the situation in the Fort. 'I was ready to go in a very short time; but before the boat could be got ready, it was

---

* Later Lieut-General Sir R. Boyd, KCB, Colonel of the 39th Foot and Lieut-Governor of Gibraltar.

within an hour of sunset,' Boyd said later. He was rowed out from St Stephen's Cove, just to the south of the harbour entrance, and near a hill 'commonly called Turk's Mount.' The French saw him, and a number of soldiers ran for their muskets and began a straggling fire. Finding the boat was soon out of range of muskets they opened fire with cannon.

'The Fleet was at that time standing on,' said Boyd, 'and I followed till it was quite dark. After night closed about two hours —not being able to see any of their lights, and there being two small [French] tartans which stood out from Cape Mola with the intention, it seemed to me, to intercept my boat—I ordered the men to lay upon their oars, in which situation I remained till after it was quite dark, and then rowed gently into St Philip's . . .'[8]

It is a sad reflection on the leadership in Fort St Philip that although Boyd made his suggestion before 10 a.m. he could not get away until an hour before sunset—but it is equally inexplicable why Blakeney did not think of it himself. The garrison were naturally puzzled at the squadron's disappearance, but there was a simple explanation: at 11 a.m. the *Phoenix* suddenly hoisted an urgent signal, firing guns to draw Byng's attention to it—the guns that the diarist thought were fired 'as friends'.

While Byng had been making his way up to Minorca, the French squadron under the Marquis de la Galissonnière, having successfully escorted the French invasion force from Toulon, was busy covering the island and the supply routes from Toulon and Marseilles against possible attacks by the British. The French Admiral was a confident commander—confident both in his own judgment and in the ability of his captains.

He had, a few days before Byng arrived off Fort St Philip, sent a stinging reply to a carping letter from the French Government which had criticized him for letting Edgcumbe's little squadron escape from Port Mahon. Galissonnière pointed out that it had taken a week to put Richelieu's troops and supplies on shore from the transport ships, and the squadron had to guard them the whole time. This was a vital task for the squadron—and anyway, the Government had also given him orders to that effect. In addition, he added, he was forbidden to split up his squadron; and they had told him that the object he was 'perpetually to keep in mind' was the safety of his ships. Nor was he to pursue British ships if it involved any risk to the squadron or the Army on shore.

Thanks to the *Gracieuse*, the French Admiral already had very recent news of the whereabouts of Byng's squadron. After disappearing over the horizon as the British arrived at Palma, she had fled in search of Galissonnière, finding him and the rest of the French squadron at 6 a.m. on May 19—just at the moment that Hervey and his three frigates approached the Lair of Mahon on their way to Fort St Philip. Flying the signal that she had seen an enemy fleet of seventeen ships, the *Gracieuse* ran close to the *Foudroyant*, and her captain, de Marquisan, had himself rowed over to report personally to Galissonnière[9] at 8 a.m.—the same time that Hervey had to order the *Phoenix*'s boats to take the frigate in tow to get clear of the land.

As soon as he heard that Byng had reached Palma, Galissonnière naturally guessed that the British Admiral's next move would be to get in touch with the besieged fort. He therefore ordered the French squadron to set a course for Port Mahon, which was to the north-west of him.

Galissonnière's squadron was in comparatively fine fettle: his ships were just out of the dockyard, shiny with fresh paint and with new rigging. Their hulls were free of weed and barnacles—and that alone meant they would be a knot or two faster than the British ships, especially in light winds. His officers were seasoned seamen, even if they lacked battle experience. It was perhaps appropriate for a fleet sailing from Toulon that a high percentage of them came from Provence*. Most of the seamen, however, were less well trained, but they had plenty of soldiers on board to help handle the guns.

Admiral Byng, knowing the names of Galissonnières' ships, realized the French had another big advantage: their ships carried far heavier guns than the British. Galissonnière's own *Foudroyant*, for instance carried 80 guns. Those on her lower-deck each threw a solid shot weighing 52 lbs, while Byng's flagship, the 90-gun *Ramillies*, carried only 32-pounders on the lower-deck. The *Foudroyant*'s upper-deck guns were 24-pounders compared with the *Ramillies*'s 9-pounders. The rest of Galissonnière's ships had the same advantage: four French battleships had 42-pounders on

---

* The author has been able to trace the birthplaces of just over half of the French officers. Forty-two of them came from Provence, three from Languedoc and two from Paris.[10]

their lower-decks and seven had 36-pounders, but only four British (including the *Ramillies*) had as much as 32-pounders and eight had only 24-pounders. The upper-deck guns showed the same differences—all the French ships had 24-pounders, while three British had 18-pounders, eight had 12-pounders and one had 9-pounders.

Thus the 796 guns in the twelve French battleships threw a much heavier broadside than the 826 of the British. It will be seen that the lightest armament in all the French ships, 24-pounders, equalled the heaviest armament of all but four of the British ships.

Compared with the French ships, not one of which had been at sea for much more than a month, Byng had ships like the leaky *Intrepid* and *Captain*, and the *Princess Louisa*, whose masts were condemned. Whatever Byng's merits as an admiral, the dice were well and truly loaded in Galissonnière's favour.

Since we have seen the British captains, it is interesting to take a brief look at their French opposite numbers. The *Foudroyant*, Galissonnière's flagship, was commanded by Froger de L'Eguille, the son of an old Navy lieutenant, who was born at Marennes. His humble background was a distinct contrast to that of his second-in-command, de Drée de la Serrée, who was a member of the house of Bourgogne—which had provided the King's mother. The ship's third lieutenant, Castellane St Jeurs, a Provençal, was the fourteenth to bear that name in the Navy and had first gone to sea as a cadet in 1733; the fifth lieutenant, Chevalier de Forbin d'Oppède, a fellow Provençal, could boast that nine of his forebears had served France at sea.

Galissonnière's second-in-command, Vice-Admiral the Chevalier de Glandevez, flying his flag in the *Redoutable*, was yet another Provençal, the sixth of his family to serve in the Navy. He outdid Byng (whose nephew John was on board the *Ramillies*) by having three nephews serving in the squadron. One of them, the Count de Broves was the *Redoutable*'s first lieutenant, while another, de Grasse Briançon was her fourth. (The third nephew served in the *Achille*, which did not rejoin the squadron until after the battle.)

The third-in-command of the squadron was Commodore de la Clue Sabran, yet another Provençal and former protégé of the Count de Toulouse, son of Louis XIV and Mme de Montespan. Two years later de la Clue was to command a squadron roundly beaten by Boscawen in Lagos Bay. For the forthcoming battle he commanded the *Couronne*, with Provençals as his second-in-command, and second and third lieutenants.

Galissonnière's individual captains were, like Byng's, a good cross-section of the Navy: men from humble homes rubbed shoulders with aristocrats. Commanding the 74-gun *Guerrier*, for instance, was Captain Villars de la Brosse, from Rochefort, nephew of an old lieutenant killed serving in the Navy; the *Lion* was commanded by the Marquis de la Ferté Saint-Aignan, the thirty-four-year-old son of the Duke de Saint-Aignan. His second lieutenant was the son of the French consul at Leghorn.

A newly-promoted young lieutenant in the *Orphée* (all six officers were Provencals) was the Chevalier Pierre-Andre de Suffren de Saint-Tropez, twenty-six years old and born at St Cannat, in Provence. He had gone to sea as a cadet at the age of twelve and had been promoted lieutenant on May 15, five days before the battle. Within thirty years Suffren was to be renowned as France's greatest sea-fighter.

Commanding the *Triton* was Captain Antoine Mercier, the Paris-born son of the King's wet-nurse. The *Hippopotame*'s captain, Rochemore la Devèze, born in Languedoc, was the son of one former Navy lieutenant and nephew of another; his third lieutenant, the Count de Barjeton Verelause, was descended from an English family who settled in the duchy d'Uzes, in Languedoc, under Louis XII.[11]

The *Phoenix* had just received the *Ramillies*'s acknowledgement of her signal that the British flag was still flying over Fort St Philip, when an excited lookout at the masthead shouted that away to the south-east he had just spotted the sails of a large number of ships. While a midshipman hastily scrambled up the rigging with a telescope the lookout counted them: there were seventeen. Hervey was in no doubt about who they were and at once ordered the signal for an enemy fleet in sight to be hoisted and three guns fired to draw attention to it.[12]

The signal was quickly repeated back to the *Ramillies* by the *Experiment* and Byng acted without a moment's hesitation: with the French squadron approaching, the *Phoenix* and the other frigates could do no good hanging about off Port Mahon, so he recalled them. It was a pity the French had arrived at this moment, before he could get in touch with Blakeney; but now they were in

sight his duty seemed clear enough—he would attack them as soon
as possible. His own ships were straggling along in no particular
formation and the wind was very light—though fortunately from
the north-west, so that he had the weather gage, which would
allow him to manoeuvre freely when he went down towards the
French. The enemy, however, being to leeward, would be restricted
because they would have to tack to get up to him. As soon as his
frigates rejoined the squadron, Byng steered his ships towards the
enemy by ordering the signal to chase to be hoisted.[13]

It was now noon, but the wind was light and the sails of his
ships frequently flapped lazily as the breeze became fitful.

The French ships had first appeared as a scattering of tiny
patches of canvas on the horizon, their hulls and lower sails hidden
below the curvature of the earth; and although by 2 p.m. they
were still several miles away, Byng decided to get his ships into
formation, ordering them to form line of battle. The wind soon
became even lighter, and several of the battleships had to lower
their boats and be towed into position. This took time and even
before the line of battle was properly formed it was becoming
obvious to Byng that unless a sudden stiff breeze sprang up, there
was no chance of the two squadrons getting to grips before sunset.

He signalled Rear-Admiral West to come on board the *Ramillies*—he wanted to have a talk with him—but the *Buckingham* was
such a long distance astern that some time elapsed before West's
boat arrived alongside.[14] Then, because several of the battleships were still very short of men, Byng ordered the frigates to
transfer some of their crews: since only the battleships would go
into action while the frigates stayed clear of the battle repeating
signals, it was less important that the smaller ships should have a
full complement.

Augustus Hervey had himself rowed over to the *Ramillies* so
that he could offer the services of the *Phoenix* to the Admiral as a
fireship 'as my ship was old and that he had ne'er a one, and I
had material on board with which I could make her one.' Byng
agreed as the *Phoenix* was 'a ship long before reported home unfit
for service'. (The one sure way of destroying an enemy battleship
was to set her on fire and, in turn, the one sure way of doing this
was to ram her with a small ship which was laden with combustibles
and which had grapnels hanging from the yards to catch in the
other ship's rigging. Just before the collision the combustibles

would be set alight, so that the ship became a floating firebrand, Drake had used successfully fireships against the Spanish Armada; the idea lingered on. However, Byng did not get a chance of making use of Hervey's offer.)

Both Byng and Glaissonnière waited anxiously, as the sun dipped down towards the horizon, for the wind to freshen; and at about seven in the evening a fine breeze did spring up—but it was from the south-east, putting Byng to leeward and giving the French the weather gage. The two opposing squadrons were about six miles apart and as darkness was falling it was now so late that neither admiral dare risk the confusion of a night battle. As if each had read the other's thoughts, both squadrons tacked at the same time—the French to keep the weather gage, and the British to try to gain it during the hours of darkness. Byng ordered the signal for the line to be hauled down, and the ships of both sides settled down for the last chance of any rest before the apparently inevitable battle next day.

11

INTO BATTLE

FOR ADMIRAL JOHN BYNG the battle he was expecting to fight as soon as daylight came would be the peak of his career: the climax for which thirty-eight years of naval service had prepared him. If he was fortunate—and skilful—he could achieve as great a victory as his father had gained at Cape Passaro. More wealth, a peerage, solid fame . . . these could be his, if all went well in the next few hours. The prospect of battle did not seem to worry him unduly, since he had done all he could to prepare his squadron. What he did not know—nor could it have affected him at this stage—was that even while he waited for the dawn Rear-Admiral Broderick, in Portsmouth, was issuing his last orders before sailing at daybreak for the Mediterranean with the reinforcement of five battleships.

Finally dawn came off Minorca, transmuting the blackness of night into a grey monochrome, and as the eastern sky turned pink the anxious eyes of the officers and lookouts of Byng's squadron searched the ever-widening circle of faint light for some sign of the enemy. They counted up their own ships and found them all present, but there was no sign of Galissonnière's squadron—in fact the only other ships in sight were two tartans—small and fast Mediterranean craft, single-masted and lateen rigged. They were astern over to the north-east, towards Minorca. Both were heading for the British squadron and were flying what at first seemed to be black flags, but as it got lighter they were seen to be blue.

They were in fact the two vessels which Boyd had seen from his boat as he rowed out towards Byng's squadron, and each one carried a hundred French soldiers intended to reinforce Galissonnière's ships: the French Admiral had sent Richelieu an urgent plea for extra men, and 700 had been sent off in seven tartans. Byng suspected that the two craft had mistaken his squadron for the French—as indeed they had—and thought they might yield some useful information. He therefore sent three of his ships to capture them, the *Defiance*, *Captain* and *Princess Louisa*.

The squadron was steering to the south-east, away from the tartans, so the three ships soon dropped astern. However, Byng did not want them to become too separated, so at 6.15 a.m. he tacked the squadron back towards them. Fifteen minutes later the *Princess Louisa* signalled that she had sighted ten ships to the north-west. Byng thought they were probably those of Galissonnière's squadron, and that the French Admiral must have tacked north-westward during the night.[1]

All available telescopes were trained in that direction when the *Trident* made a signal and fired guns to draw attention to it: she could see a fleet to the south-east—in the opposite direction to that reported by the *Princess Louisa**. Within a few minutes the lookouts at the *Ramillies*'s mastheads had spotted the ships reported by the *Trident* and reckoned them to be about twelve miles away. A little later they shouted down that it was definitely the French squadron, and Byng at once recalled the *Princess Louisa*, *Defiance* and *Captain*.

The *Defiance* had by then captured one of the tartans and taken off the French soldiers. As soon as she saw Byng's signal of recall she sank her prize and with the *Captain* began the slow sail back to the squadron. The *Princess Louisa*, however, did not see Byng's signal and continued chasing the other tartan. With three of his ships away to leeward, Byng was short of a quarter of his line of battle and obviously could not sail down towards the enemy in such a weak state. To his annoyance it was nine o'clock before the *Princess Louisa* saw the recall signal and altered course back towards the squadron.[2] By 10 a.m. Byng decided she was near enough for his ships to turn towards the enemy. The French were to the south-east and the wind was south-west, with a tendency to veer in the stronger puffs.

After fifteen minutes Byng ordered his ship to form the line-of-battle, each ship to be 400 yards from its next-ahead, and then at 10.30 a.m. 'squared my maintopsail, that the ships stationed ahead of me might the sooner get into their stations'.[3] Just after 11 a.m. he ordered the distance between each ship to be reduced to half

---

* Reports vary on the time of the *Trident*'s sighting. The *Ramillies*'s master's log says 7 a.m., the *Lancaster*'s captain's log 6.45, the *Trident*'s 6.30, and Byng at his trial said 'near about seven.'

a cable—one hundred yards. The *Ramillies* soon 'crowded sail to gain the wind of the enemy'.

Since the French had twelve ships in their line and Byng had thirteen, he ordered the weakest, the 48-gun *Deptford*, to quit the line to even up the numbers. Thus when the two lines of ships were parallel, each ship would have her own opponent—in theory, anyway.

Earlier each captain had given the order to clear his ship for action. Duplicate sheets and braces, controlling the set of the sails, were rove, and coils of spare rope were put in places where they could be snatched up in an emergency; the rope slings supporting the great yards on which the sails were set were reinforced with chains, so that an unlucky shot would not bring them crashing down.

The gunner, with his mates, and the quarter-gunner checked over the guns and made sure there were plenty of cartridges and shot ready; the carpenter and his crew collected a supply of shot-plugs—cone-shaped pieces of wood, of various sizes, covered with oakum and smeared with tallow, which would be rammed into any shot-hole below or on the waterline—and leather hides, for nailing over the big holes. The surgeon and his mates went down to the cockpit, lit battle lanterns (candles in horn containers) and cleared it of everything but the table, which would be used for operations, and a tub, which would act as a receptacle for amputated 'wings and limbs'.

Meanwhile teams of seamen working under the lieutenants were scurrying about the ship doing a variety of other jobs: bulkheads, which formed the cabins of the captain and officers were either swung up on hinges and secured to the beams overhead or taken down and stowed below the waterline, where they could not be shattered into dangerous splinters. Mess-tables and forms, with chairs and tables belonging to the officers—in fact all loose equipment not wanted when the ship was in action—were carried below. Casks of water were placed on the gun decks so that in the heat of the battle men could refresh themselves; sand was scattered over the decks, which had already been sluiced down with water as a precaution against any spilt powder igniting. The galley fire was put out, more shot was brought up from below, and axes were placed ready so they could be snatched up hurriedly to cut away damaged rigging or a fallen mast and yards.

Soon each ship was prepared for action, and the captains gave
the order to 'Beat to quarters'. The rhythmic thudding of drums
sent the men running to their stations for battle. The guns were
cast loose from their lashings; cutlasses, pistols and tomahawks
were issued, and the Fusiliers serving as Marines were drawn up
on deck ready to act as sharpshooters. Now they all had the long
wait before action, a time when men were alone with their thoughts.
Death took a pace or two nearer, and they joked with each other
in affected unconcern.

The French squadron could now be seen quite clearly, almost
hull up on the horizon and in line-of-battle, steering to the north-
west. With the British on the starboard tack and the French on
the larboard, the opposing squadrons were steering converging
courses, as if travelling down each arm of an invisible V inscribed
on the surface of the sea. The situation was similar to two lines of
coaches racing each other along separate roads which met at a
fork: whichever reached the fork first gained the best position for
the next part of the race. Each squadron was sailing as close to
the wind as possible and everything depended on the weatherliness
of the ships, because whichever squadron managed to cross ahead
of the other would be to windward and thus have the advantageous weather gage.

Byng and Galissonnière had, for the next critical round in the
preliminaries before the battle, to depend on the sail-trimming
skill of the masters of their ships, and the men steering them with
a happy blend of instinct and craft. At this stage in the struggle to
gain the weather gage, the guile of admirals mattered not at all:
they were in the hands of men who probably could not write their
own names, but whose sharp eyes, screwed up against the glare of
the Mediterranean sun, watched the luffs of the sails like a soaring
eagle's gaze in the seconds before it swooped on its prey: at the
slightest sign of the luffs lifting the helmsman would ease the
wheel a few spokes so that the ship would pay off, allowing the wind
once again to fill the arched sails along their whole length.

Now Byng watched the leading ships in the French line on his
larboard bow. Was their bearing changing? If the angle stayed the
same, then the two squadrons were keeping the same relative
positions and the leading French ship would meet the leading
British ship at the 'fork'. If the enemy's bearing drew ahead, then
they were gaining and would pass across Byng's bow to secure the

weather gage; but if the bearing drew aft then the British would
pass ahead to gain the coveted windward position.

Byng could see that in fact the bearing was hardly changing:
obviously it was going to be a close-run race. Only one thing could
definitely decide it at this stage—a change in the direction of the
wind: if it veered more to the west, the French ships would have
to pay off, to keep their sails filled, giving the advantage to Byng;
but if it backed to the southward the British ships would have to
bear away, allowing the French to draw ahead and pass to windward.

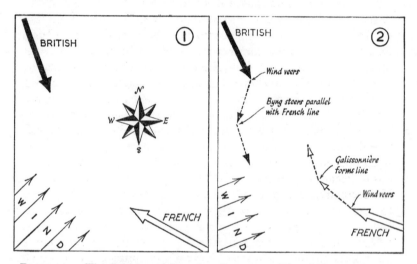

DIAGRAM 1: The British and French
squadrons sight each other—then comes
the race for the weather gage. (This and
subsequent diagrams are not to scale.)

DIAGRAM 2: The wind veers: Byng can
steer more to starboard, but the French
have to bear away. Byng then comes on
to a course parallel with the French.

And at half-past twelve the wind did change: the helmsmen of
Byng's ships found they could steer a little more to starboard—
bringing them nearer to winning the weather gage—without the
luffs of the sails quivering in protest at being starved of wind. A few
moments later there was a clear indication that the shift of wind
was also upsetting the French ships: the gaps between their masts
narrowed and their sails seemed to broaden as the helmsmen had
to pay off to leeward to keep them filled. To Galissonnière's
dismay they had to alter course more than a point, more than

eleven and a quarter degrees. He waited to see if this was just a wayward puff, but the breeze remained steady and he knew he had finally lost the race for the weather gage.[4] The *Foudroyant* hoisted several flag signals and one French ship after another turned away, like horses shying at a fence, as Galissonnière re-formed his line-of-battle to leeward. At 12.45 p.m. Byng steered his squadron a few degrees to larboard so that once more the British ships were steering almost a parallel but opposite course to the French.*

On board the *Ramillies* Admiral Byng, resplendent in uniform, made a glittering and impressive figure on the quarter-deck, giving his orders coolly and distinctly. With him were Captain Arthur Gardiner—whose responsibility was the actual handling of the *Ramillies* in obedience to the Admiral's orders—Lord Robert Bertie, whose Fusiliers were now at their quarters ready for the battle, various Army officers, the Admiral's secretary, George Lawrence, and several midshipmen acting as messengers.

Byng was holding a slim book in his hand as he watched the long line of Galissonnière's ships. By now the van, headed by the *Orphée*, had already passed the *Ramillies*, and the *Orphée* herself was almost level with the last ship in the British line, the *Defiance*. Byng opened his book—it was a copy of the Fighting Instructions —and began to read Article XVII[6] as if to refresh his memory. His secretary, George Lawrence, 'took the liberty of observing to the Admiral that agreeable to the Article the fleet should then tack.'

The Article said that when two opposing fleets were in this position, opposite each other but sailing different courses, the British squadron should tack, starting with the rear ship, so that it came on to the same tack as the enemy—i.e. had the wind on the same side. Then, under a subsequent article of the Fighting Instructions, each ship would steer down for its exact opposite number in the enemy line. But since by this time the enemy was usually waiting for the attack with little or no way on, it meant that the British ships had to approach the French ships at right angles, bows on, so that each French ship would fire her whole broadside at her opponent without the British ship being able to bring a gun to bear.

Byng was only too well aware of this dangerous disadvantage,

* It has been suggested that Galissonnière had a copy of the English 'signal book'. See note 5 on page 320.

but although usually a slave to rules and regulations, he had an idea which would get over the danger. He told Lawrence that he would let the leading ships of his squadron pass beyond the rear of the French line before tacking. This meant in fact that each British ship would sail past its particular opponent, so that when

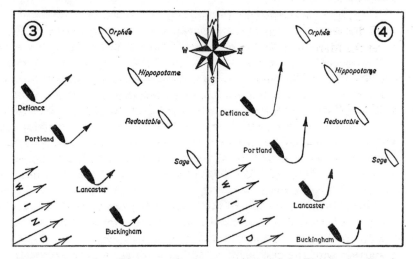

DIAGRAMS 3 and 4: Diagrammatic representation of (left, Fig 3) what Byng's squadron should have done under the Fighting Instructions and (right, Fig 4) what Byng proposed doing—a method called lasking. In these and the following diagrams the ships are shown as having worn, although they tacked. This has been done for the sake of clarity, and only the leading ships are drawn.

Byng gave the order to tack, each British captain would, on turning his ship to come on to the same tack as the French, then find his own opponent ahead and to starboard, so that to get along-side her he would have to approach diagonally, instead of at right angles, and could bring at least some of his guns to bear. The idea was good* and one that was called lasking—sailing down with the wind on the quarter.

* Though not original. As Corbett says, 'It is quite possible Byng received it as a tradition from his father' (*England in the Seven Years War*, I. 119). But not every naval officer accepted the idea of lasking: one, claiming forty years service, said in an anti-Byng pamphlet that 'It is contrary to the doctrine as well as the practise of every prudent, good or great officer I ever knew or heard of'. However, the right-angled approach can hardly be called prudent. Both methods were used at Trafalgar, but the difference was that all the captains knew what Nelson proposed doing. Hoste mentioned it in his book written in 1697.

There was, however, a snag in Byng's plan and it was to prove a considerable one: none of his captains knew what he proposed doing; nor was signalling sufficiently advanced for him to explain. He could only make certain signals and hope his captains would guess the rest and follow exactly the Fighting Instructions. If they did so, all would go well.

At 1.30 p.m. the leading British ship had passed the last ship in the French line (which was more extended than the British), and yet the Marquis de la Galissonnière, from the quarter-deck of the *Foudroyant*, could see no sign of the British line preparing to tack. This puzzled him at first; then he mistakenly decided that Byng was going to throw his whole squadron against the rear ships of the French line, overwhelming them by sheer weight of numbers before the leading French ships could turn back and go to their rescue. Galissonnière saw that the best way of thwarting this move would be to stop his ships at once, so that Byng's ships would overshoot, and he did this by ordering the squadron to throw their sails aback.

Just before Galissonnière gave this order, however, Byng had judged that his line of ships was in just the right position in relation to the French line, so that if they tacked one after the other, starting with the rear ship in his line (which was the *Defiance*) each would, after having completed the turn, then be in a perfect position to run diagonally down to tackle her opposite number. He made the signal to tack, but a few moments later he saw the French ships stop with their sails aback and, realizing his ships would now overshoot if they waited to tack one at a time, he ordered them to tack altogether. So far his plan had worked: Galissonnière had made a counter-move, and Byng had in turn beaten it.

Now, Byng expected, every one of his ships would lead down for her opponent—the *Defiance*, for example, which led the British line, would steer for the *Orphée*, which was leading the French, and so on down the line. But he was horrified to find that, when the *Defiance* tacked, instead of steering directly for the *Orphee*, she came round to starboard on to a course parallel with the French line but more than a mile away from it, and, what was worse, the *Portland*, which was the next ship, was following her—and so were the *Lancaster*, and the *Buckingham* (which was Rear-Admiral West's ship). Soon the whole squadron was following along astern of the *Defiance*, one behind the other, as if she was a stubborn Pied Piper in the pay of the French, instead of each ship heading for her opponent, as Byng had intended.

The Admiral, naturally enough, was extremely angry: the *Defiance* had spoiled an attack which up to then had been going very smoothly, and her captain, Andrews, could lead them all into a very dangerous situation. Byng commented to Lord Robert Bertie that Captain Andrews did not know the meaning of Article XIX*; to Captain Gardiner he said that he wondered why Andrews did not lead down. 'I cannot think what Captain Andrews is about.'[7]

However, this was not the time to discuss Andrews's shortcomings: something had to be done quickly. Byng told George Lawrence to look in the General Signals and 'see if there is any signal to direct her [the *Defiance*] down to the enemy'. There was none. Then Byng remembered the Fifth Article of the Additional Fighting Instructions which said that when sailing in line ahead, if the Admiral wanted the leading ship to change course to starboard, he would hoist a particular flag, firing one gun for every point (eleven and a quarter degrees) to be altered.

Byng ordered the flag to be hoisted and one gun fired, to indicate one point. 'I can't take it upon myself to direct the precise number of points he should bear away,' Byng said, 'as it is impossible for me to judge how the enemy's ships bear from the *Defiance*.'

Andrews saw the signal, heard one gun—and obediently altered the *Defiance*'s course one point to starboard. Byng soon saw that this was not nearly enough, and making little attempt to hide his anger, he ordered the signal to be repeated. Once again Andrews obeyed it punctiliously, turning a further point to starboard, and once again the rest of the ships astern followed in his wake. But the *Defiance* was still not heading for the enemy. It was obvious that the Fifth Article was never going to get the squadron into action; but Byng racked his brains for a method of preventing Andrews from leading the squadron into the distance without getting into action. There was only one way—and that was for him to hoist the red flag which was the signal to engage the enemy.

---

* Article XIX said, in effect, that Andrews should have steered directly for his opponent, after tacking. See note 7, page 320 for wording.

Byng ordered this to be done, and obediently every ship in the British squadron turned to starboard towards their opposite number in the enemy line.[8]

But the *Defiance*'s two starboard turns had made two kinks in the British line, and this combined with the original differences in the British and French courses meant the leading British ships were now much closer to the French than those in the rear, and would thus get into action sooner. The *Defiance*, at the head of the line, was a little under a mile from the *Orphée* as she finally turned

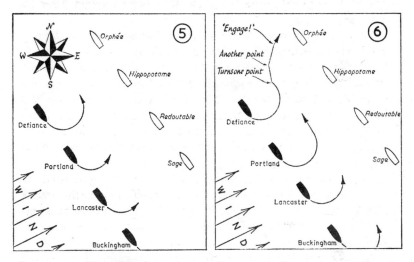

DIAGRAM 5: What Captain Andrews (*Defiance*) actually did: instead of heading for the *Orphée* after tacking, he steered a course parallel to the enemy.

DIAGRAM 6: Byng tries to bring the squadron into action by ordering the *Defiance* to turn one point to starboard, and then another. Finally he has to hoist the signal to engage the enemy.

in response to the red flag; the *Ramillies*, tenth in the line, was between two and three miles from her proper opponent in the French line, which was the Marquis de Saint-Aignan's *Lion*: while the *Kingston*, the last ship in the British line, was more than three miles from the *Triton*, which brought up the French rear.

Unfortunately not all the British ships were steering the same course: the *Intrepid*, in particular, had turned directly for the enemy line, while her next-astern, the *Revenge*, had taken a more slanting course, as did the *Princess Louisa* and the *Trident*. The next ship was the *Ramillies*, which went down directly, with the

result that Byng found his flagship forging ahead of the nearest
ships, the *Trident* to larboard and the *Culloden*—which had also
taken a slanting course—to starboard.

This did not please the Admiral: in his mind was the sanctity
of the line of battle, which must not be broken: his ships must go
into action evenly, like soldiers marching side by side in a line
abreast across the parade ground. He was not obsessed with sym-
metry or aesthetics: instead his mind went back to the hot and
stuffy cabin of a man-of-war moored in the Thames a few years
earlier, when a court martial, of which he was a member, had
condemned Admiral Mathews for breaking the line. Byng therefore told Gardiner to reduce sail for a few moments to let the
other ships catch up. Gardiner, however, was reluctant. 'I took
the liberty myself to offer my opinion', he said later, and his
opinion was that the *Ramillies* should set more sail as an example
to the *Louisa* and *Trident*, 'by which means we should be the
sooner down to the enemy, and in all probability receive less
damage in going down'.

Byng did not agree. 'You see, Captain Gardiner, that the signal
for the line is out,' he said, pointing to the flag flapping at the
mizzen peak, 'and that I am ahead of the *Louisa* and Durell
[commanding the *Trident*]. You would not have me, as Admiral of
the Fleet, run down as if I was going down to engage a single ship?
It was Mr Mathews's misfortune to be prejudiced by not carrying
down his force together, which I shall endeavour to avoid.'[9]

Gardiner replied that he would be answerable for Durell's
behaviour, but Byng took no notice—his orderly mind was made
up; indeed, it was made up for him by the events off Toulon a
dozen years earlier, and the repercussions in Parliament.

He had told Gardiner that the guns of the *Ramillies* were to be
loaded with round and grapeshot, except for the 32-pounders on
the lower-deck, which were the biggest in the ship: they were to
be double-shotted. He was sure, he added, that the French would
never stand as close an engagement as the British seamen. He
seemed quite unconcerned as the excitement round him increased.
Lining the bulwarks on the starboard side were the scarlet-coated
Fusiliers, commanded by Captain Edgar, and under the watchful
eye of their Colonel, Lord Robert Bertie, they had been given
more than twenty separate orders which were necessary for them
to load their muskets. The detachment's two drummers had left

their two unwieldy instruments below and were now handling unaccustomed muskets. Captain Edgar had, with his two lieutenants, checked that the shot were well rammed down and that the flints were good. Inevitably, in the excitement of battle, some men would eventually fire with the ramrods still left in the barrels of their muskets; but at least the first shots would be discharged in a soldierly fashion.

Meanwhile the seamen, reinforced here and there by soldiers, had obeyed the nineteen different orders required to load the big guns for the first time, starting with the injunction to 'Take heed!', and now waited for the twentieth, 'Take your match and blow on it' and then the twenty-first, 'Fire!' In the excitement of approaching battle the men forgot their misery. Those snatched up by press gangs in Portsmouth and surrounding villages, or shipped over like cattle from Ireland in the last days before the squadron sailed, were jollied along by men who had served in the Royal Navy for years, ill-fed, rarely paid,* and living in conditions little removed from those of a jail but infinitely more perilous.

Now they could only wait at their quarters, and the master-at-arms, Christopher Woodward, walked round the decks keeping a watchful eye on them, making sure that no one had left his post or was drunk—there was always a chance that a man had hoarded his tots of spirit and had now used it as a substitute for courage. Alexander Borthwick, the ship's armourer, waited until battle damage brought calls for him to exercise his skill, and behind each gun stood the individual captain, ready to take aim, while the second captain stood to one side holding the linstock, a Y-shaped staff some three feet long, and round which was wound the slow match (in effect a slow-burning fuse) with the lighted end, which was used to fire the gun, fitting into the fork.

Soon after Admiral Byng had hoisted the signal to engage and the British ships obediently turned towards the enemy, he saw spurts of flame rippling along the sides of the French ships and dissolving into clouds of smoke as they opened fire, trying the range. At 2.45 p.m., some twenty-five minutes after the signal to engage, the *Defiance* was within 300 yards of the *Orphée* and Captain Andrews turned his ship on to a parallel course, opening fire as

* The crew of the *Ramillies* were not paid their wages up to December 31, 1755, until April 19, 1757.

soon as his guns would bear. He was at a considerable disadvantage because the French ship had 36-pounders against the *Defiance*'s 24-pounders and the British ship was soon badly damaged. Within a few minutes a dozen men, including Captain Andrews,* had been killed and forty-five wounded. Masts and yards were slashed, and the heavy shot smashed holes in her hull at the waterline—'between wind and water'. But if she received damage she also inflicted it, and when some other British ships arrived, the *Orphée* dropped to leeward out of the line. By that time, however,

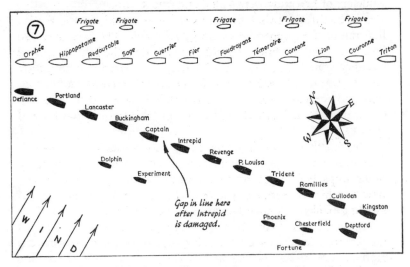

DIAGRAM 7: The battle begins—a diagrammatic representation, and not drawn to scale. Soon a gap will open up between the *Intrepid* and the *Captain*.

the *Defiance*'s masts, yards and sails were so damaged that she was slowing down out of control. The French gunners deliberately fired at the masts and rigging: it was the usual French practice, designed to immobilize their enemy and prevent pursuit.

The second ship in the British line was Captain Baird's *Portland*, whose 24-pounders were also no match for the 36-pounders of her opponent, the *Hippopotame*. Baird's log says that the leading enemy ships opened fire as he approached and 'though at a distance gawld [sic] our ship much'. He no sooner tried to turn on to a

---

* Andrews was the second captain of the ship to be killed on board in the twelve years of her life so far—the first had been Captain Thomas Grenville, a cousin of Rear-Admiral Temple West, who was killed in 1747.

parallel course to bring his guns to bear on the *Hippopotame* than she shot ahead and the *Portland* instead came level with the ship astern which was the powerful 74-gun *Redoutable*, flying the flag of Galissonnière's second-in-command, de Glandevez. The French ship's 42-pounders were soon pounding the British ship, but Baird was surprised to find that the *Redoutable* bore away, as if she had had enough of the *Portland*'s fire, and her place was taken by the *Sage*, which had 36-pounders. It was not long before the *Portland*'s sails and rigging received considerable damage, while six of her crew were killed and twenty wounded.

George Edgcumbe's *Lancaster* was the third ship in the British line and his first opponent was the *Redoutable*. The *Lancaster* had no sooner fired her first broadside into her than the French opened a withering fire but, when the *Buckingham* arrived a few minutes later to help the *Lancaster*, the *Redoutable* sheeted home her top-sails and forged ahead, as we have already seen, for a brief en-counter with the *Portland* before dropping away to leeward out of the line.[10]

The fourth British ship to get into action was Temple West's flagship, the *Buckingham*, which received broadsides from three other ships before getting into position to engage the *Sage*. By now the ships of both sides were almost completely hidden in the swirling banks of smoke from their own guns: it hung over the sea in ponderous clouds, reluctant to move or disperse in the light wind, menacing in its oily opacity yet seemingly alive with the rippling red flashes of the broadsides flickering through it like summer lightning.

Soon the *Sage* had had enough: she forged ahead to follow the *Redoutable*, opening fire on the *Portland* before going off to leeward. The *Buckingham* went on to join the *Lancaster*, helping her force de Glandevez's *Redoutable* to follow the *Sage* to leeward. The two British ships then went ahead to the aid of the badly-damaged *Defiance* and the *Portland*.[11]

But such was the sanctity of the rules for the line of battle that, with four of the leading French ships sent to leeward out of the French line, not one of the British ships dare break the line to pursue them. The French were making good use of their sanctuary which they could reach merely by dropping a few hundred yards to leeward.

The ship next to the *Buckingham* was Charles Catford's *Captain*.

Her log shows that she had fired only three or four broadsides at her opponent, the *Guerrier*, before the French ship also dropped out of the line. But the *Captain* had been badly damaged by the broadsides of other French ships as she approached the *Guerrier*: her bowsprit was smashed, the foremast shot through ten feet above the deck, and the other two masts had been hit several times. The carpenter was soon reporting 'the ship's sides and decks very much torn, and a great number of shot holes betwixt wind and water'. A lot of rigging—including the mainstay—had been cut and 'all sails which were bent very much damaged'.[12]

The *Intrepid* was the sixth ship in the British line, and she continued to experience the bad luck which had beset her from the time she left the Nore bound for Portsmouth. Captain Young had steered down directly, as we have already seen, to attack the sixth ship in the French line, which was the *Fier*. On the way, however, he ran into a withering fire from the *Fier*'s next astern, the 80-gun *Foudroyant*, and her 52-pounders soon helped the *Fier*'s 36-pounders to reduce the British ship to a wreck. Ten men were killed and another thirty-nine wounded; the jib-boom, bowsprit and mainmast were damaged and fifteen shot, many of them 52-pounders, cut into the hull at the waterline. But worst of all, a shot cut through the towering foretopmast and brought it and the yards crashing down over the side—repeating the work of the gale less than two months earlier. This sudden reduction of sail forward threw the ship's head up into the wind.

Whether the shot was fired by the gunners of the *Fier* or the *Foudroyant* we do not know; but it was, from the French point of view, the luckiest shot in the battle: from the moment the *Intrepid*'s mast started toppling, Byng's fate seemed to be sealed, for it was like the small pebble which, rolling down a mountain-side, ends up as a great avalanche.

The *Intrepid*, having come up into the wind, was now lying broadside on athwart the course of the rest of the British ships and, as they sailed along under easy canvas engaging their adversaries, they would have to pass either to windward or to leeward of her. For the moment, since the ships ahead of the *Intrepid* had gone on, and the first of those astern had not yet passed, there was now a gap opening out in the British line, separating the *Intrepid* and her next ahead, which was the *Captain*.

However, in most tragedies there is an element of farce, and this battle was to be no exception. The *Intrepid*'s seamen were busy swarming over the wreckage of the foretopmast, hacking away at the rigging to get it clear, and her gunners were still keeping up a smart fire on the enemy with those guns which could be brought to bear, when out of the smoke came a boat. The crew rowed it smartly alongside the battered *Intrepid* and an officer stepped on board, asking to speak to Captain Young. He introduced himself —he was from the *Revenge*, which was the ship next astern of the *Intrepid* in the line. Her captain, Frederick Cornwall, had sent him to ask if Captain Young would stop firing because Cornwall thought it 'for the King's service' that the *Revenge* should pass and go ahead to help the leading ships. In the meantime the *Revenge* was waiting hove-to in the smoke astern.[13]

Captain Cornwall had brought the *Revenge* down on to the enemy line to find that his 64-gun ship, with her 24-pounders, was to be pitted against the massive *Foudroyant*, whose 52-pounder guns had already given the *Intrepid* such a pounding. Cornwall explained later that he had turned a point or two to larboard 'to bring my ship properly against the French Admiral'—whose ship was his correct opponent—when he came up astern of the *Intrepid* just at the moment her foretopmast went over the side. Because he was afraid to get to leeward in case she drifted down on him, he brought-to on her weather quarter.

Cornwall then claimed that he went to the cabin window aft and looked out, and 'Great was my surprise' at seeing Byng and the other ships a considerable distance astern. He saw that the French ships were keeping up a heavy fire on the *Intrepid* so, he said, he took his ship down to the *Intrepid*'s lee quarter 'to give her all the assistance in my power', and some fifteen minutes later he saw the *Princess Louisa* emerging from the smoke astern so close 'that I apprehended her jib-boom was over my taffrail'. She soon disappeared in the smoke and Cornwall later caught a glimpse of the *Trident*, which was the ship astern of the *Princess Louisa*.

However, Cornwall still did not think he should pass the *Intrepid*. Although there was so much smoke that he had not seen the *Louisa* until she almost collided with him, and he said his only glimpse of the *Trident* had been her topsails, he claimed later, that the reason why he did not try to pass the *Intrepid* was that he thought that Admiral Byng must see his situation and 'I expected every moment that he would have made a signal for the *Intrepid* to have quitted the line, as she was the cause that I could not go on . . .' He then read the appropriate section of the Fighting Instructions, ignored them, and finally sent an officer in a boat, as we have already seen, to ask Captain Young to stop firing. Eventually, Cornwall did take the *Revenge* past the *Intrepid*, but by that time the *Foudroyant* had gone on and the rest of the enemy ships were, he subsequently admitted, 'at a pretty great distance'.[14]

Those who were charitably disposed might have thought Captain Cornwall was simply a stupid man, but some of his fellow captains regarded his tardiness as backwardness, and they were probably correct, for it is impossible to reconcile his stirring story of his defence of the *Intrepid* and his bold assault on the powerful *Foudroyant* with the fact that not one of his crew was killed or wounded and the ship received only very slight damage from three shot—especially when one recalls the damage done to the *Intrepid*. And as for his fear of passing the *Intrepid* because he had no orders, it is worth noting that when the *Defiance* came to a standstill at the head of the line the *Portland*, *Lancaster*, *Buckingham* and *Captain* all passed her without any doubts or hesitation and without waiting for any signals.

The sudden appearance of the *Princess Louisa*'s jib-boom over the *Revenge*'s taffrail was caused by the fact that her next in line, the *Trident* suddenly came up close on the *Louisa*'s starboard side, forcing her to turn to larboard, with the result that the *Louisa* came into the *Revenge*'s wake and alarmed Captain Cornwall with her jib-boom. Once the *Trident* was clear of her, the *Louisa* tried to get back into action again,[15] although her sails and rigging were badly damaged and her captain, Noel, was soon mortally wounded.

The *Trident*'s role is hard to describe because her captain, Philip Durell, never once mentioned, in his log, or his subsequent evidence at Byng's trial, that his ship got in the way of the *Louisa*: instead, he claimed that he was rescuing her.

However, since the *Trident* was the next ship to the *Ramillies*, and was the reason why Byng was subsequently accused of cowardice, we must try to discover what she did. It is clear that Durell saw that the *Intrepid* and the *Princess Louisa* were showing signs of damage, and that the enemy were still keeping up a heavy fire on them. He claimed that he then took the *Trident* down until he reached a position between them and the passing enemy ships.

There is no doubt about what he did next, since both log and evidence agree—he backed his maintopsail and, with the *Trident* stopped in the smoke, opened fire on the enemy as they passed.[16]

The first nine ships forming Byng's line of battle had now got into action. The *Defiance*, leading, was badly damaged and had dropped out of the line; the *Portland, Lancaster, Buckingham* and *Captain* were damaged but still full of fight. But the fact that the sixth ship, the *Intrepid* had come to a stop because she had lost her foretopmast, affected the seventh, eighth and ninth ships— the *Revenge*, because Cornwall was afraid to pass the *Intrepid* for a long time (even though it meant he was disobeying the Fighting Instructions); the *Princess Louisa*, who was damaged; and the *Trident*, because Durell did not attempt to pass and in doing so also disobeyed the Fighting Instructions. Now the tenth ship in the line, the *Ramillies*, was about to be affected by the motley collection of misfortune and stupidity which had preceded her.

The lower-deck guns of Byng's flagship had been double-shotted in obedience to his orders, and their crews waited impatiently. On the lower-deck Christopher Basset and Mathew Waterfall, the second and fifth lieutenants, were at their quarters supervising the 32-pounder guns; Daniel Waudby, the third lieutenant, was on the middle-deck doing a similar task. George Hamilton, the sixth lieutenant, was up forward on the upper-deck 'busily employed in getting the foremost guns pointed as far forward as possible'.*[17]

Soon stabs of red flame dissolving into smoke showed that the *Ramillies* was coming under fire: shot sighed overhead, some punching holes in the sails and cutting ropes. Rigging under strain whiplashed as it was sliced through. 'They're firing pretty smartly,' commented one of the officers near Byng.

'Let them fire,' replied the Admiral. 'I do not intend firing a gun until I get as near to them as possible.'[19]

Lord Robert Bertie was standing on an arms chest, leaning over the hammocks stowed in the nettings along the top of the bulwarks, and talking to Colonel Marcus Smith, when a shot spun through

---

* This may well have been the first big action in which locks—small pistol-like devices used to produce a spark—were used to fire some of the guns, instead of linstocks, and flannel cartridges instead of paper. See note 18 on page 321.

the air between them and crashed into the gangway on the other side of the ship.[20] Both officers affected disdain for the attentions of the *Lion*'s gunners.

Finally some seamen at the *Ramillies*'s upper-deck guns became impatient at being shot at without receiving any orders to fire back, and in the excitement first one gun fired, followed by several others. The gun-captains on the middle-deck below, hearing the guns on the deck overhead go off and rumble back from the ports in recoil, blew on their slow-matches and fired their guns before Lt Waudby could stop them. They were followed by the men at the lower-deck 32-pounders.

Hearing most of his flagship's guns firing, Byng decided not to stop them: they were masking the ship with smoke and hiding her from the enemy gunners. But although the smoke blinded the French, it also blinded the British, because it was very difficult to see other ships from the decks of the *Ramillies*.

Suddenly, amid the smoke and din, Lord Robert Bertie shouted across to Byng: 'Do you or Captain Gardiner see that ship upon our starboard bow? I apprehend her to be one of ours. If you do not take care we shall fire into her!'

Byng reacted rapidly: Gardiner was sent running to stop the forward guns from firing until they could see if the ship had French colours; Bertie rushed down into the darkness and smoke of the middle and lower decks to warn the lieutenants to cease fire. Colonel Marcus Smith had not heard Bertie's warning shout to Byng, but through the smoke he spotted part of a blue flag belonging to yet another ship and just managed to run over in time to stop one of the quarter-deck 9-pounders firing into her.[21]

Byng had, in the few seconds available, given Gardiner a second order before he ran forward: as soon as he had stopped the guns firing he was to back the foretopsail, which would stop the ship. When he had done this Gardiner had a few moments in which to glance round and see, for the first time, just what was going on: the *Trident* was about two hundred yards away on the starboard bow and the *Ramillies* was just clearing the *Princess Louisa* which was very close on the larboard bow.

With these three ships stopped and almost hidden in the smoke there was naturally a great danger that the rest of the rear division would sail down and collide with them. Byng therefore had to order the signal to be hoisted for the whole squadron to brace-to (i.e. back its sails and stop), because there was no signal for only the rear ships to brace-to. Once again, owing to the limitations of signalling, Byng could not transmit to his captains what he really wanted done.

Slowly the situation resolved itself and a few minutes later, when the *Ramillies* got clear, Byng ordered the signal to be hoisted for the squadron to fill and stand on. But the damage had been done: the hold-up caused by the stupidity or cowardice (perhaps both) of Captains Cornwall and Durell was to result in Admiral Byng being accused of cowardice in the face of the enemy: it was not difficult, if one disregarded the evidence of those on board the *Ramillies*, to declare there was no reason for the Admiral's flagship to have stopped when she did—especially when people like Cornwall and Durell had a particular interest in trying to divert attention from their own activities.

The *Deptford*, originally ordered out of the line as the thirteenth and weakest ship, so that Byng could match twelve ships against Galissonnière's twelve, was now ordered back into the line to replace the *Intrepid*, and the frigate *Chesterfield* was told to stand by in case Captain Young needed assistance.

In the meantime the French Admiral had not been idle while the British ships were held up; he could see the British line was now split in two. Well ahead were the *Lancaster*, *Portland*, *Buckingham* and *Captain*; then there was the gap where the *Intrepid* had been; then came the *Revenge*, *Princess Louisa*, *Trident*, *Ramillies*, *Culloden* and *Kingston*. The *Intrepid* and *Defiance*, both crippled, were clear of the line.

Galissonnière realized—and de Glandevez also sent a boat over to the flagship with a note to suggest it—that he should immediately break through the gap between the *Captain* and *Revenge* with his own *Foudroyant*, the *Fier*, and the five relatively undamaged ships astern of him—a move which would divide the British line in two. Breaking the line would isolate West's division and a savage attack from to windward should result in the destruction or capture of the *Lancaster*, *Portland*, *Buckingham* and *Captain*.

However, Byng's division was by now getting under way again and beginning to close the gap. Byng commented to Gardiner that the French ships, with only foresails and topsails set, 'very much outsail us'. 'On this occasion,' Byng said, 'I could not help expressing my concern to Captain Gardiner that I had not a few more ships to enable me to make the general signal to chase.'[22]

This remark was not mere bravado: Galissonnière had seen that Byng's division was getting back into action once again, slowly closing the gap, and he realized that if he tried to execute his plan for cutting the British squadron in half it would now be extremely dangerous, if not impossible. He therefore contented himself with standing on to the north-west, firing at West's ships as he passed. The *Lancaster*, which was farther to leeward than the others, noted in her log, 'tacked ship, we being in the enemy line'.[23]

From Byng's point of view, the French were now making off: they were refusing further action. The battle was over. 'After the enemy bore away and made sail,' said Byng, 'as they so much outsailed us, and a considerable part of the Fleet was unable to pursue, I judged it improper to pursue with part of the Fleet an enemy superior at first, and still all of them fit for action, according to all appearances.'[24]

The British seamen were delighted at the result of the battle: the sight of the departing French ships brought cheers and jeers. The pride of Provençe, it seemed, could not stand up to the sturdy sailors from Cornwall: the best of Languedoc were running away from the men of Kent and Dorset and a score of other shires. So much for appearances. Galissonnière was indeed retreating and refusing any further part in the fight; but the reason was not cowardice—his first task was completed. The British squadron was virtually immobilized. It was at his mercy, but he made no further attempt to destroy it.

12

SOLDIERING IN SLIPPERS

WHILE THE CREWS of the British ships busied themselves with repairs, and the captains drew up reports of the casualties and damage to send across to the Admiral, Byng wrote a brief and spontaneous note which he ordered to be sent across to Rear-Admiral Temple West. 'I hope you are well and have not received any hurt yourself,' he said, 'tho' I see that your ship has greatly suffered. I am to thank you a thousand and a thousand times for your fine and gallant behaviour this day, I wish you had been better supported . . . Your behaviour was like an angel today. God bless you.'[1]

As soon as West received the letter he went across to the *Ramillies* where, according to West, Byng told him he was dissatisfied with the behaviour of several of the ships in the rear division. West said he was very sorry to hear it, and he hoped if that was the case Byng would remove the captains concerned from their commands. The topic of the conversation was changed when Byng realized that there was something worrying West, and he discovered that West's son, who was a midshipman in the *Buckingham*, had been wounded.

Augustus Hervey soon came on board the flagship and found that Byng 'was very sensible of the many errors of some of his captains'. In addition West 'found great fault with Captain Ward [*Culloden*] and Captain Parry [*Kingston*] for not closing the Admiral, as also with Captain Cornwall of the *Revenge*, and was for bringing them to a court martial, which would have been better if the Admiral had listened'.[2]

The Admiral clearly intended to renew the battle next morning, according to Hervey, because Byng 'told me how Anson had sold him, but by God he would fight till every ship sunk before he would give this up, if the council of war did not think his instructions bound him otherwise'. Next day the weather was thick and

heavy, and several of the British ships were still busy with repairs.
'Many of them,' said Hervey, 'appeared like racks.' He was not
particularly pleased when Byng told him later that as Captain
Andrews had been killed Hervey could take over command of the
Defiance. This was, of course, promotion, since the *Defiance* was
a 60-gun ship while the *Phoenix* was only a 20-gun frigate. Hervey
accepted, but the reason for his reluctance was that the *Defiance*
was 'a perfect rack and the worst-manned ship in the service now,
and I was obliged to borrow men to fit her'. Nor was he exaggerating, because although the *Defiance* should have had a crew of
400, she had been short of fifty-three men when she left Gibraltar
and despite the twenty men she received from one of the frigates
before the battle she had subsequently lost fifty-nine men killed
and wounded.

The squadron was still busy with repairs on Saturday, two days
after the battle: the *Captain* took on board six carpenter's mates
from the *Culloden* to help repair her lower masts; the *Ramillies*
sent a carpenter's mate and five seamen to help the *Portland*'s
crew. In the afternoon the *Defiance*, Hervey's new command,
lowered her colours to half-mast for the funeral of Captain Andrews
and fired a twenty-gun salute. The *Deptford*'s master recorded
prosaically in his log that they had opened a cask of Leghorn salt
beef and found it was 120 lbs short of weight.*

The British squadron had, of course, been extremely vulnerable
all this time: had Galissonnière brought his squadron back to the
scene of the battle he would have found most of the van division
ships with damaged yards lowered down on deck and men busy
knotting torn rigging and splicing in new. But the French did not
appear again until three days later. They made no attempt to close
and, as Byng wrote in a note to West, reporting that they had been
sighted, 'I do not think, in the present situation of our squadron,
we are in a condition to lay [a course] for them'. He proposed, if
West agreed, that the British squadron should get under way that
night, and by the next day 'we shall better judge the situation and
condition of our ships'. West went on board the *Ramillies* and, for
reasons which he never subsequently made clear, (although there
is no suggestion of rancour) told Byng that 'I should be glad to
give my opinion at a council of war'.[3]

* On May 26, less than a week after the battle, an entry in the *Portland*'s
log reads: 'Punished Joseph Wood with twelve lashes for quarrelling.'

Byng called the council of war for the next day, May 24, but early that morning, before the Admiral made the signal for 'All captains', West went on board the *Ramillies* once again and told Byng that he objected to Captains Parry, Ward and Cornwall— the three that Byng considered had not done their duty—sitting at the council of war. The Admiral, however, would not agree: according to West's evidence at Byng's subsequent court martial, the Admiral 'told me he had or would reprimand them; and that it was very hard to stigmatize gentlemen for little failings— meaning with regard to their not having done their duty. I told him if that was the case I thought so too; for as it was not I who accused them, I could not possibly judge of their failings in their duty, as I could not, from my situation [in the battle] possibly know their behaviour'.*[4]

In addition to the captains, Byng also invited the four senior Army officers to attend the council of war—General Stuart, and Colonels Cornwallis, Lord Effingham and Lord Robert Bertie. Thus there were seventeen officers sitting round the table in the great cabin of the *Ramillies* making decisions which a more deter- mined commander-in-chief would have made for himself. Byng's reliance on the decision of a council of war was to go a long way towards his subsequent condemnation; yet, ironically, not one of the naval officers—including Temple West—were to suffer in any way for their part in the decisions they were about to make.†

The facts that Byng put before them were naturally many and varied. They had to consider that Byng was without a hospital ship or transports,—yet he had 411 men sick, 162 wounded, and forty-five men had been killed. Thus, apart from the problem of what to do with the sick and wounded—they would die like flies if left long in the fetid atmosphere in the battleships—he was

---

* However, West was speaking nine months later, when he appears to have been attempting to give the impression that he was not blaming the three captains. According to Hervey, West had himself already proposed the three men should be court martialled and, as we shall soon see, one of the captains demanded a court martial because of West's alleged criticisms of him.

In the Newcastle Papers is an unsigned and undated memorandum which says that at the house of the then Consul-General in Portugal about the time of Lord Torrington's death, a visitor, Dr Kennedy, was denouncing the pernicious effects of councils of war when Captain John Byng, said to him, 'Doctor, you are right; and I remember that my father once said to me, "Jack, if ever you come to have the command of a squadron, and would do anything, never call a council of war".' [5]

now deprived of another 617 men, in addition to the fact that the
ships had already left behind many sick and had been short of
more than 500 men when they sailed from Gibraltar.

Several of the ships were not in a much healthier state: the
Intrepid was so badly damaged that she would have to be towed to
Gibraltar; the *Portland*, too, would have to be docked as soon as
possible; the *Defiance*'s foretopmast would be sent up again within
a few hours; the *Captain*'s repairs were nearly completed; and the
rest of the ships were ready for action. Byng rounded off this
recital by saying he regarded the Admiralty's instructions (given
fully in Appendix III) concerning Gibraltar as peremptory.

Augustus Hervey provides the only available description of the
deliberations and this, coupled with the council's unanimous
resolutions, shows there was very little disagreement. Several of
the members criticized the Admiralty's orders to Byng—Hervey
calls them 'these absurd instructions'—before they decided that
the squadron was in no condition to attack the enemy without
risking the fate of Gibraltar. Rear-Admiral West 'particularly said
we ought on no account risk another engagement', Hervey wrote,
'on which the Admiral [Byng] said if there was any officer that
thought we ought, he would attack them tomorrow'. The council
then resolved that the squadron should go at once to Gibraltar to
cover it from a possible attack. Hervey disagreed—although he
did not vote against the resolution—saying that the squadron
should stay off Minorca, ready to attack the French once again
when more British ships arrived and, if possible, land reinforcements for Fort St Philip. However—according to Hervey—West
'particularly exclaimed against this, and said it would be risking
both places and acting directly contrary to the Admiral's instructions'.[6]

The council's final resolutions were the results of five questions
put to them by Byng—questions so worded that they suggested
the answers: perhaps Byng had, without realizing it, drafted them
in the light of his own thoughts.[7] (They are given fully in
Appendix V, page 311.) The questions and resolutions show quite
clearly that each member of the council, whether general or
admiral, colonel or captain, could think of only one way of driving
the 15,000 French soldiers out of Minorca—and that was by landing a large enough British army. Not one of them mentioned even
the possibility of blockading the island to starve out Richelieu's

army; indeed, Byng's second question had asked, 'Whether, if there was no French Fleet cruising off Minorca, the English Fleet could raise the siege?' The seventeen men could not see that this hypothetical situation would, in reality, have been a golden road to victory, with peerages and promotions for milestones; instead they recorded that they were 'Unanimously of opinion that the Fleet could not'.

However, one man understood what was really at stake, and he was the Duke de Richelieu, who appreciated the danger he was in only too well. 'Gentlemen,' he said, as the guns of the two squadrons thundered away on the horizon, 'they are playing out there a very interesting game. If M. de la Galissonnière beats the enemy, we can continue the siege in our slippers.'[8]

The Marquis de la Galissonnière had written his dispatch to the Minister of Marine on the day after the battle and sent it to Toulon on board a frigate. He could be quite confident that it would be in the hands of the French King within a very few days —and since neutral envoys in Paris would send copies to their colleagues in London, it was certain the British Government would also be reading his version of the events off Minorca long before they could possibly receive any news from Admiral Byng. Although the contents of the French dispatch will be dealt with later, when we see its effect on the politicians in London, it is worth noting at this point that Galissonnière did not claim a victory; indeed, he obviously regarded the action as little more than an almost indecisive encounter, but quite naturally phrased his dispatch to make it clear the British received the worst of it.

Byng, however, was too busy to compose his report to the Admiralty until May 25, when Augustus Hervey went on board the *Ramillies* 'and helped to write his dispatch on this lame affair'. At the same time Hervey was far from satisfied with the way the damaged ships were being repaired: 'I never saw so little activity among any set of officers. These were indeed in general the very scum of the Fleet . . . Such,' he added bitterly, 'was the situation of those ships chosen by Lord Anson to go with Mr Byng on the most important service just then that could be, but that Lord ever sacrificed the interest and service of the country to the interest and favour of a few individual favourites of his own.'[9]

The Admiral's dispatch—which enclosed a copy of the

resolutions of the council of war—was soon sent on its way to London, and with it went a letter from Augustus Hervey to Henry Fox, who was a friend of his family. The squadron in the meantime made its way towards Gibraltar and when Captain Noel died of his wounds there was some brisk manoeuvring among the junior captains, who wanted Admiral Byng to give them the command of the *Princess Louisa*. The recent battle was fought over and over again in discussions among the various officers but, Hervey noted, 'I never heard a word hinted against the Admiral's conduct until we came to Gibraltar'.

Hervey was sent on ahead in the *Defiance* to make sure the hospital at Gibraltar was ready to receive the large number of sick and wounded in the squadron. He reached there on June 16—to find five battleships and several transports at anchor: Rear-Admiral Broderick had arrived the day before.

Byng and his squadron arrived on the 20th and the sick and wounded were landed immediately. Broderick's arrival with the reinforcements naturally changed the whole situation: the resolutions of the council of war were no longer valid, since they were based on the fact that the French squadron was stronger than the British. Now the five extra battleships more than made up for the loss of the *Intrepid* and the *Portland*—for both needed considerable repairs—and once his squadron had taken on stores and water there was nothing to prevent Byng returning to Minorca. Hervey, in his usual energetic fashion, was anxious for them to be on their way. 'I pressed the Admiral much to sail the next day with all [the ships] and take some troops on board and press every seaman in the Bay, but tho' he determined to go as soon as he could, yet I was very uneasy.'

Next day, Captain Cornwall of the *Revenge*, having heard of some remarks made by certain officers about his behaviour in the battle, asked for a court martial on himself—the usual way of proving one's innocence. A court martial would take up valuable time, since the captains of the ships would be sitting round a table hearing evidence when they ought to be busy getting their ships ready to sail again, and Byng refused because it would cause too much delay. However, Cornwall was so insistent that Byng was finally forced to agree and he gave the necessary instructions, appointing Rear-Admiral West to act as president—an odd choice, for reasons which will soon become even more apparent.

Among the captains ordered to form the court were Hervey, Lloyd and Amherst. These three men, of course, commanded the frigates and, since they had been to windward of the squadron repeating signals, had a clear view of the battle. When they arrived on board the *Buckingham*, where the trial was to be held, they refused to sit, pointing out that they were bound to be called as witnesses to give evidence on Cornwall's conduct. This caused such a fuss that it was decided to adjourn for a couple of days, but before the officers left the cabin, Admiral West 'desired everyone to be attentive to him', according to Hervey, saying he had been told that he was the promoter of the inquiries into Cornwall's conduct, which he 'absolutely denied'. He knew that courts martial were always a disgrace to a fleet, although sometimes necessary. All he had said was that five of the leading British ships had beaten five of the enemy, and that they were not supported—he 'did not know the cause; that he accused no one, nor ever had; that it was true he had refused to sit at a council of war with some captains but he had accused none'.

'In short,' wrote Hervey, 'he dwelt a long time on all this, with very artful insinuations that I thought reflected on Admiral Byng.' This was too much for the young captain who promptly got up and said that he did not see what West meant by 'not accusing' when he said that five of the British van beat five of the enemy's and were not supported: it carried an accusation, he declared, against the rear of the British squadron and therefore ought to be cleared up.

'Had I been of that line,' he told the rest of the captains, 'I should think myself engaged in honour to ask Admiral West, when he objected to sitting with some captains at a council of war, whether I was one.' It was the duty of every captain there to know to whom West objected, and why. Hervey was not concerned, since he had not been in the line of battle, but 'Let those sit still who may; for my part I rise only to justify the conduct of the Commander-in-Chief, to whose conduct I was so situated as to be a judge of that day, and I can with truth and honour, and will, justify to the last.'

He told them that he knew that Rear-Admiral West had said Captain Cornwall might have passed the *Intrepid* just as West's ship, the *Buckingham*, had passed the *Defiance*. This brought West to his feet to admit that he said it, and that he still thought so.

'This occasioned two or three sharp replies between Mr West and me,' wrote Hervey, 'but I cared not, I saw what he was at.'

All this naturally caused a certain amount of coolness between Byng and West, so much so that General Fowke asked Hervey that evening if he would try to reconcile them—a task which Hervey declined. However, the unpleasant atmosphere soon cleared up because when the court sat again on June 28 no one appeared to make any accusations against Cornwall, and three days later Byng and West went on shore together, much to the relief of their captains. With Cornwall's honour satisfied, it is worth noting that there was now no murmuring or gossiping among either the Navy or the Army officers; no one criticized Admiral Byng's handling of the battle; and it seems that comments on the behaviour of the three captains died down.

Yet within a few hours the whole atmosphere had changed once again: but this time all the captains were affected and, to a certain extent, the Army officers who had taken part in Byng's council of war. Several of them, led by Captain Young and Colonel Cornwallis—turned on Byng with the quickness of a snake and bit hard in the hope that if they did so publicly perhaps their own part in the whole sad business would be overlooked.

The reason for this almost obscene exhibition of the way self-interest can overcome honour was a letter which Rear-Admiral West received from London less than twenty-four hours after resolving the coolness between himself and Admiral Byng. The letter had come overland, arriving in Gibraltar on July 1, and was from a friend in London. It warned him privately that as a result of the recent battle both he and Admiral Byng were being recalled to England in disgrace . . .[10]

The two men had only a few hours in which to mull over this shattering news because next day the *Antelope* sailed into the Bay from Portsmouth, and soon after she anchored Byng heard that he and West were not the only ones in disgrace—Generals Fowke and Stuart had also been sacked. The *Antelope*'s motley crowd of distinguished passengers were the replacements. But, as the two admirals were soon to discover, the most fantastic aspect of the whole business as far as they personally were concerned was that the Government had sacked them both entirely on the evidence of an extract from the French Admiral Galissonnière's dispatch: the dispatch had arrived on June 3, and the *Antelope* had sailed from Portsmouth on June 16. Byng's dispatch—the first news the Government received about the battle from a British source—did not arrive in London until June 23.

13

THE COURIER FROM PARIS

IN LONDON while Admiral Byng's squadron had been returning to Gibraltar after the Battle of Minorca, the Duke of Newcastle was finding himself in a very embarrassing situation owing to the death of the Lord Chief Justice, Sir Dudley Rider, on May 25. The embarrassment was caused by the Attorney-General, the Scottish-born William Murray, who had laid an immediate claim to the post and demanded a peerage to go with it. Unfortunately for the Duke, as we have seen, he had only two competent Government spokesmen in the House of Commons, Murray and Henry Fox. If Murray received a peerage and went to the House of Lords it would leave his Grace at the mercy of Fox—a prospect which alarmed him considerably.

The Duke was still trying to persuade Murray to stay on in the Commons when, on the last day of May, Lt O'Hara, Lord Tyrawley's son, drove up to the Admiralty from Portsmouth, having at last arrived with the letters from Admiral Byng and General Fowke written after Fowke's council of war, and before Byng sailed from Gibraltar for Minorca.

Clevland opened Byng's letter and took it to Lord Anson. '... The throwing men into the castle will only enable it to hold out but a little time longer ... By a council of war held by General Fowke ... it was not thought proper to send a detachment equal to a battalion to the relief of Minorca ...'

Anson read the rest of the letter and the enclosures, his anger growing, and then wrote a hurried note to the Duke of Newcastle in his untidy, sprawling writing—some of the letters were over an inch long. Telling his Grace that he had heard from Byng, he added: 'I think you won't be much pleased with his letter and less with the Governor of Gibraltar, who has sent no troops for the relief of Port Mahon, and for a very extraordinary reason, vizt because he would then have had fewer at Gibraltar.'[1]

When a copy of Fowke's dispatch was sent round to the Duke of Cumberland, his angry verdict on it was given in a letter to Henry Fox: 'an infamous council war infected with terrors and void of obedience'.[2]

Young Lt O'Hara, perhaps bearing out Augustus Hervey's poor estimate of him, was soon proclaiming that his own opinion differed from that of the General's council of war[3]—an opinion perhaps related to the fact the King and the Government reacted swiftly to the shortcomings of the Army at Gibraltar. As we have already seen, Fowke and Major-General Stuart were immediately recalled —the former to be replaced as Governor by Lord Tyrawley, the absentee Governor of Minorca and the latter by Lord Panmure. The miserable Major Mace, one of the three officers who drew up the report on Fort St Philip, was dismissed the service.

Henry Fox wrote a private letter of explanation to General Fowke. 'It may be of use to you to know particularly what has occasioned your disgrace. His Majesty could, by no means, brook you calling a council of war on orders directed to you singly ... That it would be dangerous or difficult, if not impracticable to land any succours [at Minorca] His Majesty thinks a strange reason for not attempting it.' It was remarkable, said Fox, that Major Mace had previously shown the Duke of Cumberland and other senior Army officers how it was possible to land men at Fort St Philip 'after the French should be in possession of the rest of the island and of the harbour'.[4]

For the Government these were indeed hectic days. Lt O'Hara had brought Byng's letters on Monday, May 31; on Tuesday the King had decided Fowke should be sacked; and then on Wednesday the Spanish Ambassador, the faithful Count D'Abreu, received a letter by diplomatic courier from Paris, which threw several members of the Government into something approaching panic.

There is little doubt that both the Duke of Newcastle and Henry Fox secretly feared that Byng had been sent too late with too small a squadron, and they must have been dreading the day when the first news came of an encounter with the French. It arrived from an unexpected quarter.

Galissonnière's dispatch on the recent battle had finally reached the French King at Versailles. The Spanish Ambassador in Paris had secured a copy of it which he sent off at once to his colleague

D'Abreu who received it in London on Wednesday, June 2. He in turn forwarded an extract of the dispatch to Henry Fox at the Cockpit.

From the extract (which is given in App. VI, page 312) the British Government learned that the British and French squadrons had met on May 20; that according to Galissonnière he had tried to get the weather gage but lost it to Byng when the wind shifted; and that the two squadrons were roughly equal in numbers. 'The engagement lasted about three hours and a half, or four hours, but was not general during all that time, the English ships that had suffered most from our broadsides having got to windward out of the reach of our cannon,' said the translation.

'They have always preserved this advantage, not to engage; and after having made their greatest efforts against our rear, which they found so close, and from which they received so great a fire as not to be able to break it, they resolved to retire, and appeared no more on the 21st. In general, none of their ships bore our fire for any time; the ships in our squadron have suffered very little; they were entirely repaired during the night, and fit for an engagement the next day.'[5]

Galissonnière's dispatch was written in such general terms that no one reading it could have a very exact idea of what had happened, other than that there had been a battle; a reasonable man would certainly reserve judgment until Byng's dispatch was available. The phrase that the English 'got to windward out of the reach of our cannon', for instance was more likely to be another and more tactful way of saying the French ships dropped to leeward out of the fight. Unfortunately, however, the men reading it were not reasonable because they were frightened; to them it presented a golden alibi and that which they all sought—a scapegoat.

The Inner Committee was called to a meeting next day at the Duke of Cumberland's apartments, and those present, in addition to His Royal Highness, were Hardwicke, Newcastle, Anson, Fox, Granville, Holdernesse and Robinson. According to the record, after reading the minutes of Fowke's council of war at Gibraltar, the report of the engineers, and finally the General's letter, they confirmed the decision to relieve Fowke, Stuart and Mace.

Then their Lordships dealt with Admiral Byng. It is important to remember that up to now they had not received Byng's dispatch and the only facts they had to go on were these: (1) Byng's letter of May 4 reporting Fowke's council of war and the condition of the base at Gibraltar; (2) Fowke's letter and report of the Army's council of war; and (3) the Spanish Ambassador's copy of an extract from Galissonnière's dispatch, without any proof of the truth of its claims or, indeed, of its authenticity.

On this 'evidence' they decided that 'Sir Edward Hawke be sent to succeed Admiral Byng; that Captain Saunders* be advanc'd to the rank of Rear-Admiral and sent to succeed Admiral West'.[6]

In the meantime the Government took great care that no hint of the real situation should appear in the newspapers for the time being. On June 3 they printed a bare announcement from the Admiralty dated May 31 that 'This morning Lt O'Hara of His Majesty's ship the *Dolphin* arrived here with dispatches from Admiral Byng dated the 7th of this month† at Gibraltar, giving an account of his arrival there on the 2nd, after a tedious passage occasioned by contrary winds . . .' The replacement of Fowke, Byng and the other officers was kept secret until an announcement was made in the *London Gazette* on June 6.

Just before the Inner Committee met, Henry Fox had written to the Duke of Devonshire, telling him about Galissonnière's letter and adding that nothing had been heard from Byng, 'But I doubt not that our first news will be that Byng is returned to Gibraltar, and that a council of war says he did wisely. The consternation, anger and shame of everybody here on this occasion is extreme.' As far as the hasty replacement of the two admirals was concerned, 'There is no waiting for explanations. If they can excuse themselves, amends must be made them. But the Fleet, sufficiently dispirited, I dare say, already, must not be left so till inquiries can be made'.[7]

The Duke of Newcastle, agitated by the swiftness of events, wrote to the would-be Lord Chief Justice, William Murray, pleading with him once again to stay on in the Commons for the time being, and appealing to the Scotsman's 'zeal for the King: the success of his affairs, and particularly your most sincere love and

---

* Saunders had served with Anson in the *Centurion* on the voyage round the world. Later he was to command the ships which took General Wolfe's force up the St Lawrence for the brilliant assault on Quebec.

† The letter was dated the 4th, but the Admiral had added a postscript dated the 7th. O'Hara had arrived in the *Lovell*, leaving the *Dolphin* at Gibraltar.

F

affection for me'. He added that 'the late most infamous behaviour of our Fleet' did not lessen the weight of his argument;[8] but Murray clearly thought that it did and merely renewed his claims.

Fox, meanwhile, was telling the Duke of Bedford that 'His Majesty and the Duke [of Cumberland] are struck to the greatest degree. But His Royal Highness still thinks we may save Minorca, and Lord Tyrawley (who at a minute's warning was ready to set out with great and commendable spirit) thinks so too. I heartily wish I did'.[9]

The next day was a Saturday, but Anson was busy at the Admiralty drawing up a draft of the orders for Sir Edward Hawke, which he sent to the Duke of Newcastle 'to make what alterations you think proper'.[10] Anson then went to a Board meeting attended by Bateman and Richard Edgcumbe where they decided that the captain and all six lieutenants of the *Ramillies* should also be brought home as well as Byng. The minutes[11] do not give any reason for this decision, but most likely it was already in the back of Anson's mind that Byng might be accused of cowardice—and who better to prove it than the officers on board his own ship.

William Pitt was among those who at first went more than half way towards condemning Byng on the enemy's report, and on June 5 wrote to his brother-in-law, George Grenville, that 'Byng is gone to Gibraltar, and if his own account does not differ widely from that of the French, where he ought to go next is pretty evident'.[12]

Grenville's reply on June 7 was very much in keeping with his austere, calm and deliberate personality: he had hoped for more details of the battle, he said, because as far as Byng was concerned, 'I could not believe that an officer of his rank or name would be so forgetful of what he owed to both'. He doubted if the British squadron was superior, or even equal to the French because two of Byng's ships had only 50 guns and were seldom put in the line. Yet whatever the case was against Byng, he added, 'what can be the excuse for sending a force which at the utmost is scarcely equal to the enemy, upon so important and decisive an expedition? Though in the venality of this hour it might be deemed sufficient to throw the whole of the blame upon Byng ... Whatever faults Byng may have, I believe he was not reckoned backward in point of personal courage'.[13]

Horace Walpole shared Pitt's view, telling the Earl of Strafford that 'The consternation on the behaviour of Byng, and on the amazing council of war at Gibraltar is extreme'.[14] But two days later the sage of Strawberry Hill modified his views, writing to a friend that 'The world condemns extremely the rashness of superseding admirals on no information but from our enemies ...' Within a fortnight he told Sir Horace Mann in Florence that 'If the world was scandalized at this history, it was nothing to the exasperation of the Court who, on no other foundation than an enemy's report, immediately ordered Admiral Hawke and Saunders (created an Admiral on purpose) to bridle and saddle the first ship at hand, and post away to Gibraltar to hang and drown Byng and West ... and not to be too partial to the land' [i.e. the Army]. He added that 'This expedition had so far a good effect, that the mob itself could not accuse the Ministry of want of rashness ...'[15]

On June 8 yet another bombshell arrived in London, once again via the Spanish Ambassador. An Admiralty messenger hurried round to the Duke of Newcastle's house with a letter in Anson's familiar large scrawl. It had been written in great haste, and as a result the spelling and grammar suffered, and several words and sentences were inserted after Anson read over his first attempt.

He began by saying d'Abreu had received another letter from Paris which said that although the French had found Fort St Philip better defended than they expected, Richelieu was expecting a reinforcement of five battalions and fifty battering cannon; and Byng's squadron had been seen, 'very much shattered', heading for Gibraltar.

Anson then went on to give the startling news. There was an item in d'Abreu's letter, he said, 'which he did not read, that said there is a treaty concluded between France and Vienna. I know your Grace is desirous to know all events as soon as possible, let them be ever so bad, and surely worse were never communicated. Cleveland,' he explained, 'saw the article about Vienna by looking over d'Abreu's shoulder while he was reading his letter to me.'[16]

A pact between Britain's former Austrian ally and her present enemy was what the British Government had long feared; and its significance and danger in the eyes of the Duke of Newcastle could not be exaggerated. 'If we cannot form a counter-alliance to

this most extraordinary and unnatural one between France and
the House of Austria,' he wrote to Lord Hardwicke, 'France must
soon become the masters of all Europe; we in the meantime must
be carrying on a war singly with France from whence experience
shows we can expect no success; we are unequal, I am afraid,
everywhere; and yet, I don't see how we can make peace, or when
we shall be able to make one . . .'

Nor was Austria the only problem, he told Hardwicke: Murray
would not stay in the House of Commons, and as a result his
Grace was worried about 'the means of *our* supporting the King's
business and ourselves there'. He warned the Lord Chancellor
that 'we must not deceive ourselves. Your Lordship and I are the
chief persons; and officially I am the most aim'd at, and made the
more responsible, but you will come in for your share.' Could
the pair of them take that load upon themselves 'in the distressful
condition of affairs at home and abroad' with no other support in
the Commons than Fox? Where could they get any other? The
Army—his Grace meant the Duke of Cumberland—was against
them and the Fleet 'I am afraid not in a flourishing state'. Was
there any way of having more dependence on Fox? In other words,
what further security could they have for his behaviour?

He thought that within six months they would hear of some
negotiations between Fox and Pitt and Leicester House, which of
course represented the young Prince of Wales's faction. 'And I
can answer for Your Lordship and myself, that if it could be done
with honour and ease to the King, we should be most heartily glad
of it, and to be excluded out of it. But, my Lord, if we are to go on,
we must have the means of doing it . . .'[17]

The political situation was now looking sufficiently bad for the
Government that the hack writers, who could usually pick up some
money by writing fiery and vicious pamphlets on behalf of one or
the other parties, began to rub their hands—and not without good
reason. One of the first to offer his services was the poet David
Mallet, who wrote to the Duke of Newcastle on June 10: 'In the
present universal dejection that prevails amongst almost all orders
of men whom I have conversed with, is there anything that your
Grace wishes the writer of plain sense and common honesty
should lay before the public, to reanimate and raise the spirit of
the nation?' If there was, then he was only too willing to oblige.

His motive in offering his services, he added, was solely 'a hearty love for my country'.*[18]

Colonel Joseph Yorke, writing from The Hague to his elder brother, Lord Royston, said he thought there would be a great outcry and people would complain because a greater force had not been sent, 'which I confess I don't comprehend neither, for the account we had here in April, and published in all your newspapers, agrees exactly with the account of the French Fleet in Mr Galissonnière's own letter, and consequently you must have known their force, if you had a mind'.[20] This was trenchant criticism indeed, coming from the son of the Lord Chancellor; and he wrote again a few days later that 'Your presumption [is] so strong against your own people, without hearing from them, that I see you have recalled them all … We are told too that the Admiral [Galissonnière] is to be recalled and M. de la Motte sent in his room, which if it is so will be particular enough considering what you are doing'.[21]

In the meantime a rather puzzled Lady Hervey, mother of Augustus, was writing to her old friend Henry Fox in defence of Byng. 'I have always heard Byng spoken of as a brave man; he has proved his personal courage,' she wrote, but 'what then can mean his retiring from a fleet inferior in number and in strength of all kinds to his own, where nothing but his destroying their fleet could preserve Minorca, and that gallant old man [Blakeney] who has behaved like a hero of antiquity?'

Fox answered her the same day, saying 'It is strange but it is true that Byng knew how ill the French Fleet was manned as well as Captain Hervey. I suppose the abuses and neglects he speaks of [i.e. the condition of the Gibraltar dockyard] must point at the Navy and Ordnance offices; but they have not lost the island, which nothing but a good fleet sent in time could have saved.'[22]

However, the most trenchant criticism of the day came from a totally unexpected quarter: Lord Tyrawley, while waiting at Portsmouth on board the 50-gun *Antelope* to sail for Gibraltar, wrote to Lord Albemarle and referred to the battleships there which 'are under no destination, but to lie at anchor and at stated

---

* Nevertheless this love did not stop him from accepting a hearty payment from the Secret Service Fund. In the Duke's Secret Service accounts the entry on November 9, 1756 reads 'Mr Mallet for his book—£300 0s. 0d.' It is possible this was not all remuneration because elsewhere this appears as 'Mr Mallet for the expense of printing—300'. [19]

times to go into harbour to clean. We [in the *Antelope*] have little more for it than our heels which, I am told, are not to lay the odds upon. Here are two admirals, two general officers, four sea captains, and many more officers belonging to ships in the Mediterranean, all stuffed into this small ship, and surely, my dear Lord, we should make a very queer figure to be carried into Brest and be detained there the whole war.'[23]

The *Antelope*, bearing what one wit called its 'little cargo of courage', sailed next day, the 16th. On that same day Pitt wrote to George Grenville that 'We are as helpless and childish as ever, and worse still; if any among the Ministry are disposed to be men, I hear they would be madmen; for the regret is that we have no Continent war'. As far as the Mediterranean was concerned, he said, 'probably many an innocent and gallant man's honour and fortune is to be offered up as a scapegoat for the sins of the administration'.[24]

On June 18, two months after the Duke de Richelieu and his army landed in Minorca, the French declared war. The declaration was dated exactly one month after that made by the British.

Admiral Boscawen had been far from silent all this time, and he continued writing his illuminating letters to his wife from on board the *Invincible*. 'As you say, had I been destined for Port Mahon, the French had never been there,' he wrote with scant modesty early in June. 'I find Lord Anson despairs about it, but I am of another opinion, and have told him so.' Byng had wasted time, but 'after all, why was he not ordered sooner? Everybody knew the French were arming against that place long before he was ordered, so that if he is to blame, he is not the only person to be blamed.' Later he wrote that 'I find courage of more worth than I thought it, but if a chief does not show example, the cause will hardly ever succeed. I know some with Byng to be brave; one who I find is much blamed, which led his squadron, was with me last year. He behaved very well at the taking [of the] *Lys*. Ward, Lord Romney's friend is turned out as well as Byng and West. He was always a fool and should have never had the command of a 74-gun ship . . .' (Boscawen seized the *Lys* in 1755—see page 32.)

He followed that with another verdict on Byng, saying 'they left Gibraltar with an intention not to fight or relieve Mahon, which Mr Byng must know he could do if he could beat the French. And no officer in the English service could be so well

acquainted as Mr Byng, who has been in that part of the world
from a boy till this time. He was with his father in the year
'Eighteen but a degenerate son . . . What a scandal to the Navy
that they should be premeditated cowards that have been so long
bred to arms. I should think for the future no man should command that had not given proofs of his courage. You know West
was before broke for his misbehaviour in the Mediterranean.*
Thank those that restored him, for it is believed by all that Byng
acted by his councils.'

Byng's report on the state of the Gibraltar base became, in
Boscawen's hands, turning his thoughts 'entirely how he can lay
out the Government's money that he may come in for a share of
the plunder . . . Indeed Byng's letters would have written him
coward before any jury in the world, and what possesses all the
land officers at Gibraltar I know not . . .'25

It is difficult to pin-point the exact time when the Government
realized that all the French preparation for an invasion of the
United Kingdom was either bluff or simply impractical, but on
June 20 Newcastle wrote to Holdernesse, discussing making a
common cause with Prussia and sending a fleet to the Baltic.

'But then,' he added, 'we must not neglect our fleet at home and
in the Mediterranean; those two are our capital objects . . . I begin
to think they will make a show of an attempt from Dunkirk, to
draw our Fleet from Brest, in order to send theirs to the Mediterranean; but, I repeat again, we must in all events maintain a
superiority at sea *at home* and in the Mediterranean.'26

In Gibraltar, after the *Antelope* had anchored, Sir Edward Hawke
went across to the *Ramillies* and delivered two letters from the
Admiralty to Admiral Byng. The first, harshly-worded when one
considers the source of the information on which its judgment was
based, was signed by Clevland and said:

'His Majesty having received an account that the squadron
under your command, and that of M. Galissonnière came to
action off the harbour of Mahon the 20th of last month; and
that the French, (though inferior to you in force) kept before
the harbour, and obliged you to retreat: I am commanded by

* i.e. After the Battle of Toulon: see page 20.

my Lords Commissioners of the Admiralty to send you herewith an extract of M. Galissonnière's letter to the [French]
Court, giving an account of the action, and to acquaint you that
His Majesty is so much dissatisfied with your conduct, that he
has ordered their Lordships to recall yourself and Mr West
... I am extremely sorry to be obliged to inform you of such
a disagreeable event,' concluded Clevland.

The second letter began with the time-honoured polite flourishes
and then said:

'You are hereby required and directed, upon being joined
by Sir Edward Hawke, immediately to strike your flag and
leave the command of the said ships to him; and you are to
return to England in His Majesty's ship the *Antelope* ...
Rear-Admiral West is also to proceed home in the same ship;
and Sir Edward Hawke is also ordered to discharge the
captains and lieutenants of both the ships in which your flags
are flying, and to send them likewise home in the *Antelope*.'

On reading it Byng realized with a shock that he was being
disgraced and sent home solely on the evidence of an enemy's
account of the battle (as Clevland's letter frankly admitted). The
Government had not even waited to read his own dispatch.
Infuriated and disgusted, Byng went to his cabin, angrily stripped
off his uniform, and in its place donned a plain grey suit. He was
destined never to wear uniform again.

As a pro-Byng pamphlet remarked later: 'It is not usual to take
the enemy's word for their own feats and performances; because
[it is] notorious that the bias of the story will ever be in their
favour.'[27]

According to Augustus Hervey, 'Even Sir Edward Hawke,
whom I went to see, condemned the hasty manner in which it was
done, and much more so the unprecedented infamous reports
Lord Holland [*sic*: Henry Fox], Lord Anson and the Duke of
Newcastle encouraged everywhere against Mr Byng's character in
order to raise the mob against him and turn all the resentment and
just indignation of the people from themselves to Admiral Byng.'

Despite his anger and disgust, Byng's reply to the Admiralty
was dignified. He had received their Lordship's order, which he
had 'immediately complied with, and have only to express my

surprise at being so ignominiously dismissed from my employment, in the sight of the Fleet I had commanded, in sight of the garrison, and in sight of Spain, at such a time, in such a manner, and after such conduct as I hope shall shortly appear to the whole world.

'It is not now for me to expostulate,' he said. 'I flatter myself that Mr West and I shall make evident the injury done to our characters . . .' His character had been 'most injuriously and wrongfully attacked now on the grounds of a false gasconade of an open enemy to our King and country,' instead of waiting for his own dispatch, 'in which there was nothing false, nothing vaunting, nothing shameful, nor nothing that could have prevented our receiving His Majesty's royal approbation for having with a much inferior force fought, met, attacked and beat the enemy.'

On July 2, the day Byng left the *Ramillies* to stay in Hervey's ship, the letter 'D' for 'Discharged', was entered against several names in the muster book of the *Ramillies*, including that of the Admiral and his nephew, Midshipman John Byng.

'The 8th poor Mr Byng went on board the *Antelope* with Admiral West, their captains, lieutenants, and General Fowke and his lady, and Admiral Broderick,' wrote Hervey. 'I think they were between thirty and forty in that 50-gun ship. Such was the reward of forty years service for Admiral Byng, the son of Lord Torrington, to whom this country owed so much!'[28]

14

TWISTING THE TRUTH

BY THE MIDDLE of June the murmuring of the mob and the gossip in fashionable London drawing-rooms was becoming louder and more insistent. Despite the swift sackings, the Government was still being blamed for the events in the Mediterranean, and when Admiral Byng's dispatch on the battle finally arrived in London on June 23 the Ministers were embarrassed to find that it did little to help their case.

With the dispatch Admiral Byng had sent a personal letter to Lord Anson, saying that after the battle he had decided 'that no further risk should be [taken by] His Majesty's Fleet lest by an irreparable accident Gibraltar should become exposed'. He explained quite frankly that although 'we have evidently beat the French yet it was only so that we may call the victory ours since some [of the enemy] were drove out of the line, tho' they recovered themselves to leeward . . . Indeed it was in their power to fight us on if they pleased as we continued on our spot.'

Had the French appeared again he would have engaged them, he said, but the British squadron could not hope to have fought with their crippled ships without becoming more disabled. As far as his captains were concerned, 'I wish some of our officers had been more expert at lines of battle. In engagement we should have gone down more regular and our ships would have been less exposed to have been raked in going down, and tho' we could never have hoped for a complete victory yet we might have been less disabled, and probably disabled them more.'

At the council of war after the battle the resolutions would have been more numerous, he said, 'but I put a stop to the reasons being expressed, for these resolutions were only inflaming my people at our being so weak with regard to the French Fleet, and left without stores or hospital ship, or any visible manner of being a service to Minorca when arrived there'.[1]

The Ministers now had two problems to resolve: what was to be done with Byng's dispatch, which certainly would be damaging to the Government if it was published word for word; and how to divert the blame on to Byng. They soon dealt with the Admiral, deciding that he would be brought to trial. They did not know what the charges would be, but in the meantime he was to be arrested, and the King agreed. No doubt the Ministers privately considered that the simple act of arresting the Admiral would prejudice his case in the eyes of the people—particularly as neither Mathews nor Lestock had been confined before their trial, and presumably Byng's arrest would imply great guilt.

The dispatch presented more difficulty: something had to be published in the official *London Gazette* and according to precedent it should be the Admiral's dispatch. But it contained many facts and comments, embarrassing to Ministers trying to offer up its author as a scapegoat—phrases like 'I hope indeed we shall find stores to refit us at Gibraltar; and if I have any reinforcement, will not lose a moment's time to seek the enemy again, and once more give them battle; though they have a great advantage in being clean ships that go three feet to our one.'

The Government's final solution was a simple and utterly immoral one: the dispatch would be secretly censored. Every phrase favourable to Byng would be cut out, along with anything unfavourable to the Government, but in such a way that no one would realize it had been tampered with. As Fox wrote to Wellbore Ellis*: 'You'll see in the *Gazette* an abstract of Byng's letter: he says he beat them, but they are stronger than him, and some other absurdities which we leave out.'[2]

The 'abstracting' was a cynical piece of work. The full version—with the censored portions indicated—is given in Appendix IV; here it is only necessary to draw attention to the more flagrant cuts. At the beginning of the letter Byng said he had met the *Phoenix* and confirmed the strength of the French squadron. This was cut out. So was the whole passage describing how the British squadron had gone to Mahon, seen the British colours flying, and had to leave the scene to deal with the French squadron which had just appeared. Thus anyone reading the *Gazette* version had no idea Byng had ever been near Mahon or had sent the three frigates to get information.

* MP for Weymouth and son of the Bishop of Meath. He was later created Lord Mendip.

One of the worst deletions concealed the damage the squadron had suffered. Byng had written that the *Captain, Intrepid* and *Defiance* had their masts damaged, but the rest of the paragraph was censored. It had said: '. . . so that they were endangered of not being able to secure their masts properly at sea; and also that the squadron in general were very sickly, many killed and wounded, and nowhere to put a third of their number, if I made an hospital even of the 40-gun ship, which is not easy at sea.'

The next cut was the whole passage in which Byng gave his reason for calling the council of war, 'that I might collect their opinions on the present situation' of Minorca and Gibraltar; and 'to make sure of protecting the latter, since it was found impracticable either to succour or relieve the former with the force we had. For though we may justly claim the victory, yet we are much inferior to the weight of their ships, though the numbers are equal . . .' And finally the word 'cover' was cut from the last sentence, which said that he was 'making the best of way to cover Gibraltar . . .'

But this piece of censorship—indeed, it was tantamount to a deliberate forgery—was not the only piece of villainy engineered by the Government that day: they arranged for a virulent piece of gossip, composed almost entirely of complete lies, to be inserted in several newspapers. However, in so doing they gave themselves away, for the *Gazette* with Byng's mutilated dispatch, and the piece of gossip, were published the same day, yet the gossip referred to a council of war being held after the battle—a fact known only to those members of the Government who had seen the dispatch before its publication in the *Gazette*.

The item of 'information' handed over to the newspaper was printed with the introduction: 'We have received the following circumstances, relating to the conduct of a sea officer in great command which, we are told, may be depended upon.'* It then said:

'Though he solicited the command, he *deferred* sailing from England till very pressing letters were sent him from authority; many *strange* delays happened in the course of the voyage; he *lost* seven days at Gibraltar, when the utmost expedition was necessary

---

* Headlines of each item were not used in those days: each story followed the other without a space until the column was filled. The italicized words were so printed in the original.

for the public service; he was *twelve* leagues off *Minorca* where
the *French* fleet *happened* to find him; he called a council as to the
prudence of venturing an engagement; the bad condition of the
enemy's fleet occasioned their only maintaining a running fight;
night and the cautiousness of our Admiral put an entire end to the
skirmish; after staying *four* days without seeing or seeking for the
enemy, a council was called to determine upon the *expediency* of
retrieving Fort St Philip—*the errand they were sent out upon*;
when off Mahon harbour another council was called in which it
was resolved that the endeavouring to throw in the designed
reinforcement was too dangerous . . .' So it went on, concluding
that another resolution of the council of war was 'that the non-
appearance of the enemy's fleet made it probable they were sailed
against *Gibraltar*, and therefore that it was *prudent* to get thither as
fast as possible: where the *British* admiral has since remained in
perfect security and freedom from them.'[3]

Altogether, it was a clear warning of the methods the Government were preparing to use against Byng in order to shield themselves.

Although it had been decided on the 25th to arrest the Admiral,
the actual order was not given until the 29th, when Fox wrote to
the Admiralty that it was the King's pleasure 'that Admiral Byng
be put immediately under arrest, and sent forthwith to England,
in order that he may be brought to his trial, for which purpose your
Lordships will give the necessary directions to Sir Edward
Hawke'. Hawke was also 'to inquire into Mr Byng's conduct after
his arrival before Minorca; in the action with the French; and
subsequent thereto; and particularly as to his leaving the island of
Minorca exposed to the French Fleet.'[4]

One of the first people to hear that Byng was to be arrested and
court martialled was Lady Hervey, Augustus's mother, to whom
Henry Fox wrote on June 25, the day after he had received a long
letter from Augustus in which he described the battle and made
some very frank criticisms of the Government. Hervey had said,
with his usual frankness, 'Every one here calls out loudly on the
manner this fleet was sent and how late, how equipped, no store-
ships, no stores, no hospital ship, no fireship, nor no tender.'[5]

Not surprisingly, such candour made Fox extremely angry. He
sent the letter to Lady Hervey saying that 'I have not shown it to
anybody, because the blaming people here will do neither Mr

Hervey nor them any good'. He was concerned to see how uneasy
the British had been, claiming that they were but equal to the
French, 'though in fact, let them say what they please, they are a
little superior . . .' Byng, he added, 'is sent for and will be tried for
disobedience to orders'.

In reply, Lady Hervey admitted to Fox that she was heartily
vexed about the whole thing, 'both as an English woman and as a
well-wisher to Byng. I am also frightened lest all those who composed the council of war should receive censure.'   However, she
then showed she had a better knowledge of the comparative size
and power of warships than the Secretary of State by gently cor-
recting him: 'The complaint of our Fleet that they were only equal
to that of the French doesn't seem in my opinion to turn upon the
bare equality, but that they are superior in strength whenever they
are equal in number.'[7]

A week later Fox wrote again, giving her a scarcely-veiled warning which presumably he intended she should pass on to Augustus.
He was afraid that young Hervey's gratitude to Byng, 'joined to a
lively disposition may make him talk imprudently when he finds
in how different a light his superiors here look on that Admiral's
conduct from that in which his captains, and particularly Captain
Hervey, represent it. I wish,' Fox added ominously, 'I could advise
him to do his own duty, as I dare say he will, well: and neither
write nor speak of that of others. But particularly not to write his
thoughts on such occasions.'[8]

It was not long before Fox received another letter from Augustus, describing the battle and enclosing four rough charts showing
the course of the action. Once again Fox was far from pleased and
complained to Lady Hervey that although Augustus was obliged
to Byng, 'his account is on the face of it so partial that it won't do
neither Mr Byng nor him any service to show it, but the contrary.
For instance in the list of ships on each side to show how great the
French superiority was, he swells the number and weight of their
guns beyond measure, and actually leaves the *Deptford*, a 50-gun
ship, out of our line, lessening the number of our guns, too, in a
manner every clerk in the Admiralty could contradict it . . .'*

---

* In fact Hervey was correct and Fox wrong. Byng did order the *Deptford*
out of the line, as we have seen; and the number of guns listed by Hervey for
the British squadron was accurate, several cannon having been left behind in
Port Mahon by Edgcumbe's ships before they sailed.

Many letters had arrived from Gibraltar, Fox added, and 'they agree the whole Fleet, his own division as well as West's, cry out against him. I am very sorry for it, and have not, as some of my brother Ministers have, the wretched comfort of thinking that his ill-conduct will divert the blame. We are, notwithstanding that, and shall be, much blamed. The rage of the people increases hourly. I don't deserve blame but that won't save me from it, and though I were to meet with no more than I deserve, that would not alleviate the concern I am under for this great and irretrievable loss . . .'[9]

Fox later wrote to Wellbore Ellis that he expected nothing from Byng's trial 'or, which is singular, wish any ill to him from it, for I can hardly yet believe that it could appear to the officers there as it does to us here.' But, with an eye on the attack that was bound to be made on the Government in Parliament, he added that he fancied they would have a warm session. He then suggested that Ellis should prepare for the onslaught: 'Send to Mr Clevland for materials, look into last winter's conduct, and prepare yourself for as good a defence of it as can be made. As nothing is more wanted as a champion to stand in this Minorca breach, and as nobody is more able, so I think nothing can raise you more than such an undertaking. You'll consider that great things are never attainable by pleasant paths . . .'[10] When Ellis agreed to take on the task, Fox answered: 'Beat them, Ellis . . . and you will be as high in reputation as either vanity or ambition can desire or expect in one session to raise a man.'[11] The Byng affair, he said in another letter, would be 'the subject on which five debates in six will turn'.

Once the newspapers had published news of Byng's arrest, following closely on the censored dispatch and item of 'information', the mob was well and truly roused, as the Government had intended. 'There is no describing the rage against Byng,' Walpole wrote to Sir Horace Mann. 'He has not escaped a sentence of abuse by having involved so many officers in his disgrace and his councils of war: one talks coolly of their being broke and that is all.'[12]

Byng's case was not being helped by letters that had arrived in England from Captain Young of the *Intrepid*, copies of which were being shown round in fashionable drawing-rooms and the more exclusive coffee houses. The *Evening Post*, describing the contents of a letter from Young to his wife, said the *Intrepid* 'was just on the point of sinking, and the Admiral refused sending the least assistance, till two of the captains, observing her distress, bore down betwixt her and the enemy . . . even this they did contrary to the express command of the Admiral, who threatened to break them for so doing.' Clearly Captain Young considered that as soon as the *Intrepid* was damaged (she was far from being 'on the point of sinking') it was quite in order for two other battleships to come to shield him instead of engaging the enemy.

Another letter from Young, which was also being shown round as propaganda, was made up of a garbled version of the exploits of the *Intrepid* and vague sneers at Byng. It contained such a phrase as 'Never was a fleet in better spirits, nor by the behaviour of those ships who did engage, and the eagerness of those who did not to do it, that promised great success' and yet went on to say that 'All the Fleet are open-mouthed against Byng, his own division more than ours [i.e. West's], as are all the land officers who were on board to be landed at Minorca . . . Mr West is greatly displeased.

'I suppose this affair will come to inquiry,' Young wrote. 'I say little, and as I was sufficiently employed myself had little leisure to mind what others did—however, the whole is reducible to one short question. Whether the wind that carried six of us into action would not have brought down the rest, then why did it not?'

This smug letter failed to explain why, if everyone—including West—was so critical of Byng, they all signed the resolutions of the council of war; nor did it reveal that several of the captains had stood in danger of being court martialled for cowardice—at West's instigation. The clue perhaps lies in the fact it was written immediately after the news of Byng's recall reached Gibraltar, and it seems that Young wanted to strike while his alibi was hot.

Fox soon heard of the letter and told Wellbore Ellis that if it was true it 'will go near to condemn Byng . . .' but, he added a couple of days later, 'If anybody thinks that his faults will avert all blame from his superiors [i.e. the Ministers] they will find themselves mistaken. The public anger increases hourly.'[13]

Colonel Edward Cornwallis, a Minorca absentee on board one of Byng's ships, also suddenly discovered he had some scruples and criticisms of his own when he heard that Byng had been disgraced, and promptly wrote to Henry Fox about them. He defended his action at the council of war and, getting his blow in first, said: 'The action I was witness of I am ashamed of; the thought of it hurts me sorely. The behaviour of the French could not have been equalled by anything but ours, it was so shameful.

Notwithstanding their superiority, had the Blue Flag [Byng's division] behaved as gallantly as the Red [West's], I am convinced the victory must have been ours. May the honour of the nation be retrieved by their successors, pray God.'[14]

As a commanding officer absent from his post, which was at the head of his regiment in besieged Fort St Philip, and who signed the resolutions of both Fowke's and Byng's councils of war, the Colonel can be dismissed as a hypocrite trying to save his own skin: the letter, like Captain Young's, was written from Gibraltar just four days after Hawke arrived with news of Fowke's disgrace and Byng's dismissal, and sixteen days after the squadron had arrived. For twelve days the gallant Colonel had managed to keep silent . . .

By the beginning of July the campaign against Byng was in full swing: hired hacks prepared pamphlets, suborned journalists wrote malicious articles and lampoons. Newspapers often carried on the same page one long article attacking and another defending the Admiral. Few newspapers at this time had a set policy, but most had a price. The theme of the attack against Byng, apparently, was to be cowardice: any other charge—such as incompetence— might involve the Ministers, since it involved the question of what sort of force Byng had. Cowardice was safe enough, since it was concerned only with the few hours of the actual fighting.

One of the first lampoons to be published purported to be a resolution 'By a general court of sailors . . . held at the Lyon [sic] and Anchor, in Wapping, and declared 'that Mr Byng, the Chief d'Escadre in the Middle Seas, should be exemplarily punished for cowardice . . .' A week later some verse was published 'On a Certain Most Honourable Admiral.'

> If you believe what the Frenchmen say,
> B - - g came, was beat, and run away.
> Believe what B - - g himself had said,
> He fought, he conquered, and he fled.
> To fly when beat is no new thing;
> Thousands have done it, as well as B - - g:
> But no man did, before B - - g, say,
> He conquer'd, and then run away.
> B - - g therefore is, without a fable,
> An Admiral most admirable.

In Birmingham on July 1, an effigy of Byng was burnt in the

market place with an inscription on it that 'Acts of Cowardice in those who are esteemed their country's defenders should always be treated in this manner'.

A few days later, on July 13, the *Post* came out with:

> Cries Blakeney to Byng, as he kept at a distance,
> 'You'll be hanged, you poltroon, if you don't bring assistance.'
> 'Why aye,' replied Byng, 'What you say may be true;
> But I may chance to be shot if I do:
> Sudden death I abhor; while there's life there's hope:
> Let me 'scape but the gun, I can buy off the rope.'

Lord Anson's biographer wrote that 'Poor Byng was burnt in effigy in all the great towns; his seat and park in Hertfordshire [Wrotham Park] were assaulted by the mob, and with difficulty saved. The streets and shops swarmed with injurious ballads, libels and caricature prints with some of which was mingled a little justice on the Ministers, who were accused of neglect in not dispatching a fleet sooner, and an inefficient one when they did.'[15]

As far as the Government were concerned, everything was turning out better than they had hoped: Hawke had been sent to take over from Byng, and might well save something out of the mess in the Mediterranean; Byng was to be arrested and the mob's wrath seemed to have been diverted on to his head and not the Government's; and the stage was set for the trial of Byng as soon as he was brought back. With such a scapegoat already virtually under lock and key it seemed the Ministers could relax. But within a few days all their hopes of a rest were to be shattered.

Although few people expected that Sir Edward Hawke would be able to save Minorca, the news that General Blakeney had finally surrendered Fort St Philip to the French came as a shock to both the Duke of Newcastle and the King. As usual, the first report came from the Spanish Ambassador, who sent a note round to Henry Fox on July 15[16] enclosing information he had just received from his colleague in Paris.*

The news made the old King extremely angry—a fact a nervous Duke of Newcastle reported to the Earl of Hardwicke. The Earl's

---

* The information was correct: the Fort surrendered on June 29 after a heavy attack. Under the terms of the surrender, Blakeney and all his troops were repatriated to Gibraltar. The garrison had lost 251 men killed and missing.[17]

reply gave him little comfort: 'I cannot help wishing that His Majesty would seriously look towards a peace, tho' at a distance tho' endeavouring to lay some scheme and put things in train for that purpose; for that this war is hopeless and may be ruinous I have been for some time convinced.'[18]

This was discouraging advice for his Grace, coming as it did from someone who had done as much as anybody to bring about the war, and arriving on the same day as an intelligence report from France (probably sent by Cressener) saying that he understood 'Spain will certainly be tempted by the cession of Minorca and the assurance of Gibraltar, to join in the war'.[19]

The Duke now became completely demoralized: while professing in a loud voice that he feared for the nation, he complained even louder that he was being blamed for everything. It was altogether too much: he sat down and composed a long letter to Lord Hardwicke. 'I own, my Lord, the loss of Port Mahon affects me so much that there is scarce any measure or almost any expense that I would not be for, if there could be any reasonable prospect of success. I doubt if any possession belonging to this country (except Ireland) either in Europe or in the Indies, is of much more consequence to us,' he wrote—forgetting that this had not been the view when the Inner Committee originally delayed sending out a squadron and reinforcing the garrison.

They must not expect to be without their share of the blame, he said, and no doubt the Opposition 'will endeavour (if it is possible) to fling it *singly* upon me, or if that can't be done, to make me answerable for other people's neglects or weaknesses'. However, he declared, 'I hope I have too much truth, and too much honour, to excuse myself by flinging the blame upon others'. The Cabinet should meet next day and until there was a prospect of peace 'some scheme or measure of offence and attack must be thought of, or we shall be absolutely ruined'. In addition, he hoped Hardwicke would talk seriously to Anson to prepare a defence of the Government in the Commons 'and also (which is still of more consequence) for the immediate trial and condemnation of Admiral Byng, if as I think there can be no doubt he deserves it. The sea officers should be learnt [*sic*] to talk in this manner, and not to think to fling the blame upon civil Ministers. Your Lordship knows the little share *we* have in military operations, or in the choice of military men, either at sea or land. And it would be

very unjust for us to suffer where we have scarce been consulted
(I mean this only as to operations at land),'[20] he concluded, forgetting his earlier protest that he had too much honour to 'fling
the blame upon others'.

That letter must rank as one of the most lamentable ever
written by a leading British Minister, yet the Duke's panic continued unabated as the days passed; indeed, if anything, it increased. 'Let me entreat you to think seriously of some object [for
us to attack],' he wrote to Fox on July 24. 'We had better fail in
the attempt than attempt nothing. Nothing but some attempt will
or can retrieve our situation.' What about Corsica? Or Genoa? Or
Minorca? ('I can never get it out of my head but that some way or
other we may get back Port Mahon.') Or America ('Let Lord
Loudon know that conquests in America is our point'). As far as
Byng was concerned 'the very trial would put an end at once to
many lies upon that head'.[21]

While the Duke was penning these revealing letters, the
Admiralty were worrying in case Byng had sailed for England in
the *Antelope* before Hawke received the Board's order to arrest
him. To ensure that Byng would be under arrest when he set foot
in England—with all the disgrace that it would imply—they drew
up an order which read, 'In case His Majesty's Ship the *Antelope*
or any other ship with Admiral Byng on board shall arrive at
Spithead, you are hereby required and directed in pursuance of
the King's Pleasure . . . to put him under arrest and keep him in
confinement on board that ship till further orders.'[22]

This was sent to the Commander-in-Chief at Portsmouth and
caused him much distress, for he was none other than Vice-Admiral
Henry Osborn, whose elder brother John had married Byng's
sister Sarah. A similar order was sent to Vice-Admiral Thomas
Smith, commanding in The Downs, and a third to the Commander-in-Chief at Plymouth.

The contents of these letters were revealed to the Press, who
quickly informed the mob that 'We hear there are expresses
dispatched with orders to put Admiral Byng under an arrest the
moment he arrives in any of our ports.' They added in unison a
few days later that 'Letters have been received from some captains
of the Mediterranean Fleet in which they say they signed the
resolution of the council of war to return to Gibraltar not because
they approved of such a step but because they foresaw that they

would throw away the King's ships and their own lives to no purpose if they ventured another engagement under such an admiral.'

Although the letters and the news that he was to be arrested as soon as he set foot in England roused the mob once more against Admiral Byng, an article in the *Evening Post* showed that the opponents of the Government were still on the alert. It appeared on the same day as the item referring to the letters from Gibraltar, and made a trenchant demand for an inquiry into the reasons for the loss of Minorca. 'None are so fit to lead the way towards such an inquiry as the City of London, in its corporate capacity, together with the merchants and other eminent traders, by giving instructions to their representatives to search deeply and find out domestic enemies,' it said.

The first friendly pamphlet in Admiral Byng's defence was *A Modest Apology for the Conduct of a Certain Admiral in the Mediterranean*, which was published in Paternoster Row and hawked round the streets. It was written, so its anonymous author claimed, to display 'The folly and injustice of determining in matters of moment by hearsay, an error too frequent among the English.'

He added, 'It hath heretofore been thought necessary by Power occasionally to sacrifice a victim to state policy, with intent to amuse and divert the populace from delving too deep into political mysteries and tracing effects up to their prime causes; this finesse is not badly illustrated in the fable of the monkey's hugging the cat and using her claw to scratch chestnuts out of the fire withal . . .'

No one had yet questioned 'the many absurdities, palpable falsehoods, and gross misrepresentations which public rumour has lately vented about Mr B, a gentleman who deserves a suspension from such malignant abuse, at least till proofs can support malice . . . In the present case we have seen a flood of abuse flowing in ballads, newspapers, magazines and public prints, all founded upon a letter, or rather an extract from one, written by Mr B.'

The Gazeteer joined the fray with a powerful attack on the Government by 'Britannicus', who pointed out that Minorca was an island with the two best ports in the Mediterranean which, therefore, might have been made 'the magazine of British commodities and the centre of a most extensive commerce.' Instead, the Government had lost this island, which had given Britain the respect of Spain, the confidence of Italy, and the submission of the piratical states of Barbary. Yet, he pointed out, the French while planning its capture, did not keep their intention a secret. Intelligence appeared in foreign newspapers and 'was repeated and dwelt upon in our public papers—the public papers which some have represented as canals of sedition might have been, in this and many other instances, instruments of public safety'.[23]

The *Evening Post* followed this up with an article saying that whatever Byng's faults, he could not be blamed because a fleet 'was not sent up the Mediterranean time enough to prevent the invasion of Minorca'; nor was it his fault that the garrison of Fort St Philip was not reinforced before the French invasion, and so small a fleet was sent out 'when there easily and without hazard at home might have been sent double that number'.

The outspoken and irascible Lord Tyrawley had by now taken over from General Fowke in Gibraltar and, after a good look round the base, had become extremely angry over what he found. His survey confirmed Byng's—indeed, his letter to the Secretary at War went a good deal further and in far less temperate language. 'You will see that this town is granted away in property to fellows perhaps escaped out of Newgate and their wives whipped out of Bridewell, to the utter impossibility of lodging the King's troops with tolerable convenience', he wrote.

His Lordship went on to list the base's defects. 'We are almost without powder, ball, beds or ordnance, stores of any sort, though repeatedly long since demanded; the whole extent of the line wall, above three miles in length, undefended for want of a sufficient number of cannon to plant upon it, or carriages to plant them upon.' Naval storehouses and warehouses were filled with rubbish, he declared; every gun all round the town was 'planted so high that one would imagine this town was to be approached through the middle region, and not through the earth or sea'.

But the new Governor was not finished yet. 'Former Governors put all the money arising from this town into their pockets. Bland* sent it all home to the Treasury when in truth it should go

---

* General Sir Humphrey Bland, a former Governor of Gibraltar.

neither of these ways but be strictly accounted for and all employed for the service of the place, which between the rapaciousness of governors and General Humphrey Bland's politics, is gone to ruin.

'If Gibraltar is of consequence something must be done, and that speedily too, for if it could be done today it should not be postponed till tomorrow. All the stores here demanded should be sent instantly, without the abatement of one single nail.' Gibraltar, he declared, 'must be restored to its first intention, *une place de guerre*; whereas it is dwindled into a trading town for Jews, Genoese and pickpockets from which no advantage results to England that I can find out.'[24]

This startling criticism needed to be made, and Tyrawley was the man to do it, for when Byng had made a much milder protest about the naval stores (about which Tyrawley was even more scathing) he was labelled a defeatist; indeed, Boscawen, who was a member of the Board, accused him of cheating the Government.

15

A CELL IN THE TOWER?

THE BYNG FAMILY, reading attack after savage attack on the Admiral in the newspapers and constantly hearing the shrill cries of pamphlet sellers echoing in the streets, were waiting anxiously for the Admiral's return. Sarah was still at Stratton Street but—perhaps mercifully—their mother, Lady Torrington, had died before hearing her son being accused of cowardice. The sickly Ned waited at his house in Grosvenor Street, expecting at any moment an express from Admiral Osborn saying that his brother had reached Portsmouth.

Henry Osborn was in a very difficult situation: like all admirals at this time, his future rested with the party in power; yet cutting across that consideration was his personal loyalty to Byng, and he must have been dreading the task before him.

When the little *Antelope* finally reached Spithead just before lunch on Monday, July 26, Osborn boarded his barge to carry out the most distasteful orders of his career, and was taken out to the anchorage. When the salutes and formalities were over, he asked Byng to receive him alone in his cabin. There, with all the tact he could muster, he showed him the Admiralty letter ordering his arrest. Byng was thunderstruck: already angry and resentful at being recalled, he had not received the slightest hint that he was going to be tried or, what was in many ways worse, put under arrest.

Osborn returned on shore and wrote a brief note to the Admiralty: 'I send by this express to acquaint their Lordships of the arrival of the *Antelope*, and of my having caused Admiral Byng to be in arrest [sic] on board the said ship, agreeable to their Lordships' directions.'[1]

Rear-Admiral West, too, was very angry at his recall, and he wrote to the Admiralty from his cramped cabin on board the *Antelope* that he proposed 'going soon to Town', and that 'The mortification of this public disgrace cannot but be sensibly felt by an officer whose utmost endeavour all his life long has been to serve his King and Country'. He enclosed 'in justice to myself' an extract from the letter Byng wrote to him after the battle thanking him 'a thousand and a thousand times'.[2] Nevertheless, apart from being recalled, West was not to be tried (indeed, he was employed again very soon, and as we shall see later, the King went out of his way to pay him a compliment).

The Board had to wait for another twenty-four hours before they received a letter from Byng. Commenting on his arrest, he said he could not help being surprised nor avoid 'desiring to be acquainted with the reasons of my confinement which, even if their Lordships are disposed to look upon me as a criminal, I presume I have a natural right to'.[3]

A brief acknowledgement from Clevland[4] still gave no hint of the charge, and the reason was not hard to find: the Government, despite the hue and cry they had raised against Byng, still had no idea of what the charge was going to be. When the Board met they considered Byng's letter and hedged by ordering that 'he is to be acquainted that the directions for confining him were in pursuance of the King's Pleasure, in order to his being brought to a trial for his conduct and behaviour in the Mediterranean'. The Board also ordered that Admiral Osborn was to hand Byng over to the Marshal of the Admiralty, who was to take the Admiral into his custody on board the *Antelope*.[5]

The warrant for Byng's arrest which was given to the Marshal of the High Court of Admiralty—to give Mr William Brough his full title—was an impressive document which contained a long recital of Byng's actions and omissions—actual or alleged—in the Mediterranean, and ended with an exhortation to Brough to 'safely keep him till delivered by due course of law'.[6] The captain of the *Antelope* was told to make sure Brough had all the guards he needed.[7]

However, by the time the Board's unsatisfactory reply arrived on board the *Antelope*, Admiral Byng had already more than enough to worry him. His brother Ned, warned on Tuesday by Henry Osborn that the *Antelope* had at last arrived, had set off on a hurried visit to Portsmouth. He was far from well, but the idea of staying idle in Grosvenor Street while his brother was under arrest never entered his head, and a coach was soon clattering down the hot and dusty Portsmouth road. But by the time he arrived at the harbour on Wednesday afternoon, Ned was worn out and feverish, his already sick body twisted up with worry for the safety of his brother Jack. Henry Osborn put a boat at his disposal to take him out to the *Antelope*.

A lot had happened since the two brothers parted less than four months earlier. Ned had to tell the Admiral that their mother had died. Old Lady Torrington had seemed almost immortal: the warm and whimsical personality of their childhood, sheltering them from the wrath of their father when the occasion arose, had been a considerable influence on their lives. The two brothers had much else to talk about. John was calm, convinced of the rightness of his cause, almost contemptuous of the behaviour of the Admiralty and, despite Ned's descriptions, he had not yet realized the ugly and powerful forces that were building up against him. Ned, who had been reading the virulent attacks on his brother in the newspapers, seeing the mobs and hearing the gossip, trying to sort out the truth from the lies, was probably enough of a realist to know this was not to be a straightforward court martial: his brother's real accusers were men who stayed in the shadows: men with immense power and influence: men who would be proved guilty if the Admiral was proved innocent.

Ned was too upset and ill to go on shore that night, so a cot was arranged for him in the Admiral's cabin on board the *Antelope*. Next morning he was feverish and Byng sent for the *Antelope's* surgeon. By noon Ned was lying dead in his brother's cabin—having been, according to the surgeon, seized with fatal convulsions brought about by his weak constitution, fatigue and anxiety.

Death was striking savage blows at the Byng family: of the six children of Admiral Lord Torrington who reached their twenty-first birthday, only John and Sarah now survived: the title had already reached the fourth holder—the present Lord Torrington was a boy at school. Since Sarah had written to her son Danvers in July 1751 about her 'persentiment of coming evil', Danvers himself*, Mrs Hickson, her mother, and Edward had died. And—although at this time no one in England knew it—five weeks before Admiral Byng arrived at Spithead, her nephew Robert

---

* In 1753 Danvers had been appointed Governor of New York. Sailing from England in August, he arrived in New York on October 6 and was found dead in the grounds of the Governor's House on October 12.

(son of her brother Robert, and brother of Midshipman John) had perished along with 122 others in a twenty-foot-square prison cell which a shocked world was later to call the Black Hole of Calcutta.

The day after Ned's death Byng wrote to the Admiralty saying that he hoped 'no cause can be assigned for treating me with greater severity and stricter confinement than other officers who, when their conduct was doubted of, were ordered to prepare for their trials'. He cited Admirals Mathews and Lestock, 'who were indulged with leave to regulate their affairs on shore at large, more especially as such an enlargement is to me particularly necessary at present, having an only brother who, tho' in a very bad state of health came down to see me, and now lies dead by me in the cabin.

'I presume,' he concluded, 'that it is unnecessary to represent to their Lordships the natural consequences of such an unhappy circumstance in a family which must depend on me for its regulation; and I hope that even my supposed misconduct cannot be looked upon as a misdemeanour of a higher nature than the gentlemen before-mentioned were supposed to be guilty of before their trials; or my parole or security for my personal appearance when and wherever it shall be required, less rated than theirs.'[8]

It was a dignified letter, yet from his assumption that a request for freedom would produce it, it seems certain that despite Ned's warning he still did not realize the peril in which he stood. Clevland replied next day, enclosing a copy of the warrant sent to the Admiralty Marshal and saying that 'as to your enlargement I have only to acquaint you at present that orders will be given next week for your being brought to Town'.[9]

In the meantime there was Ned's funeral to be arranged. 'What a cruel star,' wrote Lady Torrington, George's widow, 'presides over this family at present. Last Friday night an express came from Admiral Byng at Portsmouth to acquaint me with the melancholy account of Col. E. Byng's death, and to desire my leave for his body to be brought to Southill and interred in the family vault. It is some consolation to hear the Admiral makes not the least doubt but that he shall be able to show that he has acted in every respect like an officer.'[10] Fortunately the Admiral's cousin, Edmund Bramston, had by now arrived from his home at Hall Place, near Worting in Hampshire, to help him settle his affairs.

While Byng arranged his brother's funeral, the Government tried to make up its mind where to keep the Admiral. The Marshalsea was the prison for those who had committed offences on the high seas—but it was hardly the place for a man who was an admiral, a Member of Parliament, and the son of a peer. Henry Fox had a better idea: he should be lodged in the Tower of London. It was the traditional prison for traitors—indeed, even queens had gone through its Traitors' Gate, a factor which no doubt the mob would bear in mind.

Fox wrote an unambiguous letter to Anson on July 30, which, bearing in mind that Byng was an Admiralty and not a political prisoner and that people such as Mathews and Lestock had never been arrested before their trials, and General Fowke and Temple West were still at liberty, gives an indication of the single-mindedness with which Byng was being hunted down: 'I am persuaded it ought not to be left to ordinary care, which perhaps is to the Marshal of the Admiralty . . . I conjure your Lordship therefore to consider well what hands you trust him to, and I own I should advise him to be brought by land, under a strong guard, and lodged in the Tower. If your Lordship will consider what would be said and believed if he should escape, I am certain you will think it ought to be made impossible. If he should die before trial, it would be bad, and there is hardly anybody whom I more heartily wish health to till his trial shall be over, than to Mr Byng.'[11]

Anson agreed wholeheartedly with the proposal. In the Anson Papers at the British Museum there is a note in Anson's handwriting which is the draft of his reply to Fox. 'I am entirely of your opinion with regard to securing Admiral Byng in the Tower, for I do think (from his former situation in the Fleet) he might have a chance to escape if he had any such intention. A letter is wrote to the Secretary at War for a strong guard to bring him to Town from Portsmouth . . .'[12]

And an undated office memorandum in Anson's writing says: 'Whether the Marshal of the Admiralty may not be permitted to carry Admiral Byng to the Tower for his better security. And if the Constable of the Tower may not be directed to let the Marshal have a proper apartment for this purpose and to assist him with whatever he shall desire for the security of his prisoner, by ordering warders &c to guard him under direction of the Marshal.'[13]

Fox managed to infect the easily-disturbed Duke of Newcastle with his fears, and His Grace wrote to Clevland on July 31 that he had 'some very serious discourse with Mr Fox upon Admiral Byng's trial. He agrees with me that all possible care should be taken to prevent *the possibility of an escape*, and that can best be done by sending for him immediately by land under a strong guard and committing him to the Tower'.[14]

On the same day—a Saturday—a Board meeting composed of Anson, Duncannon and Richard Edgcumbe finally decided on the charge Byng was to face. The accusation was framed under the Twelfth Article of War and said: 'That he withdrew and did not do what was in his power to destroy the French Fleet, nor assist His Majesty's ships engaged with them, and that he did not do his utmost to succour St Philip's Fort in the island of Minorca.'

A letter was sent to Lord Barrington, the Secretary at War, telling him that Byng was to be brought to London and 'it will be requisite he should be escorted by a strong guard'. Osborn was ordered to shift Byng from the little *Antelope* to the *Royal Anne*, a 110-gun first-rate, and arrange for 'a proper and efficient guard of Marines'.[15]

Having persuaded Anson and the Duke of Newcastle that Admiral Byng should be lodged safely in the Tower, Fox was far from satisfied with the safety of his own position. 'The rage of the people, and considerate people, for the loss of Minorca increases hourly,' he wrote to the Duke of Devonshire. 'I have not more than my share of blame, which falls on the Duke of Newcastle in so violent a degree that if he were not a very different make from what he has been represented, he could never be so cheerful as he is.' But when Parliament met, the scene of action would be the House of Commons, 'and I, being the only figure of a Minister there, shall of course draw all the odium on me'.[16]

Fox was, indeed, in a politically difficult and dangerous situation: in the Inner Committee—which met irregularly—his advice and opinions were frequently outweighed by those of Newcastle, Hardwicke and Anson, and even in normal times the Duke distrusted him. Although friendly with the Duke of Cumberland, he was out of favour with the old King, who had declared to Newcastle that 'He is black; I know it tho' I don't show it'.[17]

Meanwhile detailed preparations were being made to bring Admiral Byng to the Tower. The War Office had ordered the commanding officer of the 3rd Regiment of Dragoons, who were stationed at Guildford and Godalming, to send a detachment of fifty men to Portsmouth 'to be aiding and assisting to the Marshal of the Admiralty in safely bringing Admiral Byng prisoner from Portsmouth to Kingston'. There the Dragoons would be relieved by a detachment of Horse Guards. The Dragoons were 'not to repel force with force unless it shall be found absolutely necessary', or ordered by the civil magistrates, who were enjoined to help provide quarters, impress carriages 'and otherwise as there shall be the occasion'.[18]

Admiral Osborn was told on August 1 to land his prisoner on Thursday morning, August 5, and hand him over to the escort, while Byng was told that the Dragoons were 'for your security'. Yet at the last minute the Ministers changed their minds, and an Admiralty messenger was sent off to Portsmouth at 3.30 p.m. on Wednesday with fresh orders for Osborn. The explanation was given in a letter from the Admiralty to the Secretary at War— 'It being uncertain whether the Marshal of the Admiralty may secure Admiral Byng in the Tower', the Board thought it necessary to keep Byng at Portsmouth for the time being.[19]

However, Admiral Byng and his escort of fifty Dragoons had already left for London, and the Admiralty messenger passed them on his way to Portsmouth, where he arrived at 3.30 a.m. Vice-Admiral Osborn, roused from his bed to receive the Admiralty's letter, told the messenger to hurry back along the London road and show it to Mr Brough, the Marshal, who was travelling in Admiral Byng's coach.[20]

Byng, already angry that soldiers—and so many of them—should be escorting him when he was in fact an Admiralty prisoner, was even angrier at being brought back to Portsmouth again, and as soon as he was taken on board the Commissioner's yacht to be returned to the *Royal Anne*, he wrote a letter of protest to the Admiralty. 'I cannot but think the whole affair has been attended with great severity towards me; exposed and tossed from one prison to another; then on shore; and now back again to the *Royal Anne*: I believe a treatment the meanest subject seldom or ever met with.'[21]

The Admiralty received this letter next day, Friday, and by then the Government had at last made up their mind: Admiral Byng was to be imprisoned at the Royal Hospital at Greenwich, and was to start his journey there on the following Monday.[22] Now that the charges, and the place where he was to be imprisoned had been decided, the Board set about getting the evidence which would prove him guilty. Neither the Admiralty nor the Government apparently considered that it would have been more usual to do it the other way round—first obtain the evidence and, on that, determine whether or not a charge should be made.

There were several officers already in England including the captains of the *Ramillies* and the *Buckingham* and they ought to be questioned at once. Orders were made out for Charles Fearne who, a year earlier, had been fifth in seniority of the Admiralty's eight clerks, at a salary of £100 a year, and who was now acting as Judge-Advocate. He was given a list of Byng's officers and told 'to examine them as to what they know of his conduct and behaviour, and of the proceedings of the squadron'.

The sudden order to Fearne was probably caused by a letter from Byng two days earlier enclosing a list 'of such evidences as at present occur to my memory as necessary for my defence'. Some were already in England and others were still in the Mediterranean but, said Byng, he had kept the list as short as possible in order 'not in any manner to distress the service'.[23]

On Monday morning, August 9, the Commissioner's yacht brought Byng on shore to the gun wharf at Portsmouth and with his guardian, Brough, and the fifty Dragoons, he started off for London once again. It was not until the Horse Guards detachment took over from the Dragoons at Kingston that he discovered he was to be imprisoned at Greenwich.[24] Darkness fell as the carriage and its escort clattered into London, and midnight had struck before it reached Greenwich Hospital (or, to give it its then full title, the Royal Hospital for Disabled Seamen).

The Hospital was commanded by Admiral Isaac Townshend, a thoroughly unpleasant officer whose main aim in life was to please the Governors—and there were dozens of them, including the Archbishop of Canterbury, three dukes, several judges, all the flag officers of the Fleet and the Lord Mayor of London. Townshend was naturally aware of the attitude of the mob and the Government towards Byng and he acted accordingly. Byng therefore found his cell was on the top floor of the Queen Anne block. As a newspaper later reported, 'On his arrival he expressed himself in this manner, "That as he was the son of a peer, a

Member of Parliament, and a Vice-Admiral in the British Fleet, to be shut up in so mean an apartment, a garret, was using him very ill; adding that he would convince the world that he had done his duty." This usage he highly resented.' He was told 'he was to accommodate himself as well as he could; which for the remainder of the night he did accordingly by making a choice of the floor and his portmanteau.'

Sentries were put at his door and changed every two hours. More guards stood on the stairs. In the next room, almost as much a prisoner as his charge, was Mr Brough, the Admiralty Marshal.

16

LIBELLING THE DUKE

MOST OF THE UPROAR against Admiral Byng had been—apart from a few demonstrations in provincial towns—confined to London, where the mob could be easily roused by Government sympathizers. But almost imperceptibly at first, like the turn of the tide, a reaction set in; not among the mob, who ranted and rioted for hard cash or noisy fun, but among the more educated folk living in provincial cities and towns, especially the solid core of responsible citizens such as the justices of the peace and leading businessmen.

After the initial outburst against Admiral Byng, these people began to ponder; and the more they pondered the more they realized that whatever Byng's shortcomings, Minorca had been completely neglected and was, in effect, lost even before Byng reached Gibraltar. In addition, they were all apparently living in peril of a French invasion of the British Isles and the news from America was also extremely disturbing.

The first rumble of provincial discontent came when Buckinghamshire's grand jury resolved at the assizes held on August 8 that the MPs for the county 'be desired to promote to the utmost of their power, an inquiry in Parliament into the present dangerous and most desperate state of the Kingdom', and into why 'the important island of Minorca, for the want of timely succour, hath been totally lost'.

Four days later, an address to the King on the subject of Minorca from the High Sheriff, grand jury, justices of the peace and gentlemen of Dorset was presented to the county's MPs, declaring 'This attempt of our national and inveterate enemy was so notorious that very few of Your Majesty's faithful subjects had the least doubt of the design, long before it was put in execution; yet the island was left defenceless.' The worthy men of Dorset hoped the King would start an inquiry and punish the guilty.

Similar and equally vociferous demands were soon coming in from all over the country: on the next day, August 13, the Bedford assizes ended with the High Sheriff and grand jury calling for a Parliamentary inquiry, and Hereford followed. Bury St Edmunds also addressed itself to its MPs, one of whom had the stirring name of Sir Cordell Firebrace, to 'exhort and conjure' them to demand an investigation, while at Huntingdon Lord Carysfoot and Mr Coulson Fellowes, knights of the shire, were told on August 21 that the grand jury 'earnestly request that you will zealously promote an inquiry'. Shropshire followed suit within a week; Bristol asked that 'those persons (if any such there be) who have either wantonly neglected or treacherously betrayed the honour of the nation may not escape punishment due to these atrocious crimes'.

In the meantime several newspapers had been calling on the City of London to assert itself: 'The whole Kingdom,' said the *Evening Post*, 'flies to the ancient and famous City of London for safety,' asking them to 'Awake, citizens, awake! Set before your eyes your glorious ancestors entreating you to bestir yourselves to preserve that security and happiness which they purchased for you with so much blood.'

Before the horrified Ministers were able to lift a finger to stop them the Lord Mayor, Aldermen and Commons of the City of London, 'in Common Council assembled', had drawn up an address to the King. The Duke of Newcastle had heard of the address too late to do anything about it, and his memorandum, dated August 12, for the resultant Inner Committee meeting opens with: 'To send Mr West to Sir John Barnard, to talk to him about the Common Council and know his opinion what should be done, and what answer should be given. To get all our friends to attend the Common Council. [It then lists eight men] To consider the answer to the City address. To get a copy of it immediately. Whether any answer at all? See the precedents of that . . .'[1]

The thought that the City was on his trail naturally dismayed the Duke, and a miserable West came back from the City to report that he found their friend Sir John Barnard, a leading Whig financier and MP for the City of London, 'in great concern at the behaviour of the Common Council. He told me he thought it a very unbecoming and improper measure entirely out of their sphere and contrary to the constitution; that when he went there he knew that

The Hon John Byng, Admiral of the Blue: 'The unfortunate
Admiral was shot because Newcastle deserved to be hanged'

A page from the log of HMS *Monarch*, the ship in which Byng was executed. Part of the entry for March 14 says: '¼ past 7 am Mr Byng's coffin was brought a bord . . . at 10 ye boats mand and armd came along side to attend the excicution of Mr Byng. Do. ye marines was all under arms. At 11 lowerd down our lower yards and at 12 Mr Byng was shot dead by 6 marines and put into his coffin.'

Captain the Hon Augustus Hervey: he risked his career to help
Admiral Byng

Mrs Sarah Osborn, Byng's sister, who had 'a persentiment of coming Evil'

Lord Anson, First Lord of the Admiralty at the time Byng
was sent to Minorca

Vice-Admiral Henry Osborn, Sarah's brother-in-law, who had to arrest his friend John Byng

Captain George Edgcumbe, later Earl Mount Edgcumbe, who commanded the *Lancaster* in the Battle of Minorca

Vice-Admiral Thomas Smith, president of the
court-martial which sentenced Admiral Byng to
death

Vice-Admiral the Hon E. Boscawen: he thought
Byng was a coward

Vice-Admiral Sir Edward Hawke: he was rushed
out to replace Byng

General Lord Blakeney, the defender of Fort St Philip

Wrotham Park: one of Byng's nephews called it a 'stare-about pile'
From a print dated 1812

Captain Augustus Keppel (painted many years after):
although one of the court who condemned Byng,
he later tried to save his life

A contemporary plan of Fort St Philip in Minorca

Marquis de la Galissonnière: he commanded
the French squadron

The Duke of Newcastle

The Earl of Hardwicke, Lord Chancellor and
the Duke of Newcastle's 'Grey Eminence'

Henry Fox

The trial of Admiral Byng on board the *St George*. The members of the court are on the far side of the table and Byng sits in front, to the right, and the witness opposite him, on the left.—*From the 'London Magazine,' 1757*

There were numerous satirical prints and broadsheets published about the Battle: this one depicts the council of war—*From a contemporary print*

The quarterdeck of HMS *Monarch*: Admiral Byng gives the signal to the firing squad for his own execution.—

From a contemporary print

it was impossible to stem the impetuosity and madness of the people.'²

It rained all day on August 20, when the City dignitaries arrived at the Palace to present their address to the King, and a sharp south-east wind was blowing. As far as the Government was concerned, it was appropriate weather for the City to deliver an address which declared that 'The loss of the important fortress of St Philip's and island of Minorca (possessions of the utmost consequence to the commerce and naval strength of Great Britain) without any attempt, by timely and effectual succours, to prevent or defeat an attack, after such early notice of the enemy's intentions, and when Your Majesty's Navy was so evidently superior to theirs will, we fear, be an indelible reproach on the honour of the British nation.' They were also apprehensive for His Majesty's possessions in America, which, they pointed out, were the object of the present war, and 'the principal source of the wealth and strength of the Kingdom'.

The address concluded with a scarcely-veiled threat from the City, without whose loans no government could wage a war: the King's love of justice, it said, would no doubt lead him to direct 'the authors of our late losses and disappointment, to be inquired into and punished'.

The King was thoroughly alarmed, and told the City dignitaries that although 'the events of war are uncertain', nothing would stop him carrying it on with vigour, and 'I will not fail to do justice upon any persons who shall have been wanting in their duty to me, and their country'.³

In the meantime, General Fowke had been punished for his behaviour at Gibraltar. The warrant for the court martial, signed by Lord Holdernesse, accused him in the name of the King of 'Disobeying our order signified by our Secretary of State at War to send a reinforcement or reinforcements of troops from the garrison of Gibraltar to the island of Minorca, in breach of the trust reposed in him'.⁴ The trial was held on Tuesday, August 10, in the Privy Garden.

Fowke claimed that he did not call the council of war 'to inquire whether His Majesty's commands should be obeyed, but to understand the orders sent me by the Secretary at War, that I might obey them punctually and precisely'. Whatever his feelings had been about the defence of Minorca the previous May, Fowke's tactics for his own defence three months later were to attack— quickly. Ignoring the fact that Barrington's orders were comprehensible when read in conjunction with those to Byng, he asked Barrington if he had not intended to recall the first letter when he wrote the second. Barrington admitted that he did not refer to it, but had he thought of it he would have recalled the first, since the second was intended to supersede it.

When Fowke asked if it was not the custom when one set of orders were substituted by another 'to recite and contradict them in the subsequent order', Barrington excused himself by saying that at the time he had been Secretary at War for only four months and 'not master of the exact forms'. He conceded that it would be usual to say 'Notwithstanding former orders'. He had not done so in this case, he said, as he 'knew that General Fowke could not have received the former order'. This was a ridiculous remark, and Fowke was quick to thank Barrington for his candour in confessing that he did not intend the first order to reach him. Since such a large part of his orders had been delivered when they should have been recalled, he pointed out, there was bound to be a great deal of confusion over the remainder. He added that, 'I cannot surely be condemned of disobedience to orders which, even by the writer himself, are thus candidly acknowledged were sent out by mistake.'

That round went to Fowke, and it is remarkable that Barrington had not been guided by the First Clerk at the War Office, Thomas Sherwin, when drawing up Fowke's orders. Sherwin's evidence did not cover this point nor did Fowke ask him about it. Rear-Admiral West* was called and asked, at Fowke's request, about the General's offer to Byng of a battalion of troops. (See page 87.) Byng was not called to give evidence, and the court, 'upon mature deliberation', decided that Fowke was 'guilty of the charge exhibited against him; and doth adjudge that he shall be suspended for the space of one year'.

'I wish your Grace joy of the decision of the court martial,' Robert Nugent, MP for Bristol, wrote to the Duke of Newcastle,

---

* The Press had previously reported that on July 28 at Kensington Palace 'where there was the greatest levee that has been known for several months', West was 'distinguished by His Majesty in a very particular manner, who was pleased to say, "Admiral West, I am glad to see you; I return you my thanks for your gallant behaviour, and wish every Admiral had followed your example".'

'which has proved more conformable to my wishes than I had reason to hope from the information given me.'[5] The King, however, had decided to dismiss Fowke altogether, saying that 'if he is unfit for service for *one* year, he is certainly so for ever.'

Many long-standing friendships stood in peril over the case of Admiral Byng as people took different sides. When Henry Fox told Lady Hervey that her son Augustus would be advised to keep out of the Byng business, she sent a spirited reply which, coming from such a valued friend, must have shaken if not shamed the Secretary of State. She said she had given Augustus the only advice she could, which was to make use of nothing but truth in justification of his unhappy friend. But 'not to employ his utmost powers with truth, to vindicate his friend, is what I can neither advise nor wish; on the contrary I would excite him to it, as it is what on like occasion I would do myself at all hazards and perils, and so the best friend I have in the world shall find if ever there is occasion for it, which on *his* account (why should I not plainly say on *yours*) I hope will never happen . . .

'These are perilous times my dear Sir; God knows what may happen. The suffering, perhaps even encouraging, a mob to declare they will have—or otherwise do themselves—what they call justice is not only the most wicked but the most weak and dangerous thing imaginable; if they are supported or allowed to make such illegal declarations, who knows whose turn it may be next . . .? I fear, be it how it will, this poor man must be the scapegoat. I am sorry for it on his account; I am offended at it for the sake of justice; but I am by it beyond all expression as an Englishwoman.'[6]

Fox, who had of course written a week earlier to Anson advising him to lock Byng in the Tower of London, was apparently abashed at this candid criticism; in his reply he purposely misunderstood her. 'The mob, dear Madam, is not excited against Byng. The greatest care has been taken at least that they should not even get a sight of him.'[7]

Nevertheless, the mobs were still rioting and a great many posters were being pasted up on the walls. Some were against Admiral Byng, others against the Government; many were against both. 'Now selling by Auction,' read one, 'By order of Thomas Holles [the Duke] of Newcastle: Great Britain and the Dominions belonging thereunto. Gibraltar and Port Mahon were disposed of the first day, and the latter is already delivered. Tomorrow comes the sale of the Royal Family.—Andrew Bung, broker and auctioneer.' The man who stuck that particular poster on a wall was sent to jail and the MP for Southwark, Mr William Hammond, in whose constituency it happened, was so angry that with more indignation than tact he took it along to show the Duke of Newcastle.

Tower Hill, traditionally the outlet for Londoners' emotions, lived up to its reputation on Thursday, August 26. As the *Evening Post* reported, the effigy of a 'certain famous admiral' in an open sedan chair, guarded by a number of young men with swords, with drums beating and colours flying, was carried to Tower Hill, where a gallows had been prepared. The crowd, which included merchants' families 'and the gentlemen of the Navy Office', cheered loudly, their enthusiasm for a spectacle not damped by the rain and chilly north-westerly wind, as the effigy, 'richly dressed in a blue and gold coat, buff waistcoat, trimmed &c in full uniform', was brought to the gallows, where it was admonished by a chimney sweep dressed up as a parson.

The effigy was then hauled up on to the gallows, which was twenty feet high, and pelted with 'stones, brickbats, &c, which occasioned in so great a crowd many accidents, but none mortal'. A crowd of sailors who arrived late on the scene—the revelry had begun at 5 p.m.—wanted to drag the effigy round the streets, but 'the tar-barrels, faggots, tables, tubs, etc' under the gallows were lit. Within half an hour the effigy was burned, but the head fell off, 'which the enraged mob knocked about the hill, and also threw pieces of flaming stick, catched out of the fire, at one another; which intimidated the inhabitants for fear of their dwellings, and cleared the hill in a few minutes.'

A man walking along Cheapside had the same haughty air as Byng and someone whispered it was indeed the Admiral himself. Very soon a large mob was following the poor fellow who, scared they would attack him, ran into a draper's shop 'to prevent his being ill-used'. He had to stay there until the mob was finally satisfied a mistake had been made.

The Duke of Newcastle was naturally far from unperturbed by those attacks aimed at the Government. Immediately a particularly savage pamphlet was published he would get legal advice on it, to see whether action could be taken against the author and printer.

On August 28, for instance, the Clerk to the Privy Council, Mr William Sharpe, wrote that 'In obedience to your Grace's request . . . I have carefully perused and considered the *Fourth Letter to the People of England* [first published on August 27] and though it appears to me throughout to be a bold, daring and unjustifiable attack upon Government . . . and to be a virulent and inflammatory libel, yet considering the great topics it principally rolls upon . . . and considering also the surprising and unaccountable spirit which at this time almost universally influences the minds of the people upon these very topics, I can by no means presume to advise your Grace to direct a prosecution . . . because I apprehend there is much too great a probability that if such a prosecution was to be commenced and brought on to trial, it would from the poison that is gone forth amongst the people end in an acquittal, as it will be hardly possible to get a jury whose prepossessions will not lead them to that way of thinking.'

The Duke had also sent him an article by 'Britannicus' in the *Evening Post* which said that the loss of Minorca 'cannot surely be looked upon by any person as an uncertain event of war, but as a certain event of the treachery, negligence, or incapacity of those who were entrusted with power, more than sufficient to preserve it'. Mr Sharpe's reaction to this was: 'I have likewise carefully perused last Thursday's *Evening Post* which your Grace sent me . . . and the same reasons . . . induce me to think that it would be equally inadvisable to commence a prosecution.'[8]

To be victim of what was agreed to be a 'virulent and inflammatory libel' in a pamphlet and to be accused in a newspaper of 'treachery, negligence or incapacity', and yet be advised not to take proceedings because any jury would have returned a verdict that the allegations were true, must have made Mr Sharpe's advice distasteful; nevertheless His Grace accepted it.

Nor was he cheered by a letter from Sir John Willes, Lord Chief Justice of the Court of Common Pleas, who wrote from Warwick that 'I am very sorry that I am obliged to tell you, (unless I concealed the truth) that I never found all sorts of people so uneasy, and so dispirited, as they are at present. The loss of Fort St Philip is looked upon by everyone in a most melancholy light . . . To be sure this matter must be cleared up, and Mr Byng must be very severely punished; otherwise the clamour will be so very great that it will be impossible to put a stop to it.

'Forgive me, that I mention two methods of trying him: by
a court martial or an impeachment. For the latter many things are
to be said, as that it will better satisfy the minds of the people . . .
But there is I think one objection against it, which I cannot
answer—it is that I think (as his case is) he cannot be capitally
convicted on an impeachment.'[9] In other words, a guilty but live
Byng would still be a danger; a guilty and executed Byng would
allow them all to sleep safer in their political beds.

Yet the loss of Minorca was not the only cause of a new wave of
riots: from all over the country, especially the Midlands, justices of
the peace and judges on circuit—indeed anyone who cared to pick
up a pen and write to the Duke or the secretaries of state—sent
reports of rioting over the rapidly-rising prices of corn. In one
incident, colliers from Bedworth and Nuneaton 'and other places
in those parts of Warwickshire', stormed into Tamworth at noon
'destroying the inside of the mills and taking the corn and meal
and destroying more than they carried away'.[10]

On August 23 the *Evening Post* was reporting riots at Birmingham, Walsall, Wednesbury, Nuneaton, Atherstone, Poleworth,
Tamworth, Badgley and Heartsall: mills and farmhouses were
wrecked and pillaged; three Quaker meeting houses were nearly
destroyed. Several of the rioters were arrested and sent to Warwick jail. Four of them were sentenced to death and two more were
due to be executed in two days' time, but Lord Chief Justice
Willes told the people that if they returned to their houses and
promised to remain quiet, the six men would be pardoned. If the
riots continued, however, 'every person who shall be taken up
and committed shall be executed on the day after he is found
guilty'.

On September 2 the Duke of Newcastle wrote to tell Lord Hardwicke that in this time of difficulty, danger and almost universal
uneasiness and discontent, he wished that 'your Lordship could
have suggested some adequate expedient for stemming the torrent
and effect of this ill-humour in the House of Commons . . .'
The Surrey address to the King was 'going through the county,
to be signed in every town, and has this remarkable prayer, *for
justice against persons, however highly dignified or distinguished. That*
may mean your humble servant, perhaps somebody more highly
dignified and distinguished than either of us.' He was inclined to
think that 'I should obtain the King's leave to retire. In all events

I am determined to let the King know that I am most ready to do it, if His Majesty should think it for his service.'[11]

Then later the same day his Grace's nerve seemed to break entirely and soon a second letter was on its way by messenger to the Lord Chancellor. 'You have left me alone, and without a compliment,' wailed his Grace, 'I have no one to apply to but yourself. I see dangers on all sides, and no means of getting out of them. I wish you would seriously think of my getting out—if things should succeed beyond our expectations, and the King should consent to anything we propose, as I rather think in the present circumstances he would do, what a figure shall we make, with Mr Pitt coming in conquest over us?

'Though there is nothing I would not yield to, for the sake of the King and the public, the Army is absolutely under other direction [i.e. the Duke of Cumberland's] and the sea [Anson] does not love to be controlled, or even advised, and yet I am to answer for any miscarriage in either . . . My dear Lord, pity me; alone as I am and in my distress, give me the comfort you only can, viz. a clear and determined opinion, and then I am easy.'[12]

Hardwicke's answer assured Newcastle that he took the attacks on him too much to heart—'I think it is advisable not to show too great a sensibility, nor to talk of one's self as distinguished from others, but treat it as a general attack upon the whole administration.'[13]

Henry Fox, still digesting Lady Hervey's well-intentioned lecture on basic morality, now received some frank letters from Lord Tyrawley. The irascible old soldier, after his crisp and detailed letter about Gibraltar to Lord Barrington, now turned his guns on Fox. As far as Gibraltar was concerned he said, 'I take it for granted it will be extremely quiet; for I do not see that we can do ourselves much good, or anybody else much hurt, by being in possession of it. If anything can tempt anybody to besiege it, it will be the fatherless and motherless defenceless state it has been suffered to run into.'[14] And, he added, he would be obliged for leave to return home.

A week later he wrote that he was not satisfied 'that Gibraltar is so formidable place as the common cry thinks it . . . That Gibraltar is the strongest town in the world, that one Englishman can beat three Frenchmen, and that London Bridge is one of the Seven Wonders of the World, are the natural prejudices of the English coffee-house politician.'[15]

The General could see no strategic value in Gibraltar: he certainly did not regard it as the key to the Mediterranean. In fairness to him it should be recalled that previous Governments had not seen any strategic value in Gibraltar as a base: Britain had tried to get rid of it four times up to then in the fifty-two years since Sir George Rooke had captured it, and Pitt was, in the next year, to offer it to Spain for the fifth time in return for Spanish help in recapturing Minorca. The British Ambassador to Madrid —still Sir Benjamin Keene—commented that Pitt must be mad,[16] but made the offer on his behalf. Fortunately for Britain the Spaniards turned it down, and it is difficult to understand what Pitt had in mind because apart from any other considerations, Minorca would be valueless without Gibraltar. However, it was to be offered to Spain a sixth time (in 1783, in exchange for Porto Rico) before the British Government became resigned to being burdened with the possession of what was perhaps the most valuable overseas naval base in the world.

The situation of Britain at the end of August was summed up neatly and ironically by Horace Walpole in a letter to his friend Sir Horace Mann. 'The rains have been excessive just now, and must occasion more inconveniences. But the warmth on the loss of Minorca has opened every sluice of opposition that has been so long dammed up. Even Jacobitism perks up those fragments of asses' ears which were not quite cut to the quick. The City of London and some counties have addressed the King on our miscarriages. Sir John Barnard, who endeavoured to stem the torrent of the former, is grown almost as unpopular as Byng. That poor simpleton, confined at Greenwich, is ridiculously easy and secure, and has even summoned on his behalf a Captain Young, his warmest accuser . . . Pamphlets and satirical prints teem; the courts are divided; the Ministers quarrel—indeed, if they agreed, one should not have much more to expect from them!'

17

BARS FOR THE CELL

AT GREENWICH, under the baleful eye of Isaac Townshend, Admiral Byng was at last beginning to understand just how perilous was his situation: patience, dignified behaviour, letters expressing gentle protests at the way he was being treated—all these, he realized, were useless: the Duke of Newcastle might be a velvet hand in an iron glove; but he was in the grip of Fox, Hardwicke and Anson. His trial had in fact already begun—and anyone doubting that had only to listen to the cry of the mobs ranging the streets, or read the newspapers.

Nor did the Opposition help him. The loss of Minorca was a good enough stick with which to belabour the Ministers, and any ill-treatment of Byng gave weight to its blows; but there was no question of them flying to the aid of an Admiral who had apparently bungled his job. They would try to ensure that the Ministers did not escape by making Byng the only scapegoat; but beyond that the question of justice for the Admiral did not at this time appear to interest them as a group.

Admiral Townshend, either out of spite or to ingratiate himself with the Government and earn his £1000-a-year salary as Governor at Greenwich, settled down to make Byng's life a misery. He did not need any orders or hints. For instance on the day after he arrived Byng asked for some furniture for his cell which, apart from his own portmanteau, was bare. Townshend told him tartly that none was available: if he wanted anything he would have to buy it.

The Admiral had arrived at Greenwich late on August 9; by the 14th an order was made by Fox that no one should remain with him after dark. A week or two later, complaints from the Governor led to the Admiralty writing to the Secretary at War on September 10 for more soldiers, explaining that Townshend, having represented that 'the guards appointed to assist the Marshal of the Admiralty in the care of Admiral Byng is not sufficient', now

desired that 'there may be an addition of eight more private men
to enable proper sentinels to be posted'.[1]

Byng's room already had two sentries always on guard at the
door and, in the courtyard below, a boatswain and twelve men
from the hospital, smart in their blue uniforms, maintained a
patrol night and day. It was not long before a boatswain reported
seeing four men at Byng's window. The alarm was raised, soldiers
ran up the steps with their muskets at the ready, and the sentries at
Byng's door rushed into his cell—to find the Admiral sound asleep.

However, this false alarm was enough to goad Admiral Townshend into further activity: next day bricklayers and blacksmiths
trooped up the stairs and cemented metal bars into the windows to
form a grille. They then went on to the roof and cemented metal
bars across the top of the chimney in case the portly Admiral
should try to climb up it to seek freedom on the rooftops. It was
later reported that Townshend, 'jealous that his care and diligence
was not sufficiently conspicuous,' reprimanded the workmen for
not having fitted the bars across the chimney so that they pro-
jected, in order that passers-by could see the tangible evidence of
his zeal.

A few days later certain newspapers were told that Byng had
tried to escape dressed in his sister Sarah's clothes—a story which
the *Evening Post* on September 16 strongly denied. 'Notwithstanding the various reports so industriously propagated in almost
all the papers to the great prejudice of Admiral Byng,' it said, 'the
whole is entirely false and has not the least foundation of truth.'
In the same edition it reported that a large crowd in Whitechapel
had been busy burning Byng in effigy when a wheel came off the
Barking stagecoach as it went by, injuring five people.

Admiral Byng had written to Edmund Bramston to tell him
where he was being imprisoned, and his cousin was soon at
Greenwich helping prepare the defence and trying to make the
Admiral's life a little less rigorous.

Byng soon realized that at his trial he was going to need every
available man that could give any evidence on his behalf, and he
therefore wrote on September 6 to the Admiralty pointing out
that his first list of witnesses comprised only those of men whose
names he could remember; in a second list which he enclosed he
had to mention some men by their posts as he did not know their
names, nor did he know 'the depth of their knowledge'.[2]

This request for more witnesses arrived at the Admiralty just before a letter to Byng, drafted by Lord Anson, had been copied out and sent off to Greenwich. This draft, in Anson's writing, was to tell Byng that 'Their Lordships are desirous of giving you the earliest opportunity of acquitting yourself if possible from so heavy a charge and to bring you to an immediate trial'.[3] However, since Byng's letter asking for more witnesses needed answering, the draft was altered to cover it. Anson did not, apparently, consider a man was innocent until he was proved guilty, and his letter when finally amended and sent to Byng said that as 'You lie under an imputation of misbehaviour, by means whereof the honour and interest of this Kingdom hath suffered . . . Their Lordships were desirous, in justice to the public as well as tenderness to yourself, to give you the earliest opportunity of acquitting yourself, if possible, from so heavy a charge.' But since there were in England no fewer than twenty officers who had served in his squadron, several of whom 'must be presumed under a particular bias (as far as truth will permit) in your favour', the Admiralty hoped they would be 'sufficient to clear up the matter according to the truth and justice of the case'.

The Board said that Byng had asked on August 4 for thirty-seven witnesses, twenty-three of whom were then in the Mediterranean, and they had been sent for. They were astonished at the new application for thirty-one more officers, and 'look upon it merely as a scheme suggested to you to delay your being brought to trial . . . By the same means you may put off your trial for ever.' By sending in a new list every month, he could conclude 'with the desire that the whole Fleet may be brought home'. Justice demanded that an accused person should have the chance of proving his defence—'this you have already had to the utmost of your own desire, and been indulged to so great an extent as to make an example very dangerous to the Service and discipline of the Navy'.

Therefore, as soon as the witnesses already sent for had arrived, the Admiralty intended to start the trial, which they could see no reason to postpone any longer, and as far as Byng's latest application was concerned, 'you have laid no grounds before their Lordships sufficient to induce them to give the least countenance to so extraordinary attempt'.[4]

This was by no means a hurriedly-written letter—indeed some of it had been drafted twice; the phrases, carefully chosen, gave an ominous indication of how Anson's mind was working. Yet by any standards it was monstrous and venomous, and Byng answered it with dignity. 'I shall not comment upon that prejudging expression of yours, *an opportunity of acquitting myself, if possible*—it seems sufficiently to explain itself; but I cannot pass by unnoticed your *presuming several of the witnesses now in England having a particular bias, as far as truth will permit, in my favour*. Whence,' he asked, 'should that bias arise? If from the hopes of reward, or fear of punishment: rewards and punishments are certainly in other hands than mine.

'And how great is my astonishment at your mentioning their Lordships tenderness to me, and their indulgence! Phrases I did not expect to meet with. Can being kept moving backward and forward from one place of confinement to another, for near three weeks after my arrival in England, so as to make it impossible for me to prepare anything relating to my defence, be called by any of these names? Or can my close confinement at Greenwich, without even suffering my menial servants to remain in the house after dark, be called so? And I think I have a right to complain of that cruel countenance and belief, which seems to be given to a groundless report, of my having attempted to make my escape, and the rigid orders given in consequence of it, as if intended to confirm it.'

He could not avoid observing 'that all the charge of keeping me in custody seems to be taken from the Marshal, and committed to the Governor of the Hospital, by orders given in his name, who seems diligent in distinguishing himself in the service of his country by imposing upon me all the indignities and inconveniences that power can enable him to do.'

His first list of witnesses had been drawn up under stress— 'It would be a matter of wonder, restrained and distressed by all the methods Power can impose, and personally disturbed night and day', if he had immediately thought of all the witnesses capable of giving evidence for him. Denying the allegation that he was trying to delay his trial, he pointed out that if he had demanded a trial immediately he arrived in England—as the Board's letter seemed to intimate—he must have done so without knowing the charge and without having any witnesses. He concluded by assuring their Lordships that he was eager to face his trial, 'but a trial without the necessary witnesses cannot be considered as any trial at all; rather an act of power than an act of justice; and must be a precedent much more dangerous than that hinted at in your letter'.[5]

Thomas Potter, the barrister son of the Archbishop of Canterbury, and MP for Aylesbury, wrote to his friend George Grenville on September 11, and gave a good picture of an autumn day in London: 'This morning I heard the whole City of Westminster disturbed by the song of a hundred ballad singers, the burthen of which was "To the block with Newcastle, and the yard-arm with Byng". Their music alarmed my devotion enough to draw from me many a hearty amen. I repeat it again here, as I think it very probable that a letter from me to you will be opened at the Post Office, in order to inform his Grace what my dispositions to him are, I will subscribe my name in capitals . . .'[6]

Ten days later, 'Civis' in *The Citizen* made a shrewd comment: 'The behaviour of the lower classes is more commonly representative of the sentiments of those of the higher than perhaps you may readily believe; and the pursuits of the Ministers are often begun and promulgated by the mob. In consequence of this, when I walk the streets the operations of the multitude frequently tell me the designs of the Ministry at St James's.

'In no instance has the observation been verified with greater certainty than in the instance of Mr Byng. He has been hanged, quartered and burnt in every part of the City. Every ballad-singing throat has been sung hoarse with his destruction, and swarms of hawkers flying abroad, astonishing the streets with their cries, have been let loose with a design to overwhelm him. Mankind have been pleased with this spirit of the people; and looking no farther than the affairs in the Mediterranean, have kept their eyes and resentment on the Admiral alone.'

But others were to blame, declared 'Civis'; those who delayed sending the squadron, and who chose the commander. To divert the people's attention from these men, 'money has been given and distributed to the mob to dress a figure in the sea uniform; to make fires and burn him; and thus to keep the popular eye on Byng alone. Tales have been invented of his designing to escape; that his head begins to be turned; and a thousand falsehoods to call all the attention of England upon him, and from them . . .'

Byng, in his new mood, saw that with much of the Press being inspired or bribed against him, and pamphleteers busy, he would have to take some steps to state his own case if he was not to be judged before his trial. He or his friends therefore hired a writer—it is not clear who it was,* but it may have been Paul Whitehead—to write pamphlets on his behalf. The first to be published[7] was extremely effective, for two reasons: it printed for the first time the whole of Byng's dispatch, showing the passages which had been censored by the Government, and it also gave Byng's earlier dispatch of May 4 which had described the situation of the dockyard at Gibraltar. This was the first indication to most people that Byng had any sort of answer to the accusations being made against him.

The second pamphlet to be published on his behalf was *An Appeal to the People*, a 76-page document in the form of a violent attack on the Government: was it not a crime equal to forgery to censor the dispatch, it asked, making Byng in the eyes of the people 'a detested object of their indignation'? And if the censoring was done purposely to avoid the Government being blamed, it could only be 'an execrable endeavour to take away the life of a less guilty, perhaps innocent man, to save their own heads from condign punishment'.

However, the most effective of all the pamphlets was one entitled *Some Further Particulars in Relation to the Case of Admiral Byng, from original papers &c*,[8] 'By a Gentleman of Oxford'. It was published at the beginning of October and sold for a shilling. Giving a timetable of events, it started with a description of the delays at Portsmouth, including the difficulty of manning Byng's ships although there were overmanned ships in harbour whose crews he could not touch. Great emphasis was laid on the fact the Government recalled Byng entirely on Galissonière's dispatch —'there is not a precedent in history to be found of any process of any kind founded upon such evidence'. Then, 'having proceeded against him as a beaten coward', the Government 'prostituted the *Gazette*' by censoring and distorting his dispatch. Much of the factual material for the pamphlet was taken from Byng's Journal.

The pamphlet described in detail Byng's treatment after arriving back in England, particularly at Greenwich, where 'The Governor played the part of jailer-in-chief, pleading sometimes Lord Anson's orders, and sometime Orders in Council for it; so that every hour

* Dr Johnson did not write any pamphlets on Byng's behalf, but he reviewed some of them in the *Literary Magazine* and *Universal Review* during 1756.

made it more and more dubious whether he was the Governor's prisoner or the Marshal's, consequently whether he was to be tried by a court martial or as an offender against the State.'

All this time, 'his character was delivered over to the populace to gratify upon it the worst passions that the worst artifices and instruments could raise, insomuch that there is not a species of libelling in prints, in verse or in prose that has not been exhausted to render him odious: the very ghost of his reverend father has been raised, advising him to lay violent hands on himself; last dying speeches and confessions have been prepared for him; mock executions have been spirited up to make the way easy for a real one . . . forgetting that the worse the case, the less need there is of aggravation, that an over charge implies a defect of real matter . . .'

The *Westminster Journal* commented, as soon as the pamphlet was published, that 'The cat is out of the bag, and Byng in his appeal has made it evidently enough appear that he is not . . . the greatest knave concerned in that indelible stain and disgrace which our country had lately fixed upon her in the Mediterranean'.

The Citizen on the same day declared that nothing was easier to demonstrate 'than that our Ministers are the chief, if not the only authors of our late disgrace . . .'

A month earlier, a large volume was published called *A Complete Body of Architecture Adorned with Plans and Elevations from original designs*, by Isaac Ware. Among the plans he published were those of Byng's house, Wrotham Park, and also the wind dial of the Berkeley Square house.

At the end of September, Anson was worrying about sending new orders to Sir Edward Hawke in the Mediterranean, and he raised the matter at a meeting of the Inner Committee. On October 1, after a long discussion in the Duke of Cumberland's apartment, it was decided that Hawke should return home 'with such a number of the great ships under his command as may secure a superiority over any Fleet he may meet in the ocean . . .'[9]

This resolution is perhaps the clearest example of the Government's almost unbelievably muddled thinking and planning. Byng was being accused of not doing his utmost to relieve Minorca, and the Government—like a neglectful husband whose wife had first cuckolded and then left him—now placed a great value on that lost possession. Although Hawke had a sufficiently strong squadron (thanks to the reinforcement sent out with Broderick) to defeat Galissonnière's squadron and, having done that, starve the French Army in Minorca into submission, he had not done so. Here were the very men who derided and condemned Byng for quitting Minorca and fussing about the defence of Gibraltar with a much weaker force actually ordering the squadron home from the Mediterranean, leaving even Gibraltar completely open to attack.

Meanwhile in the fashionable coffee houses the wagers which had been laid out on the fall of Minorca had been paid, those on the fall of Gibraltar still stood, and new ones at shorter odds were being made that Byng would meet his death at the hands of the court martial.

By this time Lord Hardwicke had entered the pamphlet war: after David Mallet offered the services of his pen to the Duke of Newcastle, he was handed over to the Lord Chancellor, who briefed him on what the Government wanted—nothing more than a fluently-written attack on Byng, well bolstered up with dates and figures. Anson arranged for Mallet to see papers from the Admiralty, and Mallet had completed his pamphlet, except for the last page, when *Some Further Particulars*, the pamphlet giving Byng's case, was published. Mallet immediately bought one, and then sent it to Hardwicke on October 3 with a draft of his own work for his Lordship's 'severest examination'. He had not sent the last sheet because he thought some notice had to be taken of the pamphlet just published—a document which he considered full of 'false and insolent insinuations'.[10]

Hardwicke read Mallet's draft and then sent it on to his son-in-law, Anson, with the comment that 'I have read it quite thro' and, upon the whole, cannot find much fault in it tho' I must own I am not much enamoured with it'. However, he had made some alterations on the draft which, if Anson approved, should be sent to Clevland at the Admiralty to copy out fair and return to Mallet. The Earl's reason for this roundabout method was, he explained, 'that I am not fond of giving a handle to be named as a joint author with this gentleman'.[11]

While the Admiralty, in the shape of Lord Anson and Clevland, helped Mallet write his attack on Byng, they were also trying to fight back against written attacks on themselves. A particularly stinging assault in *The Gazeteer* on October 19 so annoyed the

Board that Clevland was told to find out whether it was libellous and whether they could prosecute[12] the writer and the newspaper.

Sir Robert Henley, the Solicitor-General, was not encouraging in his reply: in a strict construction of the law, he wrote, it might be deemed a libel, but 'when so many more virulent papers against [the] Government have been published without any animadversion, it would be very injudicious to start with this'.[13]

Nor was the Solicitor-General exaggerating when he referred to 'more virulent' attacks, for an article in *The Gazeteer* a few days earlier belaboured the Ministers for getting effigies of Byng burned all over the country, saying 'How much money has been expended on these bonfires they can best tell who set the mob to work'.

It was left to the *Evening Post* a week later to raise a very important point—what effect must this 'severe, rigorous and seemingly unjust time-serving and oppressive treatment of Admiral Byng have upon our commanders hereafter? Will not they naturally be more careful to be able to justify their own conduct than ambitions to do their country real service. . . . What sort of officers must you hereafter expect to serve you, if you suffer him to fall a victim, to atone for the negligence, ignorance and blunders of xxxxxxxxx?'*

The newspaper then asked, 'Are not the naval Ministers Admiral Byng's prosecutors? May not they be deeply interested in finding him guilty to screen themselves?' Were not his judges to be nominated by the Admiralty? Were not these judges, as well as all the witnesses, immediately dependents on the Admiralty for now, and for all their future prospects? Might not 'an undue influence be apprehended?' (The author of these pertinent queries was 'Philo-Justitiae,' the person whose article in *The Gazeteer* nine days earlier had so provoked the Board of Admiralty.)

While the Press slashed and parried, the Duke of Newcastle continued his efforts to keep the Government together; but with Fox showing signs that he was trying to escape, and William Murray still determined to become Lord Chief Justice and get a peerage, it was difficult work.

George Bubb Dodington noted in his diary for October 2 that

---

* Unfortunately in the years that followed the verdict on Byng did have this effect on some officers.

a letter from Henry Fox told him 'things were ill', and a few days later when they dined together the Secretary of State 'appeared to be in an extraordinary perturbation.' The reason was not hard to find, for Fox had previously suggested to Newcastle that his own Secretaryship of State should be offered to Pitt, the Government's chief critic. This had been followed by a new misunderstanding over one of Fox's nephews, for whom he had been trying to get a post in the Bedchamber of the young Prince of Wales. The King was against it, but under the Duke of Newcastle's urging His Majesty had agreed 'to oblige you'.[14] But the King changed his mind, and when the Duke wrote to Fox on October 5 that someone else was to have the appointment, Fox was furious, having already told his nephew that it had been arranged for him. He vented his feelings in a draft of a letter to Andrew Stone, the Duke's secretary, saying that he did not know whether he was to conclude from this that the Duke's negotiations with Pitt (i.e. offering him Fox's job) were far advanced, but 'I retract all good humoured dealing. I may be turned out, and I suppose I shall. But I will not be used like a dog, without having given the least provocation . . . I do not consent that Mr Pitt should have my place.' Then, having written the draft, he crossed out the whole passage; but, as his biographer commented, the sentences remained to testify to his bitter feelings.[15]

Lord Hardwicke, in the meantime, wrote to the Duke discussing the various proposed ministerial changes, and commenting that 'In all the arrangements mentioned by your Grace, I see no proposal for bringing an efficient Parliamentary man into the Admiralty. This is indeed very necessary, for not only the sake of the Board of Admiralty,' he hastened to add, lest perhaps Newcastle should think he was trying to shield his son-in-law Anson, 'but of the whole administration, for on those affairs the chief stress will lie'.[16]

'For God's sake, my dear Lord, tell me what to do . . .' replied the Duke.[17]

Next day his Grace received a violent though long-feared shock: Fox had finally made up his mind to resign—a step he claimed was not only necessary but innocent, and without complaint or resentment.[18]

When handed Fox's letter the Duke cried 'What shall I do?' and immediately went off to see Lord Granville, the Lord President, and told him he would resign in Granville's favour. Granville, however, was unimpressed by this generosity. 'I thought,' he said, 'I had cured you of such offers last year: I will be hanged a little before I take your place, rather than a little after.'[19]

Writing a hurried note to tell Hardwicke about Fox he grumbled, 'He makes use of this opportunity to distress us, to put the knife to our throats, to get his own terms and all the power he wants, which he thinks *we* cannot refuse him . . . In short, he will go or insist upon more power than can be given him, except he had the Treasury, which I heartily wish he had.'[20]

On October 14 Newcastle saw the King, who spent some time denouncing Fox, and then wrote once again to Hardwicke to give the following description of the conversation:

'But,' said the King, 'what is to be done?'

'Sir, my Lord President [Granville] said there was but one of two things to do, either to gratify Fox in what he wanted' (which, said I, would perhaps be giving Mr Fox more power than Your Majesty would think proper) 'or take in Mr Pitt.'

'But,' replied the King *peevishly*, 'Mr Pitt won't come.'

'If *that* was done, we should have a quiet session.'

'*But Mr Pitt won't do my German business.*'

'If he comes into your service, Sir, he must be told he must do Your Majesty's business. I have wrote, Sir, to the Lord Chancellor [Hardwicke].'

'Well, what says the Lord Chancellor?'

'I have not his answer, but I know what he will say—if this gentleman won't continue we must go to the Opposition.'

'But I don't like Pitt: he won't do my business!'

'But unfortunately, Sir, he is the only one (in the Opposition) who has the ability to do the business.'[21]

Yet for all the old King's reluctance and fears for Pitt's possible treatment of his beloved Hanover—the 'German business' to which he referred—there was no choice; and as Richard Rigby dutifully reported to the Duke of Bedford, 'At this minute, I suppose, if they have not already been rejected by him, they have some emissary with Mr Pitt with *carte blanche*'.[22]

Rigby was correct in his supposition. 'I ask much pardon for the liberty I am now taking, which nothing can excuse but the occasion,' Hardwicke wrote to Pitt on October 16, but would

Pitt meet him at Lord Royston's house in St James's Square 'upon an affair of great consequence?'[23]

However, Pitt was determined not to join any Government which had the Duke of Newcastle at the head of it, or become involved in any plan 'to cover his retreat, in case he wishes to retire from being Minister', he told George Granville.[24]

Hardwicke's talk with Pitt was a failure; after three and a half hours of discussion—in Lord Royston's dressing-room—during which Hardwicke offered him the post of Secretary of State and assured him that the King would receive him well, Pitt refused: he would not serve with the Duke of Newcastle. 'We fought all the weapons thro' but his final answer was *totally* negative,'[25] the Lord Chancellor told his eldest son, Lord Royston.

The Government's overture to Pitt now began to sound like a *Nunc Dimittis* to the Duke of Newcastle, and with his administration on the verge of collapse he approached various other leading politicians to take office under him. They all politely refused. We need not go into detail as far as the events which followed are concerned: the Duke realized he could not go on and on October 25 announced his intention of resigning.*

The King sent for Fox and told him to see if he could form a government with Pitt, but the latter gave Fox a very chilly reply. Finally the King sent for the Duke of Devonshire, who agreed to take over the Duke of Newcastle's role as leader of the Government. Pitt then took Fox's place as one Secretary of State, but Lord Holdernesse stayed in office as the other.

Pitt's brother-in-law and very close friend, Lord Temple (a large and tall man, nicknamed 'Lord Gawky') replaced Anson as First Lord of the Admiralty and the Board—with the exception of Boscawen—was changed. The new members were Rear-Admiral Temple West, who had of course been Byng's second-in-command and was a cousin of Lord Temple and the rest of the Grenvilles; John Pitt, another cousin; Dr George Hay, Gilbert Elliot and Thomas Orby Hunter. Boscawen was the only member of Lord Anson's Board to serve on the new Board under Lord Temple.

The Duke of Newcastle resigned with ostentatious good will. 'It was assiduously propagated in all the public papers,' reported

---

* By a strange coincidence, one of the part-authors of his downfall, the Marquis de la Galissonnière, died next day, five months after the battle.

Walpole, 'that he departed without place or pension; and his enormous estate, which he had sunk from thirty to thirteen thousand pounds a year, by every ostentatious vanity, and on every womanish panic, between cooks, mobs and apothecaries, was now represented by his tools as wasted in the cause of the Government . . .' His Grace retired to Claremont, his country house near Esher, 'where,' commented Walpole, 'for about a fortnight, he played at being a country gentleman. Guns and green frocks were bought and at past sixty he affected to turn sportsman; but getting wet in his feet, he hurried back to London in a fright and his country was once more blessed with his assistance.'[26]

Among the Duke's last acts before handing over to the Duke of Devonshire was to pay David Mallet his £300 from the Secret Service fund for the anti-Byng pamphlet, and a few days earlier William Murray was finally made Lord Chief Justice and given a peerage, taking the title of Lord Mansfield. And for the prisoner at Greenwich there at last seemed some hope.

18

FRIGHTENED WITNESSES

BEFORE THE DUKE OF NEWCASTLE's collapse, the old Board of Admiralty under Lord Anson had told Admiral Byng on October 14 that the *Colchester* was returning from the Mediterranean with the first group of the witnesses he had requested; but they had not answered his protest of a month earlier over their letter saying he was to be given 'an opportunity of acquitting yourself, if possible'. Byng therefore wrote again, expressing his astonishment that his letters were completely ignored.

'My case is sufficiently hard if indulged with every legal advantage,' he wrote, 'for I have too much reason to believe that my prosecution is carried on by persons too powerful for me to contend against, whose influence must add great weight to their accusations against me.' He insisted on the right of every common subject not to be deprived of a single witness that he thought necessary for his defence. 'It cannot be supposed,' he added, 'that a person confined, oppressed and calumniated as I am can possibly be desirous of postponing his trial,' but nevertheless he insisted on justice.

Clevland replied to this letter on October 25 saying that their Lordships 'are much surprised at many passages therein', but they did not see sufficient reason or argument to alter their decision about the extra witnesses. That was the last act of the old Board as far as Byng was concerned for he did not hear again from the Admiralty until after the new Board had taken over.

He was gradually preparing his defence, helped by his cousin Edmund Bramston and his young nephew John. Looking after the Admiral was his valet, John Hutchens, but of course he had to leave the Admiral's room every evening at dusk along with all the other visitors. Sarah came down to see him when she could spare the time; another of the Admiral's nephews, the young Lord Torrington, also did what he could to help.

But sorting out the evidence was a slow task, made more difficult by the fact that several of the officers who had served in his squadron had become thoroughly frightened by the violence of the mob and the virulence of the anti-Byng newspapers and pamphlets, with the result that the Judge-Advocate was questioning them first. An indication of this was given in Byng's letter to Captain Lloyd, who had commanded the *Chesterfield*, telling him that as he was being called as a witness on the Admiral's behalf, 'I beg that you will favour me with an opportunity of asking you some questions on that subject previous to your being examined in court, and before you communicate your sentiments to any other person: a favour that you run no risk in granting because I have a legal right to demand it'.[1]

The witnesses coming home in the *Colchester*, and also the *Deptford*, were a motley collection. Among those in the *Colchester* were Cornwall of the *Revenge*, Augustus Hervey, Amherst and the Earl of Effingham and his wife; in the *Deptford* were Young, formerly of the *Intrepid*, whose letters had done Byng so much harm, and four other captains.

When the two ships arrived at Spithead, Augustus Hervey immediately went on shore and travelled to London to deliver dispatches from Sir Edward Hawke. Since Lord Temple had by now taken over Anson's place as First Lord, Hervey went to call on him. 'Mr West came in whilst I was there,' Hervey wrote, 'and they appeared to me to be much against all the proceedings that were carrying on against Mr Byng.'

He later had dinner at his mother's house, where he met many of his acquaintances and found that they talked of little else but Admiral Byng and the Mediterranean affair. The next day Lord Rochford, as Lord of the Bedchamber in Waiting, 'was so good as to call of me and carry me to Court, when I was presented, but His Majesty did not deign to speak to me, or even inquire the least about his fleet, tho' I was the only officer come from it that he was likely to see. Such was His Majesty's attention.'

Hervey soon met Henry Fox, who was now of course out of office, 'but I was well on my guard with him, tho' he insinuated to me that he had nothing to do with the proceedings against Mr Byng and disapproved Lord Anson's conduct on the whole. All this Minister's discourse with me was full of arts and endeavours to see what he could get of me, by way of weakening any part of Mr Byng's defence.'

That evening Lady Hervey gave her son a warning about 'the great imprudence there would be in me to appear too warm at this time in Mr Byng's defence, that I may be sure of making myself great enemies at St James's, but all that I little regarded'.

Hervey was cheered a little next day because when he called on Lord Temple, the First Lord told him to assure Admiral Byng that he would have all the justice possible in his trial, and that Temple thought the previous Board's behaviour towards him was quite shameful. 'Yet I did not find there was any mitigation with regard to the severity in which he was confined,' Hervey commented, but when he went to see Byng at Greenwich the next day he found the Admiral in his 'usual good spirits, and speaking with a manly contempt of all the ill-treatment he received'.[2]

Hervey's arrival in England marked something of a turning point for Byng. The young captain read over the correspondence the Admiral had been having with the Admiralty and, with characteristic drive, set to work writing and publishing pamphlets on Byng's behalf and getting articles printed in the newspapers. Now Byng had an ally who was both vigorous and in touch with leading Admiralty and political figures, and who could devote all his time to helping prepare the Admiral's defence, knowing all the facts.

The new Board of Admiralty met for the first time on November 19, and the first item on the agenda was Byng's second application for witnesses. They dealt with this by writing to Admiral Osborn at Portsmouth to find out if all the officers mentioned in Byng's first list had arrived in the *Colchester* and *Deptford*, and if any mentioned in the second list had also returned. They then discussed when to hold the trial. All the letters which had passed between the previous Board and the Admiral were read to them, and then they questioned the Judge-Advocate about the progress he had made in preparing the case.[3]

With the approach of winter the hours of daylight were shortening, and the next letter they received from Byng was a request that people be allowed to stay with him after dark. The Board sent for Brough, the Admiralty Marshal, and ask him 'if he apprehended any danger in Mr Byng's being permitted to have his friends or relations to stay with him longer in the evening than they did at present'. Brough, who appears to have been carrying out his unpleasant task of guarding Byng with great tact and discretion, replied that he 'did not apprehend any danger, and that he would be answerable for his safe custody'.

Byng's main reason for the request was of course that with the brief daylight those helping him prepare his defence had very little time for their work. But after the Board had questioned Brough (and apparently been favourably disposed towards the request) Cleveland produced 'a very express order'—the one made by Fox on August 4—directing that no one remain with Byng after dark. This order, even though it was made by the previous Ministry, was quite enough to cause the Board wash their hands of the whole business: without bothering to find out why it had been made or apply to Fox's successor, Pitt, for a reversal, they decided that 'as they do not know on what ground so express an order was founded, they do not think it proper to take on themselves to make any alterations'.

They added—as if infected by the tone of the previous Board's correspondence—that it seemed unnecessary anyway since Byng's only reason for making the request was to have more time in which to prepare his defence, and that he had 'already had so much time for that purpose'.[4]

The ridiculousness of the decision is shown by the fact that Byng had made the request on November 22, just seven days after all his witnesses arrived at Spithead. Thus he had had just a week to write to nine captains, six lieutenants, four warrant officers and two midshipmen, as well as various Army officers like Effingham, and arrange for them to visit him or be questioned by his helpers. So when Byng received the Board's answer he could be excused for despairing of getting fairer treatment under the new Temple regime, although in reply he said he hoped the Board would 'forgive my representing that the most essential time for preparing my defence can only be commenced from the arrival of my witnesses'.

However, even in that short time the Judge-Advocate had started questioning the officers before Byng had a chance to see them—a process which, as Byng pointed out to the Admiralty, 'is tending illegal to discover my defence and expose me the more to the malicious and virulent attacks of my enemies'. He also asked for a copy of the whole of Galissonnière's dispatch, 'as the

reason for the disgraces and indignities I have undergone is
founded upon an extract of it; and I have reason to apprehend an
error in the translation of that extract to my disadvantage, and',
he added in an ironical reference to his own censored dispatch
published in the *London Gazette*, 'have a very ill opinion of the
late manner of making extracts of letters'.[5]

Why was the new Board so unsympathetic? Probably not for
any one reason. The Board meeting which refused to allow Byng
to have visitors after dark was attended by all the members.
Naturally Boscawen would not be outspoken on Byng's behalf;
nor was Clevland, with his close links with Newcastle, Hardwicke
and Anson, likely to be very sympathetic in his recital of the previous events and the correspondence. More important, however,
was the slender hold that the Duke of Devonshire's new administration had on power. Put quite simply, there were not enough
Pitt-Grenville adherents to fill all the posts. The wretched Barrington, for instance, continued as Secretary at War; Holdernesse
stayed in office as Secretary of State for the Northern Province.

As Walpole wrote to Sir Horace Mann in Florence, although
Newcastle and Fox had resigned, 'the chief friends of each remain
in place; and Mr Pitt accedes with so little strength that his success
seems very precarious. If he Hanoverizes, or checks any inquiries,
he loses his popularity, and falls that way; if he humours the present
rage of the people, he provokes two powerful factions.' The
official leader of the Government, the Duke of Devonshire, was in a
quandary, because 'if he acts cordially, he disobliges his intimate
friend Mr Fox; if he does not, he offends Pitt'.[6]

As far as Byng was concerned, it was quite clear that with the
Newcastle group still needing him as a scapegoat they still had him
in their power, owing to Pitt's weakness. He was still caught in the
Duke of Newcastle's web of patronage even if the spider had for
the moment been frightened away.

Among those who had returned to England in the *Deptford* was
General Blakeney, who found himself the hero of the hour—
indeed, from the very beginning of the siege he had been praised
by the Press. The *Evening Post* had already reported that 'The
common people of Stanmore in Middlesex pay almost adoration
to an old horse left there by General Blakeney in the care of Captain Peter Durell; they seek opportunities to show their esteem of

valour and are also particularly generous to the groom.' In the same issue prints of General Blakeney, costing 1s. 6d. and 'Executed in Messo-tinto [sic] by Mr M'Ardell from an original picture painted in Minorca', were advertised for sale, and customers were warned against imitations.[7]

The General's arrival at Portsmouth was spectacular, and the Press spread itself. 'He came on shore in the evening, when hundreds of people assembled together to meet him, with loud acclamations of joy, crying "General Blakeney forever," repeating it over all the way as he went through the town to his lodgings. The bells rung to welcome him to Portsmouth; the church steeple was illuminated, and likewise the houses; bonfires were made (which lasted some hours), strong beer was brought upon a dray before the General's door, was given to the populace, and great rejoicings were made all over the town. The General went to the assembly and danced two minuets with a young lady, and afterwards played at cards.'

Honours were quickly showered on him. Within a fortnight the King had created him a Knight of the Bath; a few days later he was created a baron. Walpole wrote: 'An Irish peerage to old Blakeney, who went to Kensington [Palace] in a hackney coach, with a foot soldier behind it. As Blakeney had not only lost his government but was bed-rid while it was losing, these honours were a little ridiculed.'[8]

The senior officers who had served under Blakeney in Minorca were promoted, but General Stuart and the absentee colonels who had gone out in Byng's squadron and taken part in the councils of war were forbidden by the King to appear in his presence until an inquiry had been held into their conduct. This took place on December 8, but three days earlier Lord Barrington had a chat with Blakeney. The information the old General gave him was so useful that Barrington hurried off to Newcastle House to pass it on, and when the Duke heard it he promptly wrote to Hardwicke, with Barrington still in the room, to give news which 'tends to clear up the point about the loss of Minorca and to justify all that was done *here* more than any one which I have yet heard'.

Blakeney had assured Barrington that it had been possible to communicate with Fort St Philip and that Byng might have landed aid 'at any time, even in daytime, whilst he was master of St Philip's'. In addition, the old General had declared that had

Byng's squadron been successful in landing reinforcements, 'Marshal Richelieu and his Army must have capitulated.' In a postscript the Duke added that 'Admiral Boscawen was, and I believe is, as violent against Byng as anybody'.[9]

In their enthusiasm neither Barrington nor the Duke saw any flaws in Blakeney's extravagant claims, nor questioned how another 700 men—giving Blakeney a total of just over 3000— would have defeated a French Army of 15,000. However, Hardwicke acted swiftly when he received Newcastle's letter and replied that 'I have communicated it to my Lord Anson, who will make the best use of it he can in his present private situation'. He had also made sure that a hint was dropped to Sir John Ligonier, who was leading the inquiry on Stuart, Cornwallis and Effingham, 'that General Blakeney should be very particularly examined before the general officers upon these points'. His answers, said Hardwicke, ought to be sent to the Admiralty, who in turn should be ordered to call Blakeney as a witness at Byng's trial. 'This will be a regular method of proceeding.'[10]

However regular it was, it also illustrated the control that the Newcastle group still exercised in the workings of the administration, and the inquiry into the activities of the three Army officers dutifully called Blakeney, who repeated his original declaration and added that 'Admiral Byng made no signal perceived by the garrison, nor sent anybody off towards Fort St Philip'. Not one of the examining generals asked him about the British frigates or the position of the French Fleet at this particular time, and in their report they wrote that as far as the three officers were concerned, 'we do humbly submit to Your Majesty our unanimous opinion that . . . each of them is clear from any suspicion of disobedience of orders or neglect of duty.'[11]

Whether or not the King was gratified to find that three of his officers had been neither neglectful nor disobedient is not recorded; but the Duke of Newcastle was furious. 'I am amazed at the acquittal of these land officers when Lord Barrington says the communication was proved to be open,' he wrote to Hardwicke. 'I hope all possible care be taken about Byng's trial, for there the whole question ought to turn. Sure Clevland and Boscawen should and could make even Dr Hay [a member of the Board of Admiralty] ashamed of protecting, or conniving at Byng's acquittal, if the fact comes out, as we have the strongest reason now to think it . . .'[12]

Just before Pitt had taken office, the City of London, 'justly alarmed at the critical and unhappy situation of these kingdoms', called on its four Members of Parliament to exert their utmost ability 'towards procuring a strict and impartial Parliamentary inquiry into the causes of these national calamities'. The Borough of Ipswich soon followed suit. As if to add fresh topicality to these demands the French assembled another, but smaller, invasion force at Antibes. This time its destination was Corsica, which in the first few days of November they occupied without any difficulty. Since the Newcastle Government had brought home Sir Edward Hawke and the Mediterranean squadron, the French Government then had no further need for their Toulon squadron, which was paid off.

19

THE FOUR ADMIRALS

ON DECEMBER 2 PARLIAMENT began a new session with the King's Speech, which had been composed by Pitt and which outlined the Government's future policy. The most important items were the succour and preservation of America; an adequate and firm defence at home; and the formation of a militia. But the Hessian and Hanoverian troops, which had been brought over to defend the nation, were to be sent back home—much to the King's annoyance.

Next day Parliament was officially informed, according to custom, that one of its Members was under arrest. This was done by Vice-Admiral Boscawen, representing the Admiralty, who told the Members that: 'The King and the said Board having been dissatisfied with the conduct of Admiral Byng in the late action with the French Fleet in the Mediterranean, and for the appearance of his not having acted agreeably to his instructions for the relief of Minorca, he is now in custody in order to be tried by a court martial.'

Copies of a spurious King's Speech were circulated. Many of the hawkers in the streets were arrested, but the old King's only comment was that if the printer of the pamphlet was to be punished he hoped it would be mildly: he had read both the real and the spurious Speech, and as far as he understood either, he preferred the spurious.[1] Copies of the pamphlet were later publicly burned in Palace Yard, Westminster, by the common hangman in the presence of the Sheriffs.*

While the common hangman was doing his duty in Palace Yard, four members of the new Board of Admiralty—Lord Temple,

---

* The day that this solemn event took place was exactly a year after Lord Hardwicke had received a letter from Lord Anson saying that despite the latest intelligence from Toulon it 'would be a dangerous measure to part with your naval strength'. (See page 41)

Boscawen, West and Dr Hay—met and promoted two of their
number; Boscawen to be vice-admiral of the white, and West a
vice-admiral of the blue. They also decided that Vice-Admiral
Smith, at present commanding in The Downs, should preside
over Byng's court martial, and ordered him to go to Portsmouth
where it would be held. Soon Clevland was busy supervising the
drafting of letters and instructions. Byng was told that he would
be taken to Portsmouth and quartered in a ship, and that Smith
had been directed to assemble a court martial 'as soon as conveniently may be';[2] to the Secretary at War went a request 'to
appoint a proper guard to assist the Marshal for security of the
said Admiral in his removal to Portsmouth.'[3] Smith was sent
several Admiralty orders, letters and other papers, and also
extracts from several ships' log books, which would be needed as
evidence, and was told the Board wanted the trial to start on
Monday, December 27.[4]

Byng at once asked for permission to stay on shore during the
court martial—because of the difficulties of seeing people concerned with the trial, and also because of his bad health—and the
Board agreed, deciding that he should be lodged in Portsmouth
Dockyard.[5] Admiral Smith was soon writing from Portsmouth
that he wished the *St George* to be fitted out for the trial, and on
December 22 the Admiralty gave orders to the Navy Board to
arrange this, 'and to cause the men to work extra hard for the
greater expedition.'[6]

In the few days remaining those who had been called as witnesses at the trial had to decide whether to spend Christmas in
Portsmouth, or leave London very early on the 26th. Admiral
Byng was taken from Greenwich at 8 a.m. on December 21, and
travelled with Brough in a coach drawn by six horses, flanked by a
guard of fifty cavalry. When he arrived at Portsmouth two days
later he was taken to the house of Edward Hutchins, the Boatswain
of the Dockyard, who frequently rented rooms to officers temporarily on shore—Augustus Hervey, for instance, had often
stayed there in the past.

It stood just over a hundred yards back from the landing place,
in the centre of a triangle formed by the porter's lodge, the Master
Shipwright's house and the Clerk of the Survey's house. With a
north or north-west wind Hutchin's house reeked from the pitch
boiling in great vats beside the pitch houses on Pitch House

H

Jetty, less than two hundred yards away; with the wind anything between south and south-west there was the unpleasant smell of the large mud bank just offshore of the Camber.

Captain Arthur Gardiner, Byng's former first captain in the *Ramillies*, arrived a day or two later and lodged at Mrs Wilson's at Gosport, where he was joined on December 26 by Augustus Hervey. Old General Lord Blakeney left his house in St James's Street for Portsmouth on Christmas Eve. Those of Byng's friends and relatives who arrived at Portsmouth within a few hours were his nephews John and George, his cousin Edmond Bramston, Benjamin Gage, who had been acting as the Admiral's agent at Wrotham Park,* and Paul Whitehead, the pamphleteer and poet.

On Christmas Day there were five admirals' flags flying at Portsmouth. One was that of the Commander-in-Chief, Henry Osborn. The other four belonged to new arrivals—Smith's in the *St George*, Broderick's in the *Elizabeth*, Holburne's in the *Marlborough* and Norris's in the *Yarmouth*. It was no coincidence that brought the three last-named admirals to Portsmouth; they were there, as we shall soon see, for a serious purpose.

Admiral Byng spent Christmas in the company of his nephews and friends while in Norwich seventy of the oldest soldiers who fought in the siege of Fort St Philip and had since been repatriated were given a Christmas dinner by the Dean of Norwich, the Reverend Dr Bullock. Roast beef and 'plumb pudding', was served, with two barrels of beer, and there was a present of sixpence for each man. With their bellies full of beef, beer and Christmas pudding, the old veterans toasted Blakeney and the Dean without distinction, and cried scorn on the Duke de Richelieu. Their younger comrades stationed in the ancient city were later pleased to hear that the Reverend Dean was going to give the rest of them dinner, at the rate of forty a day, until all had been entertained.

The men who were to judge Byng had by now all arrived at Portsmouth. The most senior of them was Vice-Admiral Thomas Smith, who was probably chosen as president of the court martial

---

* Benjamin Gage married Rachel Marshall at South Mimms on April 27, 1751. Gage was a farmer, and both were friends of the Admiral, who had recently lent Benjamin £150 for some unspecified purpose. Mrs Gage was probably an old friend of the Admiral's late mistress, Mrs Hickson.

because he was related to the Grenvilles—who included, of course, Earl Temple, the First Lord.

Smith, 'a grey-headed man, of comely and respectable appearance; but of no capacity', according to Horace Walpole[7] was, like Byng, a bachelor; like Byng he had a country house and a middle-aged mistress; but there the resemblance ended, for Smith was the illegitimate son of a Mrs Smith, owner of a boarding house, and Sir Thomas Lyttelton, who had retired from Parliament in 1741 and gone to his country seat suffering from gout and complaining that 'my naughty stomach gives me no quarter, tho' I eat nothing yesterday but two wings of a boiled fowl'.*[8]

Thomas Smith was accepted by his father and his legitimate brothers, and had an amiable but weak personality. He had built Rockingham Hall, near Hagley, and this was his home while he was on half-pay. As we have already seen (page 94), he was the friend and patron of one of the captains, Amherst, and also of Everitt, who had served with Byng. (Among his other protégés were two officers later to become famous—Alexander Hood, later Lord Bridport, and his brother Samuel, later Lord Hood.)

Smith had been made Commander-in-Chief at The Downs in August 1755, but he had hoped to get a station where the chances of prize money would be greater. When Pitt and the Grenvilles entered the Government one of his brothers, the Dean of Exeter, ('seldom disturbed except when he heard of a vacant bishopric') wrote that 'Admiral Smith, who has been thought of for a seat at the Admiralty, will have what he likes much better, a station [of] his heart's content; that of the Leeward Islands, or the Western Station . . .'†[9]

Various regulations and usages governed courts martial: a court could not by then consist of more than thirteen or less than five

---

* Sir Thomas had married Christian Temple, aunt of the First Lord of the Admiralty. Admiral Smith was his eldest son, albeit illegitimate; and Sir Thomas's daughter, named Christian after her mother, married William Pitt's brother Thomas. Sir Thomas's sister Hester had married a Grenville; their daughter Hester had married William Pitt. Thus through a tangled web, William Pitt, Earl Temple, Vice-Admiral Smith, Vice-Admiral Temple West and George Grenville were all related. Sir Thomas's eldest legitimate son was the gloomy George Lyttelton, soon to become a peer.

† He added, 'with regard to myself, I have good reason to hope that I shall not be forgotten,' but less than three months later complained, 'My Lords the Bishops wrap themselves up in their virtue and their cloaks that the severe cold has carried none of them to Heaven yet, consequently your humble servant remains in status quo.'

members; and the officers chosen to sit on the court martial
were the most senior of those 'whose ships were then within the
districts and limits of the command of the flag officer, or commander-in-chief who presided at such court martial'.[10]

Any trial could, of course easily be 'rigged' by arranging that
enough senior officers known to be against the accused (or sufficiently aware of the possible damage to their future prospects if
they found in his favour) were sent to hoist their flags or command
ships in the particular harbour to form a majority just before the
trial. It seems unthinkable that anything of the sort should have
been done; but in addition to Admiral Smith, three rear-admirals
who are known to have been Anson's favourites, Holburne,
Norris and Broderick, were ordered to Portsmouth and hoisted
their flags there just before the trial; and since they were senior to
all the other officers there they were bound to be chosen. This was
the intention, according to Horace Walpole, who relates how Admiral Boscawen was dining at Sir Edward Montagu's one night
before the trial and the guests were discussing Byng's forthcoming
trial. 'It being disputed what the issue of it would be, Boscawen
said bluntly, "Well, say what you will, *we* shall have a majority,
and he will be condemned." This the Duchess of Manchester
repeated to Mrs Osborn [Byng's sister Sarah] and offered to
depose in the most solemn manner.'[11] Nevertheless, it was necessary to have some admirals at the trial of a flag officer.

Rear-Admiral Francis Holburne, next senior to Smith on the
court martial, had served with Boscawen the previous year off the
American coast, but Boscawen had no liking for him—indeed
that Admiral had written to his wife Fanny, 'He is a Scot, you
know I don't think well of that nation for upper leather, nor was
he ever thought much of in our service. He is sick and has contrived
to insinuate himself into the good graces of Lord Anson, made an
Admiral and sent here to my assistance.'[12]

Rear-Admiral Harry Norris was the youngest son of Admiral
of the Fleet Sir John Norris, and his brother Richard was the
captain who fled to Spain and disappeared after being accused,
with Mathews and Lestock, following the Battle of Toulon.

The fourth admiral, Broderick, had of course taken out the
reinforcement for Byng's squadron. Recently promoted to the
rank of rear-admiral, he, like Norris and Holburne, owed everything to Lord Anson. Of the nine captains who were finally to be

chosen to sit on the court martial, the most interesting was the Hon Augustus Keppel, who was next to the most junior member of the court.* His family was originally Dutch and he was the second son of the second Earl of Albermarle—the first Earl, his grandfather, had come over with William of Orange. Young Augustus had served under Anson in the *Centurion* and, inheriting the grace and charm which had made his father such a success at Court, he was soon one of the dour Admiral's favourites. (However, if friendship with Anson was responsible for him being at Portsmouth for the trial, he was subsequently, on Byng's behalf, to disappoint his patron.)

Augustus Hervey, referring to 'This most INFAMOUS Court', said its members 'were selected to be there at Portsmouth by Lord Anson for this purpose'.[13] This seems to be confirmed by the fact that Holburne, Norris and Broderick hauled down their flags and left Portsmouth immediately after the trial.

At Portsmouth the day of the trial began with a chilly north-easterly breeze hustling clouds low over the *St George*, which was moored off the Dockyard, squat and impressive in the early morning light. Vice-Admiral Smith's flag was soon flying from the foretopmast-head, and promptly at 8.30 a.m. a Union Flag was hoisted at the mizen-peak as the signal for a court martial to be held on board. Shortly afterwards a single gun was fired—a 'one-gun salute', as it was known—for all captains in the port to come on board.

By 9 a.m. most of the captains had trooped on board the *St George* and made their way to the great cabin, which had been fitted out as a court. The cabin was lit by the windows in the stern, and in front of them was a long table, set athwartships. Sitting at the centre of one side of the table, in full uniform of blue edged with gold, and wearing his three-cornered hat, according to custom, was Vice-Admiral Smith. Rear-Admiral Holburne, as next senior, sat on his right while Norris was on Smith's left. Next to him was Broderick, the most junior of the quartet. The captains filed into the cabin. The beams were low: a cannon on each side added a warlike appearance to the scene, squatting black and menacing on its carriage. The usual stench from the bilges

---

* But later, as Viscount Keppel and an admiral of the white, to be First Lord of the Admiralty 1782–3.

penetrated even as high as this cabin; and there was the all-pervading smell of dampness.

The captains had brought their commissions with them, and one by one the dates were read out. Captain Charles Holmes was the most senior; Francis Geary was next, followed by William Boys, John Moore, John Simcoe, James Douglas, John Bentley, Augustus Keppel and Peter Denis. The rest of the captains junior to Denis were dismissed: the court would consist of four admirals and nine captains—a total of thirteen, the maximum allowed at this period. The ritual of choosing the captains took all the morning, and the newly-formed court decided that they would not be sworn in until the next day, when the trial itself would start.

By now Portsmouth was full of notabilities: apart from Lord Blakeney, there were Lord Robert Bertie, Colonel Cornwallis and the newly-promoted Vice-Admiral Temple West, as well as people like Lord Morton and Lord Willoughby, who had come down as spectators and were described by Augustus Hervey as 'both creatures of Lord Hardwicke and who were thought, as far as they were able, to do all they could to prejudice everyone against the Admiral'.[14] Portsmouth, commented the *Evening Post*, 'has not for many years past appeared with so military a face'.

20

THE TRIAL BEGINS

PROMPTLY AT 8.15 next morning, Tuesday, December 28, the signal for a court martial was made once again from the *St George* and the three admirals and nine captains had themselves rowed over from their various ships. Although a trial was about to be held, there was plenty of bustle on board the *St George*. Two hoys came alongside as the officers arrived, and the first of fourteen butts of beer were hoisted on board, with casks containing more than 500 pounds of beef to follow.[1]

Once in the great cabin the four admirals settled down in their chairs along one side of the table. The nine captains then seated themselves, in order of senority, to the right and left of the admirals. Charles Fearne, the Judge-Advocate, sat at one end of the table on Smith's right: Byng's shorthand writer, Thomas Cook, who was also a barrister, sat at the other. Admiral Smith then ordered: 'Bring the prisoner in.'

Byng had been taken from Hutchins's house by a guard of Marines armed with muskets and bayonets: they had marched him down to the steps, where Brough escorted him into a boat. Several Marines then scrambled in and sat on the thwarts, their muskets between their knees, while more Marines boarded other boats and the little convoy then set off for the *St George*. The escort was ludicrous and more suitable for guarding a score of dangerous young mutineers then a staid, middle-aged Admiral; but the Admiralty orders to Vice-Admiral Osborn had been quite specific.

As Byng climbed up the side of *St George* no doubt his mind went back to the last time he boarded her: then sideboys had stood to attention and the bosun's pipes had twittered out a salute because, of course, he had been her commanding officer, flag captain to Sir Charles Hardy. The great cabin in which he was now to be tried for his life had been his quarters for many months, and the ship had been his last individual command, because on leaving her he had been promoted to rear-admiral.

After Byng had been brought in to the court room and shown to a chair in front of the table, to the left of the president, Smith told the Judge-Advocate to carry on. Fearne stood up and started reading from a series of documents. The first was the Admiralty's order to Admiral Smith to hold a court martial on Byng, followed by the first warrant to Brough to take Byng into custody, and then the second, which gave the charge:

> '. . . That he, the said John Byng, having the command of His Majesty's Fleet in the Mediterranean . . . on the 20th day of May last, did withdraw, or keep back, and did not do his utmost to take, seize and destroy the ships of the French King, which it was his duty to have engaged, and to assist such of His Majesty's ships as were engaged in fight with the French ships, which it was his duty to have assisted: and for that he the said John Byng did not do his utmost to relieve St Philip's Castle . . . but acted contrary to and in breach of his instructions . . .'

Fearne then administered the oath to the court: standing, they all raised their right hands and repeated after him, sentence by sentence, that they swore 'upon the Holy Evangelist', to duly administer justice 'without partiality, favour or affection'. The oath ended with a sentence which was to cause them all a great deal of trouble in the near future: 'I do further swear that I will not upon any account, at any time whatsoever, disclose or discover the vote or opinion of any particular member of this court martial, unless thereunto required by an Act of Parliament. So help me God'.

Then, to finish off the formalities, Admiral Smith administered the oath to Fearne. The witnesses were ordered to withdraw, and Byng gave a letter to Admiral Smith, asking that the Judge-Advocate should read it out, as he had 'a violent inflammation in the eyes'.

Smith agreed, and Fearne began reading.

'Gentlemen, I have earnestly wished the arrival of the time for inquiring into my conduct and behaviour, and think myself extremely happy at its approach; I doubt not to evince the falsehood of all the artful malicious aspersions cast upon me by my enemies;

and to prove that the unprecedented indignities, distresses, and oppressions I have suffered, cannot be justified by any actual demerit of mine, nor even any appearance of it.'

He had one request to make: he wished to waive the evidence of one of his officers ('because not very material, as he was stationed on the middle-deck') so that he could 'assist me in regulating my minutes, which I am unable to do myself, from an inflammation of my eyes, occasioned by a severe cold during my confinement, and to entreat the usual indulgence of a person to take the minutes of the proceedings in shorthand'.

Admiral Smith then ordered the cabin to be cleared while the court considered a certain point, and Byng was led out by Brough to a cabin set aside as a temporary cell. Two hours later the court was opened again and Byng brought back. The Judge-Advocate then read out a resolution of the court. It had been considering how far back the present inquiry into Byng's conduct ought to go, and had agreed that 'The order being general, the inquiry ought to be made from the time of the squadron's sailing from St Helen's'.

Since the charge against Byng referred only to his activities on the day of the battle, this caused something of a sensation in the court. As Augustus Hervey wrote, 'Every person present showed their surprise that the charge was not confined to the day of the action, but had a retrospection to the hour in which the Admiral sailed from St Helen's, so that the resentment of the nation which was raised against the Admiral for his supposed cowardice and all their attention which was carried on to that period was now dwindled to an inquiry into all parts of his conduct from the time he unfortunately accepted the command of that pitiful squadron'.[2]

Byng's request that Lt Edward Clark should be allowed to help him in 'regulating my minutes' was refused because he was to be a witness. This was a great hardship for Byng, as Clark had for weeks been sorting out the Admiral's papers and helping prepare the defence. Byng, hardly able to see, was forced to ask that the examination of witnesses be put off until the next day, and the court adjourned. Once again the Admiral was taken on shore to Hutchins's house, where he had a late meal and spent the rest of the afternoon and evening discussing the day's events with Edmund Bramston, Hervey, Lt Clark, his lawyer Thomas Cook, Paul Whitehead and Benjamin Gage.

The first witness, when the court met again on Wednesday, December 29, was Vice-Admiral Temple West, who had, on Christmas Eve, attended a Board meeting in London which had given him orders to go to Portsmouth and 'exert himself' in getting thirteen ships ready for sea.[3]

After Fearne had administered the oath, West sat down in the witness's chair in front of the table, with the Judge-Advocate on his left, the President of the court almost in front of him, and with Byng sitting a few feet away to the right, red-eyed but alert.

West, warned by Admiral Smith not to reply until the Judge-Advocate had written the question down, gave his evidence very carefully: he made great play about not expressing opinions ('I should choose to avoid giving my opinion as an officer—I will speak to facts,' he told the President).

Was there any delay in the passage from St Helen's to Gibraltar?—'None that appeared to me,' replied West.

The stay of six days in Gibraltar was due to the need to get water and wine on board: was there a possibility of sailing from Gibraltar sooner than they did? West at first gave a round-about answer, declaring that he was giving facts: but when asked the same question in a different form, said he did not think there was an unnecessary delay.

When the court asked him about the squadron's arrival off Minorca, West described Hervey's attempt to get in touch with Fort St Philip, and then the sighting of the French squadron. As Smith and other members of the court questioned him in detail about the French ships' activities, West's answers slowly built up a word picture of the battle, particularly the part played by the van division and his flagship, the *Buckingham*.

Finally came an all-important question from Admiral Smith: 'How did the Admiral's ships and the rest of our Fleet proceed from the time of our van beginning to engage, till the engagement was over?'

Again West did not give a direct answer, saying that he did not know anything about the movements of Byng's division until after the action with the French van had ceased, although when the French rear came towards him he 'took notice that the rear of the English Fleet was considerably astern of us, and while the French rear was coming up some of the ships of our rear appeared to me, at times, with their maintopsails aback and at other times making sail towards us . . .'

Was the wind and weather such, asked Smith, that Byng's division could have got up to the enemy and engaged as closely as West's division?—'Yes, it appeared to me so. I saw no impediments: I am not to be understood to say that there was no impediment,' he added, 'I only say I saw none.'

Then Smith asked if during the battle or after he had expressed his opinion 'of the behaviour or proceedings of any of the officers or the ships, and in particular of the behaviour or proceedings of the Admiral?'

At this West appeared outraged: 'This question appears to me of an extraordinary nature,' he declared. 'I cannot conceive that as an evidence [sic] I am at all called upon to know at what I expressed dissatisfaction.' It was not a matter of fact, he said. 'When I saw the rear of our fleet astern, I could not but be dissatisfied with that appearance. I saw the Fleet in that situation but cannot tell the reason.' He then added, ambiguously, 'There was an appearance of some want in somebody, but with whom I cannot pretend to say'.

West's evidence thus gave no inkling that he had been so dissatisfied with the conduct of Captains Ward, Parry and Cornwall that he at first refused to sit at the council of war with them; but it certainly gave the impression that he really blamed Byng but was too loyal to say so.

The court adjourned for the day, and that evening Mr John Greenway, who held the post of storekeeper at Portsmouth Dockyard at a salary of £200 a year, wrote to the Admiralty giving a report on the trial so far. 'I hear various opinions but the weight inclines against Mr Byng much, by all I can perceive; however, he may shew things in a different light when he makes his defence . . .'[4]

West resumed his evidence on Thursday morning and the court went back to the time when the squadron reached Gibraltar from England. West described how Captains Noel and Edgcumbe had come on board, after visiting the *Ramillies* when the squadron arrived, to tell him of the French invasion of Minorca.

Did Byng later tell him of this intelligence? West said he did, and hastened to add that 'with respect to the consulting me about it, he did not consult in any manner so as to divert him from the pursuing his orders, which were to proceed to Minorca'.

Did Admiral Byng, from the end of the battle until the council of war, ask 'the advice, opinion or sentiments of yourself, or any other person in your hearing, with respect to any part of his proceedings?' West ignored the question but used it as an opportunity to say that 'Immediately after the action I received a letter from Mr Byng in which he was pleased to make use of many obliging expressions with regard to me'. Going on board the *Ramillies*, West said, he found Byng 'much dissatisfied with the behaviour of some of the ships in his division. I said I was very sorry to hear that and hoped, if that was the case, he would not continue those captains in their command'.

Now it was Byng's turn to examine West, and he began with questions about Fowke's council of war. Referring to the conversations between himself and Fowke, at which West had been present, Byng asked if it was not customary to the service 'in matters of consequence relating to the service, to do it in writing, and by letter?'

'Yes, generally speaking.'

'Did you look upon this as a private conversation, or as an application on the service?'

'The manner in which this transaction passed had very little the air of business about it,' said West.

Did not West think it necessary to have sufficient water and provisions on board for the expedition, as it was known that Minorca was in enemy hands, and consequently could not supply anything?—'I think so,' said West, forgetting his earlier protests that he would speak only of fact and not voice opinions.

But Byng dragged several admissions from him: in the light airs and calms of the morning of May 19, the day the squadron arrived off Mahon, there was no chance of the squadron getting close, West said, and the enemy were 'so masters of Mahon harbour as to prevent the English Fleet from making use of it with security to themselves'.

Had it been possible to put the soldiers in Byng's squadron on shore, did he think it would have been proper, when the enemy's Fleet was in sight? West agreed that 'the weakening of that force of the Fleet would have been highly inexcusable under the circumstances of seeing the enemy's Fleet, as well as exposing the English Fleet to that of the enemy, which was at that time superior to it'.

Had it been practicable to land the Fusiliers who were acting as

Marines, would the ships then have been fit for action?—'No, I think not,' said West.

Did he think that landing one hundred officers and recruits to reinforce the garrison of St Philip's would have enabled it to have held out against enemy attacks? West said he was not a proper judge of that question, but from the opinions of Army officers to whom he spoke in Gibraltar, and from what he understood of the state of St Philip's and the enemy's strength, he thought that neither the one hundred men nor the battalion that was to have been picked up at Gibraltar 'could have defended the castle of St Philip's against the enemy in such a manner as for them not to have surrendered'.

Byng then asked him about the condition of each of the ships in the squadron, and West answered in detail: the *Captain* 'was always leaky and always sickly, and was, in my opinion, a very unfit ship to have been sent abroad upon service'; the *Portland* was a good ship but 'was very foul and for the weight of metal she carried was undermanned'; the *Trident*'s captain had complained about the quality of his crew; the *Princess Louisa*'s masts were condemned; the *Defiance* as 'remarkably ill-manned' and had a leak which they could not discover; the *Revenge* was ill-manned.

But the details West was now giving were a damning indictment of the Admiralty for having such a squadron in the Mediterranean, and some members of the court martial were so alarmed at the disclosures that they ordered the court to be cleared immediately while they discussed it. When the court was recalled, Admiral Smith said they wished to question West about the condition of several of the ships, some of which were in his own division. 'Was not their goodness and condition such as enabled them to beat the ships of the French that were opposed to them. . . ?' he asked. West explained that his own ship was considerably more powerful than her particular opponent, and when he drove the French ship out of the line he was able to help the *Captain* so that her opponent had the two British ships against him, and so on.

That ended West's evidence, and there was a stir of interest as General Lord Blakeney's name was called.

The Judge-Advocate administered the oath to Lord Blakeney, and the gout-ridden old soldier eased himself into the witness chair, conscious that he was the centre of the stage and apparently convinced that there was no aspect of the recent campaign on which he was not qualified to give an opinion.

'Was the port of St Philip's open to a communication by sea on the 19th and 20th May when the English Fleet were off Minorca?' asked Admiral Smith.

'The sally port was made up to prevent desertion with new stores, which could have been removed in very little time,' Blakeney said; but the evasiveness of this reply, which made no mention of the French guns, was lost on the court because the old man glanced down at a piece of paper in his hand, and Admiral Byng at once asked 'Whether that paper was wrote [sic] at the time to which he is examined.'

Smith turned to Blakeney. 'When did you write that paper?'

Blakeney was devastatingly frank: 'I would not depend upon my own memory, and I had this from several others.'

'Then you must put that paper into your pocket,' retorted Smith, 'and not refer to it.'

As soon as Blakeney had stuffed the paper out of sight the original question was repeated, and he said there were several other landing places where troops could have been put on shore.

Could a boat or boats have safely gone to sea from the sally port?—'I am very certain they could.'

If the one hundred officers and recruits for Minorca on board the British ships had been landed, would they have been of any considerable help in defending Fort St Philip?—'I am certain they would,' he said, 'for the duty was hard upon the officers, particularly upon the subalterns, there being forty-one commissioned officers absent . . . As to the recruits and others, I was forced to employ a number of men that could have handled their arms very well as workmen and gunners.'

Admiral Smith asked: 'How much longer do you think the fort of St Philip's might have held out if Lord Robert Bertie's battalion had been thrown into it, when the Fleet was off Mahon?'—'There are so many incidents happen in war,' replied Blakeney cagily, perhaps wondering if someone was going to point out that the French besiegers numbered more than 15,000, 'that that question cannot be answered.'

Byng then asked if he thought that troops could have been

landed 'without being incommoded and in danger from the fire of the enemy'? It was a clumsily-phrased question and Blakeney's reply was sarcastic: 'I have served these sixty-three years, and I never knew any enterprise undertaken without some danger; and this might have been effected with as little danger as any I ever knew.'

But then, as Byng questioned him about the French gun batteries round the landing places, he contradicted himself from time to time. Blakeney first said he did not know if the French had any battery on Cape Mola [opposite St Philip's] on the 19th, but if they had it was so high that 'it could not do much execution upon any boat that might have attempted to land there'. He had not heard of them firing on Boyd's boat as he left to try to reach the squadron, but admitted that the Fort had received 'considerable damage' from the battery, and the landing place was within range of its grapeshot. He reiterated that it had not fired at Boyd. As for Turk's Mount, near St Stephen's Cove, which was just south of the Fort, the French had a battery, 'but it is at such a distance that it cannot command the cove'.

Byng asked him the distance, but the General declared that he 'never measured it'.

How did he know that it was so far off it could not fire into the cove?—'Because [the] banks are pretty high and [the] water pretty low, and they could not from the Mount see any boats or anything in the cove.'

He agreed the French controlled the whole of the southern shore of the cove, and when Byng asked him whether boats could land men there without being fired on by the French, he said 'They can, if they choose a proper time of night for it.'

'Is night the proper time to land a body of men?' asked Byng. It was a stupid question and Blakeney merely said: 'I know that I have landed men in the night'—probably a reference to his part in the catastrophic attack on Cartagena, when he served under Vernon.

Byng finally asked Blakeney what time Boyd had been sent out to him. The General said it was 3 or 4 p.m.—'as soon as Captain Scrope could get the boat ready'. He admitted he had seen Byng's squadron at 10 a.m., but repeated that the boat was sent as soon as possible. With that admission the General's evidence ended.

Next day was New Year's Eve, and Robert Boyd, the storekeeper of the ordnance at Minorca, gave his evidence. He was asked by Admiral Smith if the available landing places could have 'received succours in fine weather without being greatly annoyed by the enemy's batteries?' Boyd said that most of them would be 'little annoyed'.

Boyd then described how he had suggested in the morning going off to Byng's squadron to deliver a message, and how an hour before sunset he was rowed out of St Stephen's Cove by ten sailors.

He then said that as soon as the French on Turk's Mount saw him they opened fire, first with muskets and then with three cannon, thus completely contradicting Blakeney's evidence that Turk's Mount was too far away and too high for the French to open fire from it.

Byng then asked Boyd a series of questions which did not help him at all. How many boats did he think could have landed at any time on May 19, when the weather was fair?—'As many as had been sent,' said Boyd.

'Was there room for twenty boats to land at a time?' pressed Byng, blithely disregarding the fact that whatever the answer it would obviously worsen his case. 'Yes, five times that number . . .'

Byng went on to question him about the length of time that had elapsed between Boyd suggesting he took a message out to the squadron and his actual getting away in the boat. Was it one, two or five hours? Boyd refused to be drawn. What time was the boat ordered to be prepared? He did not know. Was the boat ready at the time he received the council's letter to take out to the squadron? Boyd said that it was not—'nor for some time afterwards'.

'Can you remember how long time after it was?' demanded Byng.

'I cannot say exactly the number of hours,' said Boyd, 'but I remember that the time was so long it appeared extremely tedious to me.'

At the end of the day, when the court adjourned, Byng said he wished to have Lord Blakeney recalled as he had a question he wanted to ask him.

New Year's Day was not very festive, and when the Court assembled Byng announced that he only had one question to put to Lord Blakeney. It was brief and to the point: 'If the whole of the detachment which was ordered from Gibraltar had been landed at Minorca, could you have saved the island?'

'I do not understand the question,' said Blakeney. 'It is impossible for anybody to tell that.'

But Byng and his advisers had worked on the question too long to be put off. Had not Blakeney declared that if the detachment from Gibraltar had been landed, he could have saved the island?

Blakeney was now caught up in his own web of drawing-room heroics, but he said: 'I have declared it, that without force enough to drive the enemy out of the island, there was no saving it.'

'The question is,' said Byng patiently, 'whether you did not declare that if you had received that detachment from Gibraltar, you could not have saved the island?'

The General realized he was trapped, but he said: 'By the oath I have taken, I believe I could have held out till Sir Edward Hawke arrived, if that detachment had been landed.'*

Byng was relentless: 'The question is,' he repeated, 'whether you never declared that if that detachment from Gibraltar had been landed, you could not have saved the island?'

'I did declare so,' admitted the old General. He then made a rambling statement about it being the duty of a governor to stay in the same place and send other people out for intelligence, and 'as he remains there, can know nothing but what he receives from others . . .'

The court thanked him and said they had no further questions, and there was no objection to him going back to Town.

The first lieutenant of West's flagship, Lt John Bover, was called next. Asked if there was any delay in the passage to Gibraltar, he said: 'Not in the least that I can remember.' He was equally forthright when asked if there was any delay while watering at Gibraltar. 'As we worked there night and day, especially in watering, I think there was not.'

He was followed by the *Buckingham*'s second, third and fourth lieutenants, who gave evidence about the weather on the day of the battle. The court then adjourned.

Byng spent Sunday going through Thomas Cook's transcript of the previous evidence, and on Monday, January 3, Captain Everitt, who had commanded the *Buckingham*, gave his evidence.

Byng's questions were simple enough: Everitt agreed it would

---

* The battle was on May 20; the island surrendered on June 28th, and Hawke arrived off Minorca on July 18. Blakeney's declaration had also been made to Barrington and at the Stuart inquiry.

not have been possible to sail from Gibraltar earlier; agreed that it would not have been proper to land the troops at St Philip's when the French squadron was in sight; and agreed that if all Lord Robert Bertie's Fusiliers had been landed, the British ships would not have been fit to engage the French. Nor would putting 'such an inconsiderable reinforcement' have been a sufficient reason for losing time and delaying an attack on the French squadron once it was in sight.

That concluded the evidence of the officers of the *Buckingham*. All of them had disclaimed any knowledge of what Byng's division did during the battle. The next witness was Captain James Gilchrist, who had commanded the little *Experiment* in the battle. Gilchrist had no reason to like Byng because when Captain Noel, commanding the *Princess Louisa*, died after the battle, Gilchrist had asked to be given the ship, but Byng had instead given her to Parry. Writing later that Gilchrist's evidence at the trial was 'as unfavourable as it was possible in such a cause', Hervey said he was not surprised 'as I had ever found him the most fawning sycophant that ever cringed to power'.[5]

Nor did Hervey exaggerate. Asked to describe the action, Gilchrist said that 'The Rear-Admiral [West] and his division, except the *Defiance*, bore right down before the wind and hauled up opposite to the proper ships, and attacked the enemy'. As for the rear division, 'Admiral Byng did not bear down before the wind upon the enemy, nor any of his division'.

No one commented when, a few minutes later, asked if he saw Byng's division engaged 'at a proper distance', he contradicted himself completely by saying that 'when the Admiral's division fell in with the enemy—that is, the headmost ships, *Revenge*, *Louisa* and *Trident*—when they began to fire there was such a smoke that I could not judge of the distance'.

Rear-Admiral Broderick then questioned him. Gilchrist had said the *Revenge*, *Louisa* and *Trident* made such a smoke when they began to fire 'that you could not judge of the distance they were. Did you at that time see the *Ramillies* engage?' Gilchrist said he saw the *Ramillies* open fire 'some time after'.

Another member of the court, Captain Moore, then asked him to explain why he referred to the *Ramillies* 'firing and not engaging?'

'Where I was situated,' replied Gilchrist, 'my line of direction from me was such that I did not see any enemy near the *Ramillies*.'

The rest of his evidence made it quite clear that even then he had not understood the tactics that Byng had intended to use; nor, indeed, did he appreciate that parallel lines never meet because he declared that 'our van bore down and engaged the enemy, and came in a parallel line with them', while the rear 'went down angling upon the enemy [i.e. lasking], therefore they could not all engage the enemy so near as the van did'.

The next witness was Augustus Hervey. Whereas Gilchrist, with the *Experiment*, had been stationed near the *Buckingham* to repeat West's signals, so Hervey had been near the *Ramillies* to repeat Byng's signals. The court asked him to describe the battle, and he then proceeded to give them the most detailed description they had yet heard, only occasionally referring to a note in his hand giving times. Night had fallen by the time he had finished and questioning was put off till the next day.

Hervey went to dinner with Admiral Byng at Hutchins's house that night, and found the Admiral 'well satisfied with the manner I had related the truths of that day'.[6]

Next day he was again called 'and cross-examined with no small acrimony by several, but I had the satisfaction to find that I had not made an improper answer and had given several of them very severe ones. Nor did I ever fail to throw in everything in my power that I could to prove I thought that the failure of that day's success should have ALL laid at the door of those infamous Ministers who sent such a weak squadron out, after all the repeated intelligences they had'.

This claim seems rather an exaggeration when one reads the verbatim report of the trial; but certainly his evidence was clear and the *Phoenix*'s position as repeating frigate allowed him to be exact about times of signals and events. However, it left him open to be criticized. Mrs Elizabeth Montagu, for instance, the original 'Bluestocking', wrote to Admiral Boscawen's wife Fanny, 'I admire Captain Hervey's method of watching the battle. I have known people boil an egg with a watch in their hand, counting the minutes, but I never knew we were to do so while we basted the French'. The *Evening Post* reported that Hervey 'appeared to be very candid and much more clear and distinct than the other captains'.

The next witness was Amherst, of the *Deptford*, and he was followed by Lt Peter Foulkes, formerly first lieutenant of the

Phoenix, whose evidence showed (although Mrs Elizabeth Montagu was probably never told), why Hervey had been so accurate about times. Foulkes, answering a question about the *Ramillies*'s signals, said that Hervey 'was upon deck with a watch in his hand observing them'.

Captain Lloyd, formerly of the *Chesterfield*, followed. He was the first to give detailed evidence about the *Ramillies* having to back her topsails to avoid a collision with the *Trident*. 'The *Trident* seemed to be close under the lee bow, and they appeared to me as if they were on board each other.'

This was, of course, a very important point: if Byng was to be proved guilty of cowardice and of 'not doing his utmost' then the prosecution had, among other things, to show that there was no valid reason for the *Ramillies* stopping when she did and likewise no valid reason for Byng ordering the rest of the ships in the squadron to stop.

Under repeated questioning by Captain Moore and Admiral Smith about Byng and the amount of sail his division set, Lloyd became angry.

'You seem to be warm, which is not becoming,' observed Admiral Smith.—'I am not warm, but it behoves me to see that my evidence is consistent,' he replied.

'Captain Lloyd thinks the court endeavours to trap him, and nobody means it,' commented Captain Moore.

Lloyd's evidence—which was favourable to Byng and showed that it was necessary for the *Ramillies* to take swift measures to avoid a collision—was confirmed by the *Deptford*'s former first lieutenant, Henry John Phillips, who had been promoted captain since the battle.

On January 6th the court began its ninth day of sittings and heard several other junior officers, whose evidence was straightforward. Then Captain James Young, formerly of the *Intrepid*, was called in. On the strength of his letters to his merchant friend and to his wife attacking Byng, which the Ministers had so welcomed, he was regarded as one of the most useful of the prosecution witnesses. After a few preliminary questions, Admiral Smith asked him: 'Did the loss of your foretopmast put any ship in danger of being on board of you?'

'No,' said Young, 'not that I could perceive at all.'

'Did the loss of your foretopmast,' asked Captain Moore,

'occasion any impediment to the Admiral, and the rear division, from going down and engaging the enemy close?'

'Not that I could perceive.'

'Did you observe any ships in the rear of you backing [their sails] at the time that you lost your foretopmast?' asked Admiral Smith.

'I did not mind the ships in the rear,' replied Young. 'Just then they were not backing; they were to windward of me when I bore down.'

This was such a ridiculous answer that Smith repeated the question and Young said: 'I did not then.'

Again Smith pressed him: 'Did you see any ships backing soon after you lost your foretopmast?'

'I saw ships on the weather quarter with their topsails aback,' Young admitted.

'Do you think that they were at any time in any danger of being on board of you?'

'No,' said Young, 'we were to leeward of them; we could not drive athwart them.' He said later that Byng and the rear division did pass to leeward of him, though it was some time after—'Not much above three quarters of an hour, or an hour, I believe; it cannot be much above.'

Young was then asked about certain signals and replied with a surprising frankness, 'I took no notice of any signal after the signal to engage was made.' At this point, and perhaps not surprisingly, Captain Moore said he felt faint, and the court adjourned for the day.

Next day the questioning of Young continued and the minutes of the previous day's hearing, read over before the court proceeded, showed Young had made three main claims: he had not lost his foretopmast until he was in close action with the enemy: that losing his foretopmast had not delayed any of the ships astern; that after the signal to engage—which had, of course, been made by Byng when the *Defiance* failed to lead down on the enemy—Young had purposely ignored all other signals.

Now Captain Simcoe referred to Young's evidence that it had been three-quarters of an hour or an hour before Byng and his division passed him. Did he see anything which could have prevented Byng from passing the *Intrepid* and closing with the ship next-ahead, thus filling the gap in the line?

'No,' said Young, 'none at all appeared to me if they had the same wind and weather that I had . . .'

Admiral Holburne commented on the amount of damage the *Intrepid* had received. Was this all from one French ship?

No, replied Young; for a good part of the time he had three ships firing at him.

What was Byng's division doing while the three French ships fired at the *Intrepid*?—'I cannot be positive what they were doing, for at that time I was minding my own ship.'

Finally Byng began a relentless questioning which made Young finally change his story about the ships astern. He had said earlier that the *Revenge* had sent a boat to ask if she could pass to leeward; but now he claimed he did not know where she was at the time.

'Did you observe the *Revenge* brought-to or aback, when her boat was on board of you, or when the boat was returning to the *Revenge*?' Byng asked.

'I did not observe that, but she presently passed me after her boat was gone.'

Byng was not satisfied. What position was she in when she sent the boat?—'I answered that before. I did not see her but she passed me presently after.'

'The question is,' repeated Byng, 'when she did send her boat on board, what position was she then in?'

Young gave up. 'She was right astern of me then, rather on the lee quarter.'

'In what position?'

'With her topsails,' said Young, artfully.

'A-back or full?'

'Shivering, I think, waiting for her boat.'

Byng then asked a series of questions—aimed at proving the two ships could not have been as Young claimed—about the relative positions of the two ships and the direction of the wind.

'As you have said that you did not see the *Revenge* from the time that you lost your foretopmast till she was near you, and did not know where she was, *how do you know* that there was no impediment to our rear's closing the enemy during that time?'

Young had been neatly trapped, and he realized it at once. 'I answered as to my own ship that I made no impediment to any other ship's closing,' he said, embarrassed at having been shown to be a liar. 'I say that now [sic] appeared to me.'

Byng then forced Young into a further series of admissions:
using his boastfulness—he had said 'There were us four that were
pretty much damaged in the action'—Byng then asked if the
squadron, after the battle, was in a fit condition to go into action
again.

No, said Young, because the French squadron had gone off
seemingly without damage—in fact, only one French ship had
her maintopsail-yard carried away.

In what part of the French line did that damaged ship seem to
be? Byng asked innocently. 'Rather in the rear,' Young was
forced to admit.

21

THE FAKED LOG BOOK

IT WAS NOW Captain Frederick Cornwall's turn to tell the story
of the battle from the point of view of the *Revenge*, the ship
immediately astern of the *Intrepid*. He was still smarting under the
remarks made after the battle about his courage, and he gave his
evidence with an excited precision. He told how he had been
steering down for his particular antagonist in the French line when
he came up astern of the *Intrepid*, which had lost her foretopmast,
and he brought-up on her weather quarter. Then, he told the court,
he went to his cabin windows and was surprised to see the Admiral's ship 'at a considerable distance'.

A quarter of an hour later, he said, the *Princess Louisa* arrived
so close 'that I apprehended her jib-boom was over my taffrail'
but she subsequently vanished in the smoke, and the *Trident*
arrived astern. Cornwall had not, of course, passed the *Intrepid*,
and he was very worried about the way he was going to describe
the situation. He had engaged his French opposite number, he
said, for half an hour, expecting any minute that Byng would
signal the *Intrepid* to leave the line 'because she was the cause that
I could not go on; but upon waiting some time . . .'

He broke off, and then declared: 'What I have to tell may be
against myself; but as I am sworn to tell the truth, I must do so'
and he went on to describe how, after waiting some time, he
'thought it might be for the King's service to endeavour to go on',
so he closed with the *Intrepid* 'almost within the fire of the
Intrepid's guns'.

'When I was there,' he said, 'I had great reason to apprehend
I might have been becalmed alongside her . . . and as I had no
authority for what I did, I thought if my ship had been disabled
I might have been blamed as I should have been between two
fires.' So he sent a boat to Young to tell him 'that I thought it was
for our service to go up to the relief of the van . . .'

Admiral Smith then questioned him about the *Louisa* and *Trident*. 'When was it that you say that they were in a little confusion?'

'I did not speak of any confusion,' said Captain Cornwall primly, 'neither was there any confusion.'

When it was Byng's turn to question him, the Admiral asked why, since Cornwall had said he was apprehensive of being becalmed alongside the *Intrepid* under her lee, he could not have passed her to windward, or more to leeward?

'To windward was what I never thought of,' Cornwall replied stiffly, 'I could not think of withdrawing from the enemy I was engaged with . . . as to going to leeward, I believe I might if I had thought myself authorized; and certainly should, but must have suffered greatly between two fires.'*

Since Cornwall had by now amply demonstrated that he was very attentive to orders, Byng's next question was: 'What authorized you to lay by that ship [the *Intrepid*]? Was it by orders from the Admiral, or by a signal from the Admiral?'

Cornwall had several reasons—by Byng never making a signal for the *Intrepid* to leave the line; by his not hauling down the signal for line of battle; and 'by my instructions that order me to relieve a ship in distress'.

'What', demanded Byng, 'does the 24th Article of the Fighting Instructions command captains to do in a line of battle?'

Cornwall then read the 24th Article.† 'I have read it,' he declared, 'and I read it on the day of the action; and I tell you, I thought it was wrong, and that it [i.e. not passing the *Intrepid*] was a breach of the article. I answer to the question: to keep his station in the line and to close.'

Despite the importance of the point that Byng was trying to make, Admiral Smith hurriedly interposed: 'We have nothing to do with Captain Cornwall's duty.'

Byng protested that he would show another ship—the *Deptford* —had been ordered to protect the *Intrepid* and since he was himself accused of stopping the *Ramillies*, he must prove what caused him to do it.

---

* The *Revenge*, it should be remembered, suffered no casualties and was hit by only three shot. Cornwall was fortunate not to have been asked about this.

† No ship in the Fleet was to leave her station upon any pretence without the captain telling his flag officer of the condition of his ship and receiving his orders, 'But in case any ship shall do so, the next ships are to close up the line . . .'

Finally Cornwall said that 'as Mr Byng thinks it was my ship
was the cause, there are two gentlemen now in England that were
on board the *Revenge* at that time' [Lord Effingham and a Captain
Haley] and to them he had 'called often to observe the situation
of the Admiral'.

Obviously evidence about the next ship to the *Revenge*, which
was the *Princess Louisa*, was very important; but there were no
witnesses from that ship to give the court any information. This
was particularly unfortunate because it had a great bearing on the
role of her next astern, the *Trident*, and, of course, the *Ramillies*,
which was following.

When the court met again on Monday, January 10, it heard
about the *Trident* from her captain, Philip Durell, who was asked
if the *Trident* was impeded, while going down towards the enemy,
by her next ahead, the *Princess Louisa*. No, said Durell, 'not at
all from getting down'.

Did the *Intrepid* impede any of the ships in the rear?—'Not that
I saw.'

Durell, whose ship had been followed by Byng's flagship, then
described the situation as he saw it. The *Princess Louisa* and the
Intrepid, ahead of him in the line, were apparently badly damaged
and the French ships, as they passed, were opening a heavy fire
on them. The *Revenge*—which had been between the *Intrepid* and
the *Louisa*—was apparently going ahead and passing the *Intrepid*.
Durell had decided that he would try to help the hard-pressed
Intrepid and *Louisa* by stopping between them and the passing
French ships. He had therefore come round to starboard to clear
the *Louisa*, his next-ahead, and this had brought his ship close
under the stern of the *Revenge* but, he said, he was by then in what
he regarded as the correct position to engage the enemy, so he
stopped his ship by backing the maintopsail.

This was a startling and important admission: up to that point
it had been thought that Durell had backed the *Trident*'s maintopsail because the *Louisa* was in the way, and that she in turn had
stopped because of damage. Durell then went on to admit, under
questioning, that he had backed his maintopsail before the
Ramillies which, he had earlier said, was following him 200 yards
astern.

Captain Holmes, a member of the court, immediately asked him,
since he had backed his maintopsail before the *Ramillies*, and

without a signal from Byng, 'Might not the *Ramillies* in the heat of the battle have been liable to run on board of you' if she too had not backed her maintopsail?

Here indeed was the critical issue now that Durell had admitted his reason for stopping the *Trident*, and obviously his evidence was vital. Captain Holmes had quite correctly visualized what had in fact happened—the *Ramillies*, partly shrouded in the smoke of her guns, had suddenly found the *Trident* stopped so close ahead that she too had to back her maintopsail to avoid a collision. Durell had admitted that by stopping he had broken the 24th Article of the Fighting Instructions—he had left his station in the line without orders from Byng, albeit for humanitarian motives.

If he now admitted, in as many words, that in doing so he had made a collision with the *Ramillies* inevitable unless Byng's ship backed her maintopsail, then a great part of the prosecution's case fell to the ground—the part which accused Byng that he 'did withdraw or keep back'.

However, Durell was saved from the necessity of answering Captain Holmes's question by another member of the court, Captain Boys, who quickly interjected, 'If you think it will hurt you, don't answer it'. Durell took the hint and remained silent, and Byng made no protest.

Since there were no witnesses from the *Princess Louisa* in court, her log was not put in as evidence; but it told a vastly different story—complaining that she had been prevented from firing on the enemy by the *Trident*, which shot up between her and the French ships. Thus Durell had tried to rescue a ship which did not want to be rescued.* It was wise of the Admiralty not to produce witnesses from the *Louisa*, despite a request from Byng.

The Admiral, however, saw a way of indicating what Durell had done, and asked him if the 13th Article of the Fighting Instructions did not say that when the admiral hoisted a red flag at the foretopmast-head and fired a gun that every ship in the fleet was to engage the enemy in the order the admiral had prescribed?†

Durell agreed it did, and Byng then asked him if the Admiral could be responsible for a squadron if any particular commander,

---

* The *Princess Louisa*'s log says: 'About ½ past 3 the *Trident* shott [sic] up to leeward of us which prevented our fire for four or five minutes.'

† These were the Fighting Instructions drawn up by Admiral Edward Russell, in 1691 and modified and remembered by Rooke in 1703.[1]

or commanders, disobeyed the order; and must not this disobedience 'disconcert the Admiral's plan of operation?'

Durell said it would be wrong for anyone to get out of his
station—'except it is to relieve ships in distress'.

Was not the Admiral the best judge of which ship he would
order to help a damaged ship?—'I think,' replied Durell weakly,
'that the next ship to the disabled ship is enjoined to do it, as
probably the Admiral may not see so much of their damage as the
ship next to them'.

Was the *Trident*'s signal made to help any damaged ship? asked
Byng. 'No,' Durell admitted.

The next witness was Byng's former first captain, Arthur Gardiner. His evidence was expected to be particularly important on
two points—Byng's personal courage, and why the *Ramillies*
had backed her topsails.

The usual routine questions were asked and Gardiner described
the beginning of the action. He said that the Admiral had never
asked his advice, nor that of anyone else, but that Gardiner had
offered some advice on one occasion, which was to set more sail
as an example to certain ships to get into action quicker, at which
Byng had made his remark about 'Mr Mathews's misfortune'.

After saying that the *Ramillies* had engaged at a range of about
half a mile he added that this was not as close as the Admiral had
wished, since Byng had said several times, 'while the shot was
flying over us', that he did not intend to throw his shot away 'till
he came near the enemy'.

What stopped the *Ramillies* going nearer the enemy than half a
mile? asked Captain Keppel.

'Lord Robert Bertie's telling the Admiral there was a ship
under the lee bow, which he imagined was one of ours.'

Gardiner explained that he did not at first see this ship, but later
saw the *Trident* about 200 yards away on the starboard bow, and the
Ramillies was just paying off clear of the *Princess Louisa*, which
was 'very near us'.

Asked if it would have been 'prudent or proper' for the un-
damaged British ships to have pursued the French after the battle,
Gardiner said that he thought not 'as I saw no damage done to the
French but one topsail-yard carried away.'

Lord Robert Bertie then took over in the witness chair, and

Admiral Smith asked him for 'any information relative to the action', to which the soldier replied that not understanding anything of sea affairs, he would not give a narrative but would answer questions.

'My Lord has said,' commented Captain Moore acidly, 'that he knows nothing of sea affairs, and the court can ask him none but what relate to sea matters, so that it seems to no purpose to ask him any.'

This was brushed aside by Captain Simcoe who asked if Byng had expressed any impatience or uneasiness, 'at any accident that the Admiral judged to impede his engaging the enemy properly?'

'At the time the Admiral [i.e. *Ramillies*] lay aback, I heard the Admiral say that he wondered what the ships ahead were about,' said Lord Robert. (It is noteworthy that although Lord Robert Bertie had been the first person to see the *Trident* close under the *Ramillies*'s bow, not one member of the court asked him anything about it.)

Byng then took over the questioning. Did his Lordship think that throwing in about one hundred men—the officers and recruits —would have enabled the garrison at Fort St Philip to hold out against the enemy's attacks?—'No I apprehend they would be of much more service on board the Fleet,' his Lordship replied.

Answering Byng's questions, he said that the *Ramillies* continued to go down towards the enemy from the time the signal was made to engage until Byng laid the *Ramillies*'s maintopsail aback; that (as an indication of the range) during this time the French shot were passing over her; and 'I recollect when the French began to fire upon us, that the Admiral desired Captain Gardiner not to fire till such a time as we were down alongside of them'.

Byng then asked if he had seen a British ship through the smoke close under the starboard bow and if his Lordship had warned him about it. The soldier said he had, and repeated the words of his warning.

'I think,' said Byng ironically, turning to the four admirals and nine captains, 'that implies his Lordship saw her?'

'Yes,' they all agreed.

Byng then gave to Admiral Smith a sheet of paper, on which were written some questions, requesting that the Judge-Advocate might ask them of his Lordship. Smith said he would ask them himself.

'Was you near the Admiral's person before, during and after the action? And did you observe his behaviour?'—'I was near him the whole of the action,' said Bertie.

'Did you perceive any backwardness in the Admiral during the action, or any mark of fear or confusion, either from his countenance or behaviour?'—'He seemed to me to give his orders coolly and distinctly, and I do not apprehend that he was the least wanting in personal courage.'

'Did the Admiral appear solicitous to engage the enemy, and to assist His Majesty's ships that were engaged with the enemy?'—'Yes.'

'Did you on or after the day of action hear any murmuring or discontent amongst the officers or men upon any supposition that the Admiral had not done his duty?'—'I never heard anyone of the *Ramillies* speak the least disrespectfully of the Admiral,' said Lord Robert, 'or ever hint that the Admiral had not done his duty.'*

The next witness was another soldier, Lieut-Colonel Marcus Smith, who in answering various questions described how one of the enemy's shot passed between Lord Robert Bertie and himself, and how he had prevented a gun being fired from the quarterdeck 'which would certainly have gone through one of our own ships.'

Asked the same series of questions about Byng's personal behaviour, he said he did not see any backwardness or marks of fear or confusion—'Rather the reverse, I thought'—and that the Admiral had given his orders 'very coolly and without the least confusion'.

None of the other former officers of the *Ramillies* had anything new to add although Mr Joseph Belwaird, who had been the Master, declared that as far as the *Trident* episode was concerned, if Admiral Byng had not ordered the *Ramillies* to be brought-to, 'It is my opinion we should have been on board of her'.

One after the other they were asked if they had heard any murmuring or discontent among officers or men; and one after the other they gave their answers—'No . . . No, never . . . No, very far from it . . . No, nor anything of that kind.'

Then Captain Ward of the *Culloden* was called. He had been criticized for not keeping his ship close to the *Ramillies*—his

* The words from 'or ever' to 'duty' are given in Fearne's edition of the trial but not in Cook's.

station was next astern of the flagship—and a great deal of ill-feeling existed between him and Byng. Asked by Keppel how far the *Culloden* was from the *Ramillies*, he said the distance was the hundred yards prescribed in the signal. And, Ward added, 'as near or nearer the sternmost ship of the enemy'. Nevertheless his own ship fired only sixteen shot and as far as the French fire was concerned, 'a great number of the shot fell short of me, and some few, I believe, might go over me, but did not touch the ship or rigging that I ever heard of . . .' He did not, however, explain why at less than a hundred yards' range, only sixteen of his guns fired, and why the enemy's shot should miss the *Culloden* when at that range such ships as the *Defiance* and the *Intrepid* had been crippled; nor did the court ask him.

Ward's former first lieutenant, Lt James Worth, followed and Byng asked him: 'Did you ever take any remarks out of the ship's log book concerning the situation of the *Revenge*, and the ships ahead of the Admiral?'

When Worth said he had a copy of the remarks in his pocket, taken from the ship's log, Byng asked: 'Were not these remarks made in the log book by the order of Captain Ward, to your knowledge?'

'I think Captain Ward saw the log book marked, and gave directions to the Master to be very particular in minuting everything that he saw.'

Captain Boys asked Worth if he had seen the ship's log book on the morning after the battle. Worth said he had not: it might have been some days later.

'Give the court an account, to the best of your knowledge, when the account of that day's action was inserted in the log book,' demanded Captain Moore.

'I do not know; I was not by when it was done: I cannot recollect.'

'Are you sure it was not marked the next day?' demanded Moore.

'I can give no manner of account when it was inserted . . . whether that day, the day following or when.'

Did not Kirby, the fourth lieutenant of the *Culloden* 'ever inform you that the log of the day of the action was not entered in the log book *till four days afterwards*?' asked Moore. 'Never,' declared Worth.

No one in court mentioned the reason for Captain Moore's suspicion; but the entry for the day of the battle in the *Culloden*'s Master's log,[2] kept by John Pearcy, was almost word for word the same as the entry in the *Trident*'s Captain's log.[3]

The *Trident*'s Captain's log, for instance, says for the 'impediment' period:

'At ¼ past 3 the *Intrepid*'s foretopmast was brought by the board by the enemy's shot. ½ past 3 dropped out of the line and fell astern of the Fleet, at the same time we being in a line with the *Princess Louisa* who seemed hard pressed by the enemy made more sail and went to leeward of her and the *Intrepid* to cover them and at the same time to close the *Revenge*. The Admiral remained astern of the *Princess Louisa*.'

The *Culloden*'s Master's log for the same period says:

'At ¼ past 3 the *Intrepid*'s foretopmast was brought by the board by the enemy's shot. At ½ past 3 she dropped out of the line being disabled. At the same time we being astern of the *Princess Louisa* who seemed hard pressed by the enemy's fire, made more sail and stood up to leeward between her and the enemy to cover her and then lay upon the *Revenge*'s lee quarter. The Admiral remained astern of the *Princess Louisa*.'

Nor was the similarity between the *Trident*'s Captain's log and the *Culloden*'s Master's log the only strange thing: the *Culloden*'s Captain's log[4] is written quite normally every day and in the same handwriting until after the entry for 11.40 a.m. on the day of the battle: then suddenly the rest of the day's entries are in a different handwriting. And, curiously enough, from 3 p.m. to 4 p.m. it is vague and makes no mention of the movements of the *Culloden* or any other named ship.

It is clear that the *Culloden*'s Master's log was a copy of the *Trident*'s Captain's log; but it is far from clear why it was done. The reason for having a false entry of some sort or another is easier to understand, because Ward, apart from being criticized by Admiral Byng, was also an object of Rear-Admiral Temple West's scorn—indeed, we have already seen that West wanted Byng to court martial him for what amounted to cowardice. From Durell's point of view it was a good thing that Ward and the *Culloden*'s log confirmed his story about the *Princess Louisa* and *Revenge*; and Ward needed something plausible to explain why only sixteen shot were fired and not one enemy shot hit his ship, despite his claim about the closeness of the enemy.

The seventeenth day's sitting ended with evidence from the master's mate of the *Dolphin* and then Fearne, the Judge-Advocate, told the court there were no more prosecution witnesses. As Augustus Hervey commented tartly: 'It was observed throughout that not one question had been asked by the Court that could give an opening to favour the prisoner, and yet not one reply was given that could tend to accuse him of any one crime.'[5]

Nor was Hervey exaggerating. In the evidence so far, Young of the *Intrepid* had been proved a liar over the effect his ship had on those astern; Cornwall had been shown to be an incompetent, hidebound by the Fighting Instructions yet so stupid that he broke them from sheer lack of imagination; Durell of the *Trident* admitted he too had disobeyed the Fighting Instructions; Ward's story was clearly a pack of lies and his log had, in effect, been forged.

It was only Byng's questioning which extracted the truth from these witnesses; yet a court martial was intended—theoretically —to get at the truth of the matter, and not simply to prove an accused man guilty. However, every word in the 440 pages which form the verbatim report of the prosecution's case entirely bears out Hervey's claims.

VOLTAIRE WRITES TO BYNG

BYNG SPENT the rest of Saturday, January 15, and all of Sunday and Monday writing out his defence and among those helping him were Hervey, Edmund Bramston and Lt Clark, and possibly Paul Whitehead. When the court sat again on Tuesday morning Byng handed a sheaf of papers to Admiral Smith and said: 'I beg you will give leave to the Judge-Advocate to read my defence, not being able to do it myself on account of a violent inflammation in my eyes.'

The court agreed, and Fearne started reading. Byng had written that it was his misfortune 'to have laboured under the disadvantage of a popular, and almost national, prejudice. For what reasons this spirit has been raised, and by what means propagated, is not the business of this court to determine.' But now, he said, he had an opportunity of proving his innocence before a court, and 'By this means I am at once secured from being borne down by popular clamour, or crushed beneath the weight of an overbearing power'.

It has been said, 'and indeed very industriously echoed throughout the whole Kingdom', that the loss of Fort St Philip was due to his misconduct, and Minorca might have been saved if he had done his duty. If he could clear himself of these charges, 'the charge of personal cowardice in the action will soon vanish'.

Had it not been convenient ('nay, I say necessary') for some people to shelter themselves by accusing him of the loss of St Philip's and the failure to relieve Minorca, no man living would have thought of calling on him to prove his courage.

His first task was to prove he did his utmost to relieve Minorca, and if in doing that he should, in self-defence, 'glance some blame upon others' he hoped to be excused; especially, he added, since his innocence was, in many respects, so intimately connected with their neglect that proving his innocence also exposed their guilt.

He went on to deal with the battle. The French squadron was superior to his, but instead of him retreating from it, the superior French force retreated from him, and his squadron was unable to pursue. He was perhaps the first commander-in-chief 'whose disgrace proceeded from so unfortunate a mistake'.

Why was he sent to the Mediterranean? If it was to relieve Minorca, did those who sent him with so inadequate a squadron expect that Minorca could be invaded before he arrived and covered by a superior French squadron? If so, their conduct was unjustifiable; if not, their ignorance was inexcusable.

This, he presumed, was sufficient to unravel the political secret of why the enemy's force had been so industriously lessened, and his so extravagantly magnified, 'when at the same time it is known to almost every man in the squadron I commanded that it consisted of several of the worst-conditioned ships, and mostly the worst manned of any perhaps in His Majesty's Navy'.

Nor, he said, was it foreseen by the Government that the squadron in the Mediterranean would go into action: he outlined his orders which, with their provision for the French having gone to America and instructions for helping the Minorca garrison, supposed 'the sea to be open and the Fleet unopposed'. And he was 'positively assured before my departure from the highest naval authority [Anson] that the enemy could not fit out more than six or seven ships of the line at the most'.

Arriving in Gibraltar, he said, he discovered that Minorca had been invaded, and 'every person there concluded the place lost'. He had to agree there appeared no great probability of preserving it, and he later discovered that 'the Ministers at home, for once at least, agreed in opinion with me, since the moment intelligence came that the Toulon Fleet was sailed, and the troops landed upon the island, there was not a man who did not despair of Minorca'.

As to the battle, it might be said that he could have attacked the enemy again, but he would have almost certainly been defeated. Had he been defeated, what refuge would have been left for the shattered squadron? he asked. What security would there have been for Gibraltar, exposed to the hazard of a sudden siege without a single ship to defend it? It was a place, he pointed out, 'equally recommended to my protection'. His reason for calling a council of war was the vagueness of his orders.

Then he declared his witnesses would prove 'That I never re-treated from the island till it was impracticable to make any further attempt; and that the place was not lost by me—who was too weak to save it—but by those who might have sent double the force two months earlier, and neglected it.' Yet in order to render him criminal in the eyes of the people the *London Gazette* was 'prostituted to mangle and curtail my letter to the Admiralty on this occasion, and subscribed my own name to my own defamation'.

He began a detailed description of the events on the day of the battle, and dealt with the fighting in measured terms. There had been the difficulty of the *Defiance*, the leading ship, not steering down towards the French in compliance with the Fighting Instructions; there was the problem of the ship suddenly appearing in the smoke under the *Ramillies*'s lee bow.

With his description of the battle over, Byng referred to the witnesses who, he said, were only those mentioned in his first list to the Admiralty, plus the odd people in the second list who happened, by chance, to be in England. He pointed out that there were no witnesses from the *Princess Louisa* or the *Captain*, 'and but few from several other ships in the Fleet'. He read to the court his letters to Cleveland 'earnestly requesting such witnesses', together with the answers from the Board—answers 'which will serve to give the court a specimen of the unprecedented oppression and restriction of privileges I have had to struggle with'.

He went on to say that 'Justice to myself demands, and I hope will be thought a sufficient apology, for that freedom and plainness becoming a man in my circumstances'. He did not intend to fix any blame or imputation without reason, even on his greatest enemies, 'But the indignation and resentment of an incensed nation is a load much too heavy for me to bear, though it has been my misfortune to struggle under it so long'.

Declaring that, 'No symptom of cowardice, that odious and capital part of my charge, has hitherto appeared to the court; and my innocence and conscious discharge of my duty makes me confident that none will appear,' he added: 'Yet I have already suffered the severest penalties that can be inflicted on it, being hung up in effigy, traduced by libels, tortured by misrepresentations and calumny, disgraced and superseded upon no better authority than the gasconnade of the French Admiral, arrested and confined beyond the example of former times, treated like a felon, with every indignity, and my life pursued in the most inveterate malice. But all this I have had fortitude enough to despise, and treat with the contempt it deserves; the result of a conscience clear of all crimes . . .'

With his opening statement completed he then began questioning the first of his defence witnesses, Captain Gardiner, who did not, however, add anything of importance to his previous testimony, and the court adjourned until next day.

That night some incident occurred in the Byng entourage, but at this distance it has proved impossible to discover the exact details. Byng had previously arranged that several more officers, including Augustus Hervey, would be called again as his own witnesses; but when the court sat next day Byng gave a paper to Admiral Smith, which the President read out to the court:

'As I find the court has left me very little that seems necessary to explain further by witnesses, I shall not call any more than my secretary, who was quartered by me . . .'

Hervey, who had arrived on board the *St George* ready to be called again, gives the only clue—and that not a very plausible one—to Byng's action. 'This sudden change surprised me, and the very abrupt manner in which he closed the whole of his defence. It must have been some peck [*sic*: pique] between himself and Mr Clark [Lt. Clark, who had been helping Byng] that morning.'[1]

Hervey was so hurt that he went on shore and decided to go to London next day. However, before he left he saw the Admiral who 'Was so certain of being acquitted that he desired me to write a letter for him to be ready to send to Lord Temple, that he might [afterwards] hoist his flag for a few days, which I did, and set out the next day, and was very busy in Town giving the most favourable accounts of Mr Byng's trial.'[2]

The Admiral's secretary, George Lawrence, gave his evidence when the court met again, and Byng asked him the now-familiar question about murmurings or discontent: had Lawrence heard any on or after the day of the action?—'I never heard either officer or common man on board the *Ramillies* speak the least disrespectful word of the Admiral,' he declared.

That ended the prosecution and defence cases: there remained now only the verdict. As soon as the court was ready to give sentence, the President told Byng, they would send to let him know. . . .

The four admirals and nine captains trying Byng were heartily tired of each other's company and of living crowded together on board the *St George*. From the time the court began its sittings on December 28 they had not been allowed by law to leave the ship* and, since there was a great deal of evidence to read through, it looked as if they would not reach a verdict for several days.

The focus of the Byng tragedy now turned, of all places, to the Post Office in Lombard Street, London, where on January 19— the day the trial ended—one of the men sorting the foreign mail that had just arrived from Holland came across a letter from Switzerland addressed to '*M. l'Amiral Bing, a Portsmouth*'. The sorter at once took it to the Comptroller of the Post Office's 'Foreign Office', which dealt with all the foreign post, both inward and outward. The occupier of this £150-a-year position was Mr John Daye, who gave the letter to the Secretary, Mr Anthony Todd, who in turn sent it to Lord Holdernesse, the Secretary of State for the Northern Province.

The Minister did not hesitate to have the letter opened in such a way that the seal remained unbroken; but when he came to read the letter he had a shock: it was from the famous French writer Voltaire and, even more surprising, it enclosed a copy of a letter from the Duke de Richelieu, now in Paris after his victory in Minorca, and referring to Byng in glowing terms. Written in English from Voltaire's home near Geneva, the covering letter, dated January 2, said:

> 'Sir, Tho' I am almost unknown to you, I think 'tis my duty to send the copy of the letter which I have just received from the Marshal Duke of Richelieu. Honour, humanity and equity order me to convey it into your hands, this noble and unexpected testimony from one of the most candid, as [well as] the most generous of my countrymen makes me presume your judges will do you the same justice. I am with respect, your most humble obedient servant, Voltaire.'

* In fact they found the cramped conditions so bad that they wrote to the Admiralty, asking that the Act of Parliament obliging the members of a court martial to stay on board until a verdict was reached should be repealed. The Board made only a polite acknowledgement. [8]

Richelieu's letter to Voltaire, in French, was dated Paris, December 26. The Marshal said 'I greatly pity the fate of Admiral Byng. I do assure you all that I have seen or been informed of concerning him ought to redound to his glory; his reputation ought not to be attacked for being worsted, after having done everything that could be expected. When two men of merit contend, one of them must have the advantage, without necessarily implying dishonour to the other.

'All the measures taken by Admiral Byng were admirable. According to the unaffected accounts of our sea officers, the strength of the two fleets was at least equal, though the English had thirteen ships, and we but twelve, with a greater number of men and fresh out of port.

'Chance, which has a great share in all battles, especially those at sea, favoured us in directing a greater number of our shot to strike the English masts and rigging; and it appears to me generally acknowledged that if the English had obstinately persisted, their Fleet must have been destroyed, so that there never was a more flagrant injustice than what is attempted against Byng, and every man of honour, and in particular every military man, ought to interest himself.'

A note at the bottom of Voltaire's letter said: 'I received this original letter from Marshal Duc de Richelieu the 1st January 1757, and in witness of which I have signed my name. Voltaire.'*

Holdernesse did not waste any time: he had several copies made of both letters, and without mentioning them to Pitt, who was his fellow Secretary of State, he hurried off to St James's Palace and showed them to the King.

Presumably on the King's instructions, Holdernesse then had the original letter and its enclosure sealed up again and sent back to the Post Office with instructions that they should be enclosed in a letter to Admiral Smith at Portsmouth. This was done, and Smith received them on January 20, but, of course, had no inkling of what had been going on in London. When he saw the packet was for Byng, he sent it to the Admiralty explaining that it had been forwarded to him by the Post Office. So back the letters went to

---

* These versions of Voltaire's and Richelieu's letters are taken from those in the possession of Sir Danvers Osborn. The wording is different from that given in the British Museum copies. (Add 35985. f.34). The Marquis de la Galissonnière had, of course, died two months earlier.

London, where Clevland handed them over to the First Lord,
Lord Temple, who took them to his brother-in-law, Pitt.

Without knowing that Holdernesse had previously seen them
and taken copies, Pitt opened the packet, and when he read the
contents became very angry with the Post Office for having
intercepted it. ('Which,' Lord Anson wrote to Lord Hardwicke,
having received his information from Lord Holdernesse, 'he said
was certainly not done without looking into them.')[4]

The packet was sealed up once again and Lord Temple told
Clevland to send the letters back to Portsmouth. Smith received a
letter from the Board, dated January 22, saying that the packet,
'having been transmitted to one of His Majesty's Principal
Secretaries of State, he has opened it and I am commanded to
return it to you by express to be forthwith delivered to Admiral
Byng, that he may make such use thereof as shall be found
expedient'.[5]

Meanwhile Holdernesse had given copies of the two letters to
Anson, telling him (untruthfully) that he had mentioned them to
no one 'except the Duke of Devonshire'. Anson's own reaction—
so he wrote to Lord Hardwicke—was 'to sink them', as they
'would do harm at the court martial'. According to Anson,
Holdernesse had replied that 'there must be a sign manual to
authorize that'.

Not troubling to keep Holdernesse's secret, Anson sent off copies
to Lord Hardwicke, and also mentioned the whole thing to the
Duke of Newcastle that night; but to his astonishment his Grace
said that he had known of them for several days but had not mentioned them to anyone because he had 'never thought of them
since'.*

In relating all this to Hardwicke, Anson seemed to think that the
letters had been solicited by someone connected with Byng; and
he suspected Lady Hervey, Augustus's mother, 'especially if it
was true, as is said', that Lady Hervey was very intimate with the
Duchess D'Aiguillon, who was 'the object of M. de Richelieu's
admiration and attachment.'

Anson's secretary added a postscript to the letter saying that

---

* Holdernesse, in turn, had not been told that Admiral Smith had returned
the letters from Portsmouth and that they had eventually reached Pitt. Anson
however, had been told about this secretly by Clevland, but he too did not
pass on the information to Holdernesse.

Voltaire's endeavour 'to justify Mr Byng is systematical in Voltaire, who in his history of the last war is the advocate of Mr Mathews, and lays it down that it is very cruel and unjust to prosecute a general for his conduct, unless you could prove treachery, as otherwise it ought always to be supposed that he did as well as he could . . . It is rather unlucky though that he should in the same book assert that our sea commanders took money to let provisions into Genoa—which falls within the time of Mr Byng's command.'

Doubt has often been expressed whether or not Byng received the Richelieu and Voltaire letters, but in fact it seems certain that he did. The *Evening Post* for January 27 said that the Secretary of State 'two days ago* sent to Admiral Smith two letters to Mr Byng, one from the Duke de Richelieu, the other from Mons. Voltaire, which were delivered to him accordingly. The contents are variously reported, indeed quite oppositely; some tell you that they are reflections; and others that they are consolatory.'

While the *Evening Post*'s report is no proof that the letters were actually given to Byng, it is obvious that all and sundry now knew of their existence—Walpole, for instance, referred to them in a letter to Sir Horace Mann, dated January 30—and Byng's friends would no doubt ensure he received them. In addition, Smith had Admiralty orders that they should be 'forthwith delivered' to Byng and he is unlikely to have disobeyed; indeed, there would be no reason for him wanting to do so.

Whatever happened, they were no use to Byng. The order to Smith to deliver them arrived in Portsmouth on January 23, four days after the court martial had finished hearing evidence.

The court martial was taking a long time to reach a decision. In the meantime, Hervey reported that 'it was easily perceived there was a sullen determination in the King, the Duke of Cumberland, Lord Anson, and the Duke of Newcastle (which was artfully conducted by that determined, implacable villain, Mr Fox) to sacrifice Admiral Byng in order to screen themselves from the just resentment of the people for the loss of Minorca'.[6]

Indeed, Hervey probably did not know just how deep the determination was, for two of the chief actors in the drama were already getting their lines prepared for them. The Earl of

* Actually on January 22.

Hardwicke had already chosen a man to write a detailed defence—Philip Cartaret Webb, a fifty-six year-old solicitor, an authority on constitutional law, and the Member of Parliament for Haslemere. He owed much to Hardwicke—including his most recent appointment, a month earlier, as Secretary of Bankrupts in the Court of Chancery.

Lord Hardwicke was staying at Anson's home at Moor Park when he wrote to Webb on January 2 to 'tell you the plan, whereon I wish you would set out, in as few words as I can. You have seen Mr Clevland and Mr Stephens* and therefore must be possessed of the general idea of the affair and have many of the papers already in your hands. This enables you to see they are a confused mass, consisting of various subjects mixed together, and in want of being distinguished and brought into order; without which none but adepts in Admiralty affairs can collect any lights from them.' The 'papers' were copies of all the intelligence reports received from the Continent and the orders and instructions to Byng.

Hardwicke said he wished the papers to prove that 'consistently with the *probable safety of this country* a squadron could not have been sent sooner to the Mediterranean', nor could it have been made stronger when it was sent; and he made detailed suggestions how the papers should be arranged.[7]

By January 26, Hardwicke was writing to tell Anson that he had spent the previous evening, from 9 p.m. until midnight, reading over the papers forming the written defence, which Webb had just finished. He thought they 'are extremely well done. They are unavoidably pretty long but they show the several intelligences and facts in a clear light . . . They appear to me to make a complete justification. I am convinced we are much better prepared for the *defence* than the other side are for the *inquiry* . . .

'After that it must be considered into whose hands copies of these papers should be put, for they ought not to be spread and divulged too early because that would be *shewing our hand at whist.*'[8]

One copy was sent to the then head of the Government, the Duke of Devonshire. This has survived until the present day[9] and it shows that Webb either made a silly mistake or deliberately dis-

---

* Although Anson and Hardwicke were out of office, this shows they still had good allies in the Admiralty. Philip Stephens, second senior of the Clerks to the Board, had acted as Lord Anson's secretary when he was First Lord.

torted the facts. A nineteen-page introduction to the intelligence
reports gave an outline of events, from before Byng was ordered
to the Mediterranean until after the battle, and on pages ten and
eleven it said that the facts in the previous pages showed that 'as
things then stood' it was unnecessary to send a squadron to the
Mediterranean in December 1755. 'To this,' it said, 'may be
added the sense and opinion of other persons of knowledge and
understanding in these affairs at that time. Admiral B—— [*sic*] in
a letter from London to Lord Anson, who was then at Bath, dated
5th December 1755, expresses himself thus. "I cannot help saying
that I do not think the intelligence from Toulon so entirely to be
credited, as to give us any *uneasiness*, or to make us now send a
squadron to sea. I have told the Duke of Newcastle so, and hope it
will meet with your Lordship's approbation." '

However, the present author doubts if Byng ever wrote such a
letter, for the following reasons. We have already seen (page 41)
that Anson had told Hardwicke on December 6 that the Admiralty had sent him some intelligence from Toulon, but that 'I think
it would be a dangerous measure to part with your naval strength'
and that he was 'strongly of opinion' that any French attack would
be against the British Isles. Byng's alleged letter has similar wording and was allegedly written a day earlier.

If Byng ever wrote such a letter then it was damning evidence
against him and a powerful defence for the Ministers: yet it was
never once made public: not even a hint of its existence appeared
in gossip, newspapers, pamphlets or at the trial. Nor was any
mention made of it in the scurrilous piece of gossip which the
Ministers had inserted in the newspapers to coincide with the
publication of Byng's censored dispatch in the *London Gazette*.
But even more surprising is the fact that in the other two surviving
copies* of Webb's 'Defence' which are otherwise almost identical
in wording, the whole paragraph is omitted. In the author's view,
this letter may have been sent to Anson, but it was not written by
Byng. Had Byng written it, then it surely would have been produced at the court martial—for Byng, in his defence, made a bitter
attack on the former Ministers, blaming the loss of Minorca on to

---

* One of them in the British Museum and the other in the Admiralty Library.
The passage referring to Byng, printed here for the first time, is in the third
copy which is in the possession of the present Duke of Devonshire, but which
lacks the intelligence reports.

the fact that he was 'not sent time enough to prevent the enemy's landing . . . Let others answer why I came so late, and why I came so weak.' Had Byng ever written the alleged letter, then its publication would have damned Byng for a hypocrite. The fact this was not done—yet every other scrap of paper was combed over in efforts to compromise Byng—was, it is suggested, because after Webb compiled the defence it was found that he had wrongly attributed the letter to Byng, and that subsequent copies of the 'defence' were amended.

THE VERDICT

ON BOARD THE *St George* the thirteen men forming the court martial were still meeting day after day without coming to any agreement. 'There is as yet no appearance of the sentence,' said one newspaper on January 23, and three days later it was reporting that 'We hear the court martial cannot agree about the sentence to be passed on Mr Byng, five being for condemning him to death, four for breaking him, and four for acquitting him.'

Then, shortly after lunch on Thursday, January 27, word was sent to Admiral Byng from the *St George* that the court was about to assemble again to pronounce their sentence on him. At 2 p.m. the 'one-gun salute' was fired and the court martial flag hoisted. Once again the Marine guard escorted him from Hutchins's house to the boat, and among those with him were Edmund Bramston, Thomas Cook, his nephew John, and his secretary George Lawrence. There was a fresh south-westerly gale blowing and Byng sheltered himself from the spray with his boatcloak as, flanked by other craft carrying the rest of the Marine guard, his boat was rowed out to the *St George*.

The Admiral was in good spirits: as soon as he heard the court was ready he had commented that he expected to be reprimanded and that, at worst, he might be cashiered, 'because there must have been several controverted points'. He added that, 'The court martial has been shut up a long time, and almost all of the questions proposed by the court have tended much more to pick out faults in my conduct than to get a true state of the circumstances; but I profess I cannot conceive what they will fix upon.'

Soon he and his group had boarded the *St George*, and been taken as usual to a cabin to wait for the court to send for them. In a few minutes one of the captains who was a member of the court—it is not clear which one—came to the door of the cabin and motioned to Bramston to step outside. Once they were out of earshot of the Admiral, he told Bramston that as it was known the Admiral expected to be acquitted, he had the court's leave to inform him that the court found the Admiral guilty.

Bramston had presumably shared Byng's optimism, and with his thoughts in a whirl—for he knew that such a verdict meant, automatically, a sentence of death—he went back to the cabin, white-faced and looking distraught. Byng took one look at him and knew he had been given some hint of the verdict.

'What is the matter? Have they thrown a slur on me?' he asked with some warmth in his voice.

Bramston hesitated, his eyes avoiding those of Byng, and groping for words which could break the dreadful news as gently as possible. But the words would not come, and Byng guessed the significance of his cousin's confusion. Completely composed, and without a tremor in his voice, he said, 'Well, I understand: if nothing but my blood will satisfy, let them take it.'

Bramston and the others tried to give clumsy comfort: whatever the sentence, the fact that he was innocent meant there could be no stain on his honour: it was highly improbable a sentence of death would be carried out, considering the extraordinary circumstances: there was every chance of a pardon . . .

Byng, however, wanted no such comfort: a pardon? 'What will that signify to me?' he asked, his pride stung. 'What satisfaction can I receive from the liberty to crawl a few years longer on the earth, with the infamous load of a pardon at my back? I despise life on those terms, and would rather them take it.'

An officer came to the door of the cabin. 'Sir . . .' he said, indicating the way to the court room. Byng entered the cabin and went to his usual seat, while all the members of the court avoided looking at him. Thomas Cook, who was taking Byng's shorthand notes, went and sat at the table opposite Charles Fearne, the Judge-Advocate. Admiral Smith motioned to Fearne, who stood up and began reading a series of thirty-seven resolutions passed by the court (which will be referred to later in the narrative). Having read as far as the end of the thirty-seventh resolution, Fearne put his papers down and reached for another set: these contained the sentence, and he started reading once again:

'At a court martial assembled on board His Majesty's ship *St George*, in Portsmouth Harbour . . . to inquire into the conduct of the Honourable John Byng, Admiral of the Blue Squadron of

His Majesty's Fleet . . . [the court] unanimously agree that he falls under part of the 12th Article . . .

'And as that Article positively prescribes death, without any alternative left to the discretion of the court, under any variation of circumstances; the Court do therefore hereby unanimously adjudge the said Admiral John Byng to be shot to death, at such time, and on board such ship, as the Lords Commissioners of the Admiralty shall direct . . . The court . . . unanimously think it their duty most earnestly to recommend him as a proper object of mercy.'

The trial of Admiral Byng was over. 'When the sentence was pronounced,' reported the *Evening Post*, 'he bore it with great composure, said not a word, and went ashore again as usual. The court martial were greatly affected, and most of them could not refrain from tears.'

The court then set to work preparing a petition to the Board of Admiralty. To Clevland, Admiral Smith wrote in his own sprawling writing: 'Enclosed is the sentence . . . and a letter from every member of the court to their Lordships petitioning them to intercede with His Majesty to extend his clemency to the prisoner, which you will please immediately to lay before Lord Temple and the Board.'[1]

'We, the underwritten,' said the enclosed petition, ' . . . believe it unnecessary to inform your Lordships that in the whole course of this long trial we have done our utmost endeavours to come at truths, and to do the strictest justice to our country and the prisoner: but we cannot help laying the distress of our minds before your Lordships on this occasion in finding ourselves under a necessity of condemning a man to death, from the great severity of the 12th Article of War, part of which he falls under, and which admits no mitigation, even if the crime should be committed by an error in judgment only; and therefore, for our own consciences' sake, as well as in justice to the prisoner, we pray your Lordships, in the most earnest manner to recommend him to His Majesty's clemency.'[2]

Both the letters and the copy of the sentence were rushed to London that night by special messenger. Admiral Smith's letter is endorsed 'Received 28th at 7 a.m.', and the court's letters 'Read to the Lords the 28th January at Lord Temple's house. Sent to the King the same day'.[3]

Richard Rigby, reporting to the Duke of Bedford that Byng was sentenced to be shot, wrote 'The Monarch is, as your Grace will easily imagine, horrid angry with the court martial, who have shoved the odium of Byng's death, if he is to suffer, in some measure off their own shoulders.'[4]

Temple West was horrified when he heard the verdict, and decided to resign in protest. He wrote the same day to the First Lord of the Admiralty: 'However honourable and advantageous the situation I am placed in may be, yet I am determined and fully resolved to forgo anything rather than serve on terms which subject another officer to the treatment shown Admiral Byng, whom the court martial have convicted not for cowardice, not for treachery, but for *misconduct*—an offence never till now thought capital.' He concluded that he had therefore written to the Board resigning his command, and 'I must entreat your Lordship to facilitate it.'[5]

The reasons for the court's findings, expressed in the thirty-seven resolutions, were ludicrous because they contradicted each other; the court's verdict was absurd because it had sentenced Byng to death for something which was no crime. To understand this, one of the worst miscarriages of justice in recorded British history, we must first consider once again the charges against Admiral Byng and the penalties.

The first charge was that during the battle Byng did 'withdraw or keep back, and did not do his utmost to take, seize and destroy the ships of the French King which it was his duty to have engaged, and to assist such of His Majesty's ships as were engaged . . . which it was his duty to have assisted'.

That charge was covered by the 12th Article of War—'Every person in the Fleet, who, through *cowardice, negligence* or *disaffection*, shall in time of action withdraw or keep back, or not come into the fight or engagement; or shall not do his utmost to take or destroy every ship which it shall be his duty to engage; and to assist and relieve all and every of His Majesty's ships, or those of his allies, which it shall be his duty to assist and relieve . . . shall suffer death.'*

* Death as the sole penalty under this article had only been instituted in 1749 mainly as a result of the trials after the Battle of Toulon. Many officers had protested against its harshness at the time. Previously a lesser punishment could be given. In 1779 it was altered once again to include 'such other punishment as the nature and degree of the offence shall be found to deserve'.

The second charge was 'That he did not do his utmost to relieve St Philip's Castle . . . but acted contrary to and in breach of his instructions given to him by us, by His Majesty's command.' This charge could be dealt with only as a breach of his instructions.

The thirty-seven resolutions are an interesting part of the judgment. They give the clearest evidence of the court's reasoning and are very useful in showing its thoughts and errors.

The first resolution said: 'It does not appear that any unnecessary delay was made by Admiral Byng' from the time his squadron left England on April 6 until it arrived off Minorca on May 19. That disposed of all the gossip that Byng had wasted time on the voyage to Gibraltar and, more particularly, while the squadron watered.

Resolutions 2 to 6 merely said Byng sent three frigates to Mahon to endeavour to land a letter to General Blakeney; they were recalled when Byng sighted the French squadron; the British squadron then sailed towards the enemy; that Byng 'proceeded properly' in steering for the French; and that Stuart, Effingham and Cornwallis and about one hundred men were on board the squadron.

The seventh resolution said that as there were so many officers on board belonging to the garrison of St Philip's 'where they must necessarily be much wanted', the Admiral ought to have put them on board one of the frigates to try to land them.*

Resolutions 8 to 10 said Byng took proper measures to get the weather gage of the enemy; the British van stretched beyond the enemy's rear before Byng tacked; and having tacked the British rear was further to windward of the enemy than the van. Number 11 said Byng should have tacked when the fleets were level and steered directly for the enemy, 'the van steering for the enemy's van, the rear for their rear; each ship for her opposite ship in the enemy's line, and under such sail as might have enabled the worst sailing ship, under all her plain sail, to preserve her station'.

The court forgot—ignored the fact—that the one ship that steered direct for the enemy as they advocated, instead of lasking down as Byng intended, was the *Intrepid*, which was badly damaged before doing any damage to the French.

---

* This resolution by the court was the only one not unanimous—twelve members said Byng ought to have landed all the officers and one said only General Stuart and the field officers.

Resolutions 12, 13 and 14 were merely descriptions without comment of what Byng did.

Number 15, ignoring the criticism made in number 11, and partly contradicting it, said that when the signal for battle was made the ships of the van bore down 'properly' for the enemy. (In number 11 they had indicated that Byng had been wrong.) Sixteen merely said the *Intrepid* was damaged; 17 said the *Revenge* brought up first on the *Intrepid*'s weather quarter and then on her lee quarter.

The eighteenth referred to three ships getting to windward of the *Ramillies* while going down; the nineteenth said Byng separated the rear from the van, and retarded the rear getting into action by shortening sail because of the *Trident* and *Princess Louisa*.

But Byng's ship was the tenth ship in the British line. The separation occurred between the fifth (*Captain*) and sixth (*Intrepid*), so this resolution was nonsense; in any case a later resolution contradicted it.

Number 20 said that instead of shortening sail, the Admiral ought to have ordered the *Trident* and *Princess Louisa* to make more sail to keep in the line; 21 declared the *Ramillies* opened fire too soon but firing was continued 'by the Admiral's direction'. This ignored repeated evidence that Byng wanted to engage at close quarters. The next resolution referred to the mix-up involving the *Intrepid*, *Revenge*, *Trident* and *Princess Louisa*.

Resolutions 23 and 24 described the *Ramillies* backing her maintopsail because the *Trident* appeared under her lee bow.

The next announced that the court were unanimously of the opinion that while the *Ramillies* was firing in going down, 'the *Trident* and the ships immediately ahead of the *Ramillies*, proved an impediment to the *Ramillies* continuing to go down'. (Yet, in resolution 19, they had already said the *Ramillies* was the ship that caused the separation of the van and rear.)

Twenty-six criticized Byng for allowing the *Ramillies* to open fire before she was at 'a proper distance' from the enemy; this was despite all the evidence that enemy shots were already going over the *Ramillies* at this time. Numbers 27 to 31 merely reported events.

In Resolution 32 the court said that 'after the ships, which had received damage in the action, were as much refitted as circumstances would permit, the Admiral ought to have returned with the squadron off St Philip's; and endeavoured to open a communication with that castle; and to have used every means in his power for its relief, before he returned to Gibraltar'.

In Byng's defence, it should be noted that two admirals (Byng and West), one general (Stuart), eleven naval captains and three colonels all decided at the council of war on the spot that the fleet, damaged as it was, should proceed to cover Gibraltar, while the four admirals (all junior to Byng) and nine captains forming the court thought he should have stayed off Minorca.

Resolution 33 said, 'The court are of opinion that Admiral Byng did not do his utmost to relieve St Philip's Castle, in the island of Minorca, then besieged by the Forces of the French King.'

Resolution 34 said that the court were of the opinion that Byng did not, in the action, 'do his utmost to take, seize and destroy the ships of the French King which it was his duty to have engaged; and to assist such of His Majesty's ships as were engaged in fight [sic] with the French ships, which it was his duty to have engaged'.

Then came number 35, 'It appears by the evidence of Lord Robert Bertie, Lieut-Colonel Smith, Captain Gardiner, and other officers of the ship, who were near the person of the Admiral, that they did not perceive any backwardness in the Admiral during the action; or any marks of fear or confusion, either from the countenance or behaviour; but he seemed to give his orders coolly and distinctly, and did not seem wanting in personal courage.'

A man cannot reasonably be accused in one resolution of not 'doing his utmost' and in the next one specifically cleared of 'any backwardness'.

Yet the contradictions of these resolutions were not at all obvious to the members of the court, and ignoring all the contradictions so far they blundered on to draw the fatal conclusion in resolution 36 'That the Admiral appears to fall under the following part of the 12th Article of War; to wit, "or shall not do his utmost to take, or destroy, every ship which it shall be his duty to engage, and to assist and relieve all and every of His Majesty's ships which it shall be his duty to assist and relieve".'

Then came the final resolution: 'As that Article positively prescribes death, without any alternative left to the discretion of the court, under any variation of circumstances . . . But as it

appears by the evidence of Lord Robert Bertie, Lieut-Colonel
Smith, Captain Gardiner and other officers of the ship, who were
near the person of the Admiral, that they did not perceive any
backwardness in him during the action, or marks of fear, or confusion . . . and from other circumstances, the Court do not believe
that his misconduct arose either from cowardice or disaffection;
and do therefore unanimously think it their duty most earnestly
to recommend him as a proper object of mercy.'

Thus, to sum up: By resolution number 11 the court criticized
Admiral Byng for the way he ordered the squadron to attack on a
lasking course: but in number 15 said the van (on the lasking
course) 'bore down properly'. By number 19 they said that Byng
in the *Ramillies* separated the van and rear divisions and retarded
the rear division; that was contradicted by number 25 which
declared that the *Trident* and ships immediately ahead of the
Ramillies 'proved an impediment to the *Ramillies* continuing to go
down'. Numbers 33 and 34 said he 'did not do his utmost' to
relieve St Philip's or destroy the enemy's ships (which brought
him under the 12th Article). The thirty-fifth then contradicted
them both and said he displayed no backwardness or fear. The
thirty-sixth, however, said that Byng appeared to fall under part
of the 12th Article—that dealing with not doing his utmost—and
therefore they had to condemn him to death, there being no alternative sentence. Then the thirty-seventh resolution pointed out
that no one in the battle had seen any backwardness in Byng, or
'marks of fear or confusion'; not did he seem wanting in personal
courage. The court did 'not believe that his misconduct arose
either from cowardice or disaffection' and in its plea to the Admiralty for mercy said that Byng's crime was 'committed by an
error of judgment only'.

Yet there were only three headings to the 12th Article—
cowardice, disaffection and negligence. They had, in the thirty-
seventh resolution, cleared him of cowardice and disaffection.
This left negligence, but they did not even mention the word in
the thirty-sixth resolution. Since in the petition to the Admiralty
they say quite categorically that the crime was committed *only*
by an error of judgment, we can assume that they thought an
error of judgment was the same as negligence.

But an error of judgment was certainly no crime, under civil,
military or naval law, and the court did not seem to realize that an

error of judgment—choosing a course of action which was
subsequently judged to have been wrong—could not possibly be
the same as negligence, where a person showed lack of care, fore-
thought and attention. It was reasonable to blame Byng if he had
done wrong through carelessness; but it was quite a different
matter to sentence him to death for doing in good faith something
which, months after the event, thirteen other men—all of them
his inferiors in rank, and none with anything like his experience
—subsequently considered wrong. As a pamphleteer wrote at the
time: 'Might not a court martial who wore all black wigs have
justly condemned him for wearing a white one, because they
differed in this particular?'

Almost every British naval and military commander has committed an error of judgment at some time or another, the most
recent one at that time, apart from Byng, being Boscawen over
the *Lys* and *Alcide* affair.

Byng had undoubtedly made an error in judgment. He had done
his utmost by his own standards; the trouble was they were not
high enough. This shortcoming conveniently delivered him as a
scapecoat into the hands of the Ministers. Although many of the
people perhaps realized that the Ministers were at least partly to
blame, they knew these men—particularly the Duke of Newcastle,
Hardwicke, Fox and Anson—were well beyond their reach; but
Byng, the proffered victim, was not. In their anger the mob wanted
a sacrifice; in their anger, as is the way with all mobs, they were
not particularly concerned whether they had the right victim or
not. It was important, and quite sufficient, just to have a victim.

Had it been politically necessary to have a scapegoat after the
capture of the *Alcide* and *Lys*, when it was intended to capture the
whole French convoy bound for America, it would have been
easy to proffer Boscawen—and make out a strong case against him.
Likewise Hawke, after taking Byng's place (and knowing full well
why) in command of a much more powerful squadron, had made
no attempt to establish a close blockade of Minorca to starve out
the French; nor did he blockade Toulon. Again, a case could have
been made out against him, too, had a victim been required.

Walpole wrote years later an interesting verdict on Byng. 'I have
spoken and shall speak of him as a man most unjustly and wickedly
put to death; and as this was the moment [his brave behaviour

when sentenced] from which my opinion sprung, however lament-
ably confirmed by the event, it is necessary in my own vindication
to say a few words, lest prejudice against the persecutors, or
persecuted, should be suspected of having influenced my narrative.

'I can appeal to God that I never spoke to Mr Byng in my life,
nor had the most distant acquaintance with one of his family.
The man I never saw but in the street, or in the House of Commons, and there I thought his carriage haughty and disgusting.
From report, I had formed a mean opinion of his understanding;
and from the clamours of the world. I was carried away with the
multitude in believing he had not done his duty; and in thinking
his behaviour under *his* circumstances weak and arrogant.

'I never interested myself enough to inquire whether this
opinion was well- or ill-founded. When his pamphlet appeared
I read it, and found he had been cruelly and scandalously treated.
I knew enough not to wonder at this conduct in *some* of his
persecutors—yet it concerned not me; and I thought no more
about it till the sentence, and the behaviour of his judges which
accompanied it, struck me with astonishment. I could not conceive how men could acquit honourably and condemn to death in
the same breath!'

Walpole added that a report at the time said 'when the severer
part of the court, the steady part of Admiral Boscawen's foretold
majority, found great difficulty to wring from their associates
acquiescence in condemnation, they are said to have seduced the
latter by promising on their part, if Mr Byng was condemned, to
sign so favourable a representation of his case that it should be
impossible but he must be pardoned'.

24

SARAH'S PLEAS

AUGUSTUS HERVEY HEARD the news that Admiral Byng had been condemned to death when the Admiral's secretary, George Lawrence, banged on the door of Lady Hervey's house at three o'clock in the morning, having ridden up express to London from Portsmouth. Hervey was naturally shocked, but did not waste any time: he went that morning to see Lord Temple, Lord Egmont. and Dodington—'in short everyone I could to stir up all the assistance I could to shew a face against such an infamous violation of justice'.

He busied himself writing and publishing pamphlets on Byng's behalf and getting articles printed in the newspapers—among them *Queries Addressed to Every Englishman's Own Feelings*, by Byng's new sympathizer, Horace Walpole. He met Sir Edward Hawke, Byng's successor in command of the squadron, who said that he 'would go live in a cottage rather than serve to meet such treatment, and said that Mr West had been very false in this, and rose upon Mr Byng's ruin'. Hervey added that 'This indeed was but too true, but Sir Edward was as double in all his boastings . . .'

At Portsmouth the Commander-in-Chief, Vice-Admiral Henry Osborn, now had in his charge a condemned man who was his sister-in-law's brother and a lifelong friend, and presumably within a few days orders would come down from the Admiralty for him to have that man shot. It was an intolerable situation, and the day after the court gave its verdict Osborn wrote asking for a week's leave 'to go to Town', which the Board granted, telling him to leave 'all unexecuted orders' with Vice-Admiral Smith.[1]

On January 29, the day after they received the court's verdict, the Board met and decided that an admiral condemned to death could hardly continue to be lodged in the house of the Boatswain of the Dockyard, and they sent orders to Smith that Byng 'should be removed on board a ship in Portsmouth Harbour'.[2]

Vice-Admiral Smith chose H.M.S. *Monarch* for Byng's accommodation. She was a 74-gun ship, formerly the French *Monarque*, (which had been captured by Sir Edward Hawke off Finisterre) and her Master's log[3] noted on Monday, January 31: 'Ye joyners came on board to fit our great cabbin up for Admiral Byng.' Next day they were 'gitting all readey to receve Adml Byng on bord'. The first of the party to arrive were a captain and lieutenant of Marines, with thirty-six men—they had been ordered on board to see that Byng did not escape—and the Admiral himself arrived with Brough on Thursday afternoon, February 3. There was a good deal of anxiety in the *Monarch* because although they had now a condemned admiral on board as a prisoner, they had no captain: the new one, replacing Captain George Rodney (to be the victor, in 1782, in the great battle with Count de Grasse) had not arrived.

Next morning, by a coincidence—not the last as far as she was concerned—Byng's former flagship, the *Ramillies*, arrived back in Portsmouth and anchored near the *Monarch*. An hour or two later, in the midst of a snowstorm, Captain John Montagu came on board to take command, and the time-honoured ritual was observed—all hands were called and Montagu read his commission to them.

Quite clearly Vice-Admiral Smith, who was of course Commander-in-Chief at The Downs, could not stay on indefinitely in command at Portsmouth; and he was having more qualms about the recent verdict. He too asked for leave to go to London, and the Admiralty, perhaps appreciating that it was hardly fit that the man who had presided at the tribunal condemning Byng should then also have to act as his jailer and executioner, wrote on February 2 that they had 'ordered Admiral Boscawen to repair down to Portsmouth and hoist his flag' and Smith was therefore free to come to London.

Henry Osborn had reached London several days earlier and gone to his home in Hill Street. A few yards away in the same street, on the corner with Berkeley Square, Admiral Byng's house was closed up, a mute reminder of the situation Osborn had left behind him in Portsmouth. He visited Byng's sister Sarah and went to call on the First Lord. Later the Admiralty gave him further leave and within a fortnight told him[4] he had been made an admiral of the blue. (Others promoted to the same rank this day included Smith and Hawke.)

As soon as Boscawen arrived in Portsmouth, Smith set off for Cavendish Square, where he had his town house. He had earlier written to his brothers, George and Richard Lyttelton, begging their 'interest' in the court's plea for mercy for Byng. Richard, a Member of the House of Commons, was more than willing to do what he could; but George—who had just been made a peer—was a strong supporter of the Newcastle group. Extremely tall and thin —'his face was so ugly, his person so ill-made, his carriage so awkward, that every feature was a blemish', according to Lord Hervey[5]—he never used two words when ten would do, and always spoke them in a dreary monotone. He replied to the Admiral that 'You know my heart is inclined to mercy, but though I dare say, had I been one of his judges my eyes would have been no dryer than yours when sentence was passed upon Mr Byng, I cannot say that, without any stronger reasons than those you mentioned in the latter part of your sentence and your letter to the Admiralty, I should have thought my conscience concerned in his being saved from the penalty [but if] you have stronger reasons to urge, for God's sake lose no time but write them to the Admiralty.'[6]

The beginning of February saw those on Byng's side begin to organize themselves in an effort to save his life, while those against him kept their fingers crossed. The latter group naturally included Lords Hardwicke and Anson and, an inquiry into the loss of Minorca having been called for in Parliament, the former Lord Chancellor wrote to his son-in-law to prepare a reply in case any of their political adversaries asked why a part of the Western Squadron had not been sent to the Mediterranean in the previous March. ' 'Tis possible that they may not hit upon it; but it is necessary to be prepared with the proper answers.'[7]

Richard Rigby wrote to the Duke of Bedford that the Duke of Cumberland 'was very earnest to know your Graces's opinion' about Byng's ultimate fate. His Royal Highness was 'against his suffering'. Rigby said that he had been told the King might keep him alive as a prisoner by frequent reprieves, or by a suggestion of Lady Caroline Fox, the wife of Henry Fox, 'which I do not think a bad one', might be followed. This was to order Byng's execution, but connive at his escape.[8]

The next letter concerning Byng that the Duke of Bedford received came from the Admiral's sister, Sarah. 'The present distress of our family,' she wrote, 'must plead with your Grace for my attempting to intrude on your quiet hours at Woburn . . . Yet I should not have dared to have troubled your Grace, were not my brother's suffering already such as scarce any crime could have imposed.' He had been, she said, 'Ignominiously suspended, most ignominiously aspersed, and inhumanely traduced through the world, on suppositions which his family must have shared the disgrace of, and from which not even his father's service to this nation could have afforded a shadow of refuge, had they not been as amply disproved, and he as justly acquitted of.'

She implored the Duke to consider the sentence. 'Pity, my Lord, a distressed sister, surrounded only by weeping females, and helpless boys, who will all owe grateful acknowledgements of their future happiness to the influence the Duke of Bedford must always have, when justice and mercy are the objects of his care.'⁹

The Duke replied in guarded terms: he was just able, 'through the extreme weakness of my right hand, occasioned by the gout', to acknowledge Sarah's letter. Should the King refer the court martial's sentence to the Cabinet Council he would be very happy if he found himself able to 'adopt those sentiments of mercy which that court has so strongly recommended to His Majesty'.¹⁰

Sarah wrote again, enclosing a copy of a letter she had sent to the Admiralty as the last effort that 'an unhappy sister can make'. Sarah hoped that his Grace would think the points in her letter to the Admiralty had weight—'indeed, my Lord, it is terrible to think of my poor brother's execution being ordered in consequence of a sentence in a great degree appealed from by those who passed it, not understood by the world, and passed under a law doubtful and unexplained. The hardship of my brother's approaching fate is every hour more and more felt, though I have never yet heard of the case having been laid before His Majesty with the alleviating circumstances that attend it. A cruel and false notion that His Majesty is disinclined to mercy on this occasion has probably prevented it . . .

'It may be proper to inform your Grace that Admiral Forbes refused signing the order for the execution, and has given Lord Temple his reasons in writing for such refusal which he has desired him to lay before the King.'¹¹

Sarah's reference to Admiral Forbes—who had only recently been made a member of the Board of Admiralty—did not give a hint of the drama that had attended his refusal. Forbes had been one of the five members present when the Board met on February 9 to discuss the many criticisms which had been made about the court martial's verdict: several people had declared—for the reasons we have already discussed—that the verdict was not lawful. The Board therefore decided that 'doubts having arisen with regard to the legality of the sentence, particularly whether the crime of *negligence*, which is not expressed in any part of the proceedings can, in this case, be supplied by implication', a memorial should be presented to the King requesting that 'the opinion of the judges may be taken whether the said sentence is legal'. The Board had received a petition from Byng's nephew, Lord Torrington, and they sent this along to the Palace at the same time, with copies of the thirty-seven resolutions, the sentence, and the court's plea for mercy.

Thus, quite unwittingly, did the Board make a major move towards ensuring that Byng was shot. Had they simply sent the court's appeal for mercy to the King, it is doubtful if he could have ignored it—he would certainly have had to give a straight yes or no; but their memorial gave him a loophole because it merely asked if the *sentence* was legal. It would not take a dozen judges long to see that the sentence was legal, and that what the Admiralty really meant to ask was if the *verdict* was legal. It did not mention the word 'mercy' or ask the King to exercise his Royal prerogative and reprieve Byng.

The King ordered twelve judges to consider the sentence, and they met on Monday, February 14, at the chambers of Lord Mansfield. The two senior judges were Mansfield (the former Attorney-General, William Murray, who had insisted on his preferment and peerage from the Duke of Newcastle) and Sir John Willes, whom we have already seen advising the Duke how Byng should be tried (see page 184). It did not take long for them and their ten colleagues to reach a unanimous decision that 'it is a legal sentence'. They did not bother to give any reasons nor record any views on the other point in the Admiralty's memorial— whether negligence, though not mentioned in the sentence, 'can be supplied by implication'.

The King's reply to the Admiralty on February 16 merely enclosed the report of a Privy Council meeting held that day at St James's and the judges' report. The Privy Council had simply ordered that the judges' opinion should be sent to the Admiralty. The plea of Byng's sister Sarah to the Duke of Bedford had been in vain: he had attended the Council but had said nothing.

The Board met that night to consider the King's reply and Lord Temple told them that 'His Majesty was pleased to signify his pleasure' that the sentence on Admiral Byng should be carried into execution.

The minutes of the meeting concluded: 'Ordered that Vice-Admiral Boscawen, or the C-in-C of His Majesty's ships at Portsmouth for the time being, do carry the aforesaid sentence into execution on Monday the 28th instant, by causing the said Admiral Byng to be shot to death on board such of His Majesty's ships as he shall think proper. And the warrant was prepared accordingly.'[12]

However, Admiral Forbes had been arguing strongly all the while that the court's findings were illegal: he had maintained his argument even in face of the opinion of the twelve judges. Now, as a member of the Board, he refused to sign the warrant for Byng's execution. His reasons were quite simple and honest, and he put them in writing.

'It may be thought great presumption in me to differ from so great authority as that of the twelve judges,' he wrote, 'but when a man is called upon to sign his name to an act which is to give authority for the shedding of blood, he ought to be guided by his *own conscience*, and not by the opinion of other men.

'In the case before us, it is not the merit of Admiral *Byng* that I consider; but whether or not his life can be taken away by the sentence pronounced upon him by the court martial.' Referring to the verdict and the 12th Article of War, covering cowardice, disaffection or neglect, he said: 'The court martial does, in express words, acquit Admiral Byng of cowardice and disaffection, and does not name the word negligence,' so that Byng did not fall under the letter or description of the 12th Article.

He pointed out that the court said they had condemned Byng because they had to under the letter of the law, and earnestly recommended him to mercy. 'It is then evident that in the opinions and consciences of the judges he was not deserving death.' Should the opinions or the necessities of the court martial decide on Admiral Byng's fate? If the latter, he would be executed contrary to his judges' intentions; if the former, his life was not forfeited.

'His judges declare he is not deserving of death; but mistaking either the meaning of the law, or the nature of his offence, they bring him under an Article of War which, according to their own description of his offence, he does not, I conceive, fall under; and then they condemn him to death because, as they say, the law admits of no mitigation. Can a man's life be taken away by such a sentence?'

He concluded by saying that he was not judging Byng—that was the court's task; but he could not sign a warrant for the execution when he thought Byng's life was not forfeited under the court's sentence.[13]

One's admiration for his honesty is perhaps strengthened when one recalls that Forbes was also a man of proved courage: in battle he was, at Toulon, one of the captains who went to Admiral Mathews's aid and was court martialled for his bravery; now he was hazarding his own career in a step for which the author can find no precedent. Nevertheless, Forbes's action could only be a gesture: Temple, Hay, Hunter and Elliot signed the warrant for Byng's execution, and in any case three names would have been enough to make it legal.

The pace now began to quicken. At Portsmouth, Admiral Boscawen ordered Captain Montagu of the *Monarch* to tell Admiral Byng that the sentence of death would be carried out on the 28th—to which Byng replied, according to newspaper reports, that 'His Majesty's pleasure must be complied with; and seemed but little concerned'.[14]

The opening shots of a Parliamentary battle over Byng's fate were fired in the House of Commons when Thomas Orby Hunter, representing the Admiralty, reported that one of their fellow Members, Admiral Byng, had been sentenced to death by a court martial, the King had signified his pleasure that the sentence should be carried out, and a warrant had been signed to put him to death in eleven days' time.

The Speaker promptly produced a number of precedents for expelling Byng from membership of the House before he was executed—otherwise, he claimed, the disgrace would reflect on Parliament itself. However, several Members protested: one said that it seemed to be excluding mercy while there was still a chance for it, and another, Sir Francis Dashwood—'a man distinguished by no milkiness of temper, connected with no friends of the prisoner', according to Walpole—'took this up strongly', and asked for the court martial's plea for mercy to be produced. Henry Fox objected, saying that it would look like a censure on the court, but Sir Francis denied this, declaring that 'by considering the warmth of their recommendation', it might lead to some application for mercy. Pitt seemed to favour the idea; but Sir Francis's motion was defeated.[15]

In the Commons a few days earlier several addresses had been moved for papers to begin the inquiry into the loss of Minorca. The *Evening Post* was soon reporting that the clerks in the offices of the Secretaries of State and of the Admiralty were busy copying all intelligence reports received about the Toulon Squadron and its designs on Minorca. However, since the former Ministers still had friends like Clevland at the Admiralty, Barrington at the War Office and Holdernesse as Secretary of State for the Northern Province, it was unlikely that a single paper damning the late Ministry had been left in the files; in any case, people like Philip Cartaret Webb had already been through them and prepared the collective alibi.

In Stratton Street, Sarah was busy writing to William Pitt, and to the Admiralty. She begged Pitt to intercede with the King on behalf 'of a victim to popular clamour'.[16]

To the Admiralty she wrote a detailed letter arguing over the sentence saying: 'Why, my Lords, should my poor brother suffer, when both the sentence by which he is condemned, and the letter to your Lordships, by which he is so strongly recommended to His Majesty's mercy, fully prove his judges did not seem to think him deserving of the punishment they thought themselves obliged to sentence him to? I hope your Lordships will not think he ought to suffer, either under a law unexplained, or doubtful, or under a sentence erroneously passed.'[17]

Augustus Hervey, describing the King's action in not reprieving the Admiral, said he 'was such a hardened brute that he was determined Mr Byng should not escape'.[18] Admiral Forbes's refusal to sign the death warrant, he said, 'made a great noise'; but although Temple West had, as we have already seen, written earlier to give up his command, 'his near relation Lord Temple being First Lord prevented that timely resignation'.

THE QUALITY OF MERCY...

THE DAY SET FOR Byng's execution was fast approaching but some of the feeling which had been roused up artificially against him was now becoming sympathetic. The King, however, with Teutonic obstinacy, remained fixed in his opinion. Although His Majesty was a man whose own bravery on the field of battle had been doubted on at least one occasion, he genuinely regarded Byng as a coward and, with all the fervour of a convert to courage, was intent on making an example of him. Henry Fox, writing to Augustus Hervey's mother on February 23, five days before the date set for the execution, said: 'Don't flatter yourself, dear Madam, as you have hitherto done. Admiral Byng is not safe. The King will not pardon; nor does the House of Commons wish he should, unless some reasons are given to show Byng's innocence.'[1]

As things stood at this time, there seemed little hope that Byng's life could be saved. William Pitt was certainly sympathetic—although he had not given any public indication of it before he intervened in the Commons to support Sir Francis Dashwood after the Members were told officially that Byng was to die. Nevertheless, the Secretary of State was, as we have already seen, in a difficult situation. On one side of him was Fox, clearly one of the culprits in the loss of Minorca; on the other was the Newcastle-Hardwicke group. Although at present Fox and Newcastle were enemies, a strong attack on them by Pitt over the Minorca question would bring them together for mutual defence, and Pitt's grip on power was too weak for him to risk that happening.

At the same time, the King was anxious to keep his promise to the City of London that the guilty would be punished, and he genuinely regarded Byng as a guilty man. He was particularly careful not to upset the City at this moment since it held the purse-strings (Pitt, on his first day back in the Commons, had been forced to request the raising of hard cash for the King's 'German business'). The King was certainly not going to imperil that by annoying the City with a pardon for Byng.

As if all this was not enough to weight the scales against Byng, Pitt was of course personally unpopular with the King because of his attitude over the King's German dominions; Lord Temple, too, was equally unpopular. In fact the only people who could save Byng—the ex-Ministers who still held the power—were the very men who wanted him dead.

With Pitt stalemated, it seemed that Byng could not expect anyone in a powerful position to help him. The Duke of Bedford, a former First Lord of the Admiralty and hitherto friendly towards him, had not so far lifted a finger to help, despite Sarah's plea; the present First Lord, Temple, was apparently sympathetic but powerless. The King, with his favourites out of office, was implacable.

Then suddenly, and quite unexpectedly, someone rattled the bars of the cage: it was suggested the members of the court which tried Byng should now start a petition asking that the sentence of death should not be carried out. The move may have come from one of their number, Captain Keppel, but in any case Augustus Hervey heard about it within a few hours.

Realizing that here at last was a ray of hope, he hurried round to Cavendish Square to call on the former president of the court, Vice-Admiral Smith. Would he sign the petition? Smith said he would, and Hervey went on to see Rear-Admiral Norris and Captain Denis, both of whom also agreed to put their names to the plea. But of course, the petition was not intended to be restricted to members of the court, and Hervey went on to see Lord Temple at the Admiralty, saying it was hoped that he and the Duke of Bedford would join the petition. But Temple 'told me plainly that he thought he should hurt it, for that the King would rather be against any measure that he could recommend'. However, he promised that if the question was raised in Parliament he would try to influence people.

Helping Hervey with the petition was Captain Rodney, who had recently arrived in London after handing over the command of the *Monarch* to Captain John Montagu, and although both men saw several other members of the court martial and tried to persuade them to sign, 'we could get nothing determined'.[2]

Next day Hervey went to see Sir Francis Dashwood, who had

already spoken on Byng's behalf, and Sir John Cust joined them. The three men discussed whether some move could possibly be made in the House of Commons. The difficulty was how to raise the matter, and finally Dashwood suggested a resolution to explain the 12th Article of War, 'to blend it with Mr Byng's case, and to shew the great hardship that officer and all others lay under from the severity of that absurd article'. Dashwood said he would move it, Cust proposed to second, and George Bubb Dodington later agreed 'to take it up and speak to people's passions and to move the House'.

Next morning, Wednesday, three members of the court—Captains Keppel, Moore and Denis—went to see Lord Temple at the Admiralty and 'besought him to renew their application to the Throne for mercy',[3] and in the Commons that evening Dashwood opened the debate. He said that at first he had felt great animosity against Admiral Byng, but his opinion had been greatly changed by the trial. Now he could at most only impute misjudgment to Mr Byng; but to the court martial he must impute it more strongly because, he thought, they had condemned the Admiral unjustly. 'The Admiral's blood will lie at the door of those who do not explain what they meant by their sentence, of which no man else could give an interpretation.' He pointed out the various contradictory aspects of the court's findings and concluded by saying that the court's letter recommending mercy had been laid before the King 'where he hoped the great severity of the bungling sentence would be properly considered'.

Lord Barrington, the Secretary at War, then stood up and said he would only speak about the 12th Article, the severity of which he justified by saying that the previous war had begun 'with conduct at sea not very *honourable*', yet no court martial would condemn* the offenders: it was said nobody would be hanged but for high treason. And, he asked, was this a time when discipline should be relaxed or enforced?

Walpole, to whom we are indebted for a description of these proceedings, said George Bubb Dodington rose to ask of what the Admiral stood condemned. He '*did* know of what he was *not* condemned; and that supported him, as it was what stained neither the soldier nor the subject'. Pitt 'with true spirit avowed himself on the favourable side', but said he thought Parliament had

---

* i.e. condemn to death. Mathews, for instance, was dismissed the service.

K

nothing to do to advise the King on his peculiar prerogative, which was mercy. He wished it might be extended to Byng, and that 'it was more likely to flow from His Majesty, if he was left entirely free'.

Next day, Thursday, saw the first full account of Byng's trial put on sale—'Mr R. Manby, near Ludgate Hill' published *The Trial of the Hon Admiral John Byng* 'As taken by Mr Charles Fearne, Judge-Advocate to His Majesty's Fleet.' The price was six shillings.

In the morning, Pitt went to St James's Palace and pleaded with the King for mercy for Byng 'but was cut very short; nor did His Majesty remember to ask his *usual* question, *whether there were any favourable circumstance?*'⁴ At the same time, seven members of the court martial went to see Lord Temple at the Admiralty to ask him to plead with the King. He finally agreed and went off to St James's Palace, but when he told the King about the visit of the seven officers, and their plea, His Majesty took no notice. And on the same day the Duke of Bedford, perhaps in answer to Sarah Osborn's plea, followed in the footsteps of Pitt and Temple and made an appeal to the King, 'was better heard, but with no better success'.

That night Augustus Hervey, having spent much of the day in consultation with Sir Francis Dashwood and Horace Walpole, went to White's. There 'that infernal black demon, Mr Fox, told me he was surprised the court martial could show their faces, that he would much rather be Mr Byng than one of the thirteen members of the court martial. I made him no answer, but went away.'⁵

On Friday, February 25, with Byng due to be executed on the Monday, the situation was desperate. Parliament would rise that evening and would not sit again until after Byng was executed at noon on Monday. Several members of the court martial were becoming almost distraught in their attempts to reverse their sentence. Rear-Admiral Norris went to see George Grenville, the Treasurer of the Navy, who was Lord Temple's brother, and a man 'attached to no dissipation, never seen at White's with the gamesters or at Newmarket with the jockeys'.⁶ Norris told him he had something on his conscience that he wanted to speak about, and asked Grenville to apply to Parliament to free the members of the court from their oath of secrecy. Grenville, however, 'did not care to meddle in it'.

That morning, Sir Francis Dashwood and Lord Talbot arrived at Augustus Hervey's house while he was dressing and told him that nothing could be done in the House of Commons unless they could persuade some of the court martial to say they wanted to be released from the oath of secrecy* they had taken.[7]

Hervey went into action with his usual alacrity: he called on Captain George Rodney and asked him to go and speak to some of the members while Hervey himself went to see Captain Keppel. On his way to Keppel's house he met Captain Moore, one of the court, and quickly explained the position. A few minutes later the pair of them met Rear-Admiral Norris who, when Hervey described the proposed move in the Commons, agreed to join them. They could not find Keppel at his house, so Hervey suggested they all go to the Admiralty 'that we might know if the power of respite did not lay in them'. It was a forlorn hope, and the only people of any importance at the Admiralty were the hitherto-unsympathetic George Grenville, and also Admiral Forbes. They saw Grenville first, and Rear-Admiral Norris again asked him to raise the matter of their oath in the House. Grenville refused and Captain Moore, thoroughly exasperated, declared wrathfully: 'Then, sir, the Admiral's blood will not lie on us.'

They next went to Admiral Forbes—who, it will be recalled, had refused to sign the warrant for Byng's execution. He sent for the Secretary, Clevland, and asked him about the Board's power of respite. Clevland said that in his opinion the Board could not do anything about it, and there would have to be an Act of Parliament to free the members of the court from their oath.

There was now less than an hour left if anything was to be done: in the House of Commons the day's business was drawing to a close, and when the Members finally trooped out of the Chamber the last hope for Admiral Byng would go with them. Hervey left the others and, on going back to Keppel's house, found him at home. He described the events so far that morning and, although Keppel was a Member of Parliament, he seemed to Hervey to be 'rather irresolute about speaking on it in the House, but I rather thought him inclined to it, and therefore went down myself to the House'.[8]

Keppel had gone with him but they had parted before Hervey

* The oath said that 'I will not upon any account, at any time whatsoever, disclose or discover the vote or opinion of any particular member of this court, unless thereunto required by an Act of Parliament.'

met Horace Walpole, who takes up the tale from there, and his narrative is sufficiently concise and dramatic to quote in detail. Walpole was not then an MP* and had by chance arrived at the House of Commons rather late in the day. He was told of Rear-Admiral Norris's request to George Grenville, and began to look for Grenville to try to persuade him to do something about it. He then met Hervey, who told him that Captain Keppel also wished to be freed from his oath. Where was Keppel? Up in the Gallery, said Hervey, and Walpole, describing himself in the third person, wrote:

'Walpole ran up into the Gallery, and asked Keppel if it was true? And being true, why he did not move the House himself? Keppel replied that he was unused to speaking in public, but would willingly authorize anybody to make application for him.

' "Oh! Sir," said Walpole, "I will soon find you somebody," and hurried him to Mr Fox who, Walpole fondly imagined, could not in decency refuse such a request, and who was the more proper, from his authority in the House and as a relation of Mr Keppel. Fox was much surprised, knew not what to determine, said he was uncertain—and left the House.

'The time pressed, the Speaker was going to put the question for the Orders of the Day, after which no new motion can be made; it was Friday, too; the House would sit neither on Saturday nor Sunday, and but a possibility of two days remained to intercept the execution, which was to be on Monday; and the whole operation of what Keppel should have to say, its effects, the pardon if procured, the dispatch to Portsmouth, and the reprieve, all to be crowded into so few hours.

'Walpole was in agony what step to take—at that instant, he saw Sir Francis Dashwood going up the House, he flew down from the Gallery, called Sir Francis, hurried the notification to him, and Sir Francis, with the greatest quickness of tender apprehension, (the Speaker had actually read the question and put it while all this was passing) called out from the floor before he had time to take his place, "Mr Speaker"—and then informed the House of Mr Keppel's desire that some method might be found of empowering him and the other members of the court martial to declare what had been their intention in pronouncing Mr Byng guilty.'

* He had vacated his seat for Castle Rising in order to be elected at Lynn in place of his cousin, who had become a peer on the death of Lord Walpole.

One Member opposed the motion, while a second approved it. Pitt 'rose and begged the House would consider seriously before they proceeded on so nice a matter: he wished first to see a direct application to the House. For himself, he should probably smart for it; he had received a menacing letter that very morning. He addressed himself to Keppel, wished he would break through his bashfulness and rise: it would be a foundation to him to vote for the Bill demanded . . .'

Keppel, according to Hervey, 'stammered out something of his desires to be released from his oath', saying that they had condemned Byng 'against their conscience'. He added that many other members of the court had that very morning exhorted him to make the application. Another of the court, Captain Peter Denis, who was MP for Hedon, was also in the Chamber, but he refused to back Keppel's application.

However, Sir Richard Lyttelton said that he too had been asked by a member of the court to help, and he read out a letter he had received from his brother, Admiral Smith, 'entreating him to move in the same cause'.

George Grenville stood up to say that he thought the members of the court could speak without a special Act of Parliament because their oath only forbade them to reveal the opinion of any single man; but Keppel replied that he still had doubts. Pitt, however, said he honoured Keppel for his doubts and 'wished him to consult with his friends that night', and told him that out of regard to them the House would sit specially next day, Saturday. But for himself— he would, in their position, have no hesitation to speak without an Act. [9]

Next day, Saturday, Pitt went once again to St. James's Palace to see the King and, after saying that the House of Commons wished to have Byng pardoned, he met with a Royal snub: 'Sir, *you* have taught me to look for the sense of my subjects in another place than in the House of Commons.' Pitt was followed an hour or two later by Lord Temple who also again pressed the King for a pardon; but His Majesty—in the words of Rigby in a letter to the Duke of Bedford—told Temple flatly that he thought Byng guilty of cowardice in the action, and therefore he could not break the promise which they had forced him to give to his people. At this, according to Rigby, Temple 'walked up to his nose and said, *sans autre cérémonie*, "What shall you think if he dies courageously?"'

However, it was agreed in view of the court's move to give Byng a fortnight's reprieve, and the Inner Committee meeting at Devonshire House resolved 'that proper directions be sent to the Lords of the Admiralty to respite the execution of the sentence of death passed upon Admiral John Byng . . . until the 14th day of March next'.[10]

Pitt, as Secretary of State responsible for such matters, sent instructions to the Admiralty accordingly to respite the sentence,[11] and in turn the Board dispatched one set of orders to Admiral Boscawen by a messenger at 7 p.m., a duplicate by another messenger half an hour afterwards, and a third by post.[12] Boscawen was told to send a messenger from Portsmouth acknowledging the order as soon as he received it.

The Board had also discussed the move which had been made in the Commons, and as it was very probable that the members of the court martial 'may be examined thereon', decided that the President and members of the court 'be directed to be in London on Tuesday next in the evening'.*[13] Of the admirals, Holburne had gone down to Portsmouth, Broderick was at his home in Ripley, Surrey, Smith at his house in Cavendish Square, and Norris was also in London.

After the meeting of the Inner Committee, Pitt went to the Commons and delivered the King's message: His Majesty, he said, was determined to have let the law take its course in the case of Admiral Byng, 'and resisted all solicitations to the contrary', but being told that a Member of the House, who was also a member of the court martial, had applied to the House on behalf of himself and several others of the court to be freed from their oath, the King saw fit to respite the execution. Nevertheless, 'His Majesty is determined still to let this sentence be carried into execution, unless it shall appear, from the said examination, that Admiral Byng was unjustly condemned.'[15]

By the end of the day the Bill to free the court from its oath had passed its first and second reading and the Committee Stage, and it began to look as if Byng had a sporting chance. Yet within twenty-four hours everything was changed.

---

* They also resolved that the Navy Board should be directed to allow Charles Fearne's expenses as Judge-Advocate at the trial, amounting to £61 19s. 0d. 'except the last article for hire of post chaise upon his producing proper receipts', and also to allow him 12s. 6d. a day from August 6, 'when ordered to proceed on the business of the trial' until January 27, when the trial ended. [14]

The reason for this dramatic change was that on Sunday some of the members of the court martial who Keppel had told the House of Commons were backing his request for a Bill were now apparently denying having done so although, as Horace Walpole wrote in a letter that night, one of them, Rear-Admiral Norris 'was twice on Friday with Sir Richard Lyttelton, and once with George Grenville* for the same purpose! I have done nothing but traverse the Town tonight from Sir Richard Lyttelton's, to the Speaker's, to Mr Pitt's, to Mr Fox's, to Dodington's, to Lady Hervey's, to find out how to defeat the evil of this and to extract, if possible, some good from it. Alas! Alas! That what I meant so well should be likely only to add a fortnight to the poor man's misery'.[16]

The news that caused Walpole's despondency had spread across London very quickly and eventually it transpired that only two of the four men named by Keppel—Holmes and Geary—had in fact gone back on their word. Indeed, Rear-Admiral Norris and Captain Moore, far from breaking faith, wrote Keppel a letter in which they said, 'The world says we have varied, but we desire to adhere to what we told you.' Admiral Smith's brother, Sir Richard Lyttelton, went to see Captain Geary, 'begging him to consider the injustice and dishonourableness of retracting what he had authorized Keppel to say', and Geary's illuminating reply had been that 'It will hurt my preferment to tell.' Without examining the morality of refusing to help save a man's life because it would damage his chances of promotion, Geary was probably correct in having such fears at a time when serving officers took part in politics† ; and fortunately later he modified his attitude slightly.

In the Commons on Monday—the original date set for Byng's execution—Thomas Potter moved the third reading of the Bill, but Henry Fox rose and said he had heard that the House was going to be given some information. Keppel was thus forced to rise and explain that when he had named four other members of the court on Saturday, he had believed they commissioned him to

* Actually twice: once alone and the second time in company with Hervey and Moore.

† Hervey reports that while having supper at White's at this time, he heard Fox call all the members of the court martial 'a pack of fools and knaves', adding that 'were he now to advise the King, he should not employ one of them'. [17]

move the House on their behalf. Now one of them, Captain Holmes, claimed that Keppel had misunderstood him. Keppel had argued with him, but Holmes had said 'I am easy in my mind, and desire to say nothing further.' Keppel said he believed it would be useless to call Holmes. As for Captain Geary, he was not 'absolutely off nor on', but would have no objection to speaking if all the court were compelled to speak. However, the other two, Rear-Admiral Norris and Captain Moore, stood by what they had said, and he read an extract from their letter to him.

Henry Fox then pointed out that seven of the thirteen members of the court were in London: of them Holburne had refused to interfere; Denis had withdrawn from the House; Holmes had declared himself easy in his mind; and Geary did not want to speak unless they all did. Thus a majority of those who were actually in London did not approve of the Bill.

However, the debate went on: one Member, speaking against the Bill, said that Pitt had undone one Ministry and was going to undo another; a second, urging the Bill, made a point that many people had overlooked—that 'A man who is going to die at least has a right to know for what he is to die.' Finally the House voted, and the Bill was passed by 153 votes to 22. The first hurdle had been passed. Now the Bill had to go to the House of Lords for their approval.

They debated it next day and both Lord Hardwicke and Lord Mansfield took a prominent part (they 'seemed like two attorneys at assizes pleading for the blood of a man, and using all the dirty little quirks and tours of the law', according to Hervey). The second reading was arranged for Thursday, and all the members of the court martial were ordered to attend so that they could be called before the Lords and questioned individually.

The examination of these men was stage-managed—an appropriate phrase—by Lord Hardwicke. He proposed that each member of the court should be called to the Bar of the House—in itself an intimidating process calculated to overawe, if not frighten, all but the boldest of them—and then asked a series of questions, on the following lines: (1) Whether you know of any matter that passed previous to the sentence on Admiral Byng to show it to be unjust? (2) Whether you know any matter that passed previous to the sentence which may show that sentence to have been given through any undue practice or motive?

If they answered 'yes' to either question, they were then to be asked two further questions: (3) Whether you apprehend you are restrained by your oath from disclosing any such matter? (4) What kind of matter or things you apprehend you are restrained from your oath from disclosing?

This idea, with some modification to the questions, was adopted, and when they met again the peers decided that before each man was examined, the oath of secrecy taken at the court martial should be read to him.

Admiral Smith was called first. The oath was read, and while he stood at the Bar of the House, getting more and more nervous, it was agreed that the 12th Article of War should also be read. That was done, and then the questioning started. Smith, wrote Walpole, was 'of no capacity, of no quickness to comprehend the chicanery of such a partial examination. He and the greater part of his comrades were awed too with the presence of the great persons before whom they were brought.'[18]

The questioning was handled by Lord Mansfield, who began by asking if he knew of anything that happened, before the sentence was pronounced on Admiral Byng, which might show it to have been unjust?

'Indeed I do not,' declared Smith.

Did he know of anything which might show the sentence to have been given through any undue practice or motive?

'Indeed I do not,' Smith said.

'Whether,' asked Lord Mansfield, 'you are desirous that the Bill, now being under consideration of the House, for dispensing with the oath of secrecy, should pass into a law?'

'As for myself,' said Smith, 'I have no desire of it: but if it will be a relief to the conscience of any of my brethren it will not be disagreeable to me.'

Did the Admiral have any details to reveal about the case and the sentence which he thought necessary for His Majesty's information, and which he thought likely to incline the King to mercy?

'I have not, indeed, further than as I wrote what seemed to be at that time the sense of the whole court to a right honourable member of this House, [his brother George] signifying, if it was necessary, the members would willingly attend, to set forth the reasons that induced them to recommend him to His Majesty's mercy.'

He was then asked if he thought the oath of secrecy prevented

him laying those reasons before the King, and he replied that as
the sentence, and the application for mercy, were the unanimous
resolutions of the court, he thought he was at liberty to give the
reasons why he had asked for mercy.*

Not one of the peers asked him what the reasons were; instead
he was directed to withdraw, and Rear-Admiral Holburne was
brought in. He was asked the first four of the five questions which
had been put to Admiral Smith, and to each one he replied: 'No,
my Lords.' Rear-Admiral Norris followed. We have seen that in
the previous few days he had been a strong supporter of Keppel;
he had been twice to George Grenville, the Treasurer of the
Navy, asking that the court should be freed from its oath, and as
late as Sunday he had written to Keppel reiterating that, with
Moore, 'we desire to adhere to what we told you'. But before he
arrived at the Bar of the House something had happened to
Norris's courage. Walpole said that, 'Struck with awe of the
tribunal before which he had appeared, he showed how little
qualified he had been for a judge, when so terrified at superior
judges. He lost all comprehension, understood no questions that
were asked, nor knew how or when to apply the very answers he
came to give.' The record of the House's proceedings confirm
Walpole's verdict.[19]

Rear-Admiral Broderick said 'No, my Lords' to all the questions;
and his words were echoed by Charles Holmes. Francis Geary,
'the repenter of his repentance', according to Walpole, said 'No' to
the first two questions but, asked if he wanted the Bill, said: 'No,
my Lords, but I have no objection if it will be to the satisfaction
of any person.'

Moore also said no to the first two questions but, asked if he
wanted the Bill to become law, he stood by his word and said:
'I am very desirous it should, that I might be absolved from the
oath.' Captains Boys, Simcoe, Douglas, Bentley and Denis all
gave a determined 'No' to each question, but Augustus Keppel,
asked if he wanted the Bill, said: 'Yes, undoubtedly.'

Thus of the thirteen members of the court, only two now
admitted they wanted the Bill. The report of the day's events in
the House of Lords concluded with: 'Then the several examina-

---

* Smith had previously written to one of his brothers saying the members of
the court were prepared to go before the Privy Council or Parliament to explain
the reasons for their recommendations.

tions were read by the clerk. And it being moved to reject the said Bill; ordered that the said Bill be rejected.'[20]

'What amazed me was Lord Temple, at the end of the debate, congratulating the House that the sentence was proved to be a legal one,' wrote Hervey, 'and which made most people imagine there was some compromise between the late and present administration to screen those most infamous delinquents, Lord Anson, Mr Fox, and the Duke of Newcastle.'[21]

The efforts of Hervey, Keppel and Walpole had failed; Byng now could not expect mercy from any man and the fortnight's stay of execution was fast running out. The behaviour of eleven out of the thirteen members of the court martial was despicable because they had now proved that although they did not think Byng should be executed—they made this clear in their plea for mercy—they did not have sufficient courage or conviction to try to save him. All of them had originally made a strong official recommendation to mercy; yet now eleven of them did not stand by it. Worst perhaps was the cowardice of Admiral Smith: he was the president of the court and, as mentioned earlier, had even written that the court were prepared to go before the Privy Council or Parliament.

On Friday the Board of Admiralty met and resolved that another warrant be sent to Vice-Admiral Boscawen directing him to carry out the execution of Admiral Byng the following Monday.[22] Boscawen was also to be warned to make sure Byng did not escape: although their Lordships were 'fully sensible of your diligence and care, they cannot but recommend it to you in the strongest manner to give such further directions to the captain of the *Monarch*, and other officers belonging to that ship, as will most effectually provide for the security of the prisoner', their letter said, 'and likewise that you will order such additional officers and sentries on board as you shall judge proper to assist the Marshal of the Admiralty, and they do not doubt but you will take all other methods that shall occur to you to be advisable for this purpose'.[23]

This was the last letter the Board wrote to Boscawen on the subject of Byng's execution, and it did not specify where in the ship Byng was to be shot.

THE LAST DAYS

THE BOARD'S ORDER to Vice-Admiral Boscawen for safeguarding Admiral Byng was stringent, but it might have been more so if their Lordships had known what one of their captains, Augustus Hervey, was planning. The young captain wrote that 'I was very uneasy and unhappy at seeing my friend and benefactor so betrayed, so treated and so sacrificed, but determined to set out for Portsmouth to take my leave of Mr Byng, and to see if there was not a possibility to help him to escape out of the hands of these bloodthirsters.'

He left a set of horses at Ripley, and then went on to Petersfield, where he ordered four more horses to be ready for him at any time of the night or day, 'agreeing to pay three pounds a day for them, and determining if possible to convey Mr Byng to London as the surest place to get him off from'. He also wrote to his servant William Cradock in London to have horses constantly ready and saddled and to hire a Dutch fishing boat; but, as he wrote later, 'all this proved in vain, as I got to Portsmouth Sunday the 6th, and found Mr Byng was a prisoner very narrowly watched'.[1]

Admiral Byng had by now settled into a routine on board the *Monarch*. He was imprisoned in the Captain's quarters and very strictly guarded. There were two sentries at each door leading from his cabins on to the quarter-deck, and a sentry marched up and down the stern gallery. The Marshal, Mr Brough, had thirty-six Marines and their lieutenant and captain to help him keep a guard.

All round Byng in the *Monarch* there was the familiar bustle as the crew, working under the boatswain, went on with rigging the ship. The first two weeks of February were spent getting topmasts and yards on board; the crew then began setting up the running rigging and tarring the standing.

The Admiral liked to pace up and down the stern gallery,

enjoying the fresh air and the exercise, and this habit on February 22 saved a life. He saw a man fall from a ship—a French prize— anchored nearby and at once shouted for a boat to be lowered from the *Monarch*, which was done in time to rescue the man.

The Admiral's two nephews, John and George Byng, and Edmund Bramston, came out to the ship each day. He was reported to 'behave in a truly decent and Christian-like manner, being quite composed and resigned to the will of Providence'. He usually spent part of the morning praying (a parson friend made a daily visit), and John, George and Edmund usually arrived to join him for lunch, at which he 'refreshed himself very modestly'. He would then leave them again until supper, which was very early, when he would eat with them, again very sparingly.

When Captain Montagu came to tell Byng that the King had granted a respite of fourteen days, Bramston, John and George promptly made much of the fact that Parliament was doing something at last: his friends must be at work in London, they said, and they were sure it must lead to an honourable pardon. But Byng knew by now that he had too many implacable enemies in high places: far more was at stake than one man's life. 'I am glad you think so,' he said, 'because it makes you easy and happy; but I think it is now become an affair merely political—without any further relation to right and wrong, justice or injustice; and therefore I differ in opinion from you.'

When the new warrant for Byng's execution arrived at Portsmouth, with the Admiralty's warning to Boscawen to be sure the prisoner did not escape, the routine for what was left of his life was changed. 'Received orders to put a stronger guard on Mr Byng', it was noted in the *Monarch*'s log.[2] Boscawen ordered that from then on one of the ship's officers was to be with Byng all the time, night and day. Captain Montagu selected Lieutenants Shirley, Brograve, Uvedale (who was later to become an admiral) and Lambert. Each was to stand a four-hour watch and keep a special log book in which the names of all visitors were to be listed, with the times of their arrival and departure. All visitors had to leave the ship by 6.30 p.m. In addition there were to be two sentries in the stern gallery instead of one, and as soon as darkness fell a guard boat, commanded by a midshipman and manned by six seamen and with two Marines armed with muskets, was to be rowed round the ship until after dawn. Another thirty-two

Marines were then brought on board, so that there were now
sixty-eight in the *Monarch*, solely to guard Byng.[3]

These new measures, in all their ponderous absurdity, began
on March 6, the day Augustus Hervey arrived in Portsmouth.
The next day was Monday, the beginning of Byng's last week of
life—and is a good example of the day's routine for Byng.
The north-easterly gale which had been blowing all Sunday and
most of the night, drenching the seamen and Marines in the guard
boat, had finally blown itself out. After going to Byng's sleeping
cabin at midnight on Sunday to make sure he was safe—there was
a lantern alight all the time—Lt Brograve handed over to Lt
Lambert, who had also peered into the cabin. At the same time
the two sentries in the stern gallery and at the cabin doors were
changed, and the guard boat came alongside to change its crew.
All this made a certain amount of noise which probably woke
Byng.

Lt Lambert entered the details of the change of the guard in the
logbook and then settled down for his four-hour vigil. At 4 a.m.
Lt Shirley took over and the sentries and crew of the guard boat
were changed once again.

Byng was up by 7 a.m., and after washing and being shaved by
his valet Hutchens, he had breakfast. At 8 a.m. the guards changed
and half an hour later a boat came alongside with John and George
Byng and Mr Isaac Muckins, the parson. They told the Admiral
that Augustus Hervey was in Portsmouth, and he at once wrote a
letter requesting him to come on board. 'I found him very composed, cheerful and seemed quite rejoiced to see me,' wrote
Hervey. 'He told me 'twas hard he should pay for the crimes of
others with his blood that had never before been stained . . .
He often repeated the very harsh manner he had been treated with,
which he freely forgave. He was persuaded to petition the King to
turn his sentence into perpetual banishment, but it had no
effect. Mr Pratt drew it up.*

'I offered my services to him, and showed him two or three
schemes for his escape, but he told me that he thanked me, but
would never think of it, he would rather die than fly from death
that way.'[4]

Hervey visited the Admiral again next day, and Byng soon had

---

* Charles Pratt, later Earl Camden and Lord Chancellor. The author can
find no trace of this petition, nor any other reference to it.

him and Bramston at work drafting out a letter which he intended
to leave after he was executed. Hervey found the job heartbreak-
ing, and after he had finished, when the Admiral and Bramston
were talking in the sleeping cabin, Hervey 'stole away and begged
of them to tell him I could not bear the taking leave of him, and
only prayed earnestly that I might see him again'. The log kept
by the lieutenants recorded 'At 2 Captain Hervey went on
shore'.

The time had finally come for Byng to 'choose executors and talk
of wills,' and he drew up his will with the same calm precision and
attention to detail which had characterized his life and which had
perhaps contributed something to his coming death. His calm was
not ruffled by the certain knowledge that the will would take effect
in just forty-eight hours.

On Saturday, March 12, his first visitors came on board at
7.30 a.m., an hour earlier than usual. There were his nephew John
and Mr Muckins, his old friend and agent Benjamin Gage, making
his first visit to the Admiral on board the *Monarch*, and a solicitor
and his clerk. Byng had listed all his possessions and the people
to whom they were to be left. It remained for the solicitor to draw
up the will in the appropriate legal phraseology, a clerk to write
out a fair copy, and Byng to sign it.

'In the name of God, Amen. I the Honourable John Byng
Esquire, being of sound and disposing mind and memory (praised
be to God) do make and publish this my last will and testament . . .'
it began. Edmund Bramston and Midshipman John were appointed
executors. The two people with whom the Admiral was most
concerned were his nephews George and John, the sons of his
brother Robert. To George, the elder of the two boys, went
Wrotham Park, the great house Byng had built in Hertfordshire
and had so little time to enjoy; to John he left the house in
Berkeley Square.*

Settlements of his freehold and leasehold estates, and deeds of
appointment concerning £16,000 annuities were confirmed, and
he left his other nephew George, Lord Torrington, the money

---

* John was now seventeen. Deciding not to go to sea again, he went up to
Cambridge later in the year, renting the Berkeley Square house to Lord Robert
Bertie, whom he knew well, of course, from the Minorca campaign. John died
in Italy at the age of twenty-four.

due from a mortgage on a house and land at Southill. To Torrington's brother went the blue enamelled snuffbox given to Byng
by the Duke de Bell-Isle. The Admiral's gold-hilted sword, gold
repeating watch, all his silver plate (he had a great deal and listed
every item), and china, with three canteens of china-handled
cutlery, went to Midshipman John. His large square amethyst
ring went to William Daniel 'as a token of my regard and friendship' (Daniel was in fact already travelling down the Portsmouth
road to take his farewell*) while 'Mrs Hickson's mourning ring'—
the one he had bought with the £50 legacy from his former mistress
—went to Benjamin Gage's wife Rachel. Benjamin himself was
forgiven a £120 bond and received 'my picture which is in Mrs
Hickson's room', and also Byng's portrait of Augustus Hervey.
'My worthy and sincere friend' Augustus Hervey was left 'the
French clock ornamented with Dresden flowers, which I desire he
will accept as a small token of our friendship'.† Young Torrington
also received the 'picture of His Sacred Majesty the King of
Sardinia set with diamonds which the said King gave me as a token
of His Majesty's regard for me'. Admiral Henry Osborn and
Edmund Bramston were left certain land in trust.

The Admiral had detailed his possessions even down to 'the
ffigure of Venus in plaister of Paris . . . the ffiingures [*sic*] of which
are in the drawer in the small escrutore [*sic*] in my dressing-room,'
and when the clerk had finished writing Byng signed each page.
William Brough signed as a witness, followed by the solicitor and
clerk. Byng then realized he had forgotten the diamond ring he
was wearing, and several others, and he had to add a codicil.[5]

Their melancholy task completed, the Admiral's guests went on
shore and he sat down in the candle-lit cabin to write his last letter.
Appropriately enough it was to his sister Sarah. 'My dear, dear Sister,'
he wrote, 'I can only with my last breath thank you over and over
again for all your endeavours to serve me in my present situation.
All has proved fruitless, but nothing wanting in you that could be
done. God forever bless you is the sincere prayer of your most affectionate brother, J. Byng.'[6] He added a postscript: 'Enclosed I send
you a receipt for brother Edward's legacy, which you will do me the

---

* His sister had married Byng's brother George, the third Viscount Torrington; his mother was a Master—the same family that provided the Admiral's
mother, the whimsical Margaret.

† '. . . The Admiral had left me in his will a clock, which clock I have and
will keep as long as I live,' Hervey wrote later.

favour to accept of as a small token of my affection for you.'*

Sunday, March 13, although naturally a terrible day for Byng, was particularly harrowing for the relatives and friends who came to visit him, because of course it was his last complete day of life, for by now no one had the slightest illusion about a last-minute reprieve or a pardon. The visitors included Isaac Muckins, Benjamin Gage and Edward Clark, the former fourth lieutenant of the *Ramillies*, Bramston and William Daniel, who was making his first visit to the Admiral.

They had not been talking to Byng for long before an embarrassed and apologetic Brough appeared in the cabin: Boscawen had just sent Captain Montagu his warrant for the execution, and it had to be read over to the Admiral. Brough was relieved to find that Byng showed no sign of annoyance at the macabre interruption; on the contrary, he told the Marshal to read it there and then.

The second warrant which the Admiralty had sent to Boscawen cannot now be traced, but the first, which had been cancelled when the King gave the fortnight's respite, directed Boscawen to execute Byng 'on board such of His Majesty's ships in Portsmouth Harbour as you shall think proper'. The minutes of the Board meeting which ordered the dispatch of the second warrant—the one Brough was about to read to Byng—said that Boscawen was to carry out the sentence on the 14th 'by causing the said Admiral Byng to be shot to death by a platoon of Marines on board such of His Majesty's ships in Portsmouth Harbour as he shall think proper . . .'[7]

In other words, neither the first warrant nor the Board minutes concerning the second specify where in the ship Byng was to be shot. Boscawen could choose which ship he pleased; the Admiralty only ruled that a platoon of Marines were to form the firing squad. Presumably, since he had the choice of ship, Boscawen also had the choice of the particular place in the ship, and of course it was up to Boscawen to send a warrant to Captain Montagu directing him to carry out the execution.

All this is important, because when Brough read the warrant to Byng—with the Admiral's friends and relatives with him, listening in horrified silence—it revealed that he was to be shot on the fo'c'sle of the *Monarch*.

* Sarah later wrote on this letter: 'My brother from on board the *Monarque* [sic], the last letter from him, the 14th being the fatal day appointed for him to die, to the perpetual disgrace of public justice.'

Byng was outraged at the idea of the fo'c'sle and, turning to the others, exclaimed: 'Is not this putting me upon the footing of a common seaman, condemned to be shot? Is not this an indignity to my birth, my family, and to my rank in the service? I think I have not been treated like an officer in any instance since I was disgraced—excepting in that of being ordered to be shot.'*

Bramston and the others, although sure that the warrant could not be altered, agreed with Byng that 'it was an impropriety', but that they hoped he would 'think the place immaterial', a circumstance beneath his notice, and not let it break in upon his tranquillity of mind. This thought seemed to calm him.

'It is very true, the place or manner is of no great importance to me,' he agreed, 'but I think living admirals should consult the dignity of the rank, for their own sakes. I cannot plead a precedent,' he added, with a touch of bitterness in his voice, 'for there is no precedent of an admiral or a general officer in the Army being shot. They make a precedent of me such as admirals hereafter may feel the effects of . . .'

Having said that, his anger appeared to be spent: there was little more for anyone to say, and probably none of the others in the cabin was more upset than Brough, for by then there seemed to be a feeling of respect between the two men far removed from a jailer-prisoner relationship, and since there were several other people to choose from, one can only assume that this led Byng to ask Brough to be the first witness to his will.

The Reverend John Snow had been appointed chaplain of the *Monarch* as a result of a Board decision on June 8 the previous year, the day after orders had been sent to Byng at Gibraltar ordering him to strike his flag and return home.[8] Now, as the wind piped up from the north-west into yet another strong gale, Mr Snow conducted his most moving service. Byng and his visitors stood bareheaded in the great cabin, the makeshift altar flanked by cannon, as the chaplain read prayers; then Byng 'received the Sacrament in a very decent and devout manner'.

At lunch—his last—Byng was the most cheerful man at the table: he passed dishes to his guests, filled their glasses and drank their health while they searched desperately in their minds for safe topics of conversation.

After the meal they all sat round in the big cabin, the grey

* Seamen were hanged.

light filtering in through the windows of the stern gallery, and Byng again began to talk about his execution. He was not perturbed by the imminence of death: he was only upset that he was to meet it on the fo'c'sle. He commented that they were all avoiding talking about the execution, and when one of them said they felt it would be embarrassing for him, he quickly reassured them: 'I like to talk upon the subject. It is not to be supposed I do not think of it; why then should it be more improper to talk of it?'

A large squadron was at this time waiting to sail from Portsmouth. It was under the command of Rear-Admiral Holburne, one of those who had sat on Byng's court martial, while other members were commanding some of the ships, which were all at anchor near the *Monarch*. Byng frequently went to the stern gallery to reassure himself that the wind stayed westerly, preventing the ships from sailing, and he explained that 'I wish them to be present tomorrow when their sentence upon me is put into execution'.

At about 6 p.m. he told a steward to fetch tea as usual for his guests and himself. He then remarked that they had probably noticed that his manner and conversation were easy. 'I have observed that persons condemned to die have generally had something to be sorry for, and that they have expressed concern for having committed,' he said.

The others looked up, wondering what he was going to say next.

'I do not pretend to have been exempt from human frailties; what comes under that denomination are not crimes cognizable here or supposed to be so hereafter. I am conscious of no crimes,' he added, and then declared, with a show of feeling, 'I am particularly happy in not dying the mean, despicable wretch my enemies would have the world believe. I hope I am not supposed so now: the court martial has acquitted me of everything criminal or ignominious.'

'No one calls or thinks you so now,' one of the company said, 'except the most obstinately prejudiced, or your enemies—neither of whom would ever admit themselves convinced by reasons.'

This seemed to reassure him and so the time passed. Edmund Bramston and the others wanted to stay longer on this, their last evening with Byng, than the latest permitted time of half past six. They therefore asked for a message to be sent to Admiral Boscawen, who was flying his flag in the *Royal George*, requesting an extension. He replied that they could stay as long as they liked, and Byng, acting the part of the genial host, was delighted, but told them it would be best if they went about eight o'clock. He sent a steward to make a bowl of punch, and as soon as it was put down on the table he motioned them to sit round. He filled the glass of each one, and poured a little into his own. 'My friends,' he said, raising his glass, 'here is all your healths, and God bless you all: I am pleased to find I have some friends still, notwithstanding my misfortunes.'

He drained his glass and put it down on the table. 'I am to die tomorrow, and as my country requires my blood I am ready to resign it—though I do not as yet know what my crime is. I think my judges, in justice to posterity, to officers whom come after us, should have explained my crime a little more, and pointed out the way to avoid falling into the same errors as I did.'

As the sentence and resolutions now stood, he said, he was sure that no admiral would be any wiser, nor know better how to conduct himself on a similar occasion. He paused, and then said to one of the men who had been watching him closely, 'My friend, I understand a reproof in that grave look: it is a long time since I spoke so much upon the subject, and you now think I say too much: perhaps I do so.'

'Far from meaning any reproof,' was the hasty reply, 'I am all attention to what you say, sir, and though all of us here are satisfied of these truths, yet we must be pleased to hear you make them plainer.'

'Be it so,' said Byng, 'but I shall only add one remark more: I am supposed not to have relieved and assisted the van: who then did assist the van, and relieve the three disabled ships who were upon the brink of being attacked by the body of the enemy?' And why did the enemy bear away from these ships 'if it was not because my division was under sail close after them, in regular line of battle?'

That was all he had to say: it was the epitome of his defence. The tragedy was that he had not said it as succinctly to the court martial. He changed the subject and they talked desultorily and soon it wanted only a few minutes to eight o'clock. Byng mentioned several people to whom he wished to be remembered—to Sarah, to Benjamin Gage's wife Rachel, Augustus Hervey, and Henry Osborn . . . He then stood up and went into his sleeping cabin, motioning them to follow him, one at a time. To each, singly and alone, he gave his thanks 'in a very pathetic manner' for acts of friendship and service. He then embraced and said good-bye with the intention, he explained, of sparing them from 'the disagreeable and painful office' of seeing him next day. However, they all pleaded to be allowed to visit him in the morning, and reluctantly he agreed. One of them saw tears in the Admiral's eyes. 'Pray, sire, don't suffer yourself to be discomposed.'

Byng shook his head. 'I have not a heart of stone: I am a man, and must feel at parting with my friends: but,' he said, 'you will not see me discomposed tomorrow.'

As soon as Edmund Bramston left the *Monarch* he went on board the *Royal George* and told Admiral Boscawen that ordering the fo'c'sle as the place where Admiral Byng was to be shot was an unnecessary indignity for someone of his rank, and Byng was much hurt by it. Bramston said he hoped Boscawen would change the place to the quarter-deck. Boscawen immediately replied that the order from the Admiralty expressly appointed it so, but if it was Bramston's special request, he would consider it, to which Bramston replied that 'I do make that request, sir'. Boscawen thought awhile, and then promised to give orders that the quarter-deck would be used.

This seems to imply that it was Boscawen who gave the original order, including it in his warrant to Captain Montagu. If, as Boscawen claimed, it had been an express order from the Board, Boscawen, even though a member of the Board, would not have dared disobey it.

27

THE LAST HOURS

WHEN DAWN CAME on Monday, March 14, it lit up a wild, cold grey scene at Portsmouth and Spithead: a north-westerly gale whipped the white crests of the waves into fine spray and the *Monarch* tugged at her moorings like a great tethered beast struggling to break away from its leash. The rain was sluicing across her scrubbed decks in stinging squalls when out of the gloom came a boat, fighting its way from the shore with mainsail reefed right down. It was 7 a.m. and the crew had a struggle to get the boat alongside in the lee formed by the battleship's great bulk. In her tiny hold there was a curiously-shaped large wooden box which was so heavy that a yard-tackle had to be used to hoist it up on to the *Monarch*'s deck. Her Master's log noted: 'Mr Byng's coffin was brought on board.'[1]

It had been made in the dockyard two days earlier and consisted of an inner coffin of wood, surrounded by another of lead which was in turn enclosed by a third, also of wood. Already inscribed on the outer shell was: 'The Hon. John Byng, Esqr. Died March 14th 1757.'

Byng was up by 5 a.m. and was carefully shaved by Hutchens. He usually rose early, as did Brough, and it was a long-standing joke between them. When he saw the Marshal an hour later he smiled and said: 'Well, I think I beat you at rising this morning!' The two men then had breakfast together.

A little later Byng changed his coat (he made a habit of doing this several times a day, as if casting off unpleasant associations). He had previously requested that after the execution his body should be put into the coffin in the clothes that he wore at the time of his execution, and while changing he said to Hutchens, his valet, 'Here, take these sleeve buttons and wear them for my sake: yours will do to be buried in.'

Hutchens had begun removing his own plain ones for the

exchange when Byng suddenly said: 'But hold—as these buttons are gold, my giving them to you might be doubted and you may be drawn into a scrape.' He told Hutchens to fetch Brough and one of the other servants to be witnesses of the exchange.

At 9 a.m., wet and bedraggled from the gale, and one or two of them a little queasy from the brief trip in the boat, Byng's friends came on board. Obediently Lt Brograve, who was the guard, noted their names in the special log: they included Edmund Bramston, William Daniel, Edward Clark and Isaac Muckins. Absent—perhaps at the Admiral's request—were his two young nephews, John and George.

The scene at Portsmouth within an hour of noon is best described by the *Evening Post*, now reporting the last phase of a long story. Boats from every warship in the harbour and at Spithead, following an order from Boscawen, who was by then waiting on shore at the dockyard, were converging on the *Monarch*. The captain and several officers from each ship were in the boats, which also contained files of Marines armed with muskets.

'With the utmost difficulty and danger, it blowing a prodigious hard gale, the wind at the west-north-west, and ebbing water, it was most difficult to get up so high as the *Monarch* lay,' said the *Post*. 'Notwithstanding it blew so hard, and the sea ran very high and with great violence, there was a prodigious number of boats round the ship on the outside of the men-of-war's boats, which kept off all the others. Not a soul was suffered to be on board [the *Monarch*] except those belonging to the ship.

'But those ships that lay anywhere near her were greatly crowded with spectators, all their shrouds and tops full, although it was difficult to see anything on board the *Monarch*.'

Byng passed the time walking up and down the great cabin, as if he was taking his morning exercise in the usual way, talking with his visitors. He was wearing a light grey coat, with a white waistcoat, white breeches and white stockings. On his head he wore a large white wig.

There was one difficult subject that Bramston had to discuss with his cousin. The Admiral had declared, right from the beginning, that when the time came for him to face the firing squad he would not be blindfolded, and would himself give the Marines the order to fire. 'As it is my fate, I can look at it and receive it,' he had said.

However, Captain Murray, commanding the Marines, knew it would upset the nine men forming the firing squad, and had asked Bramston and Brough to persuade the Admiral to be blind-folded. At times they managed to get him on the point of agreeing, but at the last moment he would draw back: 'No, no, it cannot be: I cannot bear it: I must look and receive my fate.'

Bramston pointed out that the nearest rank of Marines would be only a couple of feet away and were bound to be watching his face. They would be overawed and intimidated by his rank if they saw him looking at them when the moment came for them to open fire. Bramston hinted that this might lead to him being wounded. Finally he managed to get the Admiral, with great reluctance, to agree to a blindfold. 'If it must be so, and you insist, it must be so.' But he insisted that he would give the signal to the Marines to fire by dropping a white handkerchief.

He then wanted to be told the exact details of the actual pro-cedure for the execution, so that he should not make any mistake, explaining that 'I have never attended such a ceremony before'. When he proposed removing his coat for the execution Brough said it would be unnecessary. 'But,' argued Byng, 'it may be said that I kept my coat on as if afraid to receive the blow, or feel the bullets.'

'No,' replied Brough, 'such a remark can never be made, and it must be more decent to make no alteration.'

'Very well, then,' agreed Byng, 'if it is more decent, no alteration shall be made.'

Byng was completely self-composed: a little earlier, for instance, he had noticed that Brough had put on his full uniform as Marshal of the Admiralty, complete with sword, and he commented in a low voice to one of his friends: 'Do you observe how well dressed the Marshal is?'

'Yes,' said the friend, 'I daresay, sir, he intends paying the last piece of respect to you that he can.'

Byng, touched by this gesture, which he had not at first under-stood, said 'I am sensible he means well, and I accept the compli-ment'.

'To see you so easy and composed, sir,' the friend said, 'gives me as much pleasure as I can have on this occasion; but I expected no less . . . the last actions of a man mark his character more than all the actions of his life.'

'I am sensible they do,' said Byng, 'and obliged to you for putting me in mind. I find innocence is the best foundation for firmness of mind.'

It was past eleven o'clock when Byng happened to notice, through the stern windows, that there were scores of boats round the *Monarch*, and the rigging of the ships close by were black with people. He took a telescope from a rack and looked at them. 'Curiosity is strong,' he commented. 'It draws a great number of people together. But their curiosity will be disappointed—where they are they may hear, but they will not see . . .'

He then asked the time of high water. On being told, he said the tide would not be right to have his body taken on shore when it was dark, and he was apprehensive that it 'might be insulted, on account of the prejudice of the people'. Someone quickly assured him that there was no prejudice on the part of the people of Portsmouth.

Byng inquired if Captain Murray of the Marines knew of the arrangements concerning the white handkerchief, and said he was to be told there would be a present of ten guineas to the firing squad 'to encourage them to behave properly'.

It was by now nearly noon. Byng took a folded piece of paper from his pocket and gave it to Brough. 'Sir, these are my thoughts on this occasion: I give them to you that you may authenticate them, and prevent anything spurious being published that might tend to defame me. I have given a copy to one of my relations.'

A few minutes later one of the ship's officers came to the door of the cabin and whispered to Bramston that 'The hour of twelve is drawing near'.

Byng overheard, and turning to him, said: 'It is very well,' and went into his sleeping cabin. He stayed there for some three minutes, and while he was gone one of the doors leading on to the quarter-deck was opened.

It revealed a grim sight: against a back-cloth of scudding grey clouds Marines were lined up under arms on the poop, their mitre-shaped hats giving them a quaintly clerical appearance; seamen were perched in orderly though rain-sodden rows in the rigging, like grotesque birds. In the middle of the quarter-deck were nine scarlet-jacketed Marines with muskets, drawn up in three rows, each of three men. On the deck a few feet in front of them was a cushion, and strewn round it was sawdust, now soggy and grey from the rain. All the men were waiting silently; the only noise was the discord of the wind's weird call in the rigging, the creak and groan of the masts and spars towering overhead, and the muffled thudding of the waves butting the hull.

Then they saw Admiral Byng walking out into the wind and the rain 'with a stately pace and a composed countenance'. He motioned with one hand to Brough—'Come along, my friend,' he said, 'and remember what I told you about that paper . . .'

He was carrying a neatly-folded white handkerchief in each hand, and walked with Bramston and Brough to the cushion. He then knelt down on it and, tucking one handkerchief into a pocket, folded the other into the shape of a bandage and began to secure it round his eyes. Bramston offered to tie the knot. Byng smiled— 'I am obliged to you, sir; I thank God I can do it myself. I think I can—I am sure I can.' Then he whispered, 'God bless you, my friend, don't stay here—they may shoot you, too'.

While Byng was tying the handkerchief, Captain Murray had been quietly giving his orders to the Marines, his voice almost lost in the wind. The three ranks of Marines advanced two paces towards the kneeling Admiral and the front rank knelt, while the second rank crouched above them. The third rank stood erect: they would not fire first because they might be required to give the *coup-de-grâce*. They held their muskets in front of them, the butts level with their right knees.

'Cock your firelocks!' said the captain.

Byng had by now finished tying the handkerchief—his bulky wig made it difficult for him to adjust it properly.

'Present!' said the captain.

The Marines brought their muskets up to their shoulders. The muzzles of those in the front rank were now less than two feet from Byng's breast.

The Admiral took the second white handkerchief from his pocket, and held it up with his right hand. For a few moments, when every man watching felt as if his heart would burst, Byng's hand was poised, and he seemed to say something—perhaps saying a brief and final prayer to himself. Then his handkerchief fluttered to the deck, carrying his life with it. The Marines fired. One shot missed and whined away in ricochet. Admiral Byng 'sank down motionless, gently falling on his side, as if still studious to preserve decency and dignity in his fall'.[2]

Later Mr John Paynter, the Master of the *Monarch*, wrote in his log: '*At* 12 *Mr Byng was shot dead by* 6 *Marines and put into his coffin.*'

On shore, Admiral Boscawen wrote a hasty note to the Admiralty, dating it from 'Portsmouth Dock', and saying: 'Having ordered all captains and officers from the ships at Spithead and this harbour to attend the execution of Admiral Byng, and a signal to be made [on board the *Monarch*] as soon as the execution is over, for all the boats to repair to their respective ships, I now see the signal made, the execution is over, but if I stay till I have the report made by Captain Montagu I shall lose the post.'[3]

That night Mr Paynter made another entry in his log: 'At 9.30 sent Mr Byng's corps [*sic*] ashore with all his baggage.'

His coffin was taken to the house of Hutchins, the Boatswain of the Dockyard. Next day, something happened in the gale which the local folk declared was an omen, since it concerned Byng's former flagship, and Boscawen described it in a letter to the Admiralty: 'Many ships drove at Spithead but none came on shore . . . The *Ramillies* also broke her moorings in the harbour but brought up with her own anchors without going on shore.'[4]

Byng's body was borne to Southill and buried in the family vault. A tablet there bears the following inscription:

To the perpetual Disgrace of
Public Justice
The Honourable John Byng
Admiral of the Blue,
Fell a Martyr to
Political Persecution,
On March 14, in the Year 1757;
When Bravery and Loyalty
Were insufficient Securities
For the Life and Honour
Of a Naval Officer.

EPILOGUE

THE PIECE OF PAPER which Admiral Byng gave to the Marshal contained his 'Last Thoughts', and they said:

'On board His Majesty's ship *Monarque*
'A few moments will now deliver me from the virulent persecution, and frustrate the farther malice of my enemies—nor need I envy them a life subject to the sensations my injuries and the injustice done me must create. Persuaded I am, justice will be done to my reputation hereafter.

'The manner and cause of raising and keeping up the popular clamour and prejudice against me, will be seen through—I shall be considered (as now I consider myself) a victim destroyed to divert the indignation and resentment of an injured and deluded people from the proper objects.

'Happy for me, at this my last moment, that I know my own innocence, and am conscious that no part of my country's misfortunes can be owing to me . . .'

He concluded: 'If my crime is an error of judgment, or differing in opinion from my judges, and if yet the error of judgment should be on their side—God forgive them, as I do, and may the distress of their minds, and the uneasiness of their consciences, which in justice to me they have represented, be relieved and subside, as my sentiment has done.

'The supreme judge sees all hearts and motives; and to him I must submit the justice of my cause.'

Rochester was now without a Member of Parliament. Pitt wanted to put forward Dr Hay, but the King told Lord Temple that Rochester was a Crown, not an Admiralty, borough: he did not like Hay, who had been a member of the Board of Admiralty which, His Majesty thought, had regarded his justice as cruelty. He therefore told the Duke of Devonshire to put forward Admiral Smith, who was of course related to Temple. It was an almost disgusting suggestion, since Smith had been one of the men who condemned Byng, and to his credit he refused, saying he had not sufficient estate to qualify.

But Byng's former jailer at Greenwich had no such scruples: on March 31, seventeen days after Byng had been shot, Admiral Isaac Townshend took his seat in the Commons as the Member for Rochester.

The ultimate fate of the Government can be told briefly. Lord Temple, increasingly out of sympathy and favour with the King, was sacked from the Admiralty on April 5, and when Pitt refused to resign he too was sacked next day. However, Pitt's departure caused a storm in the country: ten days after his resignation the City of London was considering a proposal to give him the freedom of the City for his 'loyal and disinterested conduct' in a 'truly honourable though short administration'. By the 21st it was agreed the Freedom should be bestowed 'in a gold box'. After that, Walpole reported, as other towns followed suit, 'it rained gold boxes'.

With the Parliamentary inquiry into the loss of Minorca due to open a few days after Pitt's dismissal, the Duke of Newcastle and Lord Hardwicke both refused to join a government and the Duke of Devonshire continued in office. The Parliamentary inquiry was of course a complete farce, owing to the Duke of Newcastle's Parliamentary interest. The Committee to whom the inquiry was referred passed a series of resolutions, the last one of which concluded 'it doth appear that no greater number of ships of war could be sent into the Mediterranean than were sent on the 6th of April, 1756; nor any greater reinforcement than the regiment that was sent, and the detachment equal to a battalion which was ordered . . .'

As Walpole wrote: 'To their great astonishment the late Cabinet is not thanked Parliamentarily for the loss of Minorca.'

Meanwhile the 'rain of gold boxes' on Pitt was alarming the Duke of Newcastle, and he went to the King and advised him to recall Pitt. The old King eventually gave the Duke permission to negotiate and Pitt came back as Secretary of State; Fox was allowed in as Paymaster; Anson went back to the Admiralty; Newcastle became First Minister.

As Sir Julian Corbett wrote: 'Everyone had been obliged to recognize at last that without Newcastle's overpowering Parliamentary interest Government was impossible, without Pitt's power of administration it was impotent. So to Newcastle was given the name of Prime Minister, to Pitt the reality.'[1]

Many years later the Earl of Shelburne met Cardinal Bernis, Pompadour's favourite and a former French Minister. The Cardinal told him that towards the end of 1755 'the cabals ran so high against him at Court that the only struggle there was how to give the most certain intelligence to England of the design against Minorca on purpose that it might fail, which carried them so far that he told me he was at last persuaded that we must believe it was given out so publicly on purpose to deceive'.[2]

Shortly after Byng's death Voltaire published his *Candide*. His hero visited Portsmouth and saw someone on board a ship facing a firing squad, and when he inquired who was the fat man being executed with such ceremony, he was told it was an admiral. Further questioning by the curious Candide elicited the answer that 'In this country it is thought well to kill an admiral from time to time to encourage the others'.[3]

APPENDIX I

The ships at Spithead and in Portsmouth harbour on March 22, 1756, besides those intended for Byng's squadron, were as follows:

Spithead	Guns	*Portsmouth Harbour*	Guns
Prince	90*	Royal Anne	90
Prince George	80*	Barfleur	80
Monmouth	64†	Duke	90
Yarmouth	64*	Bedford	64*
Invincible	74†	Swiftsure	64
Stirling Castle	64*	Elizabeth	64*
Torbay	74*	Bristol	50*
Essex	64*	Colchester	50†
Nassau	64*	Romney	40*
Prince Frederick	64*	Greyhound	20*
Nottingham	60*	Gibraltar	20*
Augusta	60*	Nightingale	20*
Firebrand (fire-ship)	—	Unicorn	20*
Anson	60‡		

List taken from Byng's Journal.

The ships marked * were fully manned or nearly so; those marked † had more than a complete crew.

‡ Arrived three days afterwards.

APPENDIX II

Letters from Lord Barrington, Secretary at War, to Lieut-General Fowke, Governor of Gibraltar.

'War Office, March 21, 1756.

'Sir,

His Majesty hath been pleased to order the Royal Regiment of Fusiliers to embark immediately for Gibraltar; and that, upon their arrival, a detachment be made from the four regiments now in the garrison, under your command, and embark for Minorca. I am to signify to you, it is His Majesty's pleasure, that upon the arrival of the Royal Regiment of Fusiliers before Gibraltar, you do cause them (with the recruits for the corps in your garrison) to disembark, and be quartered in the garrison under your command; and upon the disembarking of the said Regiment, it is His Majesty's further pleasure, that you cause a detachment, consisting of a Lieutenant-Colonel, Major, Commission, Non-Commission Officers, and private men, equal to a Battalion of Foot, on the present British Establishment, to be made from the said four Regiments, and embark on board His Majesty's ships of war for Minorca. The Lieutenant-Colonel and Major to be the eldest of their rank in the garrison, under your command.'

'War Office the 28th Day of March, 1756.

'Sir,

I am commanded by His Majesty to acquaint you, in case the island of Minorca should be in any likelyhood of being attack'd, that it is His Majesty's pleasure you cause a detachment equal to a Battalion, on the present British Establishment, to be made from the Regiments under your command in the garrison of Gibraltar; and embark on board such of His Majesty's ships of war as Admiral Byng, or the Admiral commanding in chief His Majesty's Fleet in the Mediterranean, shall think expedient, and will carry to the relief of the said island.'

'War Office, 1st of April, 1756.

'Sir,

I am commanded to signify to you it is His Majesty's pleasure, that you receive into the garrison under your command at Gibraltar, such women and children belonging to the Royal Regiment of Fusiliers, as Admiral Byng, or the Commander in Chief of His Majesty's Ships in the Mediterranean, shall think fit to land there.'

APPENDIX III

Instructions for the Honourable John Byng, Admiral of the Blue Squadron of his Majesty's Fleet.

By the Commissioners for executing the Office
of Lord High Admiral of Great Britain
and Ireland, &c.

Whereas the King's Pleasure has been signified to us by Mr Fox, one of his Majesty's Principal Secretaries of State, that, upon consideration of the several advices which have been received, relating to the supposed intention of the French to attack the Island of Minorca, a Squadron of ten ships of the line do forthwith sail to the Mediterranean, under your command; and whereas we have appointed the ships named in the margin* for this service, you are hereby required and directed immediately to put to sea with such of them as are ready (leaving orders for the rest to follow you as soon as possible) and proceed with the utmost expedition to Gibraltar.

Upon your arrival there, you are to inquire whether any French squadron is coming through the Straits; and if there is, to inform yourself, as well as possible, of their number and force: And if any part of them were transports; and as it is probable, they may be designed for North America, and as his Majesty's ships, named in the margin,† are either at, or going to Halifax; and are to cruise off Louisbourg, and at the Mouth of the Gulph [sic] of Saint Lawrence; you are immediately to take the soldiers out of so many ships of your squadron, as together with the ships at, and going to, Halifax, will make a force superior to the said French squadron, (replacing them with landmen, or ordinary seamen, from your other ships) and then detach them, under the command of Rear-Admiral West, directing him to make the best of his way off Louisbourg; and taking the aforenamed ships, which he may expect to find there, under his command, to cruize [sic] off the said place, and the entrance of the Gulph of Saint Lawrence; and use his utmost endeavours to intercept and seize the aforesaid French ships, or any other ships belonging to the French, that may be bound to, or returning from that part of North America.

If, upon your arrival at Gibraltar, you shall not gain intelligence of a French squadron having passed the Straits, you are then to go on,

* *Ramillies, Buckingham, Culloden, Captain, Revenge, Lancaster, Trident, Intrepid, Kingston, Defiance.*

† *Grafton, Stirling Castle, Fougeux, Nottingham, Litchfield, Centurion, Norwich, Success, Vulture* sloop.

without a moment's loss of time, to Minorca: or if, in consequence of such intelligence, you shall detach Rear-Admiral West, as before directed, you are to use equal expedition, in repairing thither with the ships which shall remain with you; and if you find any attack made upon that island by the French, you are to use all possible means in your power for its relief. If you find no such attack made, you are to proceed off Toulon; and station your squadron, in the best manner you shall be able, for preventing any French ships getting out of that port, or for intercepting and seizing any that may get out; and you are to exert your utmost vigilance therein, and in protecting Minorca and Gibraltar from any hostile attempt.

You are also to be very vigilant for protecting the Trade of his Majesty's subjects from being molested, either by the French, or by cruizers [sic] from Morocco, or any other of the Barbary States; and for that purpose to appoint proper convoys and cruizers.

You are likewise to be as attentive as possible to the intercepting and seizing, as well ships of war and privateers, as Merchant Ships, belonging to the French, wherever they may be met with, within the limits of your Command: But, in pursuance of the King's Order in Council, you are not to suffer any of your squadron, to take any French vessel out of any port, belonging to the Ottoman Empire, upon any pretence; nor to molest, detain, or imprison the persons of any of the subjects of the Ottoman Empire; and also not to seize, or detain, any French ship or vessel whatsoever, which they shall meet with in the Levant Seas, bound from one port to another in those seas, or to, or from, any ports of Egypt, having any effects of Turks on board.

Upon your arrival in the Mediterranean, you are to take under your command, his Majesty's ships and vessels named in the margin,* which are at present stationed there.

If any French ships of war should sail from Toulon, and escape your squadron, and proceed out of the Mediterranean, you are forthwith to send, or repair yourself to England, with a proportionable part of the ships under your command; observing, that you are never to keep more ships in the Mediterranean, than shall be necessary for executing the services recommended to you.

To enable you the better to perform the aforementioned services, you are to take care to keep the ships and vessels under your command in constant good condition, and to have them cleaned as often as shall be requisite for that purpose.

Given under our hands, the 30th of March, 1756.

By command of their Lordships, J. Clevland.

Anson, Tho. Villiers, W. Rowley, E. Boscawen, Bateman, R. Edgcumbe.

* *Princess Louisa, Portland, Deptford, Chesterfield, Dolphin, Phoenix, Experiment, Fortune* sloop.

APPENDIX IV

The passages censored before it was printed in the *London Gazette* are set in *italic*.

'RAMILLIES, off Minorca,
May 25, 1756.

'Sir,

I have the pleasure to desire you will acquaint their Lordships, that having sailed from Gibraltar the 8th, I got off Mahon the 19th, having been joined by His Majesty's Ship PHOENIX off Majorca two days before, *by whom I had confirmed the intelligence I received at Gibraltar of the strength of the French Fleet, and of their being off Mahon. His Majesty's Colours were still flying at the Castle of St Philip's, and I could perceive several bomb batteries playing upon it, from different parts; French Colours we saw flying on the west part of St Philip's: I dispatched the PHOENIX, CHESTERFIELD, and DOLPHIN, ahead, to reconnoitre the harbour's mouth, and Captain Hervey to endeavour to land a letter for General Blakeney, to let him know the Fleet was here to his assistance, tho' every one was of opinion we could be of no use to him; as by all accounts, no place was secured for covering a landing could we have spared any people. The PHOENIX was also to make the private signal between Captain Hervey and Captain Scrope, as this latter would undoubtedly come off, if it were practicable, having kept the DOLPHIN'S Barge with him;* but the Enemy's Fleet appearing to the South East, *and the wind at the same time coming strong off the land, obliged me to call those ships in, before they could get quite so near the entrance of the harbour, as to make sure what batteries or guns might be placed to prevent our having any communication with the Castle,* falling little wind, it was five before I could form my line, or distinguish any of the enemy's motions; and not at all to judge of their force more than by their numbers, which were seventeen, and thirteen appeared large; they at first stood towards us in a regular line, and tacked about seven, which I judged was to endeavour to gain the wind of us in the night; so that being late, I tacked in order to keep the weather gage of them, as well as to make sure of the land wind in the morning; being very hazey, and not above five leagues off Cape Mola. We tacked off towards the enemy at eleven; and at day light had no sight of them. But two tartans with the French private signal, being close in with the rear of our Fleet, I sent the PRINCESS LOUISA to chase one, and made the signal for the Rear Admiral, who was nearest the other, to send ships to chase her; the PRINCESS LOUISA, DEFIANCE, and CAPTAIN became at great distance; but the DEFIANCE took hers, which had two captains, two lieutenants, and one hundred and two private soldiers, who were sent out the day before with six hundred men, on board tartans, to reinforce the French Fleet, on our then appearing off the place. The PHOENIX, on Captain Hervey's offer, prepared to serve as a fire ship, but without damaging her as a frigate, till the signal was made to prime; when she was then to scuttle her decks, everything else being prepared, as the time and place allowed of. The enemy now began to appear from the mast head; I called in the cruisers, and when they had joined me, I tacked towards the enemy, and formed the line ahead. I found the French were preparing theirs to leeward, having unsuccessfully endeavoured to weather me. They were twelve large ships of the line, and five frigates. As soon as I judged the rear of our fleet to be the length of their van, we tacked altogether, and immediately made the signal for the ships that led, to lead large, and for the DEPTFORD to quit the line, that ours might become equal in number with theirs. At two I made the signal to engage, as I found it was the surest method of ordering every ship to close down on the one that fell to their lot. And here I must express my great satisfaction at the very gallant manner in which the Rear-Admiral set the van the example, by instantly bearing down on the ships he was to engage with his second; and who occasioned one of the French ships to begin the engagement, which they did by raking ours as they went down. I bore down on the ship that lay opposite to me, and began to engage him, after having received their fire for some time in going down. The INTREPID *unfortunately* in the very beginning had his foretopmast shot away, and as that hung on his foresail, and backed it, he had no command of his ship; his foretack and all his braces being cut at the same time; so that he drove on the next ship to him, and obliged that and the ships ahead of me to throw all aback. This obliged me to do so also for some minutes, to avoid their falling on board of me; though not before we had drove our adversary out of the line, who put afore the wind, and had several shot fired at him from his own admiral.

This not only caused the enemy's center to be unattacked, but left the Rear-Admiral's division rather uncovered for some very little time. I sent and called to the ships ahead of me, to make sail on, and go down on the enemy; and ordered the CHESTERFIELD to lay by the INTREPID, and the DEPTFORD to supply the INTREPID's place. I found the enemy edged away constantly; and as they went three feet to our one, they would never permit our closing with them; but took the advantage of destroying our rigging; for tho' I closed the Rear-Admiral fast, I found I could not again close the enemy, whose van were fairly drove from their line; but their Admiral was joining them by bearing away. By this time 'twas past six, and the enemy's van and ours were at too great a distance to engage. I perceived some of their ships stretching to the northward, and I imagined they were going to form a new line: I made the signal for the headmost ships to tack, and those that led before with larboard tacks, to lead with the starboard; that I might, by the first, keep (if possible) the wind of the enemy; and by the second, be between the Rear-Admiral's division and the enemy, as his had suffered most; as also to cover the INTREPID, which I perceived to be in a very bad condition, and whose loss would *very greatly* give the balance against us, if they had attacked us the next morning, as I expected. I brought to about eight that night, to join the INTREPID and to refit our ships as fast as possible, and continued so all night. The next morning we saw nothing of the enemy, tho' we were still lying to; Mahon was north north-west about ten or eleven leagues. I sent cruisers to look for the INTREPID and CHESTERFIELD, who joined me next day; and having, from a state and condition of the squadron brought me in, found that the CAPTAIN, INTREPID, and DEFIANCE (which latter has lost her Captain) were much damaged in their masts; *so that they were endangered of not being able to secure their masts properly at sea; and also that the squadron in general were very sickly, many killed and wounded, and no where to put a third of their number, if I made an Hospital even of the forty-gun ship, which was not easy at sea.* I thought it proper in this situation, to call a Council of War, before I went again to look for the enemy. I desired the attendance of General Stuart, Lord Effingham, and Lord Robert Bertie, and Colonel Cornwallis; that I might collect their opinions upon the present situation *of Minorca and Gibraltar; and make sure of protecting the latter, since it was found impracticable either to succour or relieve the former with the force we had. For though we may justly claim the victory, yet we are much inferior to the weight of their ships, though the numbers are equal: and they have the advantage of sending to Minorca their wounded, and getting reinforcements of seamen from their transports, and soldiers from their camp; all which undoubtedly has been done in this time that we have been lying-to to refit, and often in sight of Minorca; and their ships have more than once appeared in a line from our mastheads. I send their Lordships the resolution of the Council of War,* in which there was not the least contention or doubt arose. *I hope indeed we shall find stores to refit us at Gibraltar; and if I have any reinforcement, will not lose a moment's time to seek the enemy again, and once more give them battle; though they have a great advantage in being clean ships that go three feet to our one, and therefore have the choice how they will engage us, or if they will at all; and will never let us close them, as their sole view is the disabling our*

*ships, in which they have but too well succeeded, though we obliged them
to bear up.* I do not send their Lordships the particulars of our losses
and damages by this, as it would take me much time, and that I am
willing none should be lost in letting them know an event of such
consequence. *I cannot help urging their Lordships for a reinforcement,
if none are yet sailed on their knowledge of the enemy's strength in these
seas; and which, by very good intelligence, will, in a few days, be strengthened by four more large ships from Toulon, almost ready to sail, if not
already sailed to join these.* I dispatch this to Sir Benjamin Keene, by
way of Barcelona, and am making the best of way to *cover* Gibraltar;
from which place I propose sending their Lordships a more particular
account.

'P.S. I must desire you would acquaint their Lordships, that I have
appointed Captain Hervey to the command of the DEFIANCE, in the
room of Captain Andrews, slain in the action. I have just sent the defects
of the ships, as I have got it made out, whilst I was closing my letter.'

APPENDIX V

Admiral Byng's Council of War on May 24, 1756.

Having laid before the Council of War the opinion of the engineers in regard to throwing in succours in the castle of St Philip's; the result of a Council of War held by General Fowke at Gibraltar, with regard to embarking a detachment on board the Fleet; likewise Admiral Byng's Instructions for his proceedings in the Mediterranean; likewise the order with regard to the disposal of the regiment of Fusiliers, commanded by the Right Honourable Lord Robert Bertie; and the defects of the ships which received damage in action with the French Squadron, the 20th Instant; as also having laid before the Council the state of the sick and wounded men on board the ships of the Fleet, proposed to the Council the following questions, viz.

1 Whether an attack upon the French Fleet gives any prospect of relieving Minorca.
Unanimously resolved that it would not.

2 Whether, if there was no French fleet cruising off Minorca the English Fleet could raise the siege?
Unanimously the opinion that the Fleet could not.

3 Whether, Gibraltar would not be in danger by any accident that might befall this Fleet?
Unanimously agreed that it would be in danger.

4 Whether, an attack with our Fleet in the present state of it upon that of the French, will not endanger the safety of Gibraltar and expose the trade of the Mediterranean to great hazard?
Unanimously agreed that it would.

5 Whether it is not most for His Majesty's Service, that the Fleet should immediately proceed for Gibraltar?
We are unanimously of opinion that the Fleet should immediately proceed for Gibraltar.
Signed: J. Byng; Ja^s. Stuart; Temple West; H^y. Ward; Phil. Durell; Ed. Cornwallis; James Young; Chas Catford; Fred^k Cornwall; Geo. Edgcumbe; W^m. Parry; John Amherst; Arthur Gardiner; Effingham; A. Hervey; Mich^l Everitt; W^m. Lloyd; Robt. Bertie.

APPENDIX VI

Extract from the dispatch written by Admiral de la Galissonnière to the French Court after the battle. This extract was forwarded from Paris to the Spanish Minister in London. The original spelling is retained.

Le 17me May au soir, l'escadre a été informée par la frigate la Gracieuse, *qui etoit en croisiere sur Majorque, qu'elle avoit decouvert une escadre Angloise, qui pouvoit être alors à 8 ou 10 lieues dans le sud.*

Le 18, l'escadre manoeuvra pour aller à la rencontre de celle des Anglois, mais le calme l'en empecha.

Le 19, au matin on a decouvert l'escadre Angloise du haut des mâts; et les deux escadres s'approcherent asses l'une de l'autre, pendant la journée, sans cependant se trouver a portée de canon; ce qui auroit dependu des Anglois, qui se trouvoient au vent.

Le 20 M. de la Galissonnière manoeuvroit de façon à gagner le vent, mais dans le tems ou il se trouvoit avec son escadre dans une position favorable pour cela, le vent est venu a changer, de maniere que l'escadre Angloise a eu cet avantage.

A 2½ heures aprés midi, les deux escadres se son trouvés en ligne, et ont commencé le combat; celle des Anglois composée de 18 voiles, dont 13 vaisseaux; et la nôtre de 12 vaisseau et 4 frigates.

Le combat a duré 3½ ou 4 heurs, mais n'a pas eté general pendant tout ce tems: le vaisseaux Anglois qui etoient les plus mal traités de nos bordees, se remettant au vent hors de portée de canon.

Il on toujours conservé cet avantage, et aprés avoir porté leurs derniers efforts sur notre arriere garde (qu'ils ont trouvé si serrée, et dont ils on essuié un si grand feu, quils non pas peu l'entamer) Ils ont pris le Parti de s'eloigner, et non point reparce dans la journée du 21:

En general, il n'y a eu aucun de leurs vaisseaux qui ait soutenu le feu des notres: Les vaisseaux de nôtre escadre on peu souffert: Ils étoient entierement reparés pendant la nuit, et en etat de combatre le lendemian.

NOTES AND BIBLIOGRAPHY

PROLOGUE, pages 1 to 6.

1. The house still stands. Outwardly it looks much the same as when Admiral Byng owned it, except that a top floor has been added and it has been lengthened on its Hill Street side. The house opposite, No. 42, has not been altered outwardly.
2. Details of residents from rate books of 1745 and 1756; St George's Parish.
3. Details of the furnishings in Byng's house are given in his will.
4. These seventeen volumes of letters, Hoste's book on naval tactics, and the rest of Byng's original library are now at Wrotham Park, and owned by Lady Elizabeth Byng. Unfortunately, all of Byng's journals and his letter-books, containing copies of letters he wrote, are missing. (There is an abstract of Byng's journal for the period, of the Battle of Minorca in the British Museum, Martin Papers, Additional 41355.) The seventeen volumes of letters received by Byng give a fascinating picture of naval affairs, particularly volumes four and five, covering the Mediterranean command in the last phase of the War of the Austrian Succession.
5. Details from Byng's will.
6. The artist was probably Maria Giovanna Clemanti, for whom Hervey sat in Turin on October 12, 1747, while visiting the King of Sardinia on Byng's behalf.
7. Public Record Office, Admiralty 2/1331, Out Letters, Secret Orders. The three signatories were all members of the Board of Admiralty.

CHAPTER ONE, pages 7 to 15.

For much of the material contained in this chapter on the early history of the Byng family—most of it never previously published—I am indebted to Mr T. T. Barnard, who has done a great deal of research on the history of his wife's family; and to Lady Elizabeth Byng, who has allowed me to use hitherto-unpublished material at Wrotham. Published material includes the three volumes of *The Byng Papers*, edited by W. C. B. Tunstall, and *Pattee Byng's Journal*, edited by J. L. Cranmer-Byng, all taken from the Wrotham Park documents and published by the Navy Records Society. *The Byng Papers* concern the first Viscount Torrington; Pattee Byng was the brother of John Byng and his Journal covers 1718-20, when he was with his father in the Sicilian Campaign.

1. Wrotham Papers.

2. Osborn MSS, Bedford Record Office. To Sarah Osborn, 1725.

3. Wrotham Papers, letters dated January 11, February 1 and February 2, 1745/6.

CHAPTER TWO, pages 16 to 21.

The Battle of Toulon: standard sources, and from many contemporary pamphlets, including those published by both Mathews and Lestock. Among them are the following (the Admiralty Library Catalogue numbers only are given as the titles are usually long and ponderous): P 289, P 324, P 327, Pfo A 8–14, Pfo A 15, Ca 12.

The courts martial: The minutes of the Lestock and Mathews trials, and certain other officers, are given in Admiralty Library Cf 2; the court martial of Captain Richard Norris in Cf 5 and P 289; of the lieutenants of the *Dorsetshire*, and Captain George Burrish, in Cf 28; of Captains Edmund Williams, John Ambrose and George Burrish, and Lieutenants Henry Page, Charles Davids, William Griffiths and Cornelius Smelt in Cf 04.

1. See *Fighting Instructions 1530–1816*, pp. 184–98, edited by Sir Julian Corbett, Navy Records Society, 1905.

CHAPTER THREE, pages 22 to 30.

The Berkeley Square house: details from *A Complete Body of Architecture* by Isaac Ware, London, 1756, which gives (p. 612) a picture of the dial of the wind vane; St George's Parish rate books; Byng's will; and material supplied by Mr T. T. Barnard.

1. Byng to his brother Pattee, 2nd Viscount Torrington, Wrotham MSS.

2. *Ware*, Architecture.

3. *Correspondence of the Fourth Duke of Bedford*, London, 1842, I, 159, Newcastle to Bedford, October 25, 1746.

4. ibid. 164–5, Byng to the Duke of Bedford, October 25, 1746.

5. Wrotham MSS. Punctuation inserted but spelling unchanged.

6. Unpublished Bedford Papers at Woburn Abbey, in the possession of the Duke of Bedford.

7. *Augustus Hervey's Journal*, edited by David Erskine, Kimber, 1953, p. xxvii.

8. ibid, 52.

9. Bedford Corr, I, 239. Anson to the Duke of Bedford, August 22, 1747.

10. ibid, 518–19, Byng to the Duke of Bedford, September 14, 1748.

11. Details from Mr T. T. Barnard.

12. See *The Structure of Politics at the Accession of George III*, by Sir Lewis Namier, London, 1929, I, 37–47.

13. Osborn MSS, Sarah Osborn to Sir Danvers, September 3, 1751. Some of Sarah's letters are published in *Political and Social Letters of a Lady of the Eighteenth Century*, edited by Emily F. D. Osborn, London, 1890. These letters, and many more, are now in the possession of Sir Danvers Osborn, Bt.

14. Osborn MSS, Sarah Osborn to Sir Danvers, July 30, 1751.

CHAPTER FOUR, pages 31 to 43.

The intelligence reports quoted in this and successive chapters are from (a) the collection of original handwritten papers, bound up in a single volume and entitled *Papers Relating to the Trial of Admiral Byng*, in the Admiralty Library (Cf 010); and (b) another manuscript volume in the British Museum, Additional 35895, which contains some papers not in the Admiralty Library copy.

The papers form the draft the Government prepared in its defence. An edited and incomplete version of the papers, omitting several interesting reports, was published by the Navy Records Society in 1913, entitled *Papers Relating to the Loss of Minorca in 1756*.

1. Sir Julian Corbett, *England in the Seven Years' War*, I, 65, Longmans Green, 1907. See note 6 below.

2. 'Boscawen's Letters to His Wife, 1755–56,' edited from the Falmouth Papers by Peter K. Kemp, in *The Naval Miscellany*, IV, published by the Navy Records Society.

3. British Museum, Add. 32860, f. 399, Bunge to Höpken, Paris, November 7, 1755.

4. Ilchester, *Henry Fox, First Lord Ilchester*, I, 303.

5. Mrs Hickson's will was dated September 16, 1755. No executors were named. The will was eventually proved on November 3, 1756. (P.C.C. Glazier, 296. November 1756).

6. Add. 32860, f. 273, Newcastle to Lyttelton, November 30, 1755. Sir Julian Corbett says that after 'constant reports of activity in Toulon' were received in the autumn 'these preparations soon ceased' and 'no really trustworthy information' was received until February 25. He claims that before then the agents in France were dwelling on an invasion of Britain 'and if they mentioned the Toulon expedition at all it was with the assurance that it was only a feint'. Unfortunately, when Sir Julian Corbett wrote that in 1907, he had apparently not read the complete intelligence reports, one copy of which is in the British Museum and the other in the Admiralty Library, and which were later published in 1913. A perusal of these reports—several of which are given in the present narrative—show that Sir Julian was entirely mistaken in his view. (*England in the Seven Years' War*, I, 96.)

7. Ilchester, I, 324, Cumberland to Fox, April 2, 1755.
8. Add. 35359, Anson to Hardwicke, December 6, 1755.
9. G. Lacour-Gayet, *La Marine Militaire de la France sous Louis XV*, Paris, 1902. Chapter 16; E. Guillon, *Nouvelles Archives des Missions Scientifiques et Ltt*, 1893.

CHAPTER FIVE, pages 44 to 56.

All intelligence reports are from the sources referred to in the notes to Chapter Four. The description of social and meteorological events is taken from contemporary magazines and newspapers.

1. Add. 35415, f. 147; Add. 32862, ff. 383–6.
2. Add. 32945, f. 449.
3. Namier, I, 52 *note*.
4. P.R.O. Adm. 2/1331, Adm. Secy, Out-letters, Secret Orders.
5. P.R.O. Adm. 1/4120, Adm. Secy, In-letters, from Secy of State.
6. P.R.O. Adm. 1/4322, In-letters, from Secy at War.
7. P.R.O. Adm. 3/64, Board Minutes.
8. Add. 32996, f. 373.
9. Lord E. Fitzmaurice, *Life of William, Earl of Shelburne*, I, 66. London, 1875.
10. Sir John Barrow, *The Life of George, Lord Anson*, London, 1839.
11. ibid.
12. Add. 32892, ff. 94 and 96.
13. Ilchester, I, 3.
14. Add. 32724, ff. 358, 360.
15. Add. 32996, ff. 373, 375; see also Ilchester, I, 321–3.
16. Add. 32996, f. 375.
17. P.R.O. Adm. 2/1331, Out-letters, Secret Orders.
18. P.R.O. Adm. 3/64, Board Minutes.
19. Add. 41355, 'Abstract from Admiral Byng's private journal'. The original copy of Byng's journal—in which, under the terms of his orders, he was to record his daily activities—is not in the Public Record Office or British Museum, nor is it at Wrotham. The Abstract is in the Martin Papers and has not previously been published.
20. P.R.O. Adm. 36/6463 and 36/6464, Muster Lists of HMS *Ramillies*, 1755 and 1756.

CHAPTER SIX, pages 57 to 67.

1. Hervey, *Journal*, 190.
2. The council consisted of: Lieut-General Blakeney; Capt. Augustus Hervey; Lieuts-Col William Rufane (commanding the 24th Foot in the absence of Col Cornwallis); Charles Jefferies (34th Foot in absence of the Earl of Effingham); James Thorne (4th Foot in

absence of Col Rich); Major Edward Pole (23rd Foot); Major
Henry Innes, Fort Major of St Philip's; John Bastide, Chief
Engineer at Port Mahon.

3. Hervey, *Journal*, 190–7.
4. Add. 41355, Journal.
5. P.R.O. Adm. to Navy Bd, February 24, 1756.
6. Add. 41355, Journal.
7. P.R.O. Adm. 2/516, Out-letters to Public Offices and Admirals.
8. Adm. Liby, Cf 010.
9. P.R.O. Adm. 2/76; Adm. 1/4322, Letters from Secy at War, dated
   January 20, February 28, March 2, 8, 12, 22, 23, 23, and 27.
   For Minorca were: Colonel Cornwallis; seven ensigns for Effingham's regt; six ensigns for Rich's; one lieut and four ensigns for
   Cornwallis's; three ensigns for Huske's; Charles Lechmere, the
   Governor's Secretary. For Gibraltar: one captain, one lieut and
   four ensigns for Pulteney's regt; one captain and six ensigns for
   Fowke's; one lieut and two ensigns for Panmure's.
10. P.R.O. Adm. 37/6477 Muster List, HMS *Revenge*; Adm. 2/516,
    Board to the Earl of Effingham, March 20, referring to passages for
    'Your Lordship, Lady Effingham and your attendants'.
11. Add. 32863, f. 140.
12. Robert Beatson, *Naval and Military Memoirs of Great Britain,
    1727–1783*, London, 1790; The Hon T. Keppel, *The Life of
    Augustus, Viscount Keppel*, Volume I, London, 1842; Add. 41255,
    Journal.
13. P.R.O. Adm. 2/516, Out-letters, Public Offices and Admirals,
    March 23.
14. P.R.O. Adm. 2/516, March 25.
15. P.R.O. Adm. 2/1331, Out-letters, Secret Orders, March 25.
16. Horace Walpole, *Memoirs of the Last Ten Years of the Reign of
    George II*, II, 142, London, 1822.
17. Add. 35895, f. 370.
18. P.R.O. Adm. 2/517, Out-letters, Public Offices and Admirals.
19. P.R.O. Adm. 2/1331, Out-letters, Secret Orders. The copy of the
    orders is endorsed 'Signed the 31st, and sent by Tranter, the
    messenger'.
20. The log for this period is missing from the P.R.O., but the author
    has traced 'A Journal of Proceedings of H.M. ship *Intrepid*, 1.1.1756
    –30.1.1757', kept by 'Ellis', in the British Museum (Add. 24058).
    The only Ellis on board the *Intrepid* was Midshipman Usher Ellis
    (P.R.O. Adm. 36/5841, Muster List HMS *Intrepid*).
21. Adm. Liby, 'Progress Books' and 'List of Ships'.

CHAPTER SEVEN, pages 68 to 74.

1. Guillon for both order and letter.
2. ibid.
3. Lacour-Gayet, 260.
4. Guillon, 305.
5. Lacour-Gayet, 261.
6. Guillon, 305
7. Add. 42520, 'A Diary of a Siege of Minorca'. This is in manuscript and very detailed, particularly about casualties, and types and quantities of ammunition expended.
8. *The Trial of Admiral Byng*, London, 1757, the verbatim report taken by his lawyer, Thomas Cook, which also contains many other relevant letters and reports. Noel's letter is given as Appendix X of this edition. The other published report of the trial was by Charles Fearne, the Judge Advocate at the trial. There is nothing to choose between them except for the extra documents in Cook's, whose account is used in this narrative and referred to hereafter as *Trial*.
9. Adm. Liby, Cf 010.
10. Hervey, *Journal*, 190–6; and, for the minutes of the council, 313–18.

CHAPTER EIGHT, pages 75 to 90.

1. *Gentleman's Magazine*, February 3, 1756.
2. Add. 35364, f. 85.
3. Given in *The Granville Papers*, edited by W. J. Smith, London, 1852.
4. Walpole Correspondence, to George Montagu, April 20, 1756.
5. Ilchester, I, 324; in Devonshire MSS.
6. Quoted in *Chronicles of the 18th Century*, by Maud Wyndham, Hodder & Stoughton, 1924, Volume II.
7. *The Diary of the late George Bubb Dodington, Baron of Melcombe Regis*, edited by H. P. Wyndham, London, 1789.
8. Add. 32996, f. 419.
9. Add. 32864, f. 478.
10. Wyndham, *Dodington Diary*, entry for May 7.
11. Add. 32864, f. 486.
12. ibid, f. 483.
13. Walpole, *Memoirs*, II, 191–4.
14. Walpole *Correspondence*.
15. Boscawen Letters *Miscellany*, IV.
16. Add. 24058, Journal of Midshipman Ellis, *Intrep.*; P.R.O. Adm. 51/3950, 52/996 (2), logs of *Ramillies*; Adm. 51/4132, Captain's log, *Buckingham*; Adm. 51/1010, Captain's log *Trident*.
17. *Trial*, App. X.

18. ibid, App. XVI, report dated May 4, 1756.
19. ibid, App. VII.
20. P.R.O. W.O. 71/22, Report of Court Martial on General Fowke, August 10, 1756.
21. *Trial*, App. V.
22. ibid, App. VIII.

CHAPTER NINE, pages 91 to 99.
1. *Trial*, p. 44.
2. Wyndham, *Chronicles*, II, 45.
3. ibid.
4. John Charnock, *Biographia Navalis*, London, 1794-8.
5. Details of ships from Adm. Liby., 'Progress Books' and 'Lists of Ships'; of crews deficiencies from muster books and statement given to the Council of War, May 24, 1756, *Trial*, App. XXIII; and Adm. Liby Cf 010.
6. Add. 41355, Journal.
7. London *Evening Post*, July 20, 27, 1756.
8. Hervey, *Journal*, 196-8.
9. Copy of letter in Adm. Liby, Cf 010.
10. Hervey, *Journal*, 200-2.

CHAPTER TEN, pages 100 to 111.
1. Hervey, *Journal*, 203.
2. Keppel. *Viscount Keppel* I.
3. *Trial*, Defence, 14-15, Byng to Hervey, May 19, 1756.
4. ibid, 13-14, Byng to Blakeney, May 19, 1756.
5. Hervey, *Journal*, 204-5.
6. P.R.O. Adm. 52/996, *Ramillies* Master's log.
7. Add. 42520, but diarist is unnamed.
8. *Trial*, 58-9.
9. Adm. Liby Cf 010, letter from *Foudroyant*, May 21.
10. Lacour-Gayet, 479-89.
11. ibid, 487.
12. P.R.O. Adm. 51/692, Captain's log, *Phoenix*; Adm. 51/3950, Captain's log, *Ramillies*.
13. ibid.
14. *Trial*, 13, Temple West's evidence.

CHAPTER ELEVEN, pages 112 to 132.
1. P.R.O., *Ramillies*'s logs.
2. P.R.O. Adm. 51/165, Captain's log, *Captain*; Adm. 51/226 and 52/567, Captain's and Master's logs, *Defiance*; Adm. 51/4301, Captain's log, *Princess Louisa*.
3. *Trial*, Defence, 21.

4. Add. 41355, Journal; *Trial*; logs of *Ramillies* and *Buckingham*; P.R.O. Adm. 51/692, Captain's log *Phoenix*.

5. It has been suggested that Galissonnière had a copy of the English 'signal book'. Paul d'Estree, in *Le Maréchal de Richelieu d'après les Mémoires Contemporains et des documents Inédits*, 3rd edition, Paris, 1917, p. 298 says: '*Le hasard avait fait tomber entre ses mains (Galissonnière's) le tableau des signaux de l'escadre enemie. En consequence, le 19 Mai a la hauteur de l'Ile d'Aire, il attaquait avec 12 vaisseaux les 14 de la flotte Anglais.*'
D'Estree gives no authority for this statement which is not, as far as we are aware, confirmed from any other source; in any case it would seem he has confused the 'signal book' for the Fighting Instructions, of which Galissonnière might have had a copy. It is unlikely that he had a copy of the Additional Instructions. Even if he had, they would, as will be seen from the narrative, have been of no assistance.

6. The applicable part of Article No. XVII says: 'If the admiral sees the enemy's fleet standing towards him, and he has the wind of them, the van of the fleet is to make sail till they came the length of the enemy's rear, and our rear abreast of the enemy's van; then he that is in the rear of our fleet is to tack first, and every ship one after another, as fast as they can, throughout the line, that they may engage on the same tack with the enemy . . .' See *Fighting Instructions 1530–1816*, Navy Records Society, 1905, page 197.

7. *Trial*, 446, 460. Article XIX says: 'If the admiral and his fleet have the wind of the enemy, and they have stretched themselves in a line of battle, the van of the admiral's squadron is to steer with the van of the enemy's and there to engage them.'

8. Add. 41355, Journal; logs of *Ramillies* and *Defiance*.

9. *Trial*, 307.

10. ibid, 211–22, evidence of Captain Ourry; P.R.O. Adm. 51/3878, Captain's log, *Lancaster*.

11. *Trial*, evidence of Temple West, Everitt and lieutenants; Captain's log, *Buckingham*.

12. *Trial*, evidence of Young and Cornwall; P.R.O. Adm. 51/474, Captain's log, *Intrepid*.

13. *Trial*, 258–9; P.R.O. Adm. 51/782, Captain's log, *Revenge*.

14. P.R.O. Adm. 51/4301, Captain's log, *Princess Louisa; Trial*, App. XXIII.

15. P.R.O. Adm. 51/1010, Captain's log, *Trident*.

16. *Trial*, 347.

17. ibid, 331–51.

18. A Board letter of October 21, 1755 (exactly fifty years to the day before the Battle of Trafalgar) said that 'Having considered of the arguments lately made in our presence at Woolwich by firing of cannon with locks and placing the priming in a tin tube', locks were to be fitted on all quarter-deck guns. They 'will answer much better at sea than the present method of firing only with a match, and ought to be introduced on board'. They would be introduced gradually to other guns. Flannel cartridges were also to be used instead of paper because the bottoms of the paper containers were left in the gun 'till it is filled up before the touch-hole'. P.R.O. Adm. Out-letters, Lords' letters.
19. *Trial*, 161.
20. *Trial*, 326–7.
21. ibid, 301, 324–5.
22. ibid, Defence, 29.
23. P.R.O. Adm. 51/3878.
24. *Trial*, Defence, 29.

CHAPTER TWELVE, pages 133 to 141.
 1. *Trial*, App. XX.
 2. Hervey, *Journal*, 207–8.
 3. *Trial*, 36–37.
 4. ibid, 37.
 5. Add. 33056, f. 318.
 6. Hervey, *Journal*, 208–13; crew shortages etc. Adm. Liby Cf 010.
 7. *Trial*, App. XXV for minutes of Council of War.
 8. Lacour-Gayet, 217.
 9. Hervey, *Journal*, 321.
10. ibid, 216.

CHAPTER THIRTEEN, pages 142 to 153.
 1. Add. 32865, f. 159.
 2. Fox Papers, 5, 1047.
 3. *Bedford Correspondence*, II, 193.
 4. Ilchester, I, 330–1.
 5. *Trial*, App. XXXVI.
 6. Add. 32996, f. 427, minutes of June 3, 1756.
 7. Ilchester, I, 330; Fox Papers, 5, 1049.
 8. Add. 32865, f. 203.
 9. *Bedford Correspondence*, II, 195–6.
10. Add. 32865, f. 209.
11. P.R.O. Adm. 3/64.
12. Smith, *Grenville Papers*, June 5, 1756.
13. *Correspondence of William Pitt, Earl of Chatham*, by W. S. Taylor and J. H. Pringle, I. 163–4, London, 1838–40.

L*

14. Walpole, Correspondence, June 6, 1756.
15. ibid, to Sir H. Mann, June 14, 1756.
16. Add. 32865.
17. Add. 32865, June 12.
18. Add. 32866, f. 115.
19. See Add. 32997, f. 68; Add. 33044, ff. 18–26; Namier, II, 536–7.
20. Add. 35364, f. 97.
21. Add. 35364, f. 99.
22. Fox Papers, 5, 1055.
23. Keppel, *Viscount Keppel*, letter dated June 15.
24. Smith, *Grenville Papers*, June 16.
25. Boscawen Letters, *Miscellany IV*.
26. Add. 32865, f. 373.
27. *Some Further Particulars in Relation to the Case of Admiral Byng from Original Papers, &c*, by 'A Gentleman of Oxford'. This was published on Byng's behalf, and may have been written by Paul Whitehead. It contains many of Byng's letters. It is referred to from now on as 'Oxford'. The two Admiralty letters of dismissal are given in *Trial*, App. XXXIV and App. XXXV.
28. Hervey, *Journal*, 217–18.

CHAPTER FOURTEEN, pages 154 to 167.
1. Add. 35895, f. 25.
2. Fox Papers, 5, 1057.
3. Oxford.
4. P.R.O. Adm. 1/4120, In-letters, Secy of State to Board, June 29, 1756.
5. Hervey, *Journal*, App. C.
6. Fox Papers, 5, 1056. June 25, 1756.
7. Hervey, *Journal*, App. C.
8. Fox Papers, 5, 1062.
9. ibid, 5, 1074.
10. ibid, 5, 1088.
11. ibid, 5, 1061.
12. Walpole Correspondence, July 11.
13. Fox Papers, 5, 1069 and 5, 1070, July 24, 1756.
14. ibid, 5, 1077, July 7, 1756.
15. Barrow, *Anson*.
16. Add. 32866, f. 172.
17. Add. 42520.
18. Add. 32866, f. 206.
19. ibid, f. 129.
20. ibid, f. 210.

21. ibid, f. 265.
22. P.R.O. Adm. 2/76, **Out-letters**, Secret Orders.
23. *The Gazeteer*, July 28.
24. Add. 32866, f. 270.

CHAPTER FIFTEEN, pages 168 to 176.
  1. P.R.O. Adm. 1/923, In-letters, from C-in-C Portsmouth.
  2. Letter and enclosure in Adm. 1/923—presumably both were sent with Osborn's express.
  3. Oxford.
  4. P.R.O. Adm. 2/517, Out-letters.
  5. P.R.O. Adm. 3/64, Board Minutes, July 27; Adm. 2/517, Letter to Byng.
  6. Adm. Liby, Cf 010.
  7. P.R.O. Adm. 2/76, Out-letters, Secret Orders.
  8. Oxford.
  9. Adm. Liby, Cf 010.
 10. Barrow, *Anson.*
 11. Fox Papers, 5, 1081.
 12. Add. 15955.
 13. Adm. Liby, Cf 010.
 14. Add. 32866, f. 322, July 31.
 15. Both letters in P.R.O. Adm. 2/157.
 16. Ilchester, I, 335, July 31.
 17. Add. 35415.
 18. P.R.O. Adm. 1/4322, from Secy at War (copy of letter sent to Admiralty).
 19. P.R.O. Adm. 3/64, Board Minutes.
 20. Oxford.
 21. ibid.
 22. P.R.O. Adm. 3/64, Board Minutes.
 23. Oxford.
 24. ibid.

CHAPTER SIXTEEN, pages 177 to 186.
  1. Add. 32997, f. 20.
  2. *Gentleman's Magazine*, August 1756.
  3. Add. 32866, f. 496.
  4. All court martial documents in P.R.O. W.O. 71/22.
  5. Add. 32866, f. 456.
  6. Hervey, *Journal*, 324.
  7. Fox papers, 5, 1097.
  8. Add. 32867, f. 135.

9. Add. 32867, f. 5, August 21.
10. Add. 32866, Samuel Crosland to Lord Hyde, August 18, 1756; copy sent to Newcastle.
11. Add. 35376, f. 262 and Add. 35416, f. 1.
12. Add. 32867, f. 123.
13. ibid, f. 143.
14. *Pitt Correspondence.*
15. ibid.
16. W. F. Lord, *England and France in the Mediterranean, 1660–1830*, p. 19, London, 1901, gives a good description of this event.

CHAPTER SEVENTEEN, pages 187 to 199.
1. P.R.O., Adm. 2/518.
2. *Trial*, Defence, 35–36.
3. Adm. Liby, Cf 010.
4. *Trial*, Defence, 38–40. The original draft, in Anson's handwriting and with many alterations, is in Adm. Liby, Cf 010.
5. *Trial*, Defence, 40–43.
6. Smith, *Grenville Papers*, September 11.
7. *A Letter to a Member of Parliament in the Country from his friend in London Relative to the Case of Admiral Byng: With Some Original Papers and Letters Which Passed during the Expedition.* A copy is in the Adm. Liby, P (NS) 30.
8. Adm. Liby.
9. Add. 32997, f. 52.
10. Add. 35895.
11. Add. 15955.
12. P.R.O. Adm. 1/3677.
13. ibid.
14. Ilchester, I, 353.
15. ibid.
16. Add. 32868, f. 203.
17. ibid, f. 225.
18. ibid, f. 226.
19. Walpole, *Memoirs*, II, 252.
20. Add. 32868, f. 252.
21. Add. 35416, f. 106.
22. *Bedford Correspondence*, II, 201.
23. Yorke, *Hardwicke.*
24. Smith, *Grenville Papers*, October 17.
25. Yorke, *Hardwicke.*
26. Walpole, *Memoirs*, II, 272–3.

CHAPTER EIGHTEEN, pages 200 to 207.
1. Adm. Liby, Cf 010.
2. Hervey, *Journal*, 230–1.
3. P.R.O. Adm. 3/64, Board Minutes, November 19.
4. ibid, November 24.
5. Adm. Liby, Cf 010.
6. Walpole correspondence, November 13.
7. *Evening Post*, August 12.
8. Walpole, *Memoirs*, II, 275.
9. Add. 32869, f. 249.
10. ibid, f. 253.
11. P.R.O. Adm. 1/4322, In-letters, from Secy at War.
12. Add. 35416, f. 147.

CHAPTER NINETEEN, pages 208 to 214.
1. *Memoirs from 1754 to 1758*, by James, Earl Waldegrave.
2. P.R.O. Adm. 2/516, December 14.
3. ibid.
4. ibid.
5. P.R.O. Adm. 3/64.
6. P.R.O. Adm. 2/519.
7. Walpole, *Memoirs*, II, 359.
8. Wyndham, *Chronicles*, II, 8.
9. ibid.
10. Board of Admiralty to Admiral Mathews, June 17, 1746.
11. Walpole, *Memoirs*, II, 287.
12. Boscawen Letters, *Miscellany IV*.
13. Hervey, *Journal*, 232.
14. ibid, 326–7.

CHAPTER TWENTY, pages 215 to 231.
NOTE: The court martial report in this and the following chapters is
    taken from Cook's edition.
1. P.R.O. Adm. 51/834, Captain's log of *St George*.
2. Hervey, *Journal*, 233.
3. P.R.O. Adm. 3/64.
4. Adm. Liby, Cf 010.
5. Hervey, *Journal*, 234.
6. ibid.

CHAPTER TWENTY-ONE, pages 232 to 241.
1. *Fighting Instructions*, Corbett.
2. P.R.O. Adm. 52/1074.

3. P.R.O. Adm. 51/1010.
4. P.R.O. Adm. 51/219.
5. Hervey, *Journal*, 235.

CHAPTER TWENTY-TWO, pages 242 to 252.
1. Hervey, *Journal*, 235.
2. ibid.
3. P.R.O. Adm. 2/519.
4. Add. 35359, f. 387.
5. P.R.O. Adm. 2/519.
6. Hervey, *Journal*, 235.
7. Add. 35595, f. 2.
8. Add. 15956, f. 27.
9. In the possession of the Duke of Devonshire: Chatsworth Collection.

CHAPTER TWENTY-THREE, pages 253 to 262.
Note: Much of the description of Byng's confinement on board HMS
 Monarch (as well as his behaviour when he was sentenced) is taken
 from a pamphlet, *A Letter to a Gentleman in the Country from his
 friend in London* (Adm. Liby, P. 329). This pamphlet was also used
 by Mr Brian Tunstall in his *Admiral Byng and the Loss of Minorca*,
 Philip Allan, 1928, 276–83. Other sources include *Gentleman's
 Magazine*, many contemporary newspapers and the log of the
 Monarch.
1. P.R.O. Adm. 1/5296, Part I, f. 104.
2. ibid, Part II, f. 107.
3. ibid, Part II, *ff.* 105–6.
4. *Bedford Correspondence*, II, 227–9.
5. John McArthur, *Principles and Practice of Naval and Military
 Courts Martial*, II, 390–1, London, 1813.

CHAPTER TWENTY-FOUR, pages 263 to 270.
1. P.R.O. Adm. 2/519.
2. P.R.O. Adm. 3/64, January 29, 1757.
3. P.R.O. Adm. 52/660 (4).
4. P.R.O. Adm. 2/519.
5. John Lord Hervey, *Memoirs of the Reign of George II*, London,
 1848.
6. Wyndham, *Chronicles*, II.
7. Yorke, *Hardwicke*.
8. *Bedford Correspondence*, II, 233–4, February 3, 1757.
9. Letter in the possession of Sir Danvers Osborn.

10. *Bedford Correspondence*, II, 233.
11. Bedford Papers, Volume XXXIII, f. 86, February 18, 1757.
12. P.R.O., Adm. 3/64.
13. Pamphlet published by Admiral Forbes gives the wording of the letter. Copy in Adm. Liby (P. 750). The wording varies slightly from the version in McArthur, *Naval and Military Courts Martial*, II, 392–4.
14. *Evening Post*, February 19, 1757.
15. Walpole, *Memoirs*, II, 312.
16. *Pitt Correspondence*.
17. Copy in Bedford Papers, Volume XXXIII, f. 88.
18. Hervey, *Journal*, 237.

CHAPTER TWENTY-FIVE, pages 271 to 283.
1. Ilchester, II, 25–6.
2. Hervey, *Journal*, 238.
3. Walpole, *Memoirs*, II, 318.
4. ibid, 326.
5. Hervey, *Journal*, 239.
6. Smith, *Grenville Papers*.
7. Hervey, *Journal*, 240.
8. ibid.
9. Walpole, *Memoirs*, II, 327–31.
10. Add. 32997, f. 127.
11. P.R.O. Adm. 1/4121.
12. P.R.O. Adm. 3/64, and for order, Adm. 2/519.
13. ibid.
14. P.R.O. Adm. 3/64.
15. *Parliamentary History*, XV; Add. 35895, f. 53.
16. To John Chute, February 27, 1757.
17. Hervey, *Journal*, 241.
18. Walpole, *Memoirs*, II, 359.
19. ibid, 362.
20. *Proceedings of the Rt. Hon. Lords . . . in Parliament Assembled upon a Bill entitled 'An Act to Release from . . . the Oath of Secrecy etc.'*, published in Dublin, 1757. The report was published after a proposal was made in the Lords by Lord Hardwicke.
21. Hervey, *Journal*, 241.
22. P.R.O. Adm. 3/64.
23. P.R.O. Adm. 2/519, March 4, 1757.

CHAPTER TWENTY-SIX, pages 284 to 293.
1. Hervey, *Journal*, 242.

2. Add. 24058, log of Lt Richard Filkins, of the *Monarch*; P.R.O. Adm. 51/3914 and Adm. 52/660 (4), Captain's and Master's logs of the *Monarch*.
3. Logs of the *Monarch*.
4. Hervey, *Journal*, 242.
5. From a photographic copy of the will at Wrotham Park. The will was proved in London, July 7, 1757.
6. Letter in possession of Sir Danvers Osborn, Bt.
7. P.R.O. Adm. 3/64.
8. ibid, June 8, 1756.

CHAPTER TWENTY-SEVEN, pages 294 to 299.
Note: For sources concerning Byng's last days, see Note at the head of 'Notes and Bibliography' for Chapter Twenty-Three.
1. P.R.O. Adm. 52/660 (4).
2. *A Letter from a Gentleman to His Friend in the Country*.
3. P.R.O. Adm. 1/923.
4. ibid.

EPILOGUE, pages 300 to 302.
1. Corbett, *Seven Years' War*, I, 179.
2. Fitzmaurice, *Shelburne*.
3. Voltaire, *Candide*.

INDEX

Abreu, Comte, d', 54, 76, 143-5, 147, 162

Additional Fighting Instructions: see Fighting Instructions

Aiguillon, Duchesse d', 248

Albemarle, George van Keppel, Earl of, 149, 213

Amherst, Captain John RN, 94-5, 139, 201, 211, 227

Ancaster, Peregrine Bertie, 3rd Duke of, 2, 64

Ancram, Major-General the Earl of, 1-2

Andrews, Captain Thomas, RN, 92, 120, 124, 134

Anson, George, Admiral Lord, Advice to Government, 40-1; orders to Byng for Mediterranean, 47-9; chooses Byng's squadron, 48-9; attends March 9 meeting, 51-5; orders for Med squadron, 55; final instructions to Byng, 64-5 (*see* App. III, pp. 305-6); sends reinforcements, 77; receives Byng's letter, 142-3; receives Galisonnière's dispatch, 143-4; recalls Byng, 145; orders for Hawke, 146; receives Byng's dispatch, 154; orders for Byng's arrest, 164; wants Byng in Tower, 172-4; refuses more witnesses, 189-90; libels on, 194-5; plans Hawke's recall, 193-4; comments on Voltaire's letter, 248; mentioned, xi-xii, 4, 25, 63, 76-8, 92, 102, 133, 136-7, 147, 150, 152, 162, 187, 192, 198, 200-1, 204, 206, 208, 212-3, 243, 249-51, 261, 265, 283, 301

Anson, Lady Elizabeth, 51, and note

Argenson, Marc-Pierre, Comte d' (1696-1764), 42

Articles of War, 173, 255-6, 259-60, 268-9, 273, 281

Baird, Captain Patrick, RN, 92, 124-5

Banks, Consul James, 36, 46, 53

Barjeton Verelause, Lieutenant Comte de, 109

Barnard, Sir John, MP, 178-9, 186

Barrington, William Wildman, 2nd Viscount, Muddles orders to Fowke, 62-4 (orders App. II, p. 304); orders queried at Gibraltar, 83-90; at Fowke court martial, 179-80, 185, 187-8; stays Secretary at War, 204; mentioned, 48, 52 note, 166, 173-4, 205-6, 225, 270, 273

Basset, Lieutenant Christopher, RN, 129

Bateman, John, Viscount, 47-9, 146

Bedford, John Russell, 4th Duke of, Appoints Byng to Mediterranean, 23-4, 26, 87 note; mercy plea from Sarah, 265-6, 268, 272; mentioned, 146, 197, 256, 265, 274, 277

Belle-Isle, Charles, Marèchal Duc de (1684-1761), 42, 45-6, 53, 288

Belwaird, Joseph, 238

Bentley, Captain (later Vice-Admiral Sir) John, RN, 214, 282

Bernis, Cardinal, 302

Bertie, Colonel Lord Robert, Boards Byng's squadron, 62; at Fowke's council, 85-6; at the battle, 117, 120, 122, 129; warns of *Trident*, 130; at Byng's council, 135-6; evidence at Byng's trial, 236-8, 259-60; mentioned, 64, 214, 223

Birtles, Consul John, 36, 46, 53

Blakeney, General William, 1st Baron, Commands at Minorca, 39-40; warned of French landing, 53, 72; holds councils of war, 57-8; protests to Richelieu, 96; surrenders island, 162; returns to Britain, 204-5; claims sally-port open, 205-6; given barony, 205; at Byng's trial, 210, 214; confused evidence, 221-5; mentioned, 73-4, 104, 106, 149, 257

Bland, General Sir Humphrey, 166-7

Blankley, Henry, 83

Borthwick, Alexander, 123

Boscawen, Admiral Edward, Intercepts French ships, 32-3; criticizes Byng in letters, 80, 108,